DB

**W9-BGP-725**

# Biography Today

*Profiles*
*of People*
*of Interest*
*to Young*
*Readers*

Volume 16—2007
Annual Cumulation

**Cherie D. Abbey**
*Managing Editor*

## Omnigraphics

P.O. Box 31-1640
Detroit, MI 48231-1640

Cherie D. Abbey, *Managing Editor*

Joan Axelrod-Contrada, Allison A. Beckett, Peggy Daniels, Laurie DiMauro,
Sheila Fitzgerald, Joan Goldsworthy, Margaret Haerens, Jeff Hill, Laurie Hillstrom,
Anne J. Johnson, Justin Karr, Leslie Karr, Eve Nagler, Sara Pendergast,
Tom Pendergast, Diane Telgen, and Tom Wiloch, *Sketch Writers*

Allison A. Beckett and Mary Butler, *Research Staff*

\* \* \*

Peter E. Ruffner, *Publisher*
Matthew P. Barbour, *Senior Vice President*

\* \* \*

Elizabeth Collins, *Research and Permissions Coordinator*
Kevin M. Hayes, *Operations Manager*
Cherry Stockdale, *Permissions Assistant*

Shirley Amore, Martha Johns, and Kirk Kauffman, *Administrative Staff*

INDEXED IN
Children's Magazine Guide

# Contents

5

# Preface

*Biography Today* is a magazine designed and written for the young reader—ages 9 and above—and covers individuals that librarians and teachers tell us that young people want to know about most: entertainers, athletes, writers, illustrators, cartoonists, and political leaders.

## The Plan of the Work

The publication was especially created to appeal to young readers in a format they can enjoy reading and readily understand. Each issue contains approximately 10 sketches arranged alphabetically. Each entry provides at least one picture of the individual profiled, and bold-faced rubrics lead the reader to information on birth, youth, early memories, education, first jobs, marriage and family, career highlights, memorable experiences, hobbies, and honors and awards. Each of the entries ends with a list of easily accessible sources designed to lead the student to further reading on the individual and a current address. Retrospective entries are also included, written to provide a perspective on the individual's entire career.

Biographies are prepared by Omnigraphics editors after extensive research, utilizing the most current materials available. Those sources that are generally available to students appear in the list of further reading at the end of the sketch.

## Indexes

Cumulative indexes are an important component of *Biography Today*. Each issue of the *Biography Today* General Series includes a Cumulative Names Index, which comprises all individuals profiled in *Biography Today* since the series began in 1992. In addition, we compile three other indexes: the Cumulative General Index, Places of Birth Index, and Birthday Index. See our web site, www.biographytoday.com, for these three indexes, along with the Names Index. All *Biography Today* indexes are cumulative, including all individuals profiled in both the General Series and the Subject Series.

# Our Advisors

This series was reviewed by an Advisory Board comprising librarians, children's literature specialists, and reading instructors to ensure that the concept of this publication—to provide a readable and accessible biographical magazine for young readers—was on target. They evaluated the title as it developed, and their suggestions have proved invaluable. Any errors, however, are ours alone. We'd like to list the Advisory Board members, and to thank them for their efforts.

Gail Beaver
Adjunct Lecturer
University of Michigan
Ann Arbor, MI

Cindy Cares
Youth Services Librarian
Southfield Public Library
Southfield, MI

Carol A. Doll
School of Information Science and Policy
University of Albany, SUNY
Albany, NY

Kathleen Hayes-Parvin
Language Arts Teacher
Birney Middle School
Southfield, MI

Karen Imarisio
Assistant Head of Adult Services
Bloomfield Twp. Public Library
Bloomfield Hills, MI

Rosemary Orlando
Director
St. Clair Shores Public Library
St. Clair Shores, MI

Our Advisory Board stressed to us that we should not shy away from controversial or unconventional people in our profiles, and we have tried to follow their advice. The Advisory Board also mentioned that the sketches might be useful in reluctant reader and adult literacy programs, and we would value any comments librarians might have about the suitability of our magazine for those purposes.

8

## Your Comments Are Welcome

Our goal is to be accurate and up-to-date, to give young readers information they can learn from and enjoy. Now we want to know what you think. Take a look at this issue of *Biography Today*, on approval. Write or call me with your comments. We want to provide an excellent source of biographical information for young people. Let us know how you think we're doing.

Cherie Abbey
Managing Editor, *Biography Today*
Omnigraphics, Inc.
P.O. Box 31-1640
Detroit, MI 48231-1640

editor@biographytoday.com
www.biographytoday.com

# Congratulations!

Congratulations to the following individuals and libraries, who are receiving a free copy of *Biography Today* for suggesting people who appear in this volume:

Carol Arnold, Hoopeston Public Library, Hoopeston, IL
Vondell Ashton, Fairmount Heights Library, Washington, DC
Alice Bird, VandenBerge Junior High, Elk River, MN
Paul Bishette, Silas Bronson Library, Waterbury, CT
Aaron Blechert, Irondale High School, New Brighton, MN
Ellen Blumberg, Westwood High School Library, Austin, TX
Dorey Brown, Troy Middle School, Troy, MO
Judi Chelekis, Vassar High School, Vassar, MI
Rachel Q. Davis, Thomas Memorial Library, Cape Elizabeth, ME
Carrie DeForest, Roselle Middle School, Roselle, IL
Sheronnica Dunbar, West Popular Lending Library, Raleigh, NC
Anna Flora, Knox Middle School, Knox, IN
Teia Serray Hill, Rio Linda, CA
Sarah Jow, Fresno County Library, Reedley Branch, Reedley, CA
Ricza Lopez, Bronx, NY
Erin Lounsbury, Sachem Public Library, Farmingville, NY
Jasmine McKinney, Westwood School, Stockton, CA
Noel Miranda, Harmon Johnson Elementary, Sacramento, CA
Rebecca Morris, Deer Lakes Middle School, Russellton, PA
Melissa Nga, Hercules, CA
Randy Olund, Carrington Middle School Media Center, Durham, NC
Ann Pinion, Hixson Middle School, Hixson, TN
Sarah Puckett, Northville, MI
Maggie and Julia Rapai, Grosse Pointe, MI
Paige Rawl, Fox Hill Elementary, Indianapolis, IN
F.G. Ruffner, Jr., Grosse Pointe, MI
Lisa Scharf, Ridge Junior High School, Mentor, OH
S.A. Schene, Homecroft Elementary School, Indianapolis, IN
Shelly Smith, Tzouanakis Intermediate, Greencastle, IN
St. George Parish School, Fifth Grade Class, Seattle, WA
Jim Steinke, Cottage Grove High School, Cottage Grove, WI
Carolyn Torre, William L. Buck School, Valley Stream, NY

## Shaun Alexander 1977-

American Professional Football Player with
the Seattle Seahawks
NFL Most Valuable Player in 2005

### BIRTH

Shaun Alexander was born on August 30, 1977, in Florence,
Kentucky. His father, Curtis Alexander Jr., lives in Cincinnati,
Ohio, which is situated a few miles from Florence on the
north side of the Ohio River. He is employed by the chemical
division of the salt producer Morton International. Carol
Alexander, his mother, works in the truancy department of the
Boone County School District in northern Kentucky. Durran

Alexander, Shaun's older brother by one year, serves as the executive director of the Shaun Alexander Foundation. Alexander also has three older half-brothers and four older half-sisters from his father's previous marriage; all of his half-siblings were raised by their mother in Cincinnati.

## YOUTH

Alexander grew up in Boone County, Kentucky, a few miles south of Cincinnati. Although his home town of Florence at one time abounded with tobacco and dairy farms, it is now the second largest city in northern Kentucky and home to both a thoroughbred horse race track and a minor-league baseball stadium.

Alexander's parents divorced when he was 11 years old. Consequently, he and his brother Durran were raised by their mother in a two-bedroom apartment in a government housing complex. "We had that main room, that little room, and that was everything," he explained. Despite his modest upbringing, however, Alexander never considered himself underprivileged. "[Our] mom made us feel like we had everything we needed," he said. "We knew we weren't rich, but we never felt like we were poor." In his 2006 autobiography, *Touchdown Alexander,* he cited his favorite childhood memories as the annual Christmas celebrations at his grandparents' house. Everyone was made to feel welcome at these gatherings, and many gifts were exchanged. "I grew up with that sense of being a family and loving one another. For me, Christmas wasn't about presents, it was about family—our large and loving family."

> "[My mother] was the queen of discipline. She kept things very strict in our home," Alexander recalled. "But Mom balanced her discipline with love." His mother also taught him the importance of integrity of character and self-discipline. "I am who I am because I had a wise mother, who not only took me to church . . . but has lived the life she taught me to live."

Alexander's mother has always been a positive influence on his life. She was caring and loving toward her sons, but also insisted that they learn to be polite, respectful, and tidy. "Looking back, it was to my advantage to have a mother like that," he recalled. "She was the queen of discipline. She kept things very strict in our home. . . . But Mom balanced her discipline

*Alexander shares a laugh with his mother, Carol Alexander, following practice.*

with love." Among many other lessons, his mother taught him the importance of integrity of character and self-discipline. "I am who I am because I had a wise mother, who not only took me to church . . . but has lived the life she taught me to live," he affirmed.

As a boy, Alexander attended St. Stephen's Missionary Baptist Church in Cincinnati. He remembers being awestruck by the lively and inspiring sounds of the gospel choir, but admits that he did not pay much attention to the preaching until he was about 10 years old. After experiencing an emotionally uplifting worship service in the spring of 1987, though, he elected to become a baptized member of the church. His mother and pastor both encouraged him to make a spiritual pledge to live according to the principles of his Christian faith. Since the day he joined the church, he has strived to be obedient to its teachings. "Very early I learned that we make choices," he explained in his autobiography. "We have to choose which path we will follow—we have to choose to love, to forgive, and to enjoy being alive. And we show we've decided by the way we live."

### First Taste of Football

Durran and Shaun were virtually inseparable throughout their childhoods. Whether playing make-believe games in their living room or tossing a football in a field behind their apartment building, they could almost always be found together. Although they were only a year apart in age, Shaun looked up to Durran as a role model and father figure. Even today, he rarely makes an important decision without consulting his brother first, and the two have a longstanding ritual of talking by phone before every game.

Today, Alexander credits his older brother with setting a great example, both in academics and sports. "He set the pattern for me," Alexander explained. It was only after much prodding from his brother, for example, that Alexander agreed to become a member of the pee wee football team that Durran had joined. He found that while he liked playing football, he especially liked the post-game pizza parties. "And that," he said, "was my start in playing football—when I was still more interested in the pizza and fun with friends than in the game itself."

Alexander started his pee wee career in third grade as a defensive end. His coach made him a kick returner the following year. He returned two kickoffs for touchdowns in the first game of the season. Delighted by the cheers and attention he received after each return, he approached Durran after the game and asked him which position scored the most points. When Durran revealed that the running back made the most touchdowns, Shaun decided to switch positions and concentrate his efforts on scoring. By sixth grade, his family, coaches, and teammates all recognized that he possessed a special talent for carrying the football. "When people saw Shaun in Pee Wee," his father recalled, "everyone said the same thing: 'That kid's going to play [college football] on Saturdays.'"

## EDUCATION

Alexander attended Florence Elementary School, where he was usually identified by teachers as "Durran's younger brother" because of Durran's straight-A record. He admired his brother and tried to emulate him, but often felt he could not match Durran's accomplishments. Finally, in sixth grade, his teacher offered some words of wisdom that changed his perspective. "[You] don't have to be like Durran. You just have to be the best Shaun the world's ever seen," she advised. From that day on, he stopped comparing himself to Durran and focused instead on doing his best.

Alexander focused on business before setting his sights on an athletic career. His favorite subject was algebra, and he often talked about someday becoming an important business leader. By high school, his leadership qualities were on full display. He was elected president of his class at Boone County High School every year from ninth through 12th grade. He also balanced academics and athletics with ease, posting a 3.5 grade point average even as he starred in basketball, baseball, and football for the Boone County High School Rebels.

In his junior year, Alexander was asked to replace the varsity football team's injured first-string tailback. His first game as the Rebels' starting running back was a memorable one. "My first carry in the game was a touchdown," he remembered. "So was my second. At halftime, I had 214 yards rushing and four touchdowns." Later in the game, an opponent tackled him so hard that Alexander bit through his own lip. Alexander still has a scar under his chin from the incident—the only lasting scar he has ever received in all of his years of football.

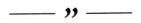

*"My friends and I would rule out schools because we didn't like their uniforms,"* Alexander joked as he described the difficult selection process. *"That was the first step. The second step was a screening committee that included my brother, my cousin and our best friend. If we didn't like a recruiter, we crossed that school off the list."*

By the end of his junior year, Alexander had tallied an astounding 2,400 yards rushing and 42 touchdowns. At the conclusion of the season, head coach Mike Murphy told him: "You'll go to a big college, and you'll play in the pros. You're going to have an outstanding career, Shaun." Until this point, Alexander had never really viewed football as a career path. But his coach's words made him realize that he had a special gift for the game.

Alexander was even more dominant as a high school senior. He led his team to its second 4A state championship in three seasons with an incredible tally of 54 touchdowns and 3,500 rushing yards. On two occasions, he scored seven touchdowns in one game. Alexander received national recognition for these gridiron exploits. He was selected as a *Parade* magazine and *USA Today* All-American, and was designated "Old Spice Athlete of the Month" by *Sports Illustrated*, which nicknamed him "Mr. Touchdown." He became known as "Alexander the Great" to high school football fans throughout the region and was honored as the Gatorade Circle of Champions Kentucky Player of the Year. Boone County High School even retired his number 37 jersey at a special ceremony staged a few weeks before his graduation.

Alexander's incredible high school career attracted the attention of major college football programs across the country. He eventually narrowed his choices down to the University of Michigan, the University of Alabama, and Notre Dame, where Durran played drums in the marching band. "My friends and I would rule out schools because we didn't like their uniforms," he joked as he described the difficult selection process. "That was the first step. The second step was a screening committee that included my brother, my cousin and our best friend. If we didn't like a recruiter, we crossed that school off the list." After visiting all three schools under consideration, he chose to accept a scholarship from the Alabama Crimson Tide because of the school's warm-weather location and the enthusiasm of the students.

Alexander began his studies at the University of Alabama in the fall of 1995. He graduated with a bachelor's degree in marketing in 1999. As a college senior, he garnered Academic All-SEC (Southeastern Conference) honors for maintaining a grade point average of 3.0 or above.

## CAREER HIGHLIGHTS

### Playing for the Alabama Crimson Tide

Alabama coaches "redshirted" Alexander during his freshman year. This designation allowed him to practice with the team throughout the season without using any of the four years of athletic eligibility allotted to college players. As a "redshirt freshman" the following year, he began the season as the team's third-string tailback. But late in the season, in a game against archrival Louisiana State University (LSU), Alexander burst into the spotlight and launched one of the greatest careers in Crimson Tide history.

Alexander began the game against the LSU Tigers on the bench, as usual. But late in the first half he entered the game and promptly rambled for a 17-yard touchdown run. On the first drive after half-time, he raced 72 yards for a second touchdown. By the end of the game, Alexander had scored a third touchdown and posted a single-game school record of 291 yards rushing to lead the Crimson Tide to victory. He finished the 1996 campaign with 589 rushing yards and six touchdowns. His surprising contributions helped lift Alabama to a solid 10-3 record for the year.

The 1997 season was a difficult one for Alexander and the Crimson Tide. Injuries dogged Alexander, who managed only 415 rushing yards and three touchdowns for the year. The team, meanwhile, posted only four wins all season long. In 1998, though, both Alexander and the Tide rebounded. The star tailback cruised to 17 touchdowns (13 rushing and four receiving) and gained 1,178 yards rushing to help guide Alabama to a win-

*During his years at the University of Alabama, Alexander
set a host of school rushing records.*

ning record (7-5). His performance earned him All-Southeast Conference honors at season's end.

As his senior year approached, Alexander was a local celebrity and the team's star player. He proved worthy of all the attention during the 1999 season. He shredded opposing defenses to rack up 1,383 rushing yards and 23 touchdowns (including 19 on the ground) despite missing three games with an ankle injury. Alexander's performance earned him SEC Offensive Player of the Year honors and helped lift the Crimson Tide to a 10-3 record and conference championship. The two most memorable victories of the season both came against the Florida Gators. Early in the season,

17

Alexander and his teammates snapped Florida's 30-game winning streak in a 40-39 thriller. Two months later, the Crimson Tide rolled over the Gators by a 34-7 score to win the conference championship.

Alexander ended his career with the Crimson Tide with a number of SEC records. He also left Alabama with 15 school records, including a school-best 3,565 career rushing yards. If he had not suffered his ankle injury, many observers believe that he would have been a serious contender for the 1999 Heisman Trophy, the prize awarded to the year's most outstanding college football player. But Alexander refused to dwell on what might have been. "We all set goals and sometimes barely miss them," he said. "Don't be depressed. Instead, be thankful for where you are. Use the near misses as fuel for later success."

> "We all set goals and sometimes barely miss them," Alexander said. "Don't be depressed. Instead, be thankful for where you are. Use the near misses as fuel for later success."

### Joining the Seattle Seahawks

In the first round of the 2000 National Football League draft, the Seattle Seahawks chose Alexander as the 19th overall pick. Many had predicted that the 5'11" and 225-pound running back would be selected sooner, even though he was neither the biggest nor the fastest running back available. For his part, Alexander quietly decided to prove that the teams that had passed him over had made a major error.

When Alexander joined the Seahawks, he was slotted behind Ricky Watters, the team's veteran tailback. Watters taught him valuable lessons, including how to avoid the crushing hit and how to respond to the long grind of an NFL season. "It turned out to be a great blessing to be mentored by one of the greatest running backs of the 1990s," Alexander later said. He played in all 16 games of his rookie season, functioning primarily as the team's short-yardage back on third and fourth downs. He scored his first professional touchdown against the Kansas City Chiefs in a game that likewise marked his first career start. Although he saw limited action in his rookie season, his 4.9 yards-per-carry average was the second highest among first-year NFL running backs.

Alexander's second season marked his emergence as an NFL star. When Watters suffered a serious shoulder injury early in the season, the former Crimson Tide star found himself in the starting lineup. He made the

*In this November 2001 game against the Oakland Raiders,
Alexander rushed for 266 yards on 35 carries.*

most of the opportunity, wracking up big yardage in nearly every game. Alexander had a particularly monumental game in November against the Oakland Raiders. In his most productive game to date, he scored three touchdowns and rushed for 266 yards on 35 carries—the fourth-best single-game total in NFL history and a franchise record. His offensive performance in that game, which included an 88-yard touchdown run, earned him recognition as the American Football Conference Player of the Week. "Shaun has gotten better with his decision-making each week. He is becoming much more aware, and a much better situational runner than he was at the beginning of the year," said Head Coach Mike Holmgren after the game.

Despite only starting in 12 games during the 2001 season, Alexander led the NFL with 14 rushing touchdowns. He finished the year with 1,318 yards on 309 attempts, the fifth-highest rushing total in the history of the team. Following the 2001 season, he was hired by the Fox Sports network to host a short-lived variety show, *Shaun Alexander Live.* In it, the writers often poked fun at Alexander's lack of recognition among fans despite his accomplishments on the field. The Christmas special, for example, included a skit set in Seattle's Factoria Mall that opened with the line: "Santa, I think all I want this year for Christmas is some people to recognize me."

## Superstar in Seattle

Watters retired at the end of the 2001 season, leaving Alexander as Seattle's undisputed backfield star entering the 2002 season. Once again, Alexander proved that he could carry the team on his broad shoulders. On September 29, 2002, for example, he scored a career- and franchise-record five touchdowns in one game against the Minnesota Vikings. Moreover, he scored all five touchdowns before the end of the second quarter, which set the NFL record for touchdowns in a single half. Alexander finished the 2002 season as the National Football Conference (NFC) leader in both rushing touchdowns (16) and overall touchdowns scored (18). (The Seahawks had switched from the AFC to the NFC prior to the 2002 campaign.)

————— **"** —————

*When Alexander angrily criticized his coach in a post-game outburst, he ignited a storm of controversy. Stung by accusations that he was just another pampered athlete, he apologized for his comments two days later. "I'm human," he confessed. "Anybody can, at one time, pop off. And I've done it several times. I'm not worried about my image."*

————— **"** —————

In 2003 Alexander tallied 16 touchdowns and a career-best 1,435 yards. This performance resulted in his first invitation to play in the Pro Bowl, the NFL's all-star game. He earned his second trip to the Pro Bowl in 2004, after recording a career-best 1,696 yards rushing (second best in the NFL) and an NFL-best 20 total touchdowns. The Seahawks qualified for the NFC playoffs in both 2003 and 2004, but lost in the first round on both occasions.

The end of the 2004 season also was marred by the first negative publicity of Alexander's career. He entered the final week of the season in a neck-and-neck duel with Curtis Martin of the New York Jets for the league rushing title. After both teams finished their last games, Alexander trailed Martin by a single yard. When the Seahawks star learned this, he angrily criticized Head Coach Mike Holmgren for ordering a quarterback sneak on the team's last offensive play—even though it resulted in a division crown-clinching touchdown. Alexander even claimed that Holmgren had "stabbed him in the back" by failing to call a running play for him.

Alexander's post-game outburst ignited a storm of controversy. Stung by accusations that he was just another selfish, pampered athlete, Alexander apologized for his comments two days later. "I'm human," he confessed. "Anybody can, at one time, pop off. And I've done it several times. I'm not worried about my image." But he also claimed that his remarks were blown out of proportion. "You take any story, and you can get confused. You can make the bad guy look like the good guy. You can make Cinderella look like the wicked stepsister. . . . That's just reality. I understand that," he said.

Since the 2004 incident, Alexander has repeatedly praised Holmgren's leadership of the team. "[He is] a man of enormous confidence . . . [who] instills that same confidence in the rest of us," Alexander declared. Before training camp in 2005, he signed a one-year, $6.32 million contract with Seattle that included an option for him to become an unrestricted free agent at the season's end.

*Alexander proudly accepts the 2005 NFL Most Valuable Player trophy.*

## Advancing to the Super Bowl

In 2005 Alexander helped guide the Seattle Seahawks to the most successful season in franchise history. Described by Dennis Dillon of the *Sporting News* as "the NFL's most underappreciated, underrated and underexposed superstar," Alexander won the NFL rushing title with 1,880 yards. In addition, his 28 total touchdowns set a new single-season NFL record in that category. On January 5, 2006, he was named Most Valuable Player in the NFL, and was recognized as the Associated Press Offensive Player of the Year the following day. He joined the ranks of Emmitt Smith, Priest Holmes, and Marshall Faulk as one of the few tailbacks in NFL history to enjoy back-to-back seasons of 20 or more touchdowns and became the only player to achieve at least 15 touchdowns for five consecutive years. He also became the first Seahawk in team history to be featured on the cover of *Sports Illustrated.*

More importantly, Alexander's terrific play was the single greatest factor in Seattle's 13-3 division-winning regular season mark. The Seahawks then toppled the Washington Redskins in the divisional playoffs. Alexander, however, suffered what the *Seattle Post-Intelligencer* termed a "franchise-chilling concussion" 10 minutes into the first quarter. He missed the rest of the Washington game, but returned to the field the following weekend for the conference championship game. He churned out 132 rushing yards to set a team playoff record and scored two touchdowns to lift the Seahawks over the Carolina Panthers. This triumph put the Seahawks in Super Bowl XL to face the AFC champion Pittsburgh Steelers. "It hasn't sunk in yet that we're one game away from being legendary," he admitted following the win.

*Alexander tried to explain the mixed emotions he felt about his Super Bowl experience. "I was sad we had lost so badly, but I had joy in the midst of disappointment," he said.* **"I had actually played at the Super Bowl."**

In the days leading up to the big Super Bowl clash, the Steelers made it clear that their top defensive priority was to shut down Alexander. "He can run you over," Steelers safety Troy Polamalu explained. "He has speed, agility and an ability to make people miss. I think his combination is far above anybody else."

As Super Bowl XL unfolded, it became clear that Pittsburgh could not completely neutralize Seattle's talented running back. Alexander rumbled for a team-high 95 yards on 20 tough carries. But despite his success on the ground, the Steelers claimed a 21-10 victory. Afterwards, Alexander tried to explain the mixed emotions he felt about his Super Bowl experience. "I was sad we had lost so badly, but I had joy in the midst of disappointment," he said. *"I had actually played at the Super Bowl."*

### "Alexander the Great"

Following his stellar 2005 season, Alexander had claimed virtually every major Seahawks career rushing record. He finished the year with 7,817 cumulative rushing yards and an amazing 100 touchdowns (89 rushing and 11 receiving) in his six seasons with the team. Accordingly, reporter Bob Brookover of the *Philadelphia Inquirer* called him "probably the greatest player to ever wear a Seahawks uniform." Alexander, however, has his sights set on the NFL record for career touchdowns. "I still don't think I've had my best year," he said. "I want to win the MVP Award a second time, a third time . . . and maybe even a fourth time! Other running backs have won it. . . . But no running back has ever won it two years in a row. I'd like to be the first to do that."

*Alexander and his team suffered a disappointing 21-10 loss against the
Pittsburgh Steelers in the Super Bowl, February 2006.*

Alexander signed a $62 million, eight-year contract extension with Seattle
in March 2006. Even though the agreement stood as the highest-paying
contract in NFL history for a running back, Seahawks President Tim Ruskell
was delighted by the deal. "We have just signed one of the best running
backs in the history of the National Football League in essence to a lifetime
deal," he said. "We couldn't be more excited and the team is excited and

Shaun is obviously excited." Alexander described the contract as a "blessing." He added, however, that "I didn't play football for money . . . the money is not going to be what drives me. It never has and it never will."

Today, Alexander ranks as one of the most popular players in the NFL. He is featured on the cover of the *Madden NFL 07* video game, and is phenomenally popular in Florence, Kentucky, where he returns every off-season. "Yes, the kids are in awe of him when he comes back. But by the same token, he's made them feel a part of it all," Boone County High School coach Rick Thompson told the *Los Angeles Times*. In fact, Alexander telephones the coach before each of the team's Friday night football games to provide encouragement. The Florence community, meanwhile, showed their high regard for their famous native son by changing the name of a street adjacent to his old high school to Shaun Alexander Way.

In August 2006 Alexander published his autobiography, co-written with Cecil Murphey. One of his motivations for writing the book, he stated, was "to show people—especially young people—that success is closer than they may think." With this in mind, he wrote at length about his commitment to ethical principles and self-discipline and emphasized how important these factors were in his professional success. "If it doesn't feel right to do—even though I can't explain the reason—I don't do it," he stated. For example, he abstained from sex prior to marriage and has refrained from using alcohol and drugs. "When you know what's right and wrong, all you have to do is make that decision to do right, avoid wrong—and follow through."

## MARRIAGE AND FAMILY

Alexander married Valerie Boyd on May 18, 2002, in Florence, Kentucky. He met Boyd at a small party hosted by a teammate the day after he arrived in Seattle to begin his NFL career. Alexander proposed to Boyd in December 2001 during a horse-drawn carriage ride through Central Park in New York City. The couple shared their first kiss, Alexander revealed in his autobiography, during their wedding ceremony. "It was worth the wait," he confirmed.

The couple's first daughter, Heaven Nashay, was born on September 21, 2003, a game day. Alexander broke his 34-game starting streak with the Seahawks to assist with the birth. "It was my first catch of the day," he told reporters. Although he missed the first quarter, he arrived in time to finish the game with 58 rushing yards. "I'll always remember that day . . . as very, very special," he said. The Alexander family expanded to include a second daughter, Trinity Monet, on July 28, 2005.

The Alexanders reside in Kirkland, Washington, where they intend to raise a large family. Valerie has disclosed that she would like nine children, and the couple has expressed an interest in adoption. The family attends the Christian Faith Center in Seattle, a nondenominational, Bible-based church. As the player attests in the opening paragraph of *Touchdown Alexander*, "[Football is] what I *do,* but that's not who I *am. . . .* I'm also a husband, a father, and a Christian man. I'm a mentor to younger men as well, because they are our future."

## HOBBIES AND OTHER INTERESTS

Alexander likes to play basketball and golf in his spare time. While on the road, he often plays cards with fellow team members. His favorite television show is "American Idol," and he also regularly watches college basketball games. His favorite actor is Eddie Murphy, and he knows all of the lines to his favorite Murphy film, *Coming to America.* He also listens to gospel music and cites Ruben Studdard and Kirk Franklin as his favorite recording artists.

> **As Alexander attests in the opening paragraph of Touchdown Alexander,** "*[Football is] what I* do, *but that's not who I* am. . . . *I'm also a husband, a father, and a Christian man. I'm a mentor to younger men as well, because they are our future.*"

Alexander also is pursuing his lifelong interest in business and advertising, and envisions himself running a real estate or marketing company following his NFL career. "I will have a few business things that will be more lucrative than the business I'm in right now," he has predicted.

Finally, Alexander sees himself as a philanthropist dedicated to the betterment of the community. He has volunteered time to such organizations as the Fellowship of Christian Athletes, and in 2000 he founded the nonprofit Shaun Alexander Foundation to help young men develop leadership skills and integrity. "This is a fatherless generation," he explained. "Young men are not taught that they're important. We're not taught how to be men, how to make decisions or how to fight for what is correct." The mission of the organization is to encourage youngsters to reach their potential as mentors and role models through education, athletics, character-building, and leadership programs. For example, the foundation offers a session for middle-school age boys that, according to

Alexander, "teaches them the values of staying in school and making wise decisions with money." It even sponsors a chess-playing program for children in the second and third grades.

When asked about his interest in extensive charity work, Alexander has explained that "that's how my mother was, and pretty much how my family is. So I was taught that. Now I'm just in a higher-income level, so we just give a little more." Alexander's efforts on behalf of those less fortunate than himself has caught the attention of other community-oriented NFL players, such as New England Patriot fullback Heath Evans. "For both of us, [football] is more a means to an end," Evans revealed. "We have a heart for kids, especially Shaun. He spends his off-season speaking to youth groups and youth rallies. I think that's Shaun's true passion."

## HONORS AND AWARDS

High School All-American (*Parade; USA Today*): 1995
SEC Player of the Year (SEC Coaches): 1999
NFC Pro Bowl Team: 2003-05
Bert Bell Award (Maxwell Football Club): 2005, Professional American
    Football Player of the Year
ESPY Award (ESPN): 2005, Best NFL Player
NFL Most Valuable Player Award (Associated Press): 2005
NFL Offensive Player of the Year (Associated Press): 2005
NFL Rushing Title: 2005

## FURTHER READING

### Books

Alexander, Shaun, with Cecil Murphey. *Touchdown Alexander,* 2006
Mentink, Jarrett. *Alexander the Great,* 2004 (juvenile)

### Periodicals

*Men's Fitness,* Dec. 2005, p.50
*New York Post,* Feb. 6, 2006, Metro section, p.89
*Seattle Post-Intelligencer,* Nov. 22, 2001, p.D1; Dec. 25, 2002, p.C1; Oct. 22,
    2003, p.D8; Aug. 24, 2006, p.D2
*Seattle Times,* Jan. 4, 2005, p.D1; Jan. 8, 2006, p.D1; July 30, 2006, p.C2
*Sporting News,* Dec. 23, 2005, p.18
*Sports Illustrated,* Jan. 10, 2005, p.28; Dec. 19, 2005, p.46
*Sports Illustrated KIDS,* Mar. 2005, p.53; Sep. 2006, p.26

## Online Articles

http://www.nfl.com/news/archive/01/2006
(NFL.com Wire Reports, "Alexander Ready to Go for NFC Championship," Jan. 18, 2006)
http://www.nfl.com/news/archive/02/2006
(NFL.com Wire Reports, "MVP Alexander Considers Seahawks, Others," Feb. 12, 2006)
http://www.nfl.com/news/archive/04/2006
(NFL News, "Alexander Selected for *Madden '07* Cover," Apr. 21, 2006)

## Online Databases

*Biography Resource Center Online,* 2007

## ADDRESS

Shaun Alexander
Seattle Seahawks
11220 N.E. 53rd Street
Kirkland, WA 98033

## WORLD WIDE WEB SITES

http://www.nfl.com
http://www.rolltide.com
http://www.seahawks.com
http://www.shaunalexander.org

# Carmelo Anthony 1984-

American Professional Basketball Player with the
Denver Nuggets
Second-Leading Scorer in the NBA for the
2006-07 Season

## BIRTH

Carmelo Kyan Anthony—known by the nickname "Melo"—
was born on May 29, 1984, in Brooklyn, a section of New York
City. When he was two years old, his Puerto Rican father,
Carmelo Iriarte, died of liver failure. From this time on,
Carmelo was raised primarily by his African-American mother, Mary Anthony, who worked as a housekeeper. He had two
older brothers, Robert and Wilford, an older sister, Michelle,

and an older half-sister, Daphne. Since all of Carmelo's siblings were more than ten years older than him, he spent much of his youth as the only child at home.

## YOUTH

When Carmelo was eight years old, his mother took a job in housekeeping at the University of Baltimore. The two of them moved to Baltimore, Maryland. They lived in a townhouse on the west side of the city, in a gritty neighborhood known as "The Pharmacy" for its large number of drug dealers.

> *"Everything in my household had God in it," Anthony recalled. "Posters with inscriptions. Two or three Bibles in every room. That was the meaning of God to me. Now that I'm older, I recognize that God is everywhere."*

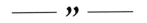

Although young Carmelo was surrounded by drugs, guns, and crime, his mother kept him out of trouble with strict discipline and strong religious values. "Everything in my household had God in it," he recalled. "Posters with inscriptions. Two or three Bibles in every room. That was the meaning of God to me. Now that I'm older, I recognize that God is everywhere."

Throughout his youth, Carmelo spent most of his spare time playing basketball. He played in the streets with neighborhood friends, at a local recreation center, and on various school teams. In fact, his mother's most effective method of discipline was to revoke his court privileges. By the time he reached high school, he had gained a reputation as one of the most talented young players in Baltimore.

## EDUCATION

Anthony attended Towson Catholic High School. It was located on the other side of Baltimore from his neighborhood, so he traveled 45 minutes each way by bus and train to get to school every day. Given his natural basketball talent and growing local reputation, he had no trouble making the varsity team at Towson as a freshman. But staying on the team turned out to be a bigger challenge for him.

Anthony did not bother to work hard on the court or in the classroom. Because of his laziness, bad attitude, and poor grades, he was being dropped

*Anthony with his mother, Mary Anthony.*

from the varsity team. "As a good player in the inner city, you're always hearing people say you're better than you really are and that you don't have to do things like everybody else," he explained. "When I was in Baltimore I took all that talk and ran with it. It distracted me from my schoolwork. I started getting suspended."

Fortunately, losing his spot on the team made an impact on Anthony. He started taking both school and basketball more seriously, and he dedicated himself to working hard and improving. During his junior season, his skills attracted the attention of Jim Boeheim, coach of the Syracuse University Orangemen. Boeheim offered the young player a scholarship, and Anthony committed to Syracuse.

Over the summer between his junior and senior years, Anthony performed well in a number of summer camps and tournaments against other talented players. He suddenly went from being considered a solid regional recruit to one of the top high-school basketball players in the country. In fact, some analysts indicated that he might be good enough to skip college and play professionally straight out of high school. "I was reading my name on the Internet. People were writing about me going to the NBA," he recalled. "I wasn't even thinking about it at first. Then I did. It's hard not to think about it."

If he did want to play college basketball, Anthony knew that he needed to improve his grades and earn a qualifying score on a standardized college aptitude test like the ACT. He took the ACT exam several times, but he always came up a few points short of the required score. "Without the score I'd have no choice," he acknowledged. "I would have gone to the NBA."

### Transferring to a National Powerhouse

For his senior year in high school, Anthony hoped to improve his academic performance and showcase his basketball talents. So he decided to transfer to Oak Hill Academy, a Baptist boarding school in rural Virginia. Oak Hill traditionally boasts one of the best high-school basketball teams in the country and has produced several NBA players over the years. The academy also emphasizes strict discipline and high academic standards. All students are required to wear uniforms, stay on campus, and observe a bedtime.

Before Anthony was accepted to Oak Hill, he had to complete five weeks of summer school in order to catch up academically. "He would go to classes from 7 A.M. to noon, six days a week, and then at 2 P.M. each day he had to meet me at the gym," recalled Coach Steve Smith. "It would be 100 degrees, with no air-conditioning, and we would work him out for two hours, all by himself. Then he would have study hall."

Anthony's hard work in the gym paid off in a terrific senior year. Averaging 21.7 points and 7.4 rebounds per game, he led Oak Hill to a 32-1 record and a number three national ranking. The highlight of the season came in February 2002, when Anthony scored 34 points in a victory over St. Vincent-St. Mary of Akron, Ohio, a top prep team. The team was led by junior standout LeBron James, who went on to star for the NBA's Cleveland Cavaliers. (For more information on James, see *Biography Today Sports,* Vol. 12.) In recognition of his great season, Anthony was named a first-team high-school All-American.

Anthony's hard work in the classroom paid off as well. After several more attempts, he managed to earn a high enough score on the ACT to enable him to go to college. No one was more thrilled about this achievement than his mother. "I didn't want him to go to the NBA," Mary Anthony admitted. "When you get all that fame and fortune, honey, you become a man, right then and there. I wanted my son to have a chance to be 18 years old." Anthony graduated from Oak Hill in 2002 and enrolled as a freshman at Syracuse University. Ultimately, he spent only one year at Syracuse before leaving college to join the NBA.

*Dunking for the Syracuse University Orangemen.*

## CAREER HIGHLIGHTS

### College—The Syracuse University Orangemen

At Syracuse, Anthony became a star from the moment he walked onto the basketball court. He scored 27 points and grabbed 11 rebounds in his first college game, then went on to start every game of the 2002-03 NCAA season at small forward. Anthony led the Orangemen in points per game, with 22.2, and in rebounds, with 10.0. His strong performance helped Syracuse post a 30-5 record for the year.

With Anthony's help, the Orangemen earned a spot in the NCAA tournament. This prestigious event features the top 64 teams in college basketball. They play a single-elimination tournament to decide the national championship. Most analysts thought that Syracuse was too young and inexperienced to advance far in the tournament. But Anthony showed great maturity and helped keep his teammates focused. The team surprised many observers by advancing through the first four rounds to reach the Final Four.

Syracuse faced the University of Texas in its Final Four matchup, and Anthony turned in his best performance of the entire year. He scored a season-high 33 points and added 14 rebounds to lead his team to a 95-84 victory and a spot in the title game. A few days later, Anthony contributed 20 points, 10 rebounds, and 7 assists to help the Orangemen defeat the University of Kansas Jayhawks by a score of 81-78. Syracuse claimed its first NCAA national basketball championship, and Anthony was named Final Four most valuable player. "When I first cut the net down, I thought it was the greatest thing that ever happened to me," he remembered. "But it didn't sink in right away. It took me two or three months to realize that I actually won a national championship."

Despite his outstanding season and spectacular tournament performance, Anthony did not win many individual awards following his freshman year. Some voters snubbed him because they believed he would only play one year for Syracuse before jumping to the NBA. They preferred to reward upperclassmen who had paid their dues in college basketball. But Coach Boeheim dismissed this argument. "If Carmelo stays one year, that's better than no years," he said. "For everyone involved." Anthony did receive his due from some sportswriters. Mike DeCourcy of the *Sporting News*, for instance, expressed the opinion that "Anthony played the college game better than any freshman in NCAA basketball. Ever."

In any case, Anthony enjoyed his college experience, which involved living a normal student lifestyle and sharing a modest apartment with one of his teammates. "I know a lot of people thought I was crazy to be here, but I liked it," he stated. "I just went out, played hard every game, enjoyed college for this one year. After that it's another decision." After completing his freshman year at Syracuse, Anthony decided to give up the remainder of his college eligibility and make himself available for the 2003 NBA draft.

## NBA—The Denver Nuggets

Anthony was selected third overall—behind high-school sensation LeBron James and Serbian seven-footer Darko Milicic—by the Denver Nuggets. He joined a struggling franchise that had tied for the worst record in the league the previous season, at a dismal 17-65, and had not reached the playoffs since 1995. Before he even stepped on the court, Anthony won over Denver fans by praising the city and waiting to sign his 3-year, $8.67 million contract so that the team would have more money to acquire free agents.

Anthony soon proved his value on the court, as well. During the first game of his rookie season, he led the Nuggets to victory over the defending NBA champion San Antonio Spurs. He went on to start every game of the 2003-04 season, averaging 36.5 minutes per game. He led the Nuggets in scoring with 21 points per game, and he also contributed 2.8 assists and 1.2 steals. Thanks to the impressive play of their rookie small forward, the Nuggets posted a vastly improved 43-39 record and earned a spot in the playoffs for the first time in nine years. Unfortunately, Denver was knocked out in the first round by the Minnesota Timberwolves. Anthony won all six Rookie of the Month awards in the Western Conference, but the NBA Rookie of the Year Award went to LeBron James.

> "As a good player in the inner city, you're always hearing people say you're better than you really are and that you don't have to do things like everybody else," Anthony explained. "When I was in Baltimore I took all that talk and ran with it. It distracted me from my schoolwork. I started getting suspended."

## Playing in the Olympic Games

Following his successful rookie NBA season, Anthony joined the U.S. Men's National Basketball Team that played in the 2004 Olympic Games in Athens, Greece. Although he was thrilled to represent his country in international competition, he joined a group of relatively young, inexperienced players that had little opportunity to practice together before the Games.

As the Olympic tournament got underway, Anthony clashed with Team USA Coach Larry Brown, who had a reputation for being hard on young players. When Anthony complained publicly about his lack of playing time, Brown responded by limiting his minutes even further, to an average of 6.7 per game. Brown also informed the media that he found Anthony to be selfish and lazy. Anthony took the criticism personally and told a reporter that he could not wait for the Games to be over. "I'm not saying I'm the greatest player in the world, but I've never sat on nobody's bench," he declared.

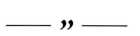

> "I had a mentality that whoever doesn't believe in me, then screw'em," Anthony acknowledged. "I'd go to practice, have an attitude the whole time, wouldn't talk to nobody."

The American men lost an unprecedented two games in the first round, but they still managed to advance to the medal round. After beating Spain in the quarterfinals, however, Team USA lost in the semifinals to the eventual gold medal winner, Argentina. The Americans then defeated Lithuania to claim a bronze medal. Although Anthony found his Olympic experience disappointing, he said that it "motivated me to come back here [to Denver] and try to prove people wrong, that I'm not the person they portrayed me to be."

### Struggling with Off-Court Controversies

Unfortunately, the period following the Olympics marked the lowest point of Anthony's basketball career. He returned to Denver for the start of the 2004-05 NBA season feeling frustrated and stressed out, and his poor attitude affected his relationship with his teammates. "I had a mentality that whoever doesn't believe in me, then screw'em," he acknowledged. "I'd go to practice, have an attitude the whole time, wouldn't talk to nobody."

Next, a series of off-court incidents brought Anthony more bad publicity. In October 2004, he was arrested at Denver International Airport when security personnel found a small bag of marijuana in his backpack before he boarded the Nuggets' team plane. He immediately proclaimed his innocence. "He passed every drug test with the Nuggets because he does not take illegal drugs," said his lawyer, Daniel Recht. "The case has upset

*Anthony is guarded by LeBron James of the Cleveland Cavaliers, December 2003.*

Carmelo a great deal because he does not want his fans, especially the kids, to get the wrong impression of him." The drug possession charge was eventually dropped when one of his friends took responsibility for leaving the marijuana in Anthony's backpack.

The following month, however, the media obtained a video that showed Anthony fighting with another man at a New York City nightclub. He explained that the brawl occurred after the man spit a drink on his girlfriend, MTV personality La La Vazquez. Later, three other men were arrested for trying to force Anthony to pay them $3 million not to release the video of the incident.

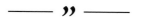

*"I was on top, and then everything was turning so bad," Anthony related. "I felt like the whole world was against me. I started isolating myself. I stopped talking to people, even my family. I was in a shell. . . . I was down, man. Really, really down."*

In December 2004 Anthony became involved in yet another controversy when he appeared in a street video called *Stop Snitching*. The video showed footage of Anthony in his old Baltimore neighborhood hanging out with a group of men, some of whom were alleged drug dealers. It seemed designed to intimidate law-abiding people and prevent them from informing the police about drug dealing and other illegal activities. Anthony insisted that he had nothing to do with the video and did not support its message. "I'm completely against drugs and violence—that's not me," he declared. "I've lost friends to violence. I would never support anybody harming anyone."

Anthony realized that the negative publicity from these incidents threatened to destroy his reputation and even his career. "I was on top, and then everything was turning so bad," he related. "I felt like the whole world was against me. I started isolating myself. I stopped talking to people, even my family. I was in a shell. . . . I was down, man. Really, really down."

### Sitting Out the All-Star Game

The first half of the 2004-05 season was tough for Anthony, as the pressure of dealing with off-court controversies, along with a nagging ankle injury, limited his production. The Nuggets struggled as well, posting a 17-25 record. These factors contributed to Anthony being left off the Western Conference roster for the NBA All-Star Game, which was held in Denver. Anthony's teammates knew that he would feel disappointed by this turn of events. "It may be a little tough for him," said Nuggets center Marcus Camby, "considering last year people were saying he should have been the rookie of the year and not LeBron because we made it to the playoffs. You look at this season, everybody's talking about LeBron and Dwyane Wade and they're barely mentioning Carmelo."

Anthony demonstrated some maturity by showing up for media events and watching the All-Star Game from the sidelines. "I made myself watch guys I play against every day—guys I could beat up on every day—play on my home court," he recalled.

*Anthony is blocked by Chris Wilcox of the Los Angeles Clippers, March 2005.*

"Laughing, joking. And I wasn't down there with them, knowing that I should have been." Anthony seemed determined to overcome his disappointment and focus on the future. "When people think of me, they think of me like I've been in the league 9, 10, 11 years," he noted. "This is only my second year. All-Star Game or not, I've still got plenty of time."

## Turning His Life Around

Both Anthony and the Nuggets started to turn their fortunes around in the second half of the 2004-05 season. Anthony got help from Kiki Vandeweghe, Denver's general manager and a former NBA star, and from Kenyon Martin, a free agent guard who joined the Nuggets. Anthony began meeting with Vandeweghe for extra shooting drills, and the two men also spent a great deal of time discussing the personal challenges of playing professional basketball. "We talked a lot about what's important and where the passion is for him. He was getting away from that at the beginning of the year," the general manager recalled. "Sometimes when you have a setback or when you don't achieve the goal you want, that can drive you even harder. I think he's starting to realize that hard work is what's really going to get him over the top."

Shortly after Martin arrived in Denver, he realized that Anthony was struggling to deal with the leadership role he was expected to play on the team. The veteran took the second-year star aside and provided words of encouragement and support. "One day Kenyon pulled me up and said, 'You look like a lot of stuff is on your mind. I just want to tell you I'm on your side,'" Anthony remembered. "That conversation really turned everything around for me, because from that point on I knew that somebody had my back."

Inspired by his general manager and teammate, Anthony worked hard, lost weight, and regained his shooting touch. He also rekindled his love for the game and became more assertive on the court and in the locker room. "It just took me time to figure things out," he explained. "I had to learn the hard way. But I learned."

In the meantime, the Nuggets hired a veteran head coach, George Karl, who gave the young team more discipline and direction. With Anthony leading the way, Denver posted a 32-8 record in the second half of the season and returned to the playoffs. Unfortunately, the Nuggets were eliminated in the first round once again, this time by the San Antonio Spurs. Anthony averaged 20.8 points, 5.7 rebounds, and 2.6 assists per game on the year.

Anthony continued to improve over the course of the 2005-06 season. He gradually grew more comfortable with Karl's coaching style and expectations, and he incorporated some of the coach's criticism into his game to become a more complete player. Anthony increased his scoring average by 5.7 points per game to average a career-high 26.5, making him the eighth-leading scorer in the NBA for the season. He added a respectable 4.9 rebounds, 2.7 assists, and 1.1 steals per game. He also established a reputation as one of the best clutch players in the league by making five game-winning shots in the last 10 seconds of play. Despite his strong performance, however, he was passed over for the All-Star Team once again. The Nuggets finished the season in their usual fashion, posting a 44-38 record and getting knocked out in the first round of the playoffs by the Los Angeles Clippers.

## Starring for Team USA

During the summer of 2006, Anthony rejoined the U.S. Men's National Basketball Team for the World Championships in Japan. From the time the team started practicing, he impressed the Team USA coaches with his hard work and leadership. "I got phone calls after the third practice of the USA team telling me he's the hardest worker, he's going to be captain of the team," said Nuggets Coach George Karl. "Four days before that, I had people say he wasn't going to make the team."

During the World Championship tournament, Anthony led Team USA in scoring with 19.9 points per game. Although the Americans posted an 8-1 record, they were forced to settle for another bronze medal after losing to Greece in the semifinals. Unlike the last time Anthony had faced international competition, though, no one questioned his level of desire and effort. "Carmelo was the ultimate team player. He had an outstanding summer, starting with our training camp in Las Vegas and ending with being a dominant player in the FIBA World Championships," said Team USA Coach Mike Krzyzewski. "I love the way he plays the game, but I love the way he carries himself as a leader on the Senior National Team even better." In recognition of his strong performance, Anthony earned the 2006 USA Basketball Male Athlete of the Year Award.

## Making Another Mistake

Anthony's outstanding play continued when he rejoined the Nuggets for the start of the 2006-07 NBA season. He led the league in scoring through mid-December, averaging 31.6 points per game. But then he was involved in another damaging incident—this one on the court. It occurred during a game against the New York Knicks at Madison Square Garden. The Nuggets were leading by a comfortable score of 123-100 with just over a minute remaining to play. Some of the Knicks' players and coaches were upset that Anthony and several other Denver starters remained in the game even though the outcome had been decided. They felt that the Nuggets were being unsportsmanlike and running up the score.

> *"Carmelo was the ultimate team player," said Team USA Coach Mike Krzyzewski. "I love the way he plays the game, but I love the way he carries himself as a leader on the Senior National Team even better."*

When Nuggets guard J.R. Smith drove toward the basket, Knicks reserve player Mardy Collins grabbed him around the neck and slammed him to the ground. Smith got up and confronted Collins about the flagrant foul, and New York reserve Nate Robinson came over and pushed Smith away from his teammate. Robinson and Smith then began exchanging punches and fell into the courtside seats. Just as it appeared that the referees and coaches were getting the situation under control, Anthony approached Collins—the player whose hard foul had started the brawl—and dropped him to the floor with a punch to the face. Another Knicks player, Jared Jeffries, followed and threatened Anthony until security guards subdued him.

Television footage of the brawl was replayed over and over on news programs and sports shows across the country. Many fans and analysts were very critical of Anthony's behavior in the incident. The following day, NBA Commissioner David Stern announced the league's penalties for all of the players involved. Anthony received a 15-game suspension—the harshest punishment handed out in the incident, and the sixth-longest suspension in NBA history. "We judged him on his actions on the court," said Stern, "and they deserved a harsh penalty." Six other players were suspended for a total of 42 games, and each team received a fine of $500,000.

Anthony issued a public apology for his role in the brawl. During his suspension, he was allowed to practice with the Nuggets but he could not travel with the team or appear in games. He found the long mid-season layoff very hard to take. "This has probably been the toughest [thing I've been through]," he noted. "As I was going through all of that stuff I went through a couple of years ago, I still had a chance to get out on the court and play." Anthony was grateful for the continued support of fans, which helped raise his spirits during the suspension. "Everywhere I go, the majority of kids, they tell me I'm still their hero, I'm still their role model, and they can't wait until I get back out there on the court," he stated. "That gets my day going."

The Nuggets attempted to make up for the loss of Anthony by trading for Allen Iverson, one of the top guards in the NBA. Nevertheless, Denver struggled to 7-8 record without the young star leading the way. When Anthony finally got back into the Nuggets' starting lineup in late January, he was determined to learn from his mistake and become a better player and person. "I try to tell myself we all make mistakes. And this is a mistake," he said. "I have to put it in the past. One thing I learned from this is you always gotta think before you act. You can't just go out there and do something and then not think about the consequences until a couple of days later."

## Finally Becoming an All-Star

Many observers felt that Anthony's suspension would hurt his chances of making the 2007 All-Star Team. When the Western Conference roster was announced, Anthony learned that he had been passed over once again in fan voting and in coaches' selections. As it turned out, though, NBA Commissioner David Stern added him as a reserve when several other players were unable to appear due to injury. Anthony was thrilled to finally make

*After the disappointment of being left off the All-Star Team in earlier years, Anthony was finally selected for his first All-Star game in 2007. He scored 20 points.*

*Anthony and his mother, Mary, pose with children at a Christmas party at the Cross Community Coalition Family Resource Center in Denver. Anthony has been a big supporter of the Family Resource Center organization.*

the All-Star Team in his fourth professional season. "Any way you can get in there is a blessing," he stated. "For me to be able to get in there—injury or votes or coaches' pick—it didn't matter."

Anthony entered the All-Star Game toward the end of the first quarter and went on to score 20 points to help lift the West to victory. "When I heard my name [announced], I told myself this was the validation of all the hard work I put in," he related. "Just to hear my name out there with the other guys, I was excited. I don't think I've been this excited in a long time."

Anthony continued to play well after the All-Star break. His scoring average of 28.9 points per game ranked second in the NBA, behind only Kobe Bryant of the Los Angeles Lakers. He also contributed 6.0 rebounds, 3.8 assists, and 1.18 steals per game. The Nuggets finished the year with a 45-37 record and made the playoffs, only to lose in the first round to San Antonio once again.

Despite the occasional mistakes that have marked his career, Anthony is still widely recognized as one of the best young players in the NBA. He possesses the speed, ball-handling ability, and outside shot to play on the perimeter, but at 6 feet 8 inches tall and 220 pounds, he also has the size and strength to be a force under the basket. This unique combination creates problems for opposing defenses.

Anthony's offensive skills have also made him one of the most popular players in the NBA, and his jersey often ranks among the best-sellers in all of sports. Given the challenges he has overcome in his life and career, he hopes to serve as an inspiration for his many fans. "Everyone will have bumps in the road, so you need to stay focused," he stated. "I'm here to tell you to stay strong. Don't give up. No matter what, today is a new chance."

## MARRIAGE AND FAMILY

Anthony is engaged to be married to Alani "La La" Vazquez, an MTV video jockey, rap artist, and actress of Puerto Rican descent. They have a son, Kiyan, who was born on March 7, 2007. Anthony and his family live in a 12,500-square-foot mansion in Lakewood, a suburb of Denver. The home features an indoor basketball court, a batting cage, a recording studio, and a large garage to hold Anthony's collection of classic muscle cars from the 1960s and 1970s.

## HOBBIES AND OTHER INTERESTS

In his spare time, Anthony enjoys watching classic TV shows and mafia movies. He is a big fan of the Baltimore Ravens football team and the Baltimore Orioles baseball team. Anthony also enjoys auto racing, and he is the co-owner of an Indy Racing League team with Ron Hemelgarn.

Anthony supports a number of charities, especially ones that help underprivileged children. For instance, he acts as a spokesperson for Family Resource Centers, a Colorado organization that helps poor families. "I came from an area where I saw poverty and hardship, and Family Resource Centers makes a big impact in helping people in those situations," he explained. "If I can make a difference in my community to help people who are struggling, then in the long run, it will make my career more fulfilling."

Anthony also spent $1.5 million to purchase and renovate a former Boys and Girls Club facility in Baltimore. When it reopened in 2007 as the Carmelo Anthony Youth Center, it provided hundreds of children with new after-school recreation and education options, including a gym, computer lab, dance studio, library, and meeting space. "There's nothing wrong with giving back," Anthony stated. "I was one of them kids years ago."

## WRITINGS

*Carmelo Anthony: It's Just the Beginning,* 2004 (with Greg Brown)

## HONORS AND AWARDS

First Team High School All-American (*Parade*): 2002
First Team High School All-American (*USA Today*): 2002
ESPY Award for Best Male College Athlete: 2003
National Freshman of the Year (U.S. Basketball Writers Association): 2003
NCAA Final Four Most Valuable Player: 2003
NCAA First Team All-American (*Sporting News*): 2003
Olympic Men's Basketball: 2004, bronze medal (with Team USA)
USA Basketball Male Athlete of the Year: 2006
World Championship Men's Basketball: 2006, bronze medal (with Team USA)
NBA All-Star Team: 2007

## FURTHER READING

### Books

Anthony, Carmelo, with Greg Brown. *Carmelo Anthony: It's Just the Beginning,* 2004 (juvenile)
*Contemporary Black Biography,* Vol. 46, 2005

### Periodicals

*Current Biography Yearbook,* 2005
*Denver Post,* Dec. 15, 2006, p.D1; Jan. 21, 2007, p.B1
*Denver Rocky Mountain News,* Nov. 1, 2006, p.C1; Feb. 10, 2007, Sports, p.1
*Esquire,* Jan. 2005, p.76; Dec. 2005, p.118
*Sports Illustrated,* Apr. 16, 2003, p.24; Dec. 20, 2004, p.91; Mar. 27, 2006, p.50
*Sports Illustrated KIDS,* May 1, 2004, p.50

### Online Articles

http://www.usabasketball.com/seniormen/2006/06_aoy_anthony.html
(*USA Basketball,* "Carmelo Anthony Honored as USA Basketball's 2006 Male Athlete of the Year," Jan. 16, 2007)
http://www.usatoday.com/sports/basketball/nba/nuggets/2005-02-07-carmelo-second-year_x.htm
(*USA Today,* "Star Nugget Anthony Aims to Regain Shine," Feb. 7, 2005)

**Online Databases**

*Biography Resource Center Online,* 2007, article from *Contemporary Black Biography,* 2005

## ADDRESS

Carmelo Anthony
Denver Nuggets
1000 Chopper Circle
Denver, CO 80204

## WORLD WIDE WEB SITES

http://www.carmeloanthony.com
http://www.nba.com
http://www.usoc.org
http://www.suathletics.com

## Drake Bell 1986-

American Actor and Musician
Co-Star of the Award-Winning Nickelodeon TV
Series "Drake & Josh"

### BIRTH

Jared Drake Bell was born on June 27, 1986, in Newport
Beach, California. He has three brothers and a sister. Bell's
parents are divorced. His father, Joe Bell, is a talent manager
for young actors. His mother, Robin Bell Dodson, is a former
world-champion billiards player whose life has been full of
twists and turns. She learned to play pool at the age of 12 and
became a professional player, but heroin addiction derailed

her career for several years. A renewal of her religious faith finally helped her end her dependence on drugs and turn her life around. In both 1990 and 1991, she won the women's WPBA (World Pool-Billiards Association) world championship in billiards. In 1995 she married Roy Dodson.

## YOUTH

In many ways, Bell had an unusual childhood. Instead of playing soccer or other sports after school, he spent much of his time auditioning for parts in television commercials, TV series, and movies. His father first got him into acting at the age of five, when he appeared in a commercial for Whirlpool Appliances. "I had to sit under a tree and eat a Popsicle," he recalled. "I thought, 'I could get used to this.'"

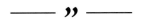

> *Bell did his first commercial at age five for Whirlpool Appliances. "I had to sit under a tree and eat a Popsicle," he recalled. "I thought, 'I could get used to this.'"*

Bell found that he enjoyed the limelight, and he spent many afternoons after school in front of the camera. In fact, he became such a familiar face at auditions that casting directors and others in the business even took to calling him "One Take Drake" for his ability to get everything right on the first try. But in other respects, his interests were those of a typical teenager. He liked listening to music, watching television, and playing video games with friends. Surprisingly, Bell never learned to play pool even though his mother was a world champion. "It's a game that can take you in the wrong direction, so my mom kinda kept us away from the table," he said.

## EDUCATION

During his years at the Vineyard Christian School in Costa Mesa, California, Bell's involvement in show business greatly influenced his attitude toward school. "I didn't want to do what other kids did," he recalled. "I wanted to build my career." As a result, he got a different kind of education from most young people his age. For example, Bell's acting jobs sometimes took him to places that most young people learn about only in textbooks. "How many kids his age get to travel to Third World countries and see the poverty first-hand?" noted Joe Bell, his father and manager. "He gets an education that 90 percent of children don't get because he gets to travel. He's a better, well-rounded child for acting."

Bell attended the Orange County High School of the Arts but he freely admits he was a poor student who did not apply himself. This disinterest in traditional school, combined with his thriving career, led him to leave school and earn a GED (general equivalency diploma) instead.

## CAREER HIGHLIGHTS

Hard work, talent, and perseverance helped Bell climb the career ladder from commercials to small acting parts. His acting credits during these early years ranged from small roles on popular TV shows such as "Seinfeld," "The Drew Carey Show," and "Home Improvement" to appearances alongside film stars Denis Leary and John Cusack. Bell appeared with Leary in the 1995 feature film *The Neon Bible,* a tale about a dysfunctional family in rural Georgia. He also played John Cusack's son in the 1999 HBO film *The Jack Bull* and won a small part in the 2000 feature film *High Fidelity.*

### Big Break with *Jerry Maguire*

It was in the 1996 blockbuster film *Jerry Maguire,* however, that Bell truly caught Hollywood's attention. In *Jerry Maguire* Bell plays Jesse Remo, an injured hockey player's son who angrily condemns the ethics and morality of a high-powered sports agent played by Tom Cruise. In real-life, Drake was awed by Cruise, who invited him into his trailer to play video games. "I, like, couldn't believe I was with Tom Cruise," he told a reporter.

Bell's role in *Jerry Maguire* also required him to use a swear word. According to Bell's father, his ten-year-old son wrestled with his conscience about it but ultimately decided that it was his professional obligation to read the line as it was written. "That's when I realized that Drake was growing up," Joe Bell recalled

Bell's next notable feature film role was in the 2001 movie *Changing Destiny.* He learned to play guitar for the role with a helping hand from fellow cast member Roger Daltrey, the front man of the legendary 1960s band The Who. Bell promptly fell in love with the guitar, started writing songs, and formed his own rock band.

### "The Amanda Show"

In 1999, the 13-year-old Bell landed a role as a regular on the Nickelodeon sketch comedy "The Amanda Show," starring Amanda Bynes. The show brought Bell together with Josh Peck, another longtime child actor. Peck and Bell had met earlier on the Nickelodeon game show "Double Dare," but they did not hit it off at first. "Our original meeting was a fiasco," Peck remembered. "It wasn't exactly love at first sight."

When the two actors were reunited on "The Amanda Show," however, Bell and Peck became friends. In addition, the show boosted both of their careers. Bell was given the opportunity to show off his guitar-playing skills as the effortlessly cool character of Totally Kyle. The heavyset Peck, in turn, unveiled a comic persona that evoked comparisons to actors such as John Candy and Jackie Gleason.

*Bell admitted that it is not a big acting stretch for him to play the role of Drake Parker. "I guess I'm not as cool as he is, but I basically just play me." The big differences between Bell and his character, he observed, are that "I'm mellower and can't fib with a straight face like Drake."*

The on-screen chemistry between Bell and Peck caught the eye of "Amanda Show" producer Dan Schneider, who had once been a child actor himself on the 1980s sitcom "Head of the Class." Within a matter of weeks, Schneider began creating a spin-off show for the two young actors.

**"Drake & Josh"**

On January 11, 2004, "Drake & Josh" debuted on Nickelodeon, complete with a theme song, "I Found a Way," co-written and performed by Bell. The show updates the old "odd couple" formula by pairing two high school students who have to adjust to living in the same house after Drake's mother marries Josh's father. Bell plays the cool, guitar-playing slacker who draws his dorky, responsible stepbrother into his shenanigans. The two forge a brotherly bond through their madcap adventures. A mischievous younger sister, played by Miranda Cosgrove, adds to the humorous mix.

The new show made an instant splash as Nickelodeon's highest rated season premiere in almost 10 years. "The girls are really going for Drake, who is an extremely handsome kid," Schneider observed happily. Bell, meanwhile, acknowledged that the part he plays on the show was not a big acting challenge. "I guess I'm not as cool as he is, but I basically just play me." Still, he did point out some differences between himself and his character: "I'm mellower and can't fib with a straight face like Drake Parker."

*Bell in several different roles: during his days on "The Amanda Show" (top); in his bedroom on the set of "Drake & Josh" (middle); and with the cast of* Yours, Mine, & Ours *(bottom).*

Bell was delighted with the success of "Drake & Josh," but he did not let it interfere with his growing interest in music. In the fall of 2005 Bell released his first album, *Telegraph,* on the Nine Yard Records label. Bell describes his band's sound as "John Mayer meets Dave Matthews." He writes all his own songs and enjoys touring with his band. "Getting the immediate re-action from the crowd is great," he said.

The year 2005 also marked Bell's return to the big screen in the feature film *Yours, Mine & Ours,* starring Dennis Quaid and Rene Russo. Bell plays Dylan, the oldest son of an artsy mother (Russo) who enters into a second marriage with an up-tight father (Quaid). The marriage brings two mismatched clans of children under the same roof. "Yeah, they're dorks in J.Crew clothes and our family is full of individuals and free spirits," Bell explained. "I'm a graffiti artist."

> *"The [car] accident showed me how much I love what I'm doing and that it can be taken away in a split second," Bell said.*

Many critics griped that the film was bland, noisy, and predictable, but others described it as a wholesome and lighthearted family film. *Daily Variety,* for example, charged that the movie was "occasionally overzealous in hard-selling its slapstick elements." But it also commented that *"Yours, Mine & Ours* ultimately emerges as generally pleasant family-friendly fare."

## Recovering from a Near-Tragedy

On December 29, 2005, Bell was seriously injured in a car accident. Another car plowed into him while he was stopped at a traffic light behind the wheel of a 1966 Ford Mustang. The Mustang did not feature a shoulder harness or airbags because such safety features did not exist in the 1960s, so Bell's injuries were quite severe. The crash fractured his neck, knocked out six teeth, and left him wondering about his future. "I was like, 'My ca-reer's over. I don't know how I'm going to look after this,'" Bell recalled.

Bell's recovery was a slow and difficult one. His jaw was wired shut for two months, which meant that smoothies became his breakfast, lunch, and dinner. "We tried putting pizza in a blender, but it smelled like vomit," he said. But friends and colleagues visited him to keep his spirits up during his convalescence. During one visit to the hospital, for instance, co-star Josh Peck told him, "You're still better looking than me, man."

*Bell and Josh Peck on the set of their hit movie,* Drake & Josh Go Hollywood.

Bell's spirits were also lifted by good news about the Drake & Josh television movie, *Drake & Josh Go Hollywood: The Movie,* which aired on January 6, 2006. It received the highest ratings with kids in the 6-11 and 9-14 age groups in Nickelodeon's entire broadcasting history. Some television reviewers, meanwhile, were critical of the movie's plot. But several critics commented on the on-screen chemistry between the movie's young stars.

After recuperating from his accident for a few months, Bell returned to the set of "Drake & Josh." He had a two-and-a-half-inch scar on his chin, but was happy to be back at work. "The accident showed me how much I love what I'm doing and that it can be taken away in a split second," he said.

## A Fan Favorite

Bell's status as one of Hollywood's most popular young actors was confirmed on April 1, 2006, when he earned the favorite actor award at Nickelodeon's annual Kids' Choice Awards. "Drake & Josh" also took best show honors, and it rode into the fall 2006 season as television's number one-rated live-action series with kids ages 2-11. Meanwhile, plans are underway for a Drake & Josh feature film. According to *Daily Variety,* the project will "follow the well-off but sheltered Josh as he gets a crash course in life experience from popular slacker Drake."

## HOME AND FAMILY

Bell lives in an apartment in Los Angeles decorated with framed Beatles posters from the 1960s. He has an extensive collection of vinyl albums, a rotary telephone, and vintage furniture and happily admits that his decorating tastes are basically "neo-grandma."

## HOBBIES AND OTHER INTERESTS

Bell spends much of his spare time playing music or relaxing to music by the Beatles and other bands from the 1960s. "Nothing today compares with that music," he said. His favorite Beatle was John Lennon, but he also admires Paul McCartney and would like to someday work with him.

When he is on break from filming, Bell says that a typical day for him is to "hang out in my pajamas and eat cereal and watch cartoons." He also enjoys the work of the classic comedy duo Laurel and Hardy and 1950s movie icon James Dean. His favorite contemporary actor is Johnny Depp.

The actor/musician also makes time for charity work "to help those not as fortunate as me." For example, Bell has volunteered his time to help Gibson Musical Instruments raise money for breast cancer. "This cause hits pretty close to home," he explained. "I lost my Aunt Sandra to breast cancer."

## SELECTED CREDITS

### Television

"The Amanda Show," 1999-2001
"Drake & Josh," 2004-

## Films

*Jerry Maguire,* 1996
*High Fidelity,* 2000
*Changing Destiny,* 2001
*Yours, Mine & Ours,* 2005
*Drake & Josh Go Hollywood: The Movie,* 2006 (TV movie)

## Recordings

*Telegraph,* 2005
*It's Only Time,* 2006

## HONORS AND AWARDS

Favorite Actor, Nickelodeon Kids Choice Awards: 2006, for "Drake & Josh"

## FURTHER READING

## Periodicals

*Girls' Life,* Feb./Mar. 2006, p.42
*New York Times,* Feb. 1, 2004, p.55
*People, Apr.* 10, 2006, p.105
*Teen People,* Apr. 2005, p.104; Sep. 2006, p.6
*TV Guide,* Apr. 10, 2005, p.2

## Online Articles

http://www.timeforkids.com
    (*Time for Kids,* "Chatting with Drake Bell," undated)

## ADDRESS

Drake Bell
Nickelodeon Studios
231 W. Olive Ave.
Burbank, CA 91502

## WORLD WIDE WEB SITES

http://www.nick.com
http://www.drakebell.com

# Chris Brown 1989-

American R&B Singer and Actor
Creator of the Popular Songs "Run It" and
"Yo (Excuse Me Miss)"

## BIRTH

Christopher Maurice Brown was born on May 5, 1989, in
Tappahannock, Virginia, a small town with a population of
about 2,000. His mother, Joyce Hawkins, operated a day-
care center, and his father, Clinton Brown, worked as a cor-

rections officer at a prison. Brown recalled that his father was tough on the inmates, "but to me he was always real lenient, letting me get away with a lot of stuff." Brown has an older sister, Lytrell Bundy, who works in a bank.

## YOUTH

Brown grew up in a family that loved music. Through his parents' music collection, he became familiar with R&B and pop singers of past and present eras, including Sam Cooke, Stevie Wonder, Michael Jackson, Anita Baker, and Aretha Franklin. Brown began dancing in front of the television at home as a small child. "When I was two," he recalled, "I knew I was bound to do something in entertainment. I was dancing and watching TV and seeing people like Michael Jackson. It just came to me, and from that point on, I was always dancing." However, it was not until his mother heard him singing along with Usher's "My Way" when he was 11 years old that she realized her son had an undeniable talent. "My mom was like, 'You can sing?' And I was like, 'Well, yeah, Mama.'"

> "It's funny: I miss my public school, because in public school you can take your test and get your work done but you're around your friends and girls, and that way you're more influenced to do [your work] instead of just being with one tutor by yourself."

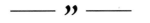

## EDUCATION

Brown attended Essex High School in Tappahannock until early 2005, when he moved to the New York area to pursue a music career. Since that time he has been home schooled and still travels with a tutor. On his web site he lists his favorite school subjects as math and biology. Public appearances and media interviews are scheduled around his school day so they do not interfere with his education. Brown has said that he sometimes misses his old school, which had about 500 students. "It's funny: I miss my public school, because in public school you can take your test and get your work done but you're around your friends and girls, and that way you're more influenced to do [your work] instead of just being with one tutor by yourself." Brown's manager, Tina Davis, said that "his education is just as important to us, so he goes to school every morning, even Saturdays and Sundays."

## CAREER HIGHLIGHTS

### Getting Started

Brown enjoyed singing for his friends and girls at school but did not do so professionally until his father met a talent agent by chance at a local gas station. Soon Brown began recording songs with a production team in Richmond, Virginia, about 45 miles from his home. He was 13 years old. He later connected with a songwriter and producer in New York and traveled there with his mother to audition for a recording contract with a national label.

In August 2004 he met Tina Davis, who was then vice president of A&R (Artists and Repertoire) for Def Jam Records, which included the artists Jay-Z, Ludacris, and LL Cool J. A&R executives like Davis scout and develop new talent. Davis was enthusiastic about Brown's potential and so was company president L.A. Reid, who had helped launch the careers of such well-known acts as TLC and Usher in the 1990s. However, before a deal could be finalized, Davis left Def Jam. She became Brown's business manager, and under her guidance he signed instead with Jive Records. Jive is part of the Zomba Label Group, which includes such top-selling performers as Justin Timberlake and R. Kelly.

> ── **"** ──
>
> *Brown was ecstatic when he heard his song "Run It!" on the radio for the first time. "I was actually at my house in New Jersey, and [radio station] Hot 97 played the record. I was just real excited. I knew it was my record when I first heard the beat, so I ran upstairs and told my mom, 'Ma, it's on, it's on, it's on!' So it was just crazy."*
>
> ── **"** ──

Brown spent the next few months recording songs for his first album. He worked with several highly sought-after songwriters and producers, including Sean Garrett and Scott Storch ("Gimme That," "Run it!" featuring Juelz Santana), Vidal Davis and Andre Harris ("Yo [Excuse Me Miss]"), Jermaine Dupri ("Run It!" Remix featuring Bow Wow and Jermaine Dupri), and Bryan Michael Cox ("Say Goodbye"). Altogether Brown recorded about 50 songs, only 15 of which would be chosen for the CD. (The rest are reserved for later release, possibly on a movie soundtrack or on a subsequent album.) Brown has said that the songs selected for the album were chosen specifically to reflect age-appropriate themes for a teenage performer, including hanging out with friends,

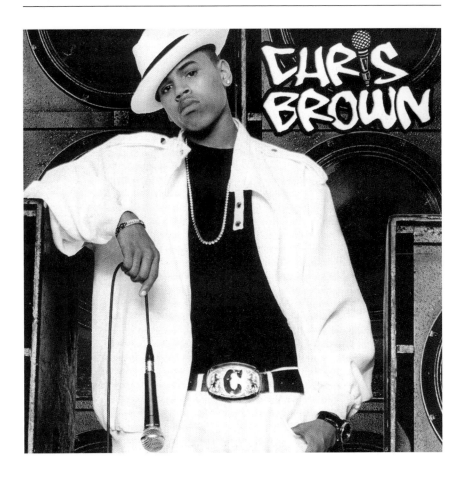

meeting girls, and falling in love. "I'm young," he explained on his web site. "I want to appeal to people my age as well as older people. This gives me time to grow with my audience."

## Releasing "Run It!"

Brown's debut single, "Run It!" featuring rapper Juelz Santana, was released on July 26, 2005. Brown was ecstatic when he heard the song on the radio for the first time. "I was actually at my house in New Jersey, and [radio station] Hot 97 played the record. I was just real excited. I knew it was my record when I first heard the beat, so I ran upstairs and told my mom, 'Ma, it's on, it's on, it's on!' So it was just crazy." The video for "Run It," which was nominated for an MTV Music Award in 2006, showcases Brown as both a singer and dancer. In the video, teenagers climb through a window into a school gym at night and hold an impromptu dance. The boys and girls face off in groups, each showing their dance moves. Brown's dancing wins the interest of his beautiful counterpart, but both groups scatter when security guards arrive. Interviewed on his web site, Brown said that he came up with the concept for the video because he "just wanted to bring to the kids and everybody just dancing, the whole feel of dancing. . . . Sneaking away and going into this abandoned school and just gettin' off, doing what you gotta do—dance, holler at girls, the girls holler at you."

The release of his self-titled debut CD, *Chris Brown,* was planned for fall 2005. But first, Jive Records sent Brown out on a tour to make personal appearances around the country. He visited schools and malls, posing for photographs and signing autographs for many young fans. With his good looks, fashion sense, and personal charm, Brown quickly established a large female fan base. He also made a favorable impression on the industry insiders who would support his career. According to Colby Colb, a radio programming director in Philadelphia, "I was taken aback by the fact that he was willing to sign autographs for three hours. But that's the key to his appeal: He's like a regular guy who gets the whole star thing but isn't diva-fied yet. He's very humble."

**""**

*Brown said that he came up with the concept for the "Run It!" video because he "just wanted to bring to the kids and everybody just dancing, the whole feel of dancing. . . . Sneaking away and going into this abandoned school and just gettin' off, doing what you gotta do—dance, holler at girls, the girls holler at you."*

**""**

By late November 2005, "Run It!" was the *Billboard* Hot 100 No. 1 single in the United States, holding that position for five weeks. It topped the *Billboard* Pop 100 chart as well, and remained in the top spot throughout the holidays and into January 2006. Meanwhile, Brown's CD, *Chris Brown,* debuted in the No. 2 position on the *Billboard* 200 hot album list in late November. In its first week of sales the CD sold 155,000 copies. During the same week, "Run It!" was downloaded more than five million times, according to Jeff Leeds in the *New York Times.* Jive Records vice president Lisa Cambridge commented on the quick success of Brown's first release. "We did [a music] industry showcase last May in front of 300 people. That was the first time he'd ever been onstage, singing into a microphone," Cam-

*Showing off his dance moves on MTV's "Total Request Live"(TRL).*

bridge said. "Chris went from singing in front of the mirror in his bedroom to having the No. 1 [single] in the country."

## Krumping

Brown's second single, "Yo (Excuse Me Miss)" was released in February 2006. The video for the song features Brown and two companions dancing down the sidewalk in pursuit of a gorgeous girl he glimpsed through a shop window. Brown dances in what is known as the krump style. Krump is a high-energy, acrobatic form of hip-hop dance that evolved in south central Los Angeles—in part as an alternative to street violence. Brown described krumping as "a new style, more aggressive dancing, releasing anger, releasing stress." It fuses funk and hip-hop styles from the 1970s through the 1990s with mock fighting postures. Among the styles it draws on are *popping,* which involves quickly contracting and relaxing muscles to create jerking movements, and *locking,* which combines rapid hand and arm movements with a relaxed lower body. Lockers include quick collapses to one or both knees, interact with the audience, and frequently incorporate props (such as a hat) into their routines. Many reviewers raved about Brown's dancing, comparing him to such innovative dancers as Michael Jackson and Usher. Commentator Melissa Ruggieri, for example, called his dancing "phenomenal, a nonstop blur of airborne sneakers and rubbery limbs."

Brown found success with other singles from the *Chris Brown* CD. "Gimme That" peaked at No. 15 on the Hot 100 chart, and "Say Goodbye" hit the *Billboard* Hot R&B/Hip Hop chart in November 2006. Both singles were supported by memorable videos. In "Gimme That," Brown falls asleep in a crowded modern train station and is transported in a dream to the same station in the 1920s. He sings and dances in an attempt to impress a beautiful older woman. The single and video feature rapper Lil' Wayne, who introduces Brown as "the 16-year-old phenom, Chris Breezy." Soon the nickname was picked up in the media and on the web by fans around the world.

In the confessional ballad "Say Goodbye," Brown searches for the right way to break up with a girl after he meets someone new. He sings: "How do you let it go? When you, / You just don't know? What's on, / The other side of the door / When you're walking out, talk about it / Girl I hope you understand / What I'm tryin' to say. / We just can't go on / Pretending that we get along." "Say Goodbye" became Brown's third single to reach the top ten on the *Billboard* Hot 100 Chart.

## Relating to Teens

Themes of romance, desire, and disappointment echo throughout the songs on *Chris Brown*. In "Ya Man Ain't Me," Brown addresses a girl hoping to convince her to leave her current boyfriend to be with him. "Winner" uses a boxing analogy to describe how he feels knocked out by a beautiful girl he has met. Discussing in particular the song "Young Love" on his web site, he explained, "Even when teenagers really are in love with each other a lot of older people are like 'Love? You're barely old enough to go outside at night!' But what they don't know is that kids our age really do have feelings for each other, so this song is basically telling older people that even though we're young, we still love each other. I think all the teenagers can relate to it." Brown's favorite song on the CD is the final one, "Thank You." As he explained, "I wrote the whole song, really, just basically thanking my fans." In it he sings, "Thank you, you mean so much to me, / I don't know what to do / (For you and you and you and you and you and you) / Thank you from my heart right to my soul."

> "[When] you dance and sing, everybody's gonna compare you to Usher or Michael. I see myself as a totally different artist, equally unique," Brown once said. "I just want to be recognized as being my own person and as being a unique artist in the game."

Because of his youth, his innovative dance moves, and his smooth vocals, Brown has often been compared to his predecessors Michael Jackson and Usher. And, like them, Brown has been embraced by legions of female fans, making him one of today's hottest teen idols. Reviewer Melissa Ruggieri described his voice in the *Richmond Times Dispatch* as "a respectable blend of Michael Jackson falsetto and Usher heftiness." Responding to such comparisons, Brown said, "[When] you dance and sing, everybody's

gonna compare you to Usher or Michael. I see myself as a totally different artist, equally unique," Brown once said. "I just want to be recognized as being my own person and as being a unique artist in the game."

In June 2006 the DVD *Chris Brown's Journey* was released. The disc includes a 25-minute documentary showing footage of his tour stops in Japan and England. It also contains performance footage, outtakes, videos, and "making of" segments for "Gimme That," "Yo (Excuse Me Miss)," and "Run It!"

In August 2006 Brown set off on a 29-city U.S. tour with R&B singer Ne-Yo, the girl group Cherish, and the rappers Lil' Wayne, Dem Franchize Boyz, and Juelz Santana. In addition to the songs from his debut CD, Brown's show included a medley of the Michael Jackson hits "Rock with You," "Billie Jean," and "Wanna Be Startin' Somethin.'" For these numbers he wore one sequined glove in a tribute to Jackson's signature look from the 1980s. Brown's wardrobe onstage featured a variety of looks, ranging from streetwear for "Run It!" to a three-piece white suit for the show's opening number "Gimme That." Throughout the show Brown created excitement with his remarkable dance moves. According to music reviewer David Lindquist, "Brown moved in ways that freshly combined leaping, spinning, gliding, stop-action and slow-motion."

## Heading in New Directions

For Brown, the success of his music career is only the beginning. "I wanna be a mogul. . . . I wanna be a singer, actor, entrepreneur, have a clothing line, be an executive everything." The young star has already begun pursuing an acting career. Brown joined the cast of the hit television show "The O.C." for about several episodes in 2006-07, the show's final season. He played Will Tutt, a lonely band geek who becomes friends with Kaitlin Cooper (played by Willa Holland). "I play, like, a band geek—I'm really stepping out of my own character," he said. "I was kind of a geek in school. . . . But [on the show] I'm geeked out all the way. I'm just trying to be myself and then be the character [the role calls for]. I don't look at it like this role takes away from who I am." After filming his first TV appearances, Brown confided that "I'm a rookie in the [acting] game, so the nervous jitters kicked in, but I had to get over it."

Brown made his feature film debut in *Stomp the Yard* (2007). This dance movie is about DJ Williams (played by Columbus Short), a troubled kid and street dancer from Los Angeles who moves to Atlanta to attend the historically black college Truth University. There, he discovers stepping, a precise form of dance based on African-American tradition, and becomes the focal point of a fierce rivalry between two fraternities. Brown had a secondary role as DJ's younger brother, Duron.

——— " ———

*"I want to be a role model— to tell kids to believe they can be something when they're older. . . . That they can follow their dreams and still be good. Innocence is good."*

——— " ———

Brown's versatility as an artist has convinced many that his success will not be short-lived. According to BET senior music director Kelly G., "There's a huge void out there. There aren't many popular teenage boys singing who can connect with teen girls. Our audience wants Chris Brown. With Usher growing up, there's a new kid on the block who can sing and dance." Those sentiments were echoed by Barry Weiss, president of the Zomba Label Group. "[Brown has the] richness of vocal tone, the million-dollar smile, the star appeal. . . . Superstars like Usher come along every 10, 15 years. Chris Brown is in that category. He's a burgeoning superstar."

The music press has greeted Brown's success enthusiastically, calling him the "new prince of pop" and the "future of R&B." He won a host of awards in 2006, including recognition at the BET Awards, the Billboard Awards, the NAACP Image Awards, the Soul Train Music Awards, and the Teen Choice Awards. Still, Brown insists that he is a normal kid. "I just try to keep the same exact way I was in Virginia. . . . I feel the need to accomplish stuff. And God will bless me if I work and can be so humble." However, he recognizes that many kids will look up to him as a role model. "I want to be a role model—to tell kids to believe they can be something when they're older. . . . That they can follow their dreams and still be good. Innocence is good."

*Brown with Columbus Short in* Stomp the Yard.

## HOME AND FAMILY

Brown lives with his mother in Cliffside Park, New Jersey.

## MAJOR INFLUENCES

Brown has cited Kim Burrell, Sam Cooke, Marvin Gaye, Donnie Hathaway, Michael Jackson, Usher, and Stevie Wonder as some of his musical influences.

## HOBBIES AND OTHER INTERESTS

In his limited free time, Brown enjoys basketball, playing video games, drawing, and hanging out with his friends.

## CREDITS

### CDs

*Chris Brown,* 2005

### TV and Movies

"One on One," 2006
"The Brandon T. Jackson Show," 2006

"The O.C.," 2006-07
*Stomp the Yard,* 2007

## DVDs

*Chris Brown's Journey,* 2006

## HONORS AND AWARDS

BET Awards: 2006 (two awards), Best New Artist and Viewer's Choice for "Yo (Excuse Me Miss)"
Billboard Music Awards: 2006 (three awards), Artist of the Year, Male Artist of the Year, New Artist of the Year
Image Award (NAACP): 2006, Outstanding New Artist
Soul Train Music Award: 2006, Best R&B/Soul or Rap New Artist for "Run It"
Teen Choice Award: 2006, Choice Breakout Music Artist (Male)

## FURTHER READING

### Periodicals

*Ebony,* June 2006, p.32
*Indianapolis Star,* Aug. 18, 2006, p.20; Aug. 19, 2006
*Jet,* Jan. 30, 2006, p.40; May 29, 2006, p.54
*Los Angeles Times,* Nov. 27, 2005, p.E46; Oct. 4, 2006, p.E3
*New York Times,* Mar. 9, 2006
*New York Times Upfront,* Nov. 28, 2005, p.6
*People,* Dec. 12, 2005, p.90
*Richmond (VA) Times Dispatch,* Dec. 25, 2005, p.H1; Aug. 22, 2006, p.C1
*Sunday Times* (London), Feb. 12, 2006, p.16

### Online Articles

http://www.allhiphop.com/Alternatives/?ID=226
(*All Hip Hop,* "Chris Brown: New Kid on the Block," Oct. 2005)
http://www.pollstar.com/news/viewhotstar.pl?Artist=CHSBRO
(Pollstar, "Chris Brown," Feb. 20, 2006)
http://www.teenpeople.com/teenpeople/article/0,22196,1553733_2,00.shtml
(*Teen People,* "Catching Up with Chris Brown and Ne-Yo," Nov. 17, 2006)

### Online Databases

*Biography Resource Center Online,* 2007

## ADDRESS

Chris Brown
Jive Records
137-139 West 25th Street
New York, NY 10001

## WORLD WIDE WEB SITES

http://www.chrisbrownworld.com
http://www.myspace.com/chrisbrown

## Regina Carter 1963?-

American Jazz Violinist
Winner of the 2006 MacArthur "Genius" Award

### BIRTH

Regina Carter was born in Detroit, Michigan. She does not reveal her age, but her birthday is believed to be August 6, 1963, although some sources say 1966. Her father, Dan Carter, worked for the Ford Motor Company, and her mother, Grace Williamson Carter, was a kindergarten teacher. Carter has two older brothers, Danny and Reginald.

## YOUTH

Carter's parents were not musical themselves, although they insisted their children receive a well-rounded education that included the arts. Carter began piano lessons at age two after surprising her brothers' piano teacher by playing back a melody by ear. However, her extreme youth made lessons problematic. At her first recital she changed the ending of the song she played. When her teacher corrected her, instead of playing it right, the little girl hit the wrong note over again, only with more emphasis. She recalled, "I just hammered down the note I had played before—like, 'No, this is the one *I* want to play.'"

*Carter champions the Suzuki method for children, saying, "Children are not always taken with an instrument; they want to play something right away. So if they can play a tune right away, then you've got them. Otherwise it's not music; it's exercise."*

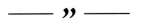

The piano teacher suggested that a Suzuki violin program might be more conducive to Carter's creativity and her uncanny ability to play by ear. Suzuki is a method developed in Japan in the mid-20th century that uses young children's natural ability to learn new things as a basis for music instruction. The Suzuki method was created by Shinichi Suzuki, a Japanese musician and teacher who created a music education program to reflect his belief that talent can be nurtured in every child. (For more information on Suzuki, see *Biography Today*, Sep. 1998.) Carter's mother enrolled her at the Detroit Community Music School, which had recently begun offering the program. She was then four years old.

For the next eight years the young musician attended a weekly solo lesson after school one day each week and a group lesson from 8:00 to 3:00 on Saturday. She later recalled that the teacher used a variety of methods to help the students learn how to improvise songs and to read music. In one exercise, the teacher would create a melody line and then call on one of the students to add a line to follow. That student would play until the teacher called on another student, who would take over and continue to develop the song. Describing the exercise, Carter said, "So it was improvisation. . . . I think that really got me started on being free from the paper, making up things." To further develop the students' music knowledge, her violin teacher gave each student classical music records to take home and listen to each week. Carter now champions the Suzuki method for children, saying, "Children are not always taken with an instrument; they want to play something right away. So if they can play a tune right away, then you've got them. Otherwise it's not music; it's exercise."

As a child, Carter led a busy life. In addition to school and violin lessons, she continued with piano and also took tap and ballet. She enjoyed violin more than her other lessons, and by age 12 she planned a career as a soloist with a symphony orchestra. Her parents fully supported her aspirations, but playmates in her neighborhood wondered at her dedication. Many of the other students in her violin program, however, were the children of professional musicians. Through her close association with these families Carter gained further insights into musical technique and the life of a performance musician. As a teenager she trained in the youth program of the Detroit Symphony Orchestra. From time to time visiting musicians provided master classes to the young students, and Carter had the opportunity to participate in workshops taught by such renowned classical violinists as Itzhak Perlman and Yehudi Menuhin.

## EDUCATION

Carter attended Cass Technical High School, a magnet school in Detroit. The school is known locally as Cass Tech and has a rich history dating back to 1861. Famous alumni of the school include the singer Diana Ross, the comedian David Alan Grier, and the musician Jack White, among many others. At Cass Tech, the music program was rigorous. In addition to violin, Carter took viola, oboe, and choir. She performed with a chamber group and the school orchestra. At Cass Tech she befriended fellow student Carla Cook, who went on to become a successful jazz singer and with whom Carter collaborated on the 2006 CD *I'll Be Seeing You: A Sentimental Journey.*

At that point Carter was following a musical education that would prepare her for a career in classical music. But occasionally the young musician would add her own ideas into the music as she practiced. According to the violinist, her mother would always call to her from another room, "Regina, that doesn't sound like your lesson to me."

### From Classical to Jazz

After studying classical music for years, Carter became acquainted with jazz as a teenager. In classical music, the performers follow a musical score and play each note as it is written, including the timing and emphasis of the notes. The song will sound essentially the same when played by different musicians at different times. In jazz music, performers play the song in a unique way each time it is performed by using variations of the melody

and the notes that comprise the chords. Musicians also might alter the timing of notes to achieve different effects or work in fragments of other songs. The basic melody often remains intact and is repeated to give the tune a recognizable structure.

As Carter began listening to jazz, her music took off in a new direction. Through friends at Cass Tech she began listening to the works of violinists Jean-Luc Ponty, Noel Pointer, and Stuff Smith. She was particularly inspired after attending a concert by the French jazz violinist Stéphane Grappelli at a jazz festival in Detroit. Carter was excited by the way Grappelli improvised onstage and by the interplay among the band members. She later recalled the impact the concert made on her as a musician. "He was having such a good time, and I felt really elated after that. I said, 'If I could feel this way all the time, that would be it.' So that's what jazz meant to me. That feeling."

While still in high school Carter began performing with the Detroit-based funk band Brainstorm. She continued her high school classes and traveled with the band on weekends. After graduating from Cass Tech, she planned to prepare for a career as a classical musician and enrolled in the music program at the New England Conservatory in Boston, Massachusetts. But her interest in jazz was growing, and after a year she transferred from the classical music department to jazz. Unfortunately, the school did not have a program for jazz violinists, and her background left her unprepared for college-level theory courses.

Carter decided to transfer to another school. She returned to the Detroit area and entered the jazz music program at Oakland University in Rochester, Michigan. There she was taught by Marcus Belgrave, a jazz trumpeter who is well known in the Detroit jazz community. He often invited current and former students to play along with professional musicians in an informal setting at his house. Through Belgrave, Carter met the organist Lyman Woodard and others active in Detroit's jazz scene.

"When I first started playing jazz, I really didn't understand the music," Carter remembered. "I felt like jazz was some kind of big secret. Unlike classical music, you couldn't study books one, two, and three and then you've got it. I found out you have to study the culture of the music as well in order to learn jazz." Jazz professor and baritone saxophonist Marvin "Doc" Holladay told her not to listen to other violin players too much "because you're so new at this you'll start to sound like them." He told her, "Only listen for pleasure." Instead he suggested that she listen to horn players to hear how they phrase the music and pause for breath. Carter completed her music studies and graduated from Oakland University in 1985.

## CAREER HIGHLIGHTS

After college, Carter taught strings in the Detroit public schools. Each week, through a program sponsored by the Detroit Symphony Orchestra, she visited schools that didn't have an orchestra teacher. Before long, however, she decided that a change of scenery would help her develop as an artist. She headed to Europe, spending the next two years in Germany. With her instrument Carter instantly made friends. In a music club on her first night in Munich she asked a jazz band if she could sit in with them to play on a tune. By the end of the night she had made a number of connections in the German jazz scene and gotten a lead on an apartment. During her stay in Germany she performed with various groups. She also spent time listening to records by saxophonist Charlie Parker and trying to imitate his solos on the violin. For a while she worked as a nanny for a German family and taught violin on a U.S. military base.

In 1987 Carter returned to Detroit and joined an all-female jazz band called Straight Ahead. The group achieved some success. They recorded two CDs and were invited to play at the Montreux Jazz Festival in Switzerland. But she eventually decided that her chances of making it in the music industry would be improved by moving to the center of the jazz recording industry—New York City. And in 1991 she did.

## Success in New York

Carter was well known in Detroit among jazz musicians, but in New York she was unknown. She was open to different musical styles and she needed to earn a living, so she performed everything from pop to country while establishing herself. Over the years she was hired to accompany a variety of performers, including Aretha Franklin, Lauryn Hill, Mary J. Blige, Billy Joel, and Dolly Parton. Still, nothing could compare with jazz, which she played with Oliver Lake, Max Roach and the String Trio of New York. Carter worked with that group on three CDs—*Intermobility* (1993), *Octagon* (1994), and *Blues . . . ?* (1996)—before leaving the trio to pursue a solo career. Her first individual effort, *Regina Carter*, was released in 1995 on Atlantic Records.

*"[I don't] approach the violin as a violin; I approach it as a jazz instrument. The minute you approach it as a violin, it has a stereotype about it and ways that you're supposed to play it. I've gotten rid of all those ideas."*

During the late 1990s Carter began solidifying her reputation as a technical, if unorthodox, musician with a unique appeal. *Something for Grace*, released in 1997, is an album dedicated to the artist's mother, Grace. In a favorable review, Hilarie Grey claimed that the songs soar and described Carter's style on the CD as "an aggressive, elemental approach to the violin." Critic Mike Joyce was equally positive. Particularly citing the cuts "Soul Eyes," "Listen Here," and "I'll Write a Song for You," he praised the album like this: "With both her pen and bow, Carter is able to imbue her music with rhythmic spirit and an all-embracing spirituality." During 1997 she toured with Wynton Marsalis's production *Blood on the Fields* and was featured in a solo that garnered attention from the press and made an indelible impression on audiences.

Building on these successes, Carter changed record companies, signing with the Verve Music Group in a contract that allowed her more artistic freedom. *Rhythms of the Heart* (1999) was her first CD issued by Verve. This release saw her moving away from the smooth jazz presented on her earlier CDs. *Rhythms of the Heart* includes a reggae arrangement of the Motown classic "Papa Was a Rolling Stone" featuring singer Cassandra Wilson and the up-tempo "Lady Be Good" that drew comparisons to her forebear Grappelli. Critics responded to the adventurous energy of the collection, which showcased her wide repertoire and technical virtuosity.

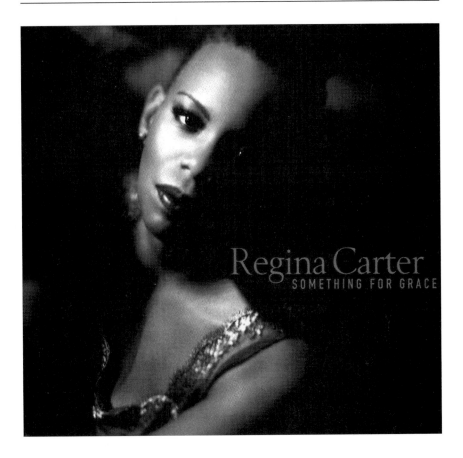

Released in 2000, *Motor City Moments* presents an homage to her home-town. Carter enjoyed selecting the songs for the CD, each one written or performed memorably by an artist with a connection to Detroit. She told an interviewer at the time, "This was a fun project. You should have seen one corner of my apartment. It was piled high with material . . . but it all boiled down to two factors: the piece had to speak to me on my instrument, and I had to feel that I could add something of my own to it." Works included Stevie Wonder's "Higher Ground" and Marvin Gaye's "Don't Mess with Mister T." Performers on the record included many musicians Carter knew from her early career in Detroit, including Belgrave on trumpet and her second-cousin James Carter on saxophone.

## Playing the Cannon

In December 2001, Carter received an offer of a lifetime. The city of Genoa, Italy, invited her to play the Cannon (Il Cannone), one of the most famous

*Carter playing the Guarneri violin, known as the Cannon. The violin was made in 1743 by Guarneri del Gesu and owned by composer Niccolo Paganini.*

violins in existence. The instrument is named for the "explosive" sound that can be achieved on it. It was crafted in 1743 and was bequeathed to the people of Genoa in 1840 upon the death of its owner, the Italian composer Niccolo Paganini. The Italians extended their invitation to Carter as a gesture of solidarity in the aftermath of the terrorist attacks on New York City and Washington DC on September 11, 2001. Carter was both the first jazz musician and the first African American to play the Cannon. The concert in Genoa on New Year's Eve 2001 was an unprecedented success, and Carter received permission to record a CD using the Cannon.

That CD, *Paganini: After a Dream*, was recorded in 2002 and released in 2003. It includes both classical compositions by Maurice Ravel and Claude DeBussy and more contemporary works, including "Cinema Paradiso" by the Italian composer Ennio Morricone. Reviewers praised her performances on the recording for bringing out the expressive sound of the violin over a range of musical styles. Carter, too, was pleased with the results. At the time she said, "I love this recording and not just because of being able to use this violin, but because there was so much magic happening when we recorded the music. You could just feel the energy in the room and many of the tunes were recorded on the first takes. It was really, really scary and we thought, 'Wow, what's happening, like what's going on here?'" Carter played a farewell concert with the Cannon in New York City in November 2003 before returning the priceless instrument to the city of Genoa.

*I'll Be Seeing You: A Sentimental Journey,* Carter's sixth CD as a solo artist, was released in 2006. The album was conceived as a tribute to her mother, who had recently passed away. The song list includes her mother's favorites as well as other American standards from the 1920s to 1940s. In addition to "I'll be Seeing You," the CD includes renditions of Duke Ellington's "Blue Rose," Les Brown's "Sentimental Journey," and Ella Fitzgerald's "A Tisket, A Tasket." The CD includes an original waltz by Carter titled "How Ruth Felt." Carter wrote this song as an expression of gratitude to Ruth Felt, an advocate of the performing arts in San Francisco, who helped support Carter through her mother's final illness. Carter has noted that she doesn't compose music often, but when she does, "it's more on a personal level. . . . I don't have a strong theory background, I have to wait for it to come to me and it can take a long time. At times I'll just sit there and think, 'OK, any day now,' just waiting for some idea to drop from the sky. There can be days where nothing happens and I have to accept that."

## The MacArthur "Genius" Award

In September 2006 Carter received one of the most famous awards in the United States—a MacArthur Fellowship, also known as a "genius grant." These awards are given annually by the John D. and Catherine T. MacArthur Foundation, an organization that is "dedicated to helping groups and individuals foster lasting improvement in the human condition." To do this, they identify individuals whose creativity and past accomplishment suggest a successful future. The selection committee told Carter they had been watching her for three years before awarding her the prize. The award includes a grant of $500,000 over five years, enough to allow the winners the financial independence to pursue further creativity. The awards committee had this to say about her achievement:

"Regina Carter is a master of improvisational jazz violin. Though her work draws upon a wide range of musical influences—including Motown, Afro-Cuban, swing, bebop, folk and world music—she has crafted a signature voice and style. . . . Carter's performances highlight the often overlooked potential of the jazz violin for its lyric, melodic, and percussive potential. Her early training as a classical musician is reflected in the fluidity, grace, and balance of her performance. Carter's repertoire retains a firm connection with the familiar while venturing in new, unexpected directions. . . . Through artistry with an instrument that has been defined predominantly by the classical tradition, Carter is pioneering new possibilities for the violin and for jazz."

Carter planned to use the prize money to continue her education in music therapy. She noticed during her mother's illness that her vital signs improved when certain music was played. Carter hoped to explore the therapeutic value of music and develop a program to share with medical professionals. "Doctors are just now starting to embrace using music to help heal their patients," she explained. "I want to work with people who have learning disabilities or terminal illnesses. There are other things I can do than just performing. Music is not just entertainment."

——— **"** ———

*"I don't think that a lot of us chose to be musicians. I didn't. It chose me. I think it's my job. I consider myself, in a way, to be a healer or to deliver a message. I definitely think it was a gift, and I don't believe in slamming the door on a gift."*

——— **"** ———

During the time covered by the MacArthur Fellowship, Carter also hopes to compose a new piece: she plans to take the poetry of Leslie Reese and set it to music in a work called *Black Bottom*. Black Bottom was the name of an African-American neighborhood in Detroit that was demolished in the 1960s to make way for urban renewal projects and a freeway.

**Hard Work and Success**

Even though practice has been a part of her daily routine since she was a small child, Carter still struggles sometimes. She leaves her instrument in the middle of the bedroom at night so that in the morning it will be among the first things she sees. Typically she does warm-up exercises on open strings and scales before working on the finer points of her technique. She still takes lessons to improve her understanding of jazz theory. She has said that the secret to her technique is that she doesn't "approach the violin as a violin; I approach it as a jazz instrument. The minute you approach it as a violin, it has a stereotype about it and ways that you're supposed to play it. I've gotten rid of all those ideas."

Asked about her decision to become a musician, Carter responded, "I don't think that a lot of us chose to be musicians. I didn't. It chose me. I

*Carter working with a student on technique.*
*A natural teacher, she often visits schools when on tour.*

think it's my job. I consider myself, in a way, to be a healer or to deliver a message. I definitely think it was a gift, and I don't believe in slamming the door on a gift." The important thing about jazz as an art form to her is "that it's a music of the people, like a voice. . . . It allows you to be creative and to take chances without having to know what the outcome is going to be and that's really the beauty of it."

Part of Carter's appeal is that her style of improvisation is enriched by many musical influences developed over the years. Her music draws techniques and sounds from diverse types of music, including classical, Motown, Middle Eastern, African, and Caribbean. She has attributed this to her upbringing in Detroit, with its rich musical history and ethnic diversity. She experiments with different sounds on the violin, incorporating bowing and pizzicato (plucking the strings), but also trying different techniques like hitting the strings with the back of the bow (the wood). Lowell Pickett, the owner of a jazz club in Minneapolis, Minnesota, believes that audiences respond so well to Carter's performances because they share in the happiness she expresses onstage. "She's a great player," he told *Strings*, "and she's so much fun. You can tell the way she just dives into the music and pulls out everything she can and then just throws it at the audience in a way that lets them share in the joy that she's feeling."

Summarizing the impact of Carter on jazz music, author Wayne Enstice described her as follows: "A fiddler who can make her four strings sing, swing, and cry the blues, Regina Carter is the most significant violinist to emerge on the jazz scene in decades." Guitarist Rodney Jones, who has performed with Carter, said this: "Regina's at the right place at the right time. She's unique because she can play mainstream jazz with authority, and she has the ability to interpret a ballad with so much emotion and nuance. She paints with the fine strokes of a master painter."

## MARRIAGE AND FAMILY

Carter married Alvester Garnett in Detroit, Michigan, on September 5, 2004. Garnett plays the drums in Carter's band. Because they work together and she is his boss, the couple maintains a strict separation between their professional and personal lives. They don't even share a hotel room when the band travels on the road to performances. Carter says that helps "keep the professional distance, and it keeps the lines from blurring. And when we get home, we are really happy to see each other and do un-band-related things."

## HOBBIES AND OTHER INTERESTS

Carter is active in music education and is pursuing studies in music therapy. She visits numerous schools across the country each year when she is on tour. She has been described as a natural teacher who easily connects with children. At Olympic Hills School in Seattle, Washington, principal Zoe Jenkins welcomed her visit: "There are 18 different languages represented at our school, but everybody here speaks music. . . . Music teaches focus, self esteem, a strong work ethic and self-expression. That's why we're so happy to have Regina here." Carter believes that music can have a positive impact on people. She has said, "Since I was a child, I've believed that there would be less angst, prejudice, and ignorance if everyone learned to play an instrument. We're all so guarded, but I know that when I play my violin, people can hear and see my real, complete self."

## SELECTED RECORDINGS

### As a Solo Artist

*Regina Carter*, 1995
*Something for Grace*, 1997
*Rhythms of the Heart*, 1999

*Motor City Moments*, 2000
*Paganini: After a Dream*, 2003
*I'll Be Seeing You: A Sentimental Journey*, 2006

### With Straight Ahead

*Look Straight Ahead*, 1992
*Body and Soul*, 1993

### With the String Trio of New York

*Intermobility*, 1993
*Octagon*, 1994
*Blues . . . ?*, 1996

### With Kenny Barron

*Freefall*, 2001

## HONORS AND AWARDS

MacArthur Fellowship (John D. and Catherine T. MacArthur Foundation): 2006

## FURTHER READING

### Books

*Contemporary Black Biography*, Vol. 23, 1999
*Contemporary Musicians*, Vol. 22, 1998
Enstice, Wayne and Janis Stockhouse, *Jazzwomen: Conversations with Twenty-One Musicians*, 2004
Peterson, Lloyd, *Music and the Creative Spirit: Innovators in Jazz, Improvisation, and the Avant Garde*, 2006
Stokes, W. Royal, *Living the Jazz Life: Conversations with Forty Musicians about Their Careers in Jazz*, 2000

### Periodicals

*Atlanta Journal-Constitution*, June 27, 2004, p.JJ3
*Billboard*, Apr. 3, 1999
*Current Biography Yearbook*, 2003
*Detroit Free Press*, Aug. 30, 1998, p.E1; Jan. 11, 2004, p.G1; Sep. 19, 2006
*Detroit News*, Nov. 12, 2003, p.D1
*Down Beat*, June 1999, p.20; Apr. 2003, p.34; Oct. 2006, p.26
*Essence*, July 2003, p.98
*Jazz Times*, July/Aug. 1999
*Jet*, Dec. 1, 2003, p.24

*Los Angeles Times,* Sep. 26, 1999, p.9; Feb. 14, 2001, p.B6
*Michigan Chronicle,* July 5, 2006, p.D2
*Minneapolis Star Tribune,* Apr. 9, 2004, p.E5
*New York Times,* Jan. 2, 2002, p.E2; Nov. 2, 2003, p.B17; Sep. 12, 2004, p.I17
*O, The Oprah Magazine,* Apr. 2002, p.93
*Orange County Register,* Jan. 12, 2007
*San Francisco Chronicle,* Sep. 12, 1999, p.46
*Seattle Post-Intelligencer,* Sep. 11, 1999
*Time,* July 26, 1999, p.76
*Utne Reader,* Jan./Feb. 2001, p.98
*Washington Post,* Feb. 20, 1998, p.N10

## Online Articles

http://www.allaboutjazz.com
   (*All About Jazz,* "Regina Carter: Improvising a Life in Jazz," Feb. 18, 2006)
http://jazztimes.com
   (*Jazz Times Magazine,* "Regina Carter: Something for Grace," June 1997)
http://jazzusa.com
   (*JazzUSA.com,* "A Conversation with Violinist Regina Carter," 1999; "Re-
   lating Her 'Motor City Moments': Regina Carter," 2000; "Regina Carter
   Interview: Queen of the Jazz Violin," 2006; "Interview with Regina
   Carter," undated)
http://www.npr.org
   (*NPR,* "Regina Carter's Encounter with a 'Cannon,'" May 14, 2003;
   "Musicians in Their Own Words: Regina Carter," May 19, 2005; "Jazz
   Violinist Regina Carter: 'I'll Be Seeing You,'" June 21, 2006)
http://www.stringsmagazine.com
   (*Strings,* "Motor City Maverick," Feb./Mar. 2002)

## Online Databases

*Biography Resource Center Online,* 2007

## ADDRESS

Regina Carter
Verve Music Group
1755 Broadway
New York, NY 10019

## WORLD WIDE WEB SITES

http://www.vervemusicgroup.com
http://www.reginacarter.com

## Kortney Clemons 1980-

U.S. Army Veteran and Paralympic Athlete
Winner of the 100-Meter Sprint at the 2006 and 2007
U.S. Paralympic Track and Field Championships

### BIRTH AND YOUTH

Kortney R. Clemons was born on June 23, 1980, in Meridien, Mississippi. Throughout his childhood, he spent much of his spare time playing sports. "I always loved sports," he recalled. "I always wanted to be part of a team." He particularly enjoyed playing football, and he spent hours practicing his moves in the backyard with his father, Mitch Clemons. Although Kortney was always small for his age, he was also fast and strong, which helped him excel at the position of defensive back.

## EDUCATION

Clemons attended The King's Academy in Meridien, where he was a solid player on the school's baseball, basketball, and football teams. After graduating from high school in the late 1990s, he went on to attend East Central Mississippi Community College. Disappointed that his small size prevented him from playing college football, he decided to quit school and join the U.S. Army. He attained the rank of sergeant and served as a combat medic in the Iraq War. Following his discharge from the military, Clemons returned to school in January 2006. He enrolled at Pennsylvania State University, known as Penn State. His field of study is therapeutic recreation, and his career goal is to work with disabled athletes.

## CAREER HIGHLIGHTS

### Serving in the Iraq War

After leaving college in the early 2000s, Clemons enlisted in the U.S. Army. He initially hoped to receive training to become a pharmacist. Instead, the army gave him basic medical training to enable him to treat wounded soldiers in combat situations. He earned the rank of sergeant in the First Cavalry Division and was sent overseas to serve as a combat medic in the Iraq War.

This conflict began in March 2003, when the United States launched a military attack against the Middle Eastern nation of Iraq. President George W. Bush claimed that the war was necessary to prevent Iraqi dictator Saddam Hussein from arming international terrorist groups with weapons of mass destruction. The U.S. war effort succeeded in removing Hussein from power within a few short weeks, but American troops did not find any evidence that Iraq possessed chemical or nuclear weapons.

In the months and years following the U.S. capture of the Iraqi capital of Baghdad, it became increasingly clear that the war had created many problems in Iraq. The Iraqi people struggled to reconstruct their country and establish a democratic government in the face of violent postwar confrontations between rival religious and ethnic groups. Security became a serious concern as Iraqi insurgents and foreign fighters launched a series of attacks against American troops, international aid workers, and people connected to the new Iraqi government. These attacks became more sophisticated and deadly as the U.S. occupation of Iraq dragged on.

This was the situation Clemons faced when the U.S. Army sent him to Iraq, and he witnessed the effects of the continuing violence many times in his work as a combat medic. Just a few days before he was scheduled to return home, Clemons himself became a casualty. On February 21, 2005, his patrol came across an overturned U.S. Army vehicle on a dirt road outside Baghdad. It had run over a roadside bomb that had been placed there by insurgents. Clemons rushed to assist the driver of the vehicle, who had been wounded in the blast. As he prepared the soldier to be evacuated by helicopter, however, a second bomb exploded nearby. The explosion killed three fellow medics and inflicted serious wounds to Clemons's legs. "I crawled to the other side of the road where my friends were, and they covered me up," he remembered. "I was sitting, talking to them, and they were trying to keep me alert."

*Clemons became a casualty of the war when a bomb exploded and inflicted serious wounds to his legs. "I crawled to the other side of the road where my friends were, and they covered me up," he remembered. "I was sitting, talking to them, and they were trying to keep me alert."*

Clemons was evacuated to the U.S. military hospital in Landstuhl, Germany. When he woke up several hours later, he knew that something was wrong. "My cousin, who was in the military, came in and told me that I would see my family soon and that I needed to understand what had happened before they saw me," he recalled. "'You have to be strong for them,' she said. I lifted up the blankets and for the first time looked down where my leg had been." The injuries to Clemons's right leg had been so severe that doctors were forced to amputate the limb above the knee.

## Coming to Terms with His Loss

As soon as he recovered from the surgery to remove his leg, Clemons was shipped back to the United States. He immediately entered a rehabilitation program for injured veterans at the Brooke Army Medical Center (BAMC) in San Antonio, Texas. Clemons worked hard physically to adapt to his disability. Within a few days of his arrival at BAMC, he began trying to walk again. He also had to learn new strategies for accomplishing everyday tasks that he had once done without thinking, like getting into and out of the shower safely. "It was like starting all over," he explained. "It was like a new beginning for me."

*Clemons is one of the many amputees who have been treated at
Brooke Army Medical Center (BAMC) in San Antonio, Texas.*

In some ways, though, Clemons found it more difficult to adjust to the loss
of his leg mentally than physically. "In the very beginning, you're happy
you're still alive, but after that wears off, you hit the period of 'Why me?'"
he acknowledged. "I had so many plans." Clemons felt particularly disappointed when he thought that his days of playing sports could be over.
"Serving my country worked in my favor," he noted. "I kind of got stronger
and quicker, and I was looking forward to coming back and at least playing
softball or basketball here or there."

It took some time for Clemons to come to terms with his injury. He struggled to face his disability with determination and optimism and to find a
way to feel normal again. "I had to reintroduce myself to myself," he stated. "When I was in the hospital, I thought I must have done something re-

ally bad in my life to deserve this. I went over everything that had happened to me, searching for a reason why God would want to take my leg. I came to the realization that He did this for a reason. He wanted me to make something more of myself. I had to lose my leg to find the real me."

In April 2005, just a few weeks after he arrived at BAMC, Clemons received some of the inspiration he needed to face the challenge of living with one leg. He saw John Register, a fellow amputee and head of the Paralympics Military Program, running around a track on his prosthetic leg. Even though Clemons was still learning to walk at that time, he was thrilled to discover that he might be able to run again someday. "I was so excited I couldn't sleep that night," he remembered. "I knew I could do this. I knew that I could accomplish great things."

## Using Advanced Prosthetic Limb Technology

Before he could accomplish his goal of running, Clemons had to be fitted for a special prosthetic leg. The technology behind artificial limbs has advanced rapidly in the 21st century. Experts in prosthetic devices use computers to take three-dimensional measurements of the amputee's residual limb. They use these measurements to mold a custom socket that fits the stump perfectly. The other side of the socket connects to the prosthetic limb, which is likely to be made of carbon fiber or other advanced materials that are strong, yet lightweight and flexible. Many artificial limbs are battery powered, while others feature hydraulic shock absorbers or sophisticated electronic sensors.

Given his interest in running, Clemons was fitted for a "sprinter" leg. It consists of a thin carbon-fiber calf section and a metal flat-spring foot that curves up in the front like a sled. It also features a mini hydraulic system in the knee joint. The socket contains tiny electronic sensors that connect to Clemons's thigh muscles. These sensors detect which muscles are working in the front or back of his thigh, and then send messages to a computer chip that instantly adjusts the hydraulic joint to compensate. This system was designed to give Clemons the maximum balance and speed for running. Similar custom limbs have allowed other amputees to ride bicycles, ski, and engage in a variety of other activities.

In the near future, Clemons and other amputees may benefit from further exciting advances in prosthetic technology. Experts predict that it soon will become possible to connect artificial limbs directly to the bone in an amputee's residual limb. They also believe that new technology will allow electronic sensors to be attached to nerve endings, enabling amputees to control their prosthetic limbs with their brains. All of these advances have

*Clemons stretches after a workout at the Multisport Indoor Facility at Penn State.*

helped change the way that doctors view amputation. "Rather than being considered a treatment failure, [amputation] is viewed by our staff as one of the treatment options aimed at maximizing the soldier's rehabilitation potential," declared Colonel Mark Bagg, chief of orthopedics and rehabilitation at BAMC.

Only six months after sustaining his injury, Clemons ran for the first time at BAMC. He compared the sensation of running on his prosthetic "sprinter" leg to hopping on a pogo stick. Even though it felt different, Clemons found the experience exhilarating. "I had tried it for a few strides before that moment, but I had never gone full speed," he recalled. "I took off down the track, and it was the most wonderful feeling, the wind in my face, moving by my own power."

## Becoming Involved in the Paralympics

Almost as soon as Clemons began running, he started dreaming about competing in the Paralympic Games. This international athletic competition for disabled athletes was founded in England following World War II as a way to give injured war veterans a chance to compete in sporting events. Like the Olympic Games, it is held every four years and features the top athletes from around the world. In fact, the competition takes place in the same location and uses the same facilities as the Olympics, but it is generally held a few weeks later. The U.S. Paralympic Team placed fifth overall at the 2000 Games in Sydney, Australia, and fourth at the 2004 Games in Athens, Greece.

Organizers of the American Paralympic program understand that they tend to get a larger pool of disabled athletes to draw from during times of war. This is particularly true of 21st century conflicts like the Iraq War, because U.S. soldiers are less likely to die in combat than in previous wars. Whereas 24 percent of wounded American troops died from their injuries during the Vietnam War in the 1970s, this number has decreased to 10 percent during the Iraq War. Analysts attribute the declining death rate to the development of body armor made of Kevlar, a form of lightweight plastic that is five times stronger than steel. Worn in the form of a vest, Kevlar protects soldiers' bodies and vital organs from bullets and shrapnel.

> "People in Iraq are still getting injured every day, and if I can give them something to strive for, [show them] that it can be done, give them some type of hope, that would be my greatest accomplishment," Clemons stated. "The more I can help someone else, it gives me more energy to keep going."

Unfortunately, Kevlar is too bulky for soldiers to wear on their entire bodies. The technology protects their torsos—and thus reduces the number of combat deaths. But it also leaves their extremities exposed—and thus increases the number of limb injuries and amputations. Making the most of a bad situation, soldiers who are injured in combat can provide a good source of athletic talent for the U.S. Paralympic Team. "We have a population of young amputees who were very fit and very athletic before they got wounded," said Captain Justin LeFerrier, who manages the physical therapy facility at BAMC. "Our job here is to get them back to whatever level they want to get to. If they've lost both legs and want to run, they'll run. As far as we're concerned here, the word impossible just means it hasn't been done yet."

The U.S. Paralympic Team launched a special program, called the Paralympic Military Summit, so the growing number of injured Iraq War veterans could become involved in disabled sports. The program encourages the veterans to take up sports in order to relearn skills, build confidence, and return to a healthy, active lifestyle. During a three-day training session, they get to participate in such events as wheelchair fencing, sitting volley-

*Getting ready to race at Penn State.*

ball, and sled hockey. "These types of sports allow us to know we might have bad days, just like anybody else, but we can continue to move on in life and still compete," Clemons noted. "You can't get stuck in that rut, start feeling pity for yourself, and let life pass you by."

Clemons attended a Paralympic Military Summit in Colorado in October 2005. Although less than a year had passed since his injury, he was inspired to begin training to compete in the 100-meter sprint event at the 2008 Paralympic Games in Beijing, China. Since he had done a lot of weightlifting in the army, Clemons also began training for the Paralympic powerlifting event.

## Inspiring Other Injured Veterans

In January 2006, when Clemons enrolled at Penn State, he had the opportunity to work with some of the top coaches in adaptive sports as part of the school's Ability Athletics Program. By May, he was ready to compete in the powerlifting event at the 2006 International Paralympic Committee World Championships in Korea. Clemons set a new U.S. Paralympic record of 340 pounds in the 155-pound senior division. He placed 11th overall and qualified for the 2008 Paralympics in the event.

In the meantime, Clemons continued improving his skills on the track. In July 2006 he became the first Iraq War veteran to compete in the U.S. Paralympics Track and Field National Championships, which were held in Atlanta, Georgia. This event would help determine the U.S. team for the 2008 Paralympic Games. Clemons won the national championship in the 100 meters with a personal-best time of 15.61 seconds. Although he was thrilled to qualify for the 2008 Paralympic Games in a second event, he was more excited about setting a good example for other injured veterans. "I'm not in this to beat other people," he explained. "I just want to set records. There are a lot of guys who have come back from Iraq like me. I want them to look at those records and see what is possible. I'm living proof that you can accomplish anything."

Clemons hopes that a strong showing at the 2008 Paralympic Games in Beijing will also help motivate people facing similar challenges. "People in Iraq are still getting injured every day, and if I can give them something to strive for, [show them] that it can be done, give them some type of hope, that would be my greatest accomplishment," he stated. "The more I can help someone else, it gives me more energy to keep going."

## HOME AND FAMILY

Clemons, who is single, lives and trains on the campus of Penn State University. He has a ten-year-old daughter, Daytriona.

## AWARDS AND HONORS

U.S. Paralympics Track and Field National Championships, 100-Meter Sprint: 2006, gold medal; 2007, gold medal

## FURTHER READING

### Periodicals

*Atlanta Journal-Constitution,* June 30, 2006, p.A1
*Current Science,* Feb. 10, 2006, p.10
*New York Times,* Oct. 9, 2005, sec. 8, p.1
*Soldiers Magazine,* Mar. 2006, p.28
*USA Today,* Nov. 21, 2006, p.C3

### Online Articles

http://www.msnbc.com.msn.com/id/13051084
    (*MSNBC.com,* "Iraq War Amputee Seeks Track Success," June 20, 2006)

## ADDRESS

Kortney Clemons
United States Olympic Committee
U.S. Paralympics Division
One Olympic Plaza
Colorado Springs, CO 80909

## WORLD WIDE WEB SITE

http://www.usolympicteam.com/paralympics

# Taylor Crabtree 1990-

American Student and Charitable Entrepreneur
Founder and Owner of TayBear Company, which
Provides Free Teddy Bears to Sick Children

### EARLY YEARS

Taylor Marie Crabtree was born on September 20, 1990, in San
Diego, California. Her father, Ken Crabtree, is an engineer,
and her mother, Tricia Crabtree, is an office manager. She lives
with her parents in Rancho Santa Fe, California, not far from
San Diego. She has one older sister, Rhiannon.

An athletic girl, Crabtree was an avid gymnast when she was younger. During grade school, she also enjoyed track, tennis, and swimming. Since enrolling at La Costa Canyon High School in Carlsbad, California, she has become a talented volleyball player. A straight A student, Crabtree is a member of her school's debate team and is learning American Sign Language. After graduating from high school, she hopes to attend an Ivy League college and eventually to forge a career in politics.

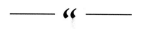

*Crabtree set a goal of providing teddy bears—"pre-hugged" by her or one of her helpers—to 50 children. "I thought her too-high goal was that of a child who didn't really understand [the challenges involved]," her mother recalled. "I was the one who didn't understand."*

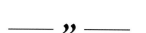

## MAJOR ACCOMPLISHMENTS

Crabtree first became involved in charitable activities when she was just seven years old. In October 1997 she and her mother began hand-painting hairclips for her to wear to gymnastics class. "They were so pretty I thought I could sell them," she said. Just as she was reaching that conclusion, two events increased her determination to earn money. First, her grandmother was diagnosed with colon cancer. She eventually made a full recovery, but Crabtree saw how hard it was for her to fight the disease. Crabtree then saw a TV news report about city police programs that provided teddy bears to frightened children.

These two events inspired Crabtree to comfort younger cancer patients by giving them teddy bears to hug when they were frightened or in pain. She set an initial goal of earning enough money to provide teddy bears to 50 children. "I thought her too-high goal was that of a child who didn't really understand [the challenges involved]," her mother recalled. "*I* was the one who didn't understand."

## A Community Effort

Crabtree decided she would hand-paint and sell hairclips at local stores to buy bears for the children. She set up her little craft operation in her bedroom and the family kitchen, and within a matter of weeks local media outlets were publicizing the project. The growing publicity about her efforts to buy "TayBears" (a playful blend of "teddybear" and Crabtree's first name) helped get the whole community involved. Local supermarkets stuffed bags with her fliers and kept donation canisters near the checkouts, and word-of-mouth about her efforts spread through local schools and churches alike.

"Pretty soon I found out that I couldn't keep up with the inventory," Crabtree recalled. "I knew that people wanted to buy my hairclips but I was selling them faster than I could make them. I needed help fast! So I asked my friends to help and set up several 'painting parties' at my house." Eventually hundreds of other children, including special-needs children, became helpers. "Taylor wanted other kids to feel they too were capable of helping others in their own way," her mother said. "It has been rather like a chain letter from the heart."

The project finally became so big that it outgrew the Crabtree household. The youngster promptly moved her art sessions into schools and community centers, both to accommodate her growing army of helpers and to let her mother reclaim the family kitchen for meals.

Crabtree is very proud that so many other kids have become involved in the project. In fact, only children are permitted to prepare the bears for shipping. They give each one a name, a special tag with the TayBear logo, and a big hug. "That's so they're delivered with love," Crabtree said. "By being part of TayBear, hundreds of kids have already proven that it is possible to make a difference-even if you are under five feet tall and haven't finished middle school yet."

Crabtree's efforts to get teddy bears to children who have cancer and chronic blood diseases have been heartily embraced by area hospitals, which provide her with estimates of how many children with cancer or blood diseases they see in a year. TayBear tries to provide that many bears. Crabtree visits hospitals to deliver bears in person whenever she can. Otherwise, bears are given to nurses who present the bears to young patients.

## Learning about Business

Crabtree freely admits that the early days of TayBear were extremely challenging. "When I started I didn't know anything about business," she said. "In school I was learning to add small numbers and stuff. That worked fine in the beginning. There were only two small numbers to add. $2.50 per hair clip times 2 makes $5, and I could add by 5s pretty well. Then the numbers started getting bigger and I learned to add bigger numbers. It happened just like that."

Crabtree realized that she needed to know how all her money was being spent. "So I learned some Quicken [a computer-software program for busi-

*Crabtree with some of the stuffed animals collected by her organization.*

ness] to keep better control of my money and went to the bank to get a business account," she said. "I learned that it is hard to start a business with very little money. I started to look at my expenses in a way that I could understand. For every $5 spent . . . that would be one child without a bear."

Crabtree eagerly sought out ideas and suggestions from others to help run and improve her business. "By talking to a lot of people I'm able to get more ideas than I could have on my own. I really learned a lot about running a business," she said. She keeps careful records of all her supplies, sales donations, and of her business checking account. Crabtree also solicited companies and individuals to donate money to pay for the cost of shipping TayBears across the country. These displays of business skills have been a real eye-opener for Crabtree's mother. "I've listened with amazement as she's discussed the huggability of the teddy bears with vendors and later ordered 700 teddy bears after negotiating a lower price," she said.

## Promoting TayBear

Once TayBear was firmly established, Crabtree began visiting elementary schools and middle schools across the United States to meet principals who could help her get students involved. At first, her mother went into the meetings with her. But soon she handled them on her own. "My parents have taught me that shyness doesn't get you anywhere," Crabtree said. "You just got to go for everything with all you got."

Crabtree also has shared her vision by making speeches to people—from small groups of kids to audiences of hundreds of adults. In 2000, for example, an international association of financial and insurance executives called the Million Dollar Round Table asked her to speak at its convention in San Francisco. She was their youngest-ever speaker. After asking the audience of nearly 7,000 to buy hairclips, they bought out her supply of 500 in just a few hours. The following year she received a $10,000 grant from the foundation to continue her work.

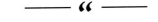

Crabtree says that another one of her most memorable speeches was delivered to the Young Entrepreneurs Organization in San Diego. Afterwards, she said, "People kept coming from the back and pulling money out, the money kept piling higher and higher on the table. My mom was crying and my dad was laughing. Here I was, just giving a normal speech and all of a sudden here were all these donations." TayBear received $3,700 that

*A nine-year-old patient from Oklahoma wrote to Crabtree after receiving one of her bears, which he named Little Scotty. "Any time I have a nightmare, I squeeze Little Scotty, and he gets rid of my bad dreams," the boy wrote.*

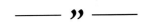

day in cash gifts. Later that day, Crabtree received a promise of $10,000 from a businessman who heard her speech. The money allowed her to list her business with the U.S. government and to set up a board of directors—with herself as chairperson, president, and founder of TayBear Co.

Crabtree has continued to work on TayBear since that time. Since starting the organization in 1997, she and her hundreds of young helpers ("and a few grownups," she adds) have given away more than 20,000 bears to children in hospitals all over the United States and in Canada. "It's really kind of fun and inspiring to watch her," her father said. "She's had to cut back on some of the sports, but TayBear is another opportunity for her to develop skills other children might not and carry them into adulthood."

In January 2006, *People* magazine highlighted Crabtree and TayBear. The article featured one of the bear's recipients, a four-year-old named Andrew Granger. The little boy hugged his bear through long and difficult medical treatment, including chemotherapy, radiation, and two stem-cell transplants. He's well now, and keeps his bear in his bedroom. "It's just unbelievable that a kid did this for another kid," said Andrew's mother, Margaret. A nine-year-old patient from Oklahoma also wrote to Crabtree after receiving one of her bears, which he named Little Scotty. "Any time I have a nightmare, I squeeze Little Scotty, and he gets rid of my bad dreams," the boy wrote. Needless to say, these stories are welcome confirmation to Crabtree that her years of hard work are making a difference in the lives of young people across North America.

## HONORS AND AWARDS

Entrepreneurial Achievement Award (Ernst & Young): 1999
George Washington Honor Medal (Freedom Foundation at Valley Forge): 1999
Honorary Membership (Young Entrepreneurs' Organization): 1999
Born Hero (Lands' End): 2000
Star Kid (*American Girl* magazine): 2001
Angels in Action Award (Angel Soft): 2004

## FURTHER READING

### Books

Giovagnoli, Melissa. *Angels in the Workplace,* 1999

### Periodicals

*Business Journal,* Feb. 18, 2000, p.1
*People,* Jan. 16, 2006, p.97

### Online Articles

http://www.signonsandiego.com/news/solutions/20041126-9999-
1mc26bears.html
(*San Diego Union Tribune,* "Bear Business Keeps Girl Busy, Helps Cancer Patients," Nov. 26, 2004)

## ADDRESS

Taylor Crabtree
TayBear
993 South Santa Fe Avenue, #C339
Vista, CA 92083

## WORLD WIDE WEB SITES

http://www.taybearhugs.org

## Miley Cyrus 1992-

American Actress and Singer
Star of the Disney Channel Television Program
"Hannah Montana"

### BIRTH

Miley Cyrus was born in Franklin, Tennessee, on November 23, 1992. Her birth name is Destiny Hope Cyrus, but she was such a happy baby that her dad called her "Smiley Miley," and the nickname Miley stuck. Her parents are Billy Ray Cyrus, a singer, songwriter, and actor, and Letitia "Tish" Finley Cyrus. Miley has five siblings: an older half-sister, Brandi, two older half-brothers, Trace and Christopher; a younger brother, Braison Chance, and a younger sister, Noah Lindsey.

## YOUTH

Miley was born in the same year that her dad shot to stardom on the strength of his catchy, country-flavored tune, "Achy Breaky Heart." The song climbed to the No. 4 spot on the *Billboard* Hot 100 list in 1992 and was a mainstay of the line-dancing fad of the early 1990s. The album on which it appeared, *Some Gave All*, sold 14 million copies. Billy Ray Cyrus was never able to recapture the success of his first hit, but he has continued to record music and tour. Eventually, he became a television star, recognized around the world because of "Doc," a program broadcast on Pax TV. In it, Cyrus played a country doctor who works in New York City.

> *Even as a young child, Miley was convinced that she wanted a career in entertainment, just like her father. Billy Ray recalled, "Since she was little, she would look at me confidently and say, 'I'm going to blow by you, Daddy. I'm going to be a singer, songwriter, entertainer.'"*

Her dad's celebrity status taught Miley a lot about life in the spotlight—both the good and bad sides of it. It also gave her opportunities to get used to being in front of an audience. She always liked performing with her father. As a toddler, she would dash on stage during his concerts if she got the chance. When she did this, he would go along with it, singing a few duets with her before sending her back offstage.

Miley's love of performing lasted beyond her toddler years. As she got older, she became convinced that she wanted a career in entertainment, just like her father. Billy Ray recalled, "Since she was little, she would look at me confidently and say, 'I'm going to blow by you, Daddy. I'm going to be a singer, songwriter, entertainer.'" At first he discouraged her, knowing that show business can involve a lot of heartbreak. But Miley was persistent. When Billy Ray Cyrus began filming "Doc," he allowed her to act in a few episodes. These experiences gave her confidence and strengthened her feeling that show business was right for her. When her parents realized how determined she was, they allowed her to start taking lessons from an acting coach and going to auditions. They also gave her a Daisy Rock guitar, and she became an endorser for the company, which makes guitars especially for girls.

*Cyrus with her father and the rest of the cast from "Hannah Montana."*

Miley's experiences on "Doc" showed her "how much fun, joy, and encouragement there is on the set," she recalled. "It's great seeing everyone working together as a team on the show. You are all together and you're all a family and it's a really great place to be." In addition to her TV performances, Miley also worked in some music videos, had a part in the movie *Big Fish*, and appeared on another show her dad was involved with, "Colgate Country Showdown," a country music talent search.

## EDUCATION

Because of her commitment to her TV show, Miley doesn't have time to attend regular school. She is tutored on the set of "Hannah Montana" in Burbank, California.

## CAREER HIGHLIGHTS

### "Hannah Montana"

Miley was 11 years old when she first auditioned for a new show being planned by the Disney Channel. The series would feature a middle-school age girl who is a pop superstar, but who hides her identity at school because she wants to have a normal life. Disney executives were eager to produce the show, but they knew they had to find the right actress to play the part before they could get started.

The Disney Company has proven to be very good at training young performers and managing their careers for maximum success. Justin Timberlake, Britney Spears, Hilary Duff, and Raven are just some of the entertainers who got a lot of experience and exposure at an early age on the Disney Channel. (For more information on these performers, see the following issues of *Biography Today*: for Timberlake, see N Sync in *Biography Today*, Jan. 2001; for Spears, see *Biography Today*, Jan. 2001; for Duff, see *Biography Today*, Sep. 2002; for Raven, see *Biography Today*, Apr. 2004.) In the case of Hilary Duff ("Lizzie McGuire") and Raven ("That's so Raven"), Disney first gave them lead roles in television. After they had gained an audience, the girls were launched on singing careers.

>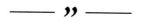
>
> *"[The Miley Stewart character] is just like me, but she's also like any other average girl going through love stuff, friend stuff, and family stuff. But she is trying to get through the pressure of being a universal super star. Everyone loves Hannah, but she just wants to have her friends and her family."*

"Hannah Montana," the new Disney show, would combine those two steps. Its star would have to be confident and funny enough to handle the comedy scenes in the show, and a strong enough singer to be a convincing superstar. According to Gary Marsh, the president of entertainment for Disney Channel Worldwide, "We decided we would not go through with this series until we found a kid who could carry a sitcom as well as she could carry a tune."

## Perfect for the Part

Miley's first audition for "Hannah Montana" went well. Decision-makers at Disney thought she was a good actress and singer, and a stable, down-to-earth person. But they needed someone who could handle the pressures of life in the spotlight, and they thought that an 11-year-old probably would have a hard time dealing with the long hours and demanding pace of filming the show, making publicity appearances, and keeping up

*Two views of Cyrus: as herself (left) and as Hannah Montana (right).*

with schoolwork. Besides, Miley was small for her age, too small to play the part of a teenager. Although her audition was good, she didn't get the part.

A year passed, and Disney still hadn't found the right girl. The "Hannah Montana" show was on hold. "I kept going after this part, because it is really something I wanted to do," Miley remembered. When she was 12, she got another chance to audition. This time, she won the role. Gary Marsh praised Miley, saying, "She has the everyday relatability of Hilary Duff and the stage presence of Shania Twain, and that's an explosive combination." Miley was thrilled to have achieved her goal. "I've always loved singing, and I've always loved acting and dancing," she said. "Getting this opportunity with Disney, I get to do it all. They let you do everything you love." Miley and her family left their Tennessee farm and moved to California so she could work on "Hannah Montana" at the Disney studios there. Her grandmother stayed behind to look after their horses, dogs, and other pets.

There are some parallels between the life of Miley Cyrus and the setup of "Hannah Montana." In the show, Miley's character—a bubbly teenager named Miley Stewart—moves from Nashville to California to pursue her career. Unlike Miley Cyrus, however, Miley Stewart wants to keep her identity as Hannah Montana, the pop superstar, a secret. Only her two best friends know about Miley's other life; the rest of the students at Sea-view Middle School hardly notice her, even though most of them are huge fans of Hannah Montana.

## Double Identity

"Hannah Montana" doesn't try to be particularly realistic. In the show, Miley just has to toss on her blonde stage wig and a little makeup to trans-form into Hannah, and her classmates don't seem to recognize her. Episodes involve such goofy antics as Miley spying on her dad while he picks out a dress for her, Miley parasailing in a chicken suit, and Miley being asked out on a date—to attend a Hannah Montana concert.

Comedy is an important ingredient in "Hannah Montana," but so is music. The show has lots of footage of Hannah in concert. To get it, Disney started by having Miley perform as Hannah at Walt Disney World. Though they already had confidence in her appeal, Disney executives were im-pressed by the way the crowd went wild over the singer. "They didn't know who she was. The show wasn't on the air yet, so that was another sign that we had something really, really special," said Adam Bonnett, an executive responsible for programming at the Disney Channel.

In addition to Miley, "Hannah Montana" features Billy Ray Cyrus in the role of her father and manager, a musician named Robbie Stewart. Also appearing are Mitchel Musso and Emily Osment as her friends Oliver and Lilly, and Jason Earles as her older brother Jackson. The character's mother is dead, but she has appeared on the show in a dream sequence, played by Brooke Shields. Other guest stars have included Jesse McCartney and Dolly Parton.

## Success on TV and the Music Charts

"Hannah Montana" debuted in March 2006. That first show drew the biggest audience in the history of the Disney Channel—more than five million viewers. But that strong start was only the beginning. Disney gave Miley lots of support, featuring her music and videos on Radio Disney and the Disney Channel, which reaches more than 100 countries. She was the opening act on a 40-city tour with The Cheetah Girls, another popular Disney-produced group which, like "Hannah Montana," is aimed at the "tween" audience (children between 8 and 12 years old). Many types of Hannah Montana merchandise were created, including clothing, cosmet-ics, dolls, and video games.

*Miley has had some success as a recording artist, including this CD soundtrack* Hannah Montana 2: Meet Miley Cyrus.

That promotional effort paid off. "Hannah Montana" is consistently ranked as one of the most popular programs among girls ages 9 to 14, and it also has a huge following among younger children, both boys and girls. When a CD titled *Hannah Montana: Songs From and Inspired By the Hit TV Series* was released, it entered the Billboard 200 chart in the No. 1 spot. The CD featured eight songs by Miley and a few by other artists, including Jesse McCartney and The Click Five. Miley's contributions included the "Hannah Montana" theme song, "Best of Both Worlds," "Pumpin' Up the Party," "The Other Side of Me," "This Is the Life," and "Just Like You." The CD had seven singles on the *Billboard* Hot 100 at one time and sold 1.6 million copies in just two months. Sales eventually passed 2 million.

Miley is enjoying her success. "There's nothing more fun than being out on stage and getting the vibe from the crowd. There's nothing like being on a set where you are there to make other people happy and to make them laugh. That's the best job in the world," she said. She enjoys performing as Hannah, whose sound she has compared to that of singer and "American Idol" winner Kelly Clarkson. (For more information on Clarkson, see *Biography Today*, Jan. 2003.) But Miley wants to be recognized for her own musical style too. "I get on my own thing—a little country and then pop and rock and some bluegrass," she said. In 2007, she performed her own music and Hannah's on her second CD, *Hannah Montana 2: Meet Miley Cyrus*, which immediately rose to No. 1 on the pop charts.

———— " ————

*"We have a good family," Miley said. "I still go to church every Sunday with my family and really just want to learn, because I don't want to blend in with everyone. I just want to give a good image and a good message to girls, and guys, too."*

———— " ————

## Miley on Miley

Describing the Miley Stewart character, she said, "Miley is just like me, but she's also like any other average girl going through love stuff, friend stuff, and family stuff. But she is trying to get through the pressure of being a universal super star. Everyone loves Hannah, but she just wants to have her friends and her family." As for why "Hannah Montana" is so popular, she said, "I think everybody has a goal or a dream, and just showing an average girl having her dream come true and still being able to balance her friends and her school is something they relate to."

Despite her fame and her apparent confidence, Miley admits that—like most teenagers—she sometimes feels very self-conscious. "I freak out," she said. "I look in the mirror and think, 'This shirt is ugly. These pants are stupid.' It's a lot easier when I have someone to put my makeup on and fix my hair. People on TV have a lotta people pulling it together for us. It makes all the difference. Honestly, I hate getting dressed up. I'm holding my shoes in most pictures you see of me at red-carpet events. If I could go to premieres in my sweats, I would!"

Being recognized wherever she goes has presented some challenges, but so far Miley likes it. Her father has always treated his fans well, and she wants to do the same. "Say 'hi' to me," she said. "I love it. Everyone I have a chance to take a picture with or sign an autograph for—just a quick way to make them smile—that's awesome."

## HOME AND FAMILY

Miley lives with her family in California and works with her father on the set of "Hannah Montana." The chemistry between the two of them has been called one of the best things about the show, but she has said that working together isn't always easy. Discussing the daily drive to work with her dad, Miley joked, "I want to play my music and he just talks and talks about anything. Finally, I turn on my little iPod and let him talk to himself. I'm like any other teenage girl who doesn't necessarily want her dad around all the time. But—and I would never let him know that—he's really cool." Billy Ray Cyrus said that he and his daughter have always communicated best through their music: "Since Miley was a little girl we've been writing songs together. We sing together. We do a whole lot more of it off-stage than on stage," he said.

Miley knows that it can be hard to handle the pressures of fame, but she is confident that she can handle it, thanks to her strong family life and her faith in God. "We have a good family," she said. "I still go to church every Sunday with my family and really just want to learn, because I don't want to blend in with everyone. I just want to give a good image and a good message to girls, and guys, too."

## HOBBIES AND OTHER INTERESTS

In her free time, Miley likes to shop, swim, play basketball, and go skate-boarding. Before moving to California, she was active as a cheerleader. She enjoys horses and other pets. She is a vegetarian and likes Thai food, as well as cookie dough, Gummi bears, Cheetos, and candy.

## SELECTED CREDITS

### Television

"Hannah Montana," 2006-

### Recordings

*Hannah Montana: Songs from and Inspired by the Hit TV Series*, 2006
*Hannah Montana 2: Meet Miley Cyrus*, 2007

### DVDs

*Hannah Montana: Livin' the Rock Star Life!*, 2006
*Hannah Montana: Pop Star Profile*, 2007

## Films

*Big Fish,* 2003 (as Destiny Cyrus)

## HONORS AND AWARDS

Nickleodeon Kids Choice Awards: 2007, Favorite Television Actress, for "Hannah Montana"
Teen Choice Awards: 2007, TV Actress—Comedy, for "Hannah Montana"

## FURTHER READING

### Periodicals

*Boston Globe,* Nov. 6, 2006, Metro section, p.A1
*Fort Worth Star-Telegram,* Feb. 13, 2007, p.E1
*Girls' Life,* Dec. 2006, p.47
*Houston Chronicle,* Mar. 4, 2007, Star section, p.1
*Los Angeles Times,* July 8, 2007, p.E1
*New York Times,* Apr. 20, 2006, p.E1
*People,* July 2, 2007, p.72
*Philadelphia Inquirer,* May 17, 2006
*Time,* Nov. 30, 2006
*USA Today,* Jan. 11, 2007, p.D1
*Variety,* Feb. 20, 2006, p.18

## ADDRESS

Miley Cyrus
Disney Channel
Attn: Fan Mail Dept.
3800 West Alameda Ave
Burbank, CA 91505

## WORLD WIDE WEB SITES

http://www.mileycyrus.com
http://tv.disney.go.com/disneychannel/hannahmontana

## Aaron Dworkin 1970-

American Activist, Arts Administrator, and Musician
Founder and President of the Sphinx Organization

### BIRTH

Aaron Paul Dworkin was born on September 11, 1970, in
Monticello, New York. His birth parents were Vaughn Moore
and Audeen Moore, who decided to put their newborn son up
for adoption. Aaron was adopted at two weeks of age by Barry
and Susan Dworkin, who were both New York City college
professors specializing in neuroscience. They also had another
son. Though he did not know his birth parents as he grew up,

Aaron was reunited with them as an adult and now enjoys a close relationship with them.

## YOUTH

Because of the circumstances of his birth and adoption, Aaron Dworkin's upbringing was somewhat unique. His birth father was black and his birth mother was white, so he was of biracial heritage. But in his adoptive home, both of his parents were white, and he had a white older brother. Also, his adoptive parents were Jewish and taught Aaron about their religion as he grew up. "I'm black, white, Irish, Jewish," he later explained. "So I've been exposed to a lot of different perspectives on the world."

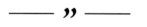

> "I'm black, white, Irish, Jewish," Dworkin explained. "So I've been exposed to a lot of different perspectives on the world."

In addition, Dworkin came in regular contact with people from a wide range of races, religions, and nationalities in his hometown of New York City. This type of community is often described as "diverse"—meaning that it includes many different kinds of people. One of the positive aspects of diversity is that it can make a person more accepting of others and less likely to fear those who have a different appearance or who practice different beliefs. This was true for Dworkin, who paid little attention to such issues as skin color. "[Race] had no significance to me," he explained about his early years. "I went to school with kids of differing backgrounds. My parents were white, my brother was white, so I just really didn't understand how there was any big deal about that." The value of diversity would become very important to Dworkin later in life.

Of the many ideas and traditions that Dworkin experienced while growing up, it was the sound of classical music that really caught his attention. His adoptive mother had been an amateur violinist before he was born. When he was about five years old, she took up her instrument once more, and the Bach compositions that she played at home excited Dworkin so much that he decided that he wanted to play too. "I thought it was the coolest thing," he said, "and so I started to play and I had a natural knack for it. It got me going pretty quick." He began formal lessons and quickly developed into a promising musician.

At age 10, Dworkin's life underwent a profound change. His family moved from Manhattan to Hershey, Pennsylvania, so that his parents could take new jobs at the Hershey Medical Center. He had to face the difficulty of enrolling in a new school and making new friends, and Dworkin soon found that Hershey was a much different place than New York City. The most jarring change had to do with race: suddenly, his biracial heritage made him different from almost everyone else in town. "At the time, there was one black family, outside of myself, living in Hershey," he recalled. "And although it's a good town, for the first time I began to understand and grasp the feeling of racial prejudice." Certain people treated him differently because of his skin color, sometimes engaging in racist name-calling, sometimes excluding him from activities. Dworkin responded to the hostility by spending even more time immersed in his violin studies. "I used music to escape," he explained. "I could always go to my violin and play."

> **"**
>
> *"I was on a downhill spiral, rebelling, feeling totally alienated," Dworkin said about his early high school years. "I felt isolated, I think, because of, you know, dating issues and being the only black kid in school and playing the violin and all these things."*
>
> **"**

## EDUCATION

As a young person intent on a career in music, Dworkin took private music lessons in addition to his regular school studies. While living in Manhattan, he studied with his first teacher, the well-known violin instructor Vladimir Graffman, and in the years that followed, he studied with a long list of other accomplished musicians and music educators. He was also able to enroll in several prestigious performing arts programs, including those at the Peabody Preparatory Institute in Baltimore and the New School of Music in Philadelphia. To build his musical skills, Dworkin engaged in hours of daily practice, even though he sometimes longed for more carefree activities. As he later explained, "You want to run around with crazy kids or your friends, you don't want to practice scales or etudes."

By his teens, Dworkin was holding his own among some of the finest young musicians in the country. He performed regularly with both the Hershey Youth Orchestra and the Harrisburg Youth Symphony and attained the position of concertmaster or first violin with the Harrisburg en-

*Dworkin with the Harlem Quartet after their performance at the Apollo Theater (left to right): Desmond Morris, Juan-Miguel Hernandez, Melissa White, Ilmar Gavalin, and Dworkin.*

semble, meaning he was judged the most skilled violinist in the orchestra. But he came to understand that race could be an issue in the musical world, just as it was elsewhere. He often found himself to be "the only black person in every classical music situation" he encountered, and a few of his fellow musicians treated him badly because of his ethnic heritage. One of his responsibilities as concertmaster was to oversee the tuning of the instruments prior to rehearsal and performances, but some symphony members refused to cooperate. "Because I was black, they were purposefully ignoring me," he recalled.

Dworkin continued to do well in his musical activities. But by the time he reached high school, he was feeling discouraged about his life in Hershey. "I was on a downhill spiral, rebelling, feeling totally alienated," he said. "I felt isolated, I think, because of, you know, dating issues and being the only black kid in school and playing the violin and all these things." After completing two years at his Pennsylvania high school, his parents convinced him that he needed to try something new. It turned out to be just what he needed. "For my junior and senior year, I went to

Interlochen Arts Academy, which literally saved my life." The prestigious arts school in northern Michigan, which includes a boarding school so students can live on campus, allowed Dworkin to refocus on his music. "All of a sudden I went to this place where all they really cared about was what art form you were doing and it was this utter transformation. . . . I was astounded." Interlochen also brought him in contact with a dozen or so other black arts students, which eased some of his feelings of racial isolation. Dworkin graduated from Interlochen Arts Academy in about 1988.

Dworkin then enrolled at Pennsylvania State University, where he served as concertmaster for the Penn State Philharmonic Orchestra. Rather than majoring in music, however, he studied business at the college until he withdrew without earning a degree because of financial reasons. Dworkin then moved to Michigan and spent several years working at various jobs before deciding to return to college at the University of Michigan (U-M) in the mid-1990s. There, he once more dedicated himself to his violin studies, earning his bachelor's degree (B.M.) in music in 1997 and a master's degree (M.M.) in 1998, graduating with high honors.

During his time at U-M, Dworkin began to think more carefully about the subject of race and classical music. This was partly inspired by his discovery of works of music that had been written by African-American composers, including William Grant Still. "All the time growing up as a young black violinist, I never knew there was music by black composers," he said. "I thought how could I have not known about this music?" Dworkin decided that more people—particularly young black musicians—should be exposed to this work. He also considered the fact that there were very few people of color involved with the classical music concerts where he performed. "I'd see 4,000 white faces in the audience," he remembered. "And I'd see no minorities on the stage. I wondered why there should be no place for minorities in classical music, something that was very important to me—something I loved." After spending a long time pondering the lack of racial and cultural diversity among the nation's orchestras, Dworkin asked himself an important question: "What can I do about it?"

## CAREER HIGHLIGHTS

Dworkin's answer was to create the Sphinx Organization in 1996, while he was still an undergraduate at the university. This nonprofit group has been his life's work ever since. The goal of the Sphinx Organization is to increase minority participation in classical music. From his own experience, Dworkin knew that there were a limited number of black and Hispanic music students, and the numbers are even more striking on the professional level. According to most estimates, less than 4 percent of orchestral players in the United States are of either African-American or Latino heritage, even though blacks and Hispanics form about a quarter of the U.S. population. In other words, orchestras are mostly made up of white musicians, along with some members of Asian heritage. As a result, most orchestras fail to reflect the diversity that's found in the United States.

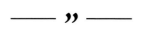

*"I'd see 4,000 white faces in the audience," Dworkin remembered. "And I'd see no minorities on the stage. I wondered why there should be no place for minorities in classical music, something that was very important to me—something I loved."*

This can be bad for several reasons. First, it allows little minority input into classical music and can discourage talented minority musicians from pursuing professional careers because they feel out of place. Second, it gives some people the false idea that blacks and Hispanics aren't capable of performing classical music and that they are in some way culturally inferior. Third, with few minority musicians in the professional ranks, the larger African-American and Latino population is less likely to feel interested in classical music, which means that they often miss out on an important art form. Dworkin feels that the lack of diversity hurts the orchestras as well. Without participation from the minority population, the orchestras are out of touch with their communities, and this often contributes to the low attendance at classical concerts.

Some music authorities argue that the lack of diversity is caused by the fact that there are simply very few blacks and Hispanics who choose to study classical music and that little can be done to increase their numbers. Dworkin, however, knew that there were skilled minority musicians like himself throughout the country, even if their numbers were relatively small. He believed that if these players were given more attention and support, they could make it as professionals. To accomplish this, he came up with the idea of staging a competition that would showcase talented minority musicians, specifically strings players, and help them to develop their skills.

*Sphinx Competition participant Gareth Johnson playing at Carnegie Hall.*

## Launching the Sphinx Competition

After hatching the idea for the contest, Dworkin faced a key challenge: raising money. Having worked for nonprofit groups before attending U-M, he knew that the Sphinx Organization wouldn't succeed without proper financing. He began his work by sending letters to a long list of celebrities and corporate leaders—anyone who might be able to help. Many of them ignored Dworkin's request for a contribution, but one person—James Wolfensohn, the president of the World Bank—had a much more positive reaction. "I got a letter back that basically said, 'This sounds like a great project. Here's a one-time contribution of $10,000 to help things get going,'" remembers Dworkin. "And I was like, 'This is gonna happen.'"

The first Sphinx Competition was held in 1998, and it set the basic framework that the event has followed ever since. Classically trained African-American and Latino musicians send in audition tapes that include specific musical selections. Based on these recordings, a jury of experts selects the semifinalists who get to attend the competition, which takes place in Ann Arbor and Detroit, Michigan. Early competitions featured musicians ages 13-19, and this was later adapted to include a junior division (for players up to age 17) and a senior division (ages 18-26). From the beginning, Dworkin has made sure that the jurors are very demanding in choosing the semifinalists. The young musicians are expected to be able to hold their own against the top national performers in their age group.

At the competition, the attendees perform before the jurors, and these performances are used to choose three finalists in each division. The finalists get the opportunity to play with a full orchestra in a special concert, which often features the work of minority composers. Based on these concert performances, the jurors select the winner and the second and third-place finishers. The finalists receive cash prizes, and many of them later get the opportunity to perform with various symphonies around the country. All of the semifinalists invited to Michigan are provided with a scholarship to attend a music camp later in the year. The value of the prizes and scholarships now totals more than $100,000 annually, with a top cash award of $10,000 for the first place winner in the senior division. As another feature of the program, Sphinx musicians who lack a professional-quality instrument can receive assistance in obtaining one.

## Creating Connections

Though it is a contest, the Sphinx Competition is intended to create a nurturing environment rather than a competitive one. The participants spend a lot of time with one another during the week-long event and attend classes with the professionals who serve as the jury for the competition. By designing the competition in this way, Dworkin tried to make the event an educational experience and one that encourages the participants to bond with one another. By fostering a communal spirit, Dworkin hopes the young musicians will escape the type of isolation that he felt in his earlier years.

The participants have found this to be one of the most enjoyable aspects of the contest. "The competition was like camp—it was so much fun," said Elena Urioste, who finished first in the junior division in 2003. "I pretty much forgot it was a competition the second I got there, because everyone was so nurturing and supportive. . . . They really promote the group mentality." Another participant, Patrice Jackson, also valued the time she got to spend with other musicians. "I can't express how it is to learn that you're not alone, that there are other African Americans your age doing the same thing," she explained.

Dworkin also helps the participants connect with minorities who have already become professional musicians. This is accomplished by bringing in black and Hispanic players who are members of orchestras and chamber ensembles around the country. They form the Sphinx Orchestra, which supports the senior division finalists in their concert performance. These professionals serve as role models and teach the young musicians what it takes to succeed in the classical music world. "The Sphinx helped me be more aware of minority musicians who are excelling," noted Bryan Hernandez-Luch, "and their success has helped motivate me."

Ultimately, the Sphinx Competition aims to link talented minority musicians with the decision-makers who run the professional orchestras. The contest gives young players a chance to meet and perform for important figures in the classical music industry, and those musicians who place in the top spots often enjoy an even better showcase when they are featured in special symphony concerts throughout the United States. "The contacts are just great," explained Sphinx winner Gareth Johnson, "because you meet these very well-known and respected musicians and conductors, and they can continue to promote you throughout the years." Johnson added that, "It's not an exaggeration to say the competition changed my life. . . . It started my career."

> "The competition was like camp—it was so much fun," said participant Elena Urioste, who finished first in the junior division in 2003. "I pretty much forgot it was a competition the second I got there, because everyone was so nurturing and supportive. . . . They really promote the group mentality."

From the beginning, Dworkin received support from some important figures in classical music. The legendary violinist Isaac Stern visited Ann Arbor during the inaugural competition in 1998 and gave free coaching sessions to Sphinx winners each year until his death in 2001. Classical stars Yo Yo Ma and Itzhak Perlman have also backed the competition. Thanks to hard work by Dworkin and his staff, the number of professional orchestras that host Sphinx winners for special performances has steadily increased, with 25 symphonies now taking part, including the well-known ensembles in Atlanta, Boston, Detroit, Baltimore, Cleveland, and St. Louis.

The organization has also had a lot of success in raising funds for its projects, which is what Dworkin calls "the biggest challenge" of his work. Such large corporations as Texaco, General Motors, Target, and American

Express have supported Sphinx, as have such nonprofit organizations as the W. K. Kellogg Foundation and the National Endowment for the Arts. At times, the grants have reached into the millions, with the Bingham Trust pledging $1.5 million to Sphinx in 2005 and JPMorgan Chase offering $1 million in 2006.

## Expanding the Sphinx Mission

As the financial resources of the Sphinx Organization have improved, the group has been able to begin a variety of new programs that promote its goal of increasing minority participation in classical music. To help mentor promising young musicians, Dworkin launched the Sphinx Performance Academy, a two-week summer program that takes place at Walnut Hill School near Boston. Founded in 2005, it offers intensive music education for 40 students each year who range between the ages of 12 and 18.

Other Sphinx programs focus on a broader issue: "The problem of bringing young people into classical music," to use Dworkin's own words. "For the kids to be motivated to play classical music in the first place, there has to be some connection," he explained. "They have to have heard it somewhere." Moreover, he believes that children's lives are enriched when they're exposed to the classics, regardless of whether they go on to pursue a music career. To help create interest in the music, the Sphinx Musical Encounters program arranges for participants in the competition to visit schools and to deliver other presentations and concerts. "We ask our kids to go back to their communities and be ambassadors for the music," Dworkin explained. "Because the same thing that sparked them to start [learning an instrument] is what's going to happen when they play."

The organization has also developed a curriculum guide and interactive CD-ROM for use by school educators. During the 2005-2006 school year, these materials were used to teach 10,000 students about classical music. In Detroit, where Sphinx is based, the organization operates the Sphinx Preparatory Music Institute, which started in 2004. It offers introductory music classes to interested students, most whom are in middle school, and brings them together each Saturday for 20 weeks. Both the Detroit academy and the teaching materials are intended to reach children in disadvantaged urban areas. "In inner-city schools it's difficult getting kids access to good music programs," Dworkin said, because "the arts are treated as a kind of luxury" that the impoverished school districts can't afford.

These programs also help to overcome the bias that many young people have against classical music. Dworkin feels that this comes from the "stiff, sterile" way that the classics are usually presented to young people. "In that atmosphere," he said, "the last thing they will think is that classical music is fun." But when minority students get close-up exposure to the music and see it played by Sphinx contestants who share their own background, opinions often change. "It's not the music that's a barrier to young people and minorities," Dworkin argued. "When we go into schools, we find that kids just love it."

In 2004, Dworkin's organization staged the first of an ongoing series of gala concerts at Carnegie Hall in New York City. These performances, which feature winners of the Sphinx Competition, have helped reinforce the message that the Sphinx contestants possess top-level talent. In a review of the 2004 concert, a *New York Times* writer noted that "this student ensemble produced a more beautiful, precise, and carefully shaped sound than some professional orchestras that come through Carnegie Hall in the course of a year." The Carnegie concerts are yet another means of highlighting the country's skilled black and Latino classical musicians, which is all part of Dworkin's ultimate goal. "Orchestras have traditionally insisted that the minority talent simply wasn't out there," Dworkin has pointed out. "Now at least they're saying, 'Yes, the talent's there but we're not seeing those musicians at our auditions.' Getting these kids spotlighted in front of orchestras is going to change all that."

> "Orchestras have traditionally insisted that the minority talent simply wasn't out there," Dworkin has pointed out. "Now at least they're saying, 'Yes, the talent's there but we're not seeing those musicians at our auditions.' Getting these kids spotlighted in front of orchestras is going to change all that."

## Awards and Rewards

As the Sphinx Organization has expanded its programs, Dworkin has received increasing attention for his groundbreaking work. He was featured in the Black Entertainment Television series *History Makers in the Making* in 2003 and garnered a number of regional and national awards. Then, in September 2005, he received a phone call notifying him that he had been

*The 2006 Annual Sphinx Competition First Place Laureate, Gabriel Cabezas, with the Sphinx Chamber Orchestra.*

selected to receive one of the prestigious fellowships from the John D. and Catherine T. MacArthur Foundation. Often described as a "genius grant," a MacArthur Fellowship gives the recipient $500,000 over five years to use in any way they wish. Because the nominations for the award are kept secret, Dworkin had no idea he was being considered. "I'm rarely at a loss for words, but I couldn't even speak," he said of the moment when he heard that he had been selected. "Ideally this will raise the visibility of these kids [the musicians in the Sphinx Competition], because in the end it's the kids who are truly fantastic."

The year 2005 also brought about another landmark for the Sphinx Organization: three musicians who had previously been finalists in the competition landed jobs in professional orchestras, a clear sign that Dworkin's efforts were showing real results. A number of other Sphinx contestants are now enrolled in highly regarded music schools and may join the professional ranks in the near future.

Many observers believe that Dworkin has already had a big impact on the classical music world, even if the number of professional minority players still remains relatively small. "When Aaron started, you would rarely see a black or Hispanic soloist with a major orchestra," noted

Steve Shipps, one of Dworkin's former professors. "Now it's become routine." The Sphinx Organization's efforts have caused symphonies and chamber-music groups to make a more determined effort to hire a more diverse group of musicians, which is likely to bring more minorities into these organizations in the coming years. Benjamin Zander, the conductor of the Boston Philharmonic, stated that "Aaron Dworkin has established—singlehandedly—the need for every classical music organization to commit to diversity."

Despite his successes, Dworkin knows that there is more work to be done. "From my perspective, we have not been successful yet, ultimately successful yet, in addressing this problem of the lack of diversity in classical music," he explained. "What I'm looking forward to is when we can go to an orchestra and there's five or ten minorities onstage, and nobody's making a big deal about it." Dworkin has vowed to continue his efforts until that mission is accomplished. "For me there really is no other option. I feel like I have to do this work," he said. "If I were to win the lottery tomorrow, I would still be doing this work and [the lottery money] would just help in making the dream come true."

> "From my perspective, we have not been successful yet, ultimately successful yet, in addressing this problem of the lack of diversity in classical music," Dworkin explained. "What I'm looking forward to is when we can go to an orchestra and there's five or ten minorities onstage, and nobody's making a big deal about it."

## HOME AND FAMILY

Dworkin met his first wife, Carrie, during his time at the Interlochen Arts Academy. The two were wed in 1997 and their son, Noah, was born in the late 1990s. They divorced in 2003, and Dworkin later married Afa Sadykhly, who serves as the vice president of programming for the Sphinx Organization. They reside in Ann Arbor, Michigan.

After seeking information about his birth parents for many years, Dworkin was able to locate them in 2001 through an adoption web site. His father, Vaughn Moore, is a hospital worker and his mother, Audeen Moore, is an emergency-management administrator. Though Vaughn and Audeen were not married when Aaron was born, they later were wed and had another child. So when Dworkin located his birth parents, he learned that he has a sister. He is on good terms with all members of his birth family and visits with them regularly.

## HOBBIES AND OTHER INTERESTS

Because the Sphinx Organization quickly became a full-time job for Dworkin, he has not pursued a professional career as a musician. He has, however, continued to play violin and has recorded two CDs, *Ebony Rhythm,* which mixes classical music with dramatic readings about the historical experiences of African Americans, and *Bar-Talk,* a collaboration with his wife, Afa Sadykhly. Dworkin often plays electric violin in addition to the standard acoustic instrument, and he has developed a college-level preparatory class in electric string performance. Interested in literature as well as music, Dworkin composes poetry and has published one collection, *They Said I Wasn't Really Black,* which addresses his experiences growing up. He also founded *The Bard,* a literary magazine in Michigan, and has produced and directed a movie entitled *Deliberation.*

## HONORS AND AWARDS

Alain Locke Award (The Friends of African and African-American Art): 2003
History Makers in the Making Award (Black Entertainment Television): 2003
John D. and Catherine T. MacArthur Foundation Fellowship: 2005
National Governors Association Award for Distinguished Service to the Arts: 2005
Giving Back Award (*Newsweek* magazine): 2006

## FURTHER READING

### Books

*Contemporary Black Biography,* Vol. 52, 2006

### Periodicals

*Chamber Music,* Aug. 2006
*Chronicle of Philanthropy,* Oct. 27, 2005
*Detroit Free Press,* Feb. 7, 2003; Aug. 4, 2006
*Detroit News,* Feb. 17, 2004
*New York Newsday,* Dec. 5, 2004, p.C19
*New York Times,* Mar. 3, 2002
*People,* Nov. 22, 2004, p.123

## Online Databases

*Biography Resource Center Online,* 2007, article from *Contemporary Black Biography,* 2006

## Online Articles

http://sitemaker.umich.edu/livingmusic/home
   (*Living Music* interview with Aaron Dworkin, Oct. 21, 2005)
http://www.macfound.org/site/c.lkLXJ8MQKrH/b.1038727/apps/s/
   content.asp?ct=1470799
   (MacArthur Foundation, "Aaron Dworkin," no date)
http://www.metrotimes.com/editorial/story.asp?id=4626
   (*Metro Times,* "Mystery of the Sphinx," Feb. 26, 2003)
http://www.umich.edu/news/MT/06/Spring06/story.html?MusicalGenius
   (*Michigan Today,* "Musical Genius," Spring 2006)

## ADDRESS

Aaron Dworkin
Sphinx Organization
400 Renaissance Center, Suite 2550
Detroit, MI 48243
Email info@sphinxmusic.org

## WORLD WIDE WEB SITE

http://www.sphinxmusic.org

# FALL OUT BOY

**Andy Hurley 1980-**
**Patrick Stump 1984-**
**Joe Trohman 1984-**
**Pete Wentz 1979-**

American Pop-Punk Band

### EARLY YEARS

Fall Out Boy is a four-man pop-punk band that formed in 2001 in the suburbs of Chicago, Illinois. The members are Andy Hurley (drums), Patrick Stump (vocals and guitar), Joe Trohman (guitar), and Pete Wentz (bass and backup vocals).

## Andy Hurley

Andrew John Hurley was born on May 31, 1980, in Menominee Falls, Wisconsin. His mother, Ann Hurley, is a nurse; his father died when he was five years old. Hurley attended Menominee Falls High School, where he gained a reputation as a gifted percussionist in the school band who was also a bit of a troublemaker. According to his mother, "He had a lot of anger in him as a youngster. . . . He was afraid to become close to people. A band to him was safe and was a family that wouldn't leave him." Before joining Fall Out Boy he attended the University of Wisconsin, Madison, where he studied history and anthropology. Hurley is a vegan (he doesn't eat or wear anything derived from animal products). In addition, like his band mates Patrick Stump and Pete Wentz, Hurley adheres to what is known as a "straight-edge" lifestyle. Straight edge is a commitment not to drink alcohol, smoke, or use drugs.

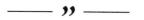

*"[The hardcore scene] focused too much on negative energy," said Wentz, "and that bogs you down after a while and gets really tiring."*

## Patrick Stump

Patrick Martin Stumph was born on April 27, 1984, in Glenview, Illinois. As a teenager, he changed the spelling of his last name from "Stumph" to "Stump" to prevent confusion about the pronunciation. His parents are Patricia Vaughn and Dave Stumph, an amateur folk musician who works as an association manager. They divorced when Stump was a child, and one of his earliest musical memories is of helping his father move his record collection out of their house. Stump has an older brother, Kevin, who is a violinist. Stump attended Glenbrook South High School and graduated in 2002.

## Joe Trohman

Joseph Mark Trohman, the youngest member of Fall Out Boy, was born on September 1, 1984, in Hollywood, Florida. His father, Richard Trohman, is a cardiologist who moved the family to the Cleveland, Ohio, area when Joe was about five years old. Trohman attended Chagrin Falls Middle School and played trombone in the school band. He also took piano lessons and began playing guitar before the family relocated once again. When he was 12, they moved to the affluent North Shore suburbs of Chicago. There Trohman attended New Trier High School in Winnetka, Illinois, graduating in 2002. According to his father, "Joe did play guitar for hours upon hours

*The members of Fall Out Boy (left to right):*
*Joe Trohman, Pete Wentz, Andy Hurley, and Patrick Stump.*

from age eight or nine. . . . He got good fast. . . . Joe would wake up in the middle of the night and start playing."

## Pete Wentz

Peter Lewis Kingston Wentz III was born on June 5, 1979. His father, Peter Wentz II, is a law professor, and his mother, Dale, is a private school administrator. Pete has a sister, Hilary, and a brother, Andrew. He attended New Trier High School before transferring to North Shore Country Day, a private school also in Winnetka. He excelled in soccer and was named to the all-state team during his senior year. After graduating from high school in 1997, Wentz attended DePaul University to pursue an interest in political science, but he soon dropped out to focus on music.

## FORMING THE BAND

Fall Out Boy got started in the Chicago area, where all four members were involved in music. What brought them together was their shared interest in hardcore music. Hardcore derives from the punk rock genre that developed during the 1970s with such bands as the Sex Pistols in England and the Ramones in the United States. Songs are noted for being characteristically loud, fast, and short. The lyrics often express anger or dissatisfaction with the government or society.

The members of Fall Out Boy were all involved with various bands before starting their own, and they crossed paths at several points. Wentz, who is the oldest member of Fall Out Boy, had played in several hardcore bands in Chicago, including xfirstbornx and 7 Angels of the Apocalypse. He was well known in the area as the lead singer of the band Arma Angelus. Wentz and Hurley played together in Arma Angelus and also in another band, Racetraitor, and Trohman toured one summer with Arma Angelus when he was just 16. After that, Trohman met Stump, who was also in a band, at a local bookstore where Stump worked. They were both high school juniors at the time. Trohman introduced Stump to Wentz, and the three of them began hanging out together and eventually began playing music together for fun.

In Stump's opinion, "I don't consider it Fall Out Boy until Andy joined."

When they first got together, Wentz, Trohman, and Stump were just having fun pursuing a new musical direction. The music they developed was more melodic and less pessimistic than the intense, hard-driving music they had been playing in their other bands. According to Wentz, "[The hardcore scene] focused too much on negative energy and that bogs you down after a while and gets really tiring."

What started out as merely an amusing break from their other projects soon led to performances at local venues. But they had difficulty finding a drummer who fit well with the group. They began using the name Fall Out Boy after they asked for suggestions from the audience at one of their early shows. Someone in the crowd shouted out "Fall Out Boy," the name of a comic book that Bart reads on the animated television show "The Simpsons." The name stuck.

Eventually an early version of the group produced a CD titled *Evening Out with Your Girlfriend*. This 2002 release includes the songs "Pretty in Punk" and "Parker Lewis Can't Lose (But I'm Gunna Give It My Best Shot)." The band, however, has since disavowed this record. In interviews they've explained that its production and musical quality do not

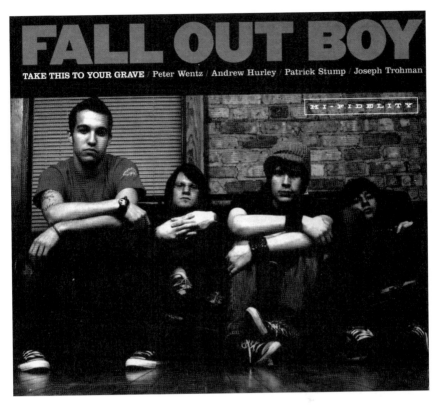

Take This to Your Grave *was the first CD with the full lineup of Fall Out Boy.*

meet with the standards they hold for their work. Also, it was recorded before Hurley joined the band, so they don't regard it as a true Fall Out Boy CD. The band tried several drummers before Hurley joined Fall Out Boy in 2003 when they needed a replacement drummer to go out on tour. Stump surely spoke for the group when he said, "I don't consider it Fall Out Boy until Andy joined."

## CAREER HIGHLIGHTS

With the lineup finally settled, Fall Out Boy worked hard touring, writing songs, and recording new music. Hoping to be signed to a recording contract, they uploaded MP3s to the web and submitted demos—self-recorded CDs that include a sample of the band's repertoire—to numerous record labels. In 2003 they signed with the Florida-based company Fueled by Ramen, which is co-owned by Vinnie Fiorello, the drummer of the band Less Than Jake. They also impressed Island Records, which advanced them

131

money to pay for recording and touring expenses. Island also acquired the rights to sign the band if their first CD did well.

In 2003 Fall Out Boy released the CD *Take This to Your Grave* on the Fueled by Ramen label. The music was hard-driving and guitar based, revealing their past in the hardcore scene. But the lyrics and song titles were not filled with rage, as in much hardcore music, but were instead filled with irony, humor, and clever puns. Songs on the disc include "Reinventing the Wheel to Run Myself Over," "Tell That Mick He Just Made My List of Things to Do Today," "Homesick at Space Camp," and "The Pros and Cons of Breathing." Many of the songs were about a bad breakup between Wentz and his girlfriend.

Because of the personal revelation in the lyrics, Fall Out Boy became associated with emo, another music genre. Emo evolved from hardcore punk and is characterized by highly personal lyrics fraught with emotion. The term is usually used for bands and musicians who perform songs with confessional lyrics that are characterized by their emotional intimacy, intensity, and sincerity. But the music accompanying those lyrics can take a variety of forms, including both softer acoustic sounds and pounding rock with loud guitars and vocals.

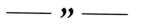

*According to Wentz, "When people come up to me and say 'Fall Out Boy saved my life,' my only response is that Fall Out Boy saved my life, too."*

Through near-constant touring, Fall Out Boy built a loyal following of fans who knew the words to all the songs and sang with them at live performances. The band's outrageous stage antics drew even more people to its shows. Wentz is known for throwing his bass all the way around his neck and catching it, tossing the bass through the air, shaking his whole body like an electric current is shocking him, and diving from the stage to surf the crowd. Trohman and Wentz often electrify the audience by jumping off monitor cabinets. Describing the bassist's performance at a concert in Tempe, Arizona, reviewer Christina Fuoco wrote, "Wentz proved that original bass-playing styles can still be found and thrown into the mix; he seemingly strums all of the strings while still picking out the correct notes, while spinning around like a six-year-old child." The fans, too, can get wild at Fall Out Boy shows. At one performance the surging crowd pushed a female fan up against the stage so hard that her arm was visibly broken. Stump recalled, "She's like 'I'm not leaving until you play my favorite song,' so we were like, 'Let's play it as fast as we can. We have to get her to the hospital!'"

As their fan base and celebrity increased, the band released *My Heart Will Always Be the B-Side to My Tongue* in 2004. This package contained a five-song EP and accompanying DVD. Included on the music disc are acoustic versions of "Nobody Puts Baby in a Corner" (based on a line from the 1987 movie *Dirty Dancing*) and "Grand Theft Autumn." In addition, the EP offers a cover of the Joy Division classic "Love Will Tear Us Apart." The DVD includes videos, concert footage, a slide show, and interviews.

At about this time Wentz was seeing a psychiatrist for depression; he was hospitalized in 2005 after taking too many prescription pills. His reasons for taking the pills are unclear, but he later said that he merely wanted to sleep, not to commit suicide. "I was isolating myself further and further," he said, "and the more I isolated myself, the more isolated I'd feel. I wasn't sleeping. I just wanted my head to shut off." Wentz has continued therapy and is a spokesperson for Half of Us, a campaign to help college students deal with depression. He credits the band with his own recovery. According to Wentz, "When people come up to me and say 'Fall Out Boy saved my life,' my only response is that Fall Out Boy saved my life, too."

### From Under the Cork Tree

Fall Out Boy's next release, the 2005 CD *From Under the Cork Tree*, was a great success both musically and commercially. The singles "Dance, Dance" and "Sugar, We're Goin' Down" were among the biggest hits of the year on MTV and on such music web sites as I-Tunes and Napster.

In addition to the mega-hits, the CD again showcased the band's humor in such song titles as "Our Lawyer Made Us Change the Name of This Song So We Wouldn't Get Sued," "A Little Less 'Sixteen Candles,' A Little More 'Touch Me,'" and "Champagne for My Real Friends, Real Pain for My Sham Friends."

For the band, however, *From Under the Cork Tree* represented an artistic breakthrough, as well. During preparation of the CD they developed a new songwriting formula. For earlier efforts, singer Stump had written the lyrics and Wentz and the others developed the music to go along with them. On *From Under the Cork Tree* they reversed their roles. Wentz provided poetry to Stump, who then put the verses to music. Since that time this process has remained in place: Wentz writes the lyrics, Stump uses the Apple software GarageBand to develop a rough version of the

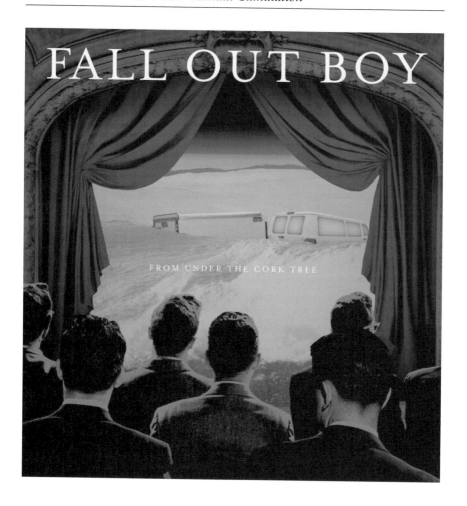

song, then the band refines it. Trohman praised Stump's creative ability, saying, "I guess Patrick is some kind of genius—he's a total mad scientist." Stump's mother, Patricia Vaughn, agreed that the band has success with this method. According to Vaughn, "Patrick is the sound of Fall Out Boy. . . . He's the guy that hears it, and Pete presents it. The combination of the two is the perfect storm."

Critics and audiences responded favorably to *From Under the Cork Tree*, which went on to sell more than three million copies. Hometown music journalist Jim DeRogatis of the *Chicago Sun-Times* raved, "Fall Out Boy boasts the hooks of a great pop-punk band, but it plays with the intensity of a hardcore group." The band even gained fans among music industry executives, including Jay-Z, the rapper and president of Island/ Def Jam Records, who went to see them when they played in New York. He said,

"Everyone knew the words and was singing. It was like a cult following. I watched them and thought, 'These guys are stars. This is genuine.'"

Awards soon followed. "Sugar, We're Goin' Down" won the MTV2 Award in 2005, and "Dance, Dance" won the MTV Viewers' Choice Award in 2006. At the 2006 Teen Choice Awards the group took prizes in three categories. Wentz and Stump accepted the honors on behalf of the group, but as usual, Wentz did the talking. "We always feel like we're kinda sneaking into these things. It's kinda like we're just getting away with it, I guess." He thanked all the fans who voted, especially the fans who posted messages for the band at their web site and all the fans who have started bands of their own. "You guys are awesome," he concluded.

### Infinity on High

After the success of *From Under the Cork Tree*, the group's next release was highly anticipated. "The Carpal Tunnel of Love," the first track from the new album to be made public, was available in December 2006 as a download on I-Tunes and from absolutepunk.net. The first official single, "This Ain't a Scene, It's an Arms Race," was released in January 2007. *Infinity on High* debuted as the No. 1 album in the country in February 2007, selling more than half a million copies during its first month of re-

*"Fall Out Boy is just an honest band with humble origins whose members are as surprised as anyone at their new-found success,"* said reviewer Chris Rolls.

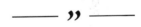

lease. The title of the CD is taken from a letter by the 19th-century Dutch artist Vincent Van Gogh, who wrote, "Be clearly aware of the stars and infinity on high. Then life seems almost enchanted after all."

Many reviewers commented on the album's clever and witty lyrics. The songs talk about the band members' personal struggles in a self-mocking, self-deprecating way, bolstering their reputation for sincerity. This approach has allowed the band members to hang on to their credibility as indie artists as they sell millions of records and forge deals with corporate sponsors. Many of the songs seem to poke fun at their celebrity while also seeming to enjoy it. They manage to combine sincerity with a sense of ironic detachment, what critic Jody Rosen called "songs that both wallow in and lampoon emo angst."

Reviewers also commented on a shift in the band's musical style, with more variation in tempo and clear R&B and traditional rock influences.

The songs on the CD take advantage of Stump's wide vocal range, including the gospel-inspired "Hum Hallelujah" and the melodic piano ballad "Golden." Critic Sasha Frere-Jones declared, "The album is deeply pleasurable, consisting of compressed, torqued-up rock songs that rarely detour into instrumental passages and return single mindedly to choruses that range from the reasonably hummable to the eminently hummable." "It's a natural progression," said Wentz. "It's our growth as songwriters and our experiences in the world. All of a sudden, our eyes have adjusted to the dark and we can see different things."

To achieve their new sound the band worked in the studio with producer Kenneth "Babyface" Edmonds and several guest artists, including Jay-Z and guitarist Ryan Ross of Panic! At the Disco. They wanted to work with Edmonds, according to Wentz, because the band appreciates "his approach to melody. . . . Patrick [sings] with a greater range and more soul in our new songs, and we wanted to find someone to drive that." Reviewer Barry Nicolson especially praised the uptempo "Don't You Know Who I Think I Am," calling it brilliant. With breaks punctuated by hand claps, Stump sings, "A penny for your thoughts / But a dollar for your insides / Oh, a fortune for your disaster / I'm, just a painter and I'm drawing a blank." According to Nicolson, "If you don't like it, you're either deaf or a liar."

> **"** 
>
> *"We mean a lot to each other as musicians and as people,"* Trohman admitted. *"But sometimes we start believing what people write about us: That the band is just one guy or two guys. That can be harsh for the soul."*
>
> **"**

## Celebrity and Success

The band's success has brought celebrity to some of its members, mostly to Wentz. Fall Out Boy breaks the typical pattern for many bands. Stump is the lead singer, but he is not the public face of the band. Instead, Wentz is unquestionably the most visible member of the group—he does most of the media interviews, he's become a favorite of many pre-teen and teenage girls, and his every move is covered in magazines. He is also well known for his business pursuits outside of Fall Out Boy, including the record label Decaydance Records and the clothing line Clandestine Industries. Describing Wentz's drive for business, Stump has said, "It scares me sometimes, watching him. The two

*Fall Out Boy performing at the House of Blues in Chicago, 2007.*

seconds you're not with that dude he's made 30 decisions that are going to affect us for the rest of the year."

Stump has not seemed jealous of all the attention Wentz gets. "I don't know if my contribution is recognized, and I don't care," he declared. "I know what I do and I'm busy doing it. I'm not one of these guys who sets out to take charge of things. That's how Pete is: He's a born leader." Besides, according to Stump, he's "horribly uncomfortable with being the frontman." Trohman has indicated that the friendship at the core of the band helps. Still, he admitted that "We mean a lot to each other as musicians and as people. But sometimes we start believing what people write about us: That the band is just one guy or two guys. That can be harsh for the soul." According to Wentz, "In the vacuum away from all the press and away from all that camera flashing, we are still just best friends and that's how it will continue to be, I hope, all the way into the future."

Fall Out Boy has devoted a lot of time to connecting with their fans, including meeting them at shows, offering web-exclusive previews of their new material, uploading personal blog entries, and using message boards and personal networking sites to correspond with the public. Their MySpace page listed 1.8 million friends as of spring 2007. Sometimes when Fall Out Boy arrives early in a city for an arena show they announce a free afternoon show at a small club in the same town. They post a message online about where and when the surprise performance will take place, and fans spread the word through text messages and IMs. According to Wentz, "We feel indebted to our fans and will always try to pay them back."

Trying to explain their appeal, reviewer Chris Rolls has suggested that fans relate to the band because of the sincerity evident in their music. "Rest assured that this merry band of melodic, heavy-riff pop players is not a carbon copy of their contemporaries, nor are they a product of producers hell-bent on making a buck off popular trends. No, Fall Out Boy is just an honest band with humble origins whose members are as surprised as anyone at their new-found success." Wentz believes their audience responds to being treated with respect. "There is an honesty in our music and I think people appreciate it. We have never dumbed down to teenagers by writing songs about being in high school and having your locker jammed. . . . We have always written what we are really feeling. We have always had the respect that they are going to figure out these songs for themselves and come up with their own interpretations."

## HOME AND FAMILY

When not touring with Fall Out Boy, Hurley lives in Germantown, Wisconsin. Stump still lives in Glenview, Illinois, and also owns a condominium in Los Angeles, California. Trohman lives in a townhouse in Chicago. Wentz lives in Los Angeles, California.

## MAJOR INFLUENCES

In an interview in 2004, Wentz talked about the band's major influences. "In the beginning," he said, "it was The Descendants, Green Day, the Police, Elvis Costello. Now with our newer stuff it's like Joy Division, The Cure, Nick Drake—stuff like that. . . . We like a lot of hardcore too." Stump has mentioned Michael Jackson's album *Thriller* as well.

## RECORDINGS

*Evening Out with Your Girlfriend*, 2002
*Take This to Your Grave*, 2003
*My Heart Will Always Be the B-Side to My Tongue*, 2004 (EP)
*From Under the Cork Tree*, 2005
*Infinity on High*, 2007

## HONORS AND AWARDS

MTV Video Music Awards: 2005, MTV2 Award, for "Sugar, We're Goin' Down"; 2006, Viewers' Choice Award, for "Dance, Dance"
XM Nation Music Awards: 2005, "On the Rise" Most Important Mainstream Emerging Artist Award
Napster Awards: 2006, Most Played Song Award, for "Dance, Dance"
Teen Choice Awards: 2006 (three awards), Choice Single Award and Choice Rock Track Award, for "Dance, Dance," Choice Rock Group Award; 2007 (two awards), Choice Music—Rock Group and Choice Music—Rock Track, for "Thnks Fr Th Mmrs"

## FURTHER READING

### Books

*Contemporary Musicians*, Vol. 57, 2005

### Periodicals

*Billboard*, Jan. 27, 2007
*Chicago Sun-Times*, May 2, 2003, p.5
*Chicago Tribune*, Mar. 30, 2006, p.28
*CosmoGIRL!*, June/July 2006, p.102
*Entertainment Weekly*, Feb. 9, 2007, p.71
*Independent* (London), Apr. 28, 2006, p.12
*Kansas City Star*, Apr. 13, 2006, p.G7
*Minneapolis Star Tribune*, Apr. 14, 2006, p.F1
*New Yorker*, Mar. 12, 2007, p.86
*People*, Feb. 26, 2007, p.90
*Rolling Stone*, Nov. 30, 2006, p.17; Mar. 8, 2007, p.50

*Spin*, Dec. 2005, p.62; Mar. 2007, p.52
*Teen People*, June/July 2006, p.30

## Online Articles

http://www.blender.com
　(*Blender*, "Boy Crazy!" June 2006)
http://www.cleveland.com
　(*Cleveland Plain Dealer*, "Fall Out Boy's Trohman Ready to Play 'Big Rock'
　at Blossom," May 18, 2007)
http://www.designerpunk.co.uk
　(*Designer Punk.co.uk*, "Interviews," Mar. 17, 2004)
http://www.livedaily.com
　(*LiveDaily*, "LiveDaily Interview: Fall Out Boy's Pete Wentz," Dec.14, 2006)
http://www.mp3.com
　(*MP3.com*, "Fall Out Boy: With or Without You," Apr. 10, 2006)
http://www.mtv.com
　(*MTV News.com*, "Pete Wentz: The Boy with the Thorn in His Side," May
　31, 2006)
http://www.nme.com
　(*NME.com*, "Fall Out Boy: *Infinity on High*," May 23, 2007)
http://www.onmilwaukee.com
　(*OnMilwaukee.com*, "Milwaukee Native Hurley Keeps the Beat for Fall
　Out Boy," May 17, 2007)
http://www.rollingstone.com
　(*Rollingstone.com*, "Let's Hear It for Fall Out Boy," Feb. 24, 2006; "The
　Boys with the Car Crash Hearts," Feb. 21, 2007)

## Online Databases

*Biography Resource Center Online*, 2007, article from *Contemporary Musi-
　cians*, 2005

## ADDRESS

Fall Out Boy
Island Records
825 Eighth Avenue
New York, NY 10019

## WORLD WIDE WEB SITES

http://www.falloutboyrock.com
http://fueledbyramen.com
http://www.myspace.com/falloutboy
http://www.islandrecords.com

## Roger Federer 1981-

Swiss Professional Tennis Player
Five-Time Wimbledon Men's Champion and Winner
of 12 Grand Slam Titles

### BIRTH

Roger Federer was born in Bern, Switzerland, on August 8, 1981. His mother, Lynette, is South African, and his father, Robert, is Swiss. Federer's parents were both employed by the Swiss pharmaceutical company Ciba-Geigy; they met when his father was on a business trip to South Africa. Roger Federer has one older sister, Diana.

## YOUTH

Federer was raised in Münchenstein, Switzerland, a German-speaking town. As a young child, he accompanied his parents to the tennis courts on weekends, but he spent most of the time running around with the other children while the adults played. By age four or so, however, he was playing himself, and when he was eight years old he joined a tennis club. He loved tennis from the start. "I always loved to play against the garage door or against the cupboard doors inside," he recalled. "My mum got fed up because it was bang, bang, bang all day."

*Federer struggled during his early teens, when tennis took him away from his family for extended periods. But his mother says that "those struggles were good for him, a challenge. He learned to be independent, and to develop as a person."*

Federer's development as a player was greatly aided by Peter Carter, an Australian coach who instructed the youngster from ages 10 to 14. Carter helped Federer develop his one-handed backhand and emphasized technique and professionalism, and by his early teens the youngster was one of the top junior players in all of Switzerland.

Federer's game received another boost when he reluctantly decided to leave soccer—another game he loved—behind to focus on tennis. "I prefer to be in control of what's happening, whereas in soccer if the goalie makes a mistake, everyone has to pay for it," he explained. "I also thought I was better at tennis, and I got results faster. I think in the end I probably enjoyed playing tennis more." Besides, as he pointed out on another occasion, "I was pretty good at soccer, but I was the Swiss national junior champ in tennis, so there was no way I could quit."

At age 13 Federer left home to be trained with other promising junior players at the Swiss national tennis center in the French-speaking town of Ecublens. He lived at the training center during the week and visited his family only on weekends. These periods of separation, combined with the challenges of learning a new language, left him extremely homesick during the first few months. His mother recalled that her son often cried on Sunday evenings when it was time for him to return to Ecublens. But she says that "those struggles were good for him, a challenge. He learned to be independent, and to develop as a person."

## EDUCATION

Federer combined tennis instruction and school until age 16, when he decided to quit school to concentrate on his sports training. "I felt school was disturbing me of being 100 percent focused on tennis," he claimed. His parents understood his decision, but according to Federer, they also said "that if, in the next few years, you don't have any results, you go back to school."

Federer resumed training with Carter, who had moved on to a coaching position at the Swiss tennis training center in Biel. The promising young star quickly proved that his self-confidence had not been misplaced. "I finished as No. 1 junior in the summer and everything was going my way," he recalled.

## CAREER HIGHLIGHTS

Federer made his professional debut in March 1998, playing doubles in the Greece F1 tournament with Martin Verkerk of The Netherlands. They were soundly beaten in the first round. Later that summer, though, the 16-year-old Federer won both the junior singles and junior doubles championships at Wimbledon. He was delighted with the victories, but skipped the gala winners' reception in London. Instead, he flew home to Switzerland to play in his first professional singles match at the Gstaad International Series tournament. He lost in straight sets, and had very limited success in other pro events that year. But in December Federer won the RADO Orange Bowl Tennis Championship, a junior-level hard-court event held in Key Biscayne, Florida. He thus finished his first year of professional play with only two wins and four losses—hardly a sensational debut. But the RADO championship also enabled him to end the year as the top-ranked junior men's player in the world.

In 1999 Federer left junior competition behind and began showing his talents on the professional stage. He advanced to the quarterfinals and semifinals of a number of smaller tournaments, showing flashes of tremendous ability. In November 1999 Federer even won his first professional title, defeating the Belorussian Max Mirnyi to claim the Brest International Tournament Championship with a score of 7-6, 6-3.

Tennis scoring can seem complicated. In men's tennis, players usually play best 3 out of 5 sets, though some tournaments use a best 2-out-of-3 format. The first player to win 6 games usually wins the set, but if their margin of victory is less than 2 games, the set is decided by a tiebreaker. Shorthand notation is often used to show the score of a tennis match. For example, 6-2, 6-3, 4-6, 7-6 means that the player in question won the first set by a

*Federer in action during the French Open in 1999.*

score of 6 games to 2, won the second set by a score of 6 games to 3, lost the third set by a score of 4 games to 6, and clinched the match by winning in a fourth-set tiebreaker. In a tiebreaker, the winner is the first player to score seven or more points and lead by two.

After he moved to the professional circuit, Federer was less successful in the tour's "Grand Slam" events. These are the four biggest annual events in professional tennis—the Australian Open, the French Open, the U.S. Open, and Wimbledon (England). To his great disappointment, he was knocked out of both the French Open and Wimbledon in the opening round of competition. Still, the 18-year-old Federer ended the year 1999 as the 64th ranked player in the world in men's play, according to the Association of Tennis Professionals (ATP).

### High Expectations

Despite Federer's youth and modest early success in the professional ranks, many observers claimed that he had the potential to become a top-ranked player. This buzz actually proved to be a distraction. "Because people were constantly saying I was talented and that I was going to make it, I always had that burden," Federer recalled. "It was like, if I make it, then I'm only doing what's expected of me, and if I don't, then I'm a disaster because I missed on a great career or wasted my talent."

The pressure to meet expectations—both his own and those of tennis "experts"—sometimes resulted in temper tantrums and other losses of composure during Federer's first couple of years on the ATP tour. "I used to have a very bad temper on court," he admitted. "I was so disappointed with the way I played, even my opponents would comfort me." Over time, however, Federer learned to keep his emotions under control out on the court. "Today I'm much more in control of myself," he said in 2006, "whereas before it was a weak point of my tennis. People would say, 'If you can get to him mentally, you've got it.' And now it's become a strong point in my game."

Another step forward in Federer's professional growth took place in September 2000, when he represented his country in the Sydney Summer Olympic Games. He missed out on a medal, losing 7-6, 6-7, 6-3 in the bronze-medal match to Arnaud Di Pasquale of France. Still, Federer recalls the Sydney Olympics fondly. "It was one of the best experiences I've had as an athlete," he insisted. "There's nothing like the vibe in the Olympic Village, and I had a great time." Federer closed out the 2000 campaign with a 34-29 win-loss record and a ranking of 29th in the world.

> **"**
>
> *"Because people were constantly saying I was talented and that I was going to make it, I always had that burden," Federer recalled. "It was like, if I make it, then I'm only doing what's expected of me, and if I don't, then I'm a disaster because I wasted my talent."*
>
> **"**

## Toppling a Hero

Federer began the 2001 season with a bang, earning the Milan Indoor Championship in February with a victory over Julien Boutter of France (6-4, 6-7, 6-4). A few months later, he advanced all the way to the quarterfinals of the prestigious French Open before losing to Spain's Alex Corretja in straight sets (7-5, 6-4, 7-5).

But despite these promising results, no one was prepared for Federer's performance at the Wimbledon Championships a few weeks later. He rolled through his first three opponents, then defeated defending Wimbledon champion Pete Sampras in a hard-fought, five-set stunner (7-6, 5-7, 6-4, 6-7, 7-5). The shocking upset ended Sampras's 31-match winning streak at Wimbledon and served notice that the 19-year-old Federer was going to be a force to be reckoned with for years to come. "There are a lot of young guys coming up, but Roger is a bit extra-special," Sampras conceded. "He has a great all-around game."

Federer was knocked out of Wimbledon in the quarterfinals by Tim Henman of Great Britain, but he played consistently well for the next several months. He ended the year as the 13th ranked player in the world, with a record of 46 wins and 20 losses. Federer's roll continued in early 2002 as he claimed the championship of the Adidas International tournament in Sydney, Australia, and advanced to the fourth round of the Australian Open before losing a tough, five-set battle to Tommy Haas of Germany (7-6, 4-6, 3-6, 6-4, 8-6). At midseason, though, Federer went into a slump, exiting both the French Open and Wimbledon in the first round. It was at this moment that he was rocked by tragic news from Africa.

In the summer of 2002 Federer learned that Peter Carter, his mentor and former coach, had been killed in an automobile accident while on safari in South Africa. At first, it appeared that the news of Carter's death struck yet another blow to the young player's state of mind. In late August 2002 Federer appeared at the TD Waterhouse Cup tournament in Long Island, New York. He lost in his first match, falling to Chilean Nicolas Massu in a performance that Charles Bricker described in the *South Florida Sun-Sentinel* as "wild-swinging" and "confounding." "I've lost all confidence," Federer admitted afterward. "I feel like I'm missing energy."

Over the next several weeks, though, Federer came to grips with the death of his friend and coach. Some observers even believe that the tragedy forced him to grow up and to commit himself to tennis in a more disciplined manner. He regained his competitive spirit and put together a string of impressive finishes to close out the year, including the championship of the CA Tennis Trophy tournament in Vienna, Austria. By season's end he had a 55-22 record in match play, good enough to vault him to sixth place in the men's ranks.

## Winning a Grand Slam

When the 2003 season began, many tennis experts believed that Federer was poised for a big year. He proved that their forecasts were on target, winning four tournaments in the season's opening weeks. Federer entered the prestigious Wimbledon Championships brimming with confidence, and he lost only one set in six matches to earn a spot in the men's singles final. Facing Australian Mark Philippoussis on tennis's biggest stage, Federer showed no signs of self-doubt or nervousness. Instead, he pounded Philippoussis in straight sets (7-6, 6-2, 7-6) in less

*Federer returns a shot to Andre Agassi during the finals of the Masters Cup, 2003.*

than two hours. With this win Federer became the first Swiss man ever to win Wimbledon and the first to win a Grand Slam singles title. After the match was over, he broke down in tears and dedicated his historic victory to his former coach, Peter Carter. "I think of him every day," he said. "In these big matches, I thank him also inside. It gives me strength somehow."

Federer closed out the season in strong fashion, capping his terrific year with a straight set victory over Andre Agassi (6-3, 6-0, 6-4) in December to claim the Masters Cup Championship. *Sports Illustrated* writer L. Jon Wertheim expressed amazement at Federer's dominant win over Agassi, one of the game's legendary players: "Federer . . . showcased the manifold qualities required to succeed at tennis's highest level: athleticism, accuracy, cunning, power, and concentration. And, in his case, grace."

Federer ended the year ranked No. 2 in the world in men's tennis behind Andy Roddick. He also won $4 million in prize money in 2003 alone. But despite his growing fame and fortune, Federer refused to hire public relations agents or travel with a large entourage. "The more people you have around you, the less it becomes about the tennis," he explained. Federer did surprise the tennis world by firing his coach, Peter Lundgren, at the end of the 2003 season. "There was a benefit to figuring things out for myself and being more responsible for my preparation," he said. Since that time, Federer has played without a full-time coach.

## World No. 1

After a holiday break, Federer was back on tour in early 2004. He won the first Grand Slam event of the year, the hard-court Australian Open in early February. In the final match he defeated Marat Safin of Russia (7-6, 6-4, 6-2). After the match, Safin told reporters that "I just lost to a magician."

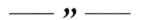

*After Federer defeated Andy Roddick in the 2004 Wimbledon finals, Roddick joked that "I threw the kitchen sink at him, but he went to the bathroom and got his tub."*

*Sports Illustrated* reached a similar conclusion after watching him in Australia, declaring that "[Federer] can execute every shot in the book— and a good many that aren't. He is equally adept at hitting with power and with touch; he is as cozy at the net as he is on the baseline."

Federer's victory in the Australian Open enabled him to slip past Andy Roddick as the top-ranked player in the ATP men's rankings. Over the next several weeks, he showed that he had no intention of giving up that spot. Federer successfully defended his title at the Dubai Tennis Open in March and won the Pacific Life Open in Indian Wells, California, two weeks later. He seemed nearly unstoppable as he rolled over opponents. He won on clay in Hamburg, Germany, and then on grass in the Gerry Weber Open in Halle, Germany (some tournaments, such as Wimbledon, are played on grass; others are played on clay and hardcourt).

In June 2004 Federer returned to the All-England Lawn Tennis Club in Wimbledon to defend his title. He beat Lleyton Hewitt of Australia and Sebastian Grosjean of France on the way to a finals match-up with Roddick. Using his powerful serve, which has been clocked at more than 150 miles per hour, Roddick won the first set. Federer, though, came back to win the second. With Roddick leading the third set four games to two, rain interrupted play. After the delay, Federer abandoned his usual baseline game in favor of a serve and volley strategy. (Serve and volley is when a player serves and then quickly moves toward the net to hit the return ball before it bounces.) Using a variety of tactics, Federer eventually triumphed 4-6, 7-5, 7-6, 6-4 to claim his second straight Wimbledon title. Afterward, Roddick joked, "I threw the kitchen sink at him, but he went to the bathroom and got his tub."

*Federer and Agassi shaking hands during the 2004 U.S. Open.*

Federer also won the final Grand Slam event of the year, the 2004 U.S. Open in Flushing Meadows, New York. Federer defeated Lleyton Hewitt, who had won 16 matches in a row coming into the championship, in straight sets (6-0, 7-6, 6-0) in the men's final. With this triumph, Federer became the first player since Sweden's Mats Wilander in 1988 to win three Grand Slam events in the same year. Federer finished the year with a total of 70 wins, 5 losses, and 11 singles championships.

## Going for the Records

As the 2005 season got underway, the 23-year-old Federer stood as the undisputed number one player in the world. "There's no one who can play with him today," claimed Sampras. "For the next four or five years, his competition will be the record books." A semifinal loss to Safin at the Australian Open, however, put to rest any talk that Federer might make a sweep of the year's Grand Slam events. "It is really unfortunate," Federer said after the loss. "I thought I played really well and a point here and there changed the match. That was a pity, but at least I gave it a fight."

Putting this disappointment behind him, Federer went on to dominate the men's tour for much of the year. He won 11 titles, including two Grand Slam events: Wimbledon and the U.S. Open. His U.S. Open victory over Andre Agassi was particularly important to Federer. "This is the most special one for me, to play Andre in the final of the U.S. Open," he said. "He's one of the only living legends in tennis we still have." For his part, Agassi was very gracious in defeat, calling Federer "the best I've ever played against. . . . He plays the game in a very special way. I haven't seen it before."

> *Federer admitted that his triumph over Rafael Nadal in the 2006 Wimbledon final "was important for me. . . . When we play so often in finals, it adds something to the game. He's up-and-coming. I used to be the youngster. Now I'm sort of getting older. But it's a great rivalry."*

Federer ended the 2005 season with a record of 80 wins and only four losses. In naming him the player of the year, *Tennis* magazine noted that Federer "put together a special season, one that will be nearly impossible for anyone to match in the near future-except, perhaps, Federer himself. . . . [It's] clear that fans are witnessing an unprecedented stretch of dominance in the men's game."

### The Emergence of a Rival

One of Federer's few defeats in 2005 had come in the French Open against 19-year-old Rafael Nadal of Spain, who eventually won the tournament. As the 2006 season began, it was clear that Federer wanted to earn a French Open title—the only one of the Grand Slam events that he had yet to win. But observers pointed out that of the 41 singles titles earned by Federer to that point, only five had been played on clay, the surface for the French Open. In addition, Nadal defeated Federer twice in the weeks leading up to the French Open. The stage was set for an exciting duel in Paris.

Federer and Nadal, who were ranked No. 1 and No. 2 in the world, cruised through the early rounds of the French Open to face each other in the final. The match was highly anticipated because if Federer won he would

*Wearing his custom sport coat, Federer holds the trophy after winning the men's final match against Rafael Nadal at Wimbledon, 2006.*

become the first player to simultaneously hold all Grand Slam titles since 1969. Federer quickly won the first set, but Nadal fought back to win his second French Open (1-6, 6-1, 6-4, 7-6). After the match, Nadal praised Federer, describing him as "the best player I ever played, the best in history, the most complete."

One month later, on the grass courts at Wimbledon, Federer faced his rival once again in the men's final. But this time Federer prevailed, defeating Nadal in four hard-fought sets (6-0, 7-6, 6-7, 6-3) to win a record fourth-straight Wimbledon singles title. "It was important for me to win a final against him for a change," admitted Federer. "When we play so often in finals, it adds something to the game. He's up-and-coming. I used to be the youngster. Now I'm sort of getting older. But it's a great rivalry." In September 2006 Federer beat Roddick to clinch his third consecutive U.S. Open and ninth Grand Slam title.

## Among the Best of All Time

Federer followed that up with an equally impressive series in 2007. The year started in January at the Australian Open, where he beat Fernando Gonzales in the finals 7-6 (2), 6-4, 6-4. At the French Open in June, he once again lost to his rival Nadal, 3-6, 6-4, 3-6, 4-6. But he turned that defeat to victory at Wimbledon. In his fifth straight win there, he beat Nadal 7-6, 4-6, 7-6, 2-6, 6-2. He followed that up with a win in September at the U.S. Open, defeating Novak Djokovic 7-6 (4), 7-6 (2), 6-4 as he earned his fourth straight title. With that win, Federer notched an incredible 12 Grand Slam wins in just five years, now only two fewer than Pete Sampras, the all-time leader in Grand Slam victories with 14 wins.

Many people now view Federer as perhaps the best player in the history of the game, with the same level of dominance over his sport that Michael Jordan enjoyed in basketball and Tiger Woods has in golf. As former Australian tennis great Rod Laver said, "he has all the ingredients. With the way he plays under pressure, he has every chance of real greatness."

> *"I would like to be remembered as a fair player," Federer said. "Also being polite with the people, because in life you can count on the elevator going in both directions—you always meet people twice, once on the way up and once on the way down."*

Many of these same observers give special recognition to the graceful but powerful way that Federer plays tennis. "Federer is the sport's jazz virtuoso, a living legend admired by tennis classicists," wrote Stephen Tignor in *Tennis*. "He moves beautifully and wins comprehensively." Sportswriter Scott Athorne agreed, writing in the *Sunday Times* that "Federer is playing a brand of tennis that has never been seen before. He is combining the classic grace and artistry of yesteryear with the modern power game. . . . Technically, he is perfect."

In assessing his own legacy, though, Federer likes to dwell on the way he carries himself in the swirl of money and stardom that surrounds him on a daily basis. "I would like to be remembered as a fair player," he said. "Also being polite with the people, because in life you can count on the elevator going in both directions—you always meet people twice, once on the way up and once on the way down."

## HOME AND FAMILY

Federer lives in Oberwil, Switzerland, with Miroslava Vavrinec, a former tennis player whom he met while both were representing Switzerland in the 2000 Summer Olympics in Sydney, Australia. Given his tour schedule, promotional events, and other engagements, Federer spends most of the year traveling. He estimates that he only spends about 60 days a year at his home.

## HOBBIES AND OTHER INTERESTS

Federer enjoys beach vacations, deep-sea fishing, ping-pong, playing cards, video games, and musical theater. During tournaments he communicates with his fans worldwide through an online diary on his official web site (http://www.rogerfederer.com/en). He owns the RF Cosmetics company, which produces aftershave, cologne, and other products for men. In 2003 Federer founded a charitable organization to benefit children in South Africa and to support sports for children throughout the world. Since April 2006 he has also served as a Goodwill Ambassador for UNICEF.

## HONORS AND AWARDS

ITF World Junior Champion: 1998
Wimbledon Junior Championship: 1998
Wimbledon Championship: 2003, 2004, 2005, 2006, 2007
ATP Player of the Year: 2004, 2005
Australian Open Tennis Championship: 2004, 2006, 2007
ITF World Champion: 2004, 2005
Player of the Year (*Sports Illustrated*): 2004
U.S. Open Championship: 2004, 2005, 2006, 2007
ESPY Best Male Tennis Player: 2005, 2006
Laureus World Sports Awards: 2005, 2006, for sportsman of the year
Men's Player of the Year (*Tennis*): 2005
Player of the Year (*Tennis*): 2006

## FURTHER READING

### Periodicals

*Atlantic Monthly,* July-Aug. 2006, p.164
*Current Biography International Yearbook,* 2004
*Interview,* July 2006, p.64
*New York Times,* July 9, 2006; Aug. 20, 2006, p.47; Sep. 11, 2006, p.D1
*South Florida Sun-Sentinel,* Aug. 25, 2002, p.C16
*Sports Illustrated,* July 14, 2003; Dec. 29, 2003, p.106; Feb. 9, 2004, p.64; July 12, 2004, p.46; Oct. 4, 2004, p.78; Jan. 17, 2005, p.62; Sep. 19, 2005; June 19, 2006, p.56; July 17, 2006, p.56
*Sports Illustrated KIDS,* Sep. 1, 2005, p.56

*Sunday Times* (London), June 20, 2004, p.13; Mar. 5, 2006, p.48
*Tennis,* June 1999, p.16; Jan.-Feb.2006, p.34; June 2006, p. 44; July 2006, p.62
*Time,* Sep. 4, 2006, p. 60
*Time Atlantic,* Aug. 16, 2004, p.53
*Time International;* Jan. 24, 2005, p.36
*Vogue,* Dec. 2004, p.348

## Online Articles

http://news.bbc.co.uk/sport2/hi/in_depth/2001/wimbledon_2001/1418928.
  stm
  (*BBC Sport,* "Federer Ends Sampras Reign," July 2, 2001)
http://news.bbc.co.uk/sport2/hi/tennis/4207905.stm
  (*BBC Sport,* "Safin Stuns Federer in Epic Semi," Jan. 27, 2005)
http://www.tennis-x.com/fun/federerfile.php
  (*Extreme Tennis News,* "The Roger Federer File," Feb. 17, 2004)
http://www.rolandgarros.com/en_FR/news/articles/2006-06-11/20060611
  1150039906600.html
  (*Roland Garros: The 2006 French Open Official Site,* "Nadal Faces Down
  Federer to Defend Crown," June 11, 2006)

## Online Databases

*Biography Resource Center Online,* 2006, article from *Newsmakers,* 2004
Additional information for this profile came from an interview with Roger
  Federer for "The Charlie Rose Show" (conducted on September 13,
  2004).

## ADDRESS

Roger Federer
Postfach
4103 Bottmingen
Switzerland

## WORLD WIDE WEB SITES

http://www.atptennis.com
http://www.rogerfederer.com
http://www.tennis.com
http://www.usopen.org
http://www.wimbledon.org

# Will Ferrell 1967-

American Actor
Star of the Hit Films *Old School, Elf, Anchorman,* and
*Talladega Nights*

## BIRTH

John William Ferrell was born on July 16, 1967, in Irvine, California. Irvine, 40 miles south of Los Angeles, is one of the larger cities in densely populated Orange County. Will's father, Lee Ferrell, is a professional musician who worked for years with a rock group called the Righteous Brothers. His mother has served as a professor and administrator at Santa Ana Community College. He has one younger brother, Patrick.

## YOUTH

Some comedians draw upon their difficult childhoods for comic material. Ferrell remembers his own childhood fondly. He was happy living in Irvine, he got along well with his brother and both of his parents, and he was popular in school. In an interview, Ferrell's mother described him as "very even tempered, very easygoing. His father and I kinda went, 'How'd he get like that?' You know those little Matchbox cars? Will would line up his Matchbox cars, by himself, and be totally happy. You'd say, 'You wanna go to Disneyland today or line up your cars?' And he'd have to think about it."

*Ferrell's mother described him as "very even tempered, very easygoing. His father and I kinda went, 'How'd he get like that?' You know those little Matchbox cars? Will would line up his Matchbox cars, by himself, and be totally happy. You'd say, 'You wanna go to Disneyland today or line up your cars?' And he'd have to think about it."*

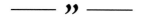

When Ferrell was eight years old, his parents divorced. Even this setback had little effect on Ferrell's sunny personality. "I was the type of kid who would say, 'Hey! Look at the bright side! We'll have two Christmases,'" he recalled. His parents came through the divorce with no hostility and animosity and with a commitment to their children. The biggest difficulty stemmed from Lee Ferrell's line of work. As an entertainer, he had to go on the road with the Righteous Brothers for months at a time. He could not establish a successful solo career. He always struggled to make enough money to support his family. The son of a struggling musician, Will Ferrell grew up determined *not* to go into show business. Will wanted a stable, stay-at-home sort of job. He wanted to go into business.

## EARLY MEMORIES

Ferrell has called third grade "a pivotal year" for him. He learned that he could make his classmates laugh if he pretended to smash his head against the wall, or if he tripped and fell on purpose. "That was a great way to make friends," he later said. At the same time, Ferrell realized that overdoing his comedy might get him in trouble with his teachers. He learned to be serious when necessary and to clown when possible—when it would not disrupt the classroom. "I wasn't obnoxious," he said. "I never got kicked out of class. I knew when enough was enough."

As he progressed through grade school and into high school, Ferrell grew tall and athletic. Standing six-foot-three by his late teens, he played basketball, soccer, and football. He was sometimes joined on teams by his brother, who grew to be six-foot-five. But the urge to make people laugh never left him. As a high school prank he formed a reptile club, even though he did not know anyone who owned a reptile. The club lasted for two meetings.

## EDUCATION

Ferrell attended University High School in Irvine. He kept a busy schedule there, serving on the student council, becoming the team captain of his basketball squad, and serving as the kicker on the football team. All the while he earned good grades. He still knew how to get laughs without causing trouble, yet he never dreamed of a career in comedy. "I grew up around the entertainment industry and it took away all my illusions," he recalled. "I didn't want to do the same as my dad. I realized it was a month-to-month existence, with no real security."

Ferrell could not stop being funny, though. In his senior year of high school, he and a friend began making comedy skits out of the school's morning announcements and piping them through the intercom system. They did this with the full cooperation of the principal. Of course they had to write the material, and this proved to be another education for Ferrell in the art of comedy. He also did comic skits in school talent shows. When he graduated from University High, his classmates named him "Best Personality."

In 1986 Ferrell entered the University of Southern California, one of the state's largest colleges. He decided to major in sports information, leading to a career in public relations or broadcasting. This seemed like a safe and sensible plan. At the same time, he did not lose his sense of humor. As he progressed through college his pranks grew bolder. One of his favorites was dressing in a janitor's uniform and strolling into his friends' classes. He also engaged in "streaking"—running naked in public places, usually with a small group of his fraternity brothers from Delta Tau Delta.

Ferrell was not a top student academically at the University of Southern California, but he was easygoing and good looking. He earned an internship at a local television station in the sports department. To his great dis-

*Ferrell first found success on "SNL," particularly with his impressions of George W. Bush. In this mock presidential debate shortly before the 2000 election, Ferrell plays Bush and Darrell Hammond plays Vice President Al Gore.*

appointment, he found he did not like the work. The only aspect of the job that appealed to him was the opportunity to appear on the air. "Midway through my training I realized I enjoyed performing for the camera much more than I enjoyed reporting," he said. Ferrell graduated from USC in 1990 with a bachelor's degree in sports broadcasting, but his internship convinced him not to seek employment as a sportscaster.

## FIRST JOBS

Uncertain about the direction he should take in life, Ferrell moved back in with his mother. He passed through a series of jobs and hated them all. He worked as a hotel valet, moving guests' cars to a parking garage. On his second day at work he tore a baggage rack off the top of a van by trying to drive it under a low-lying beam. A worse fate awaited him at another position—as a teller at the Wells Fargo Bank. After his first day on the job he was short $300. The following day he was short $280. He did not steal the money—he was just careless and error-prone as he served customers.

Ferrell's mother recognized his frustration with this series of unfulfilling jobs. She encouraged him to try his hand at comedy, even if he was worried about being able to make a living in the field. In 1991 he took her advice. He moved to Los Angeles, found an apartment, and auditioned for an improvisational group called The Groundlings.

## CAREER HIGHLIGHTS

### Early Comedy Work with
### The Groundlings

The Groundlings is a Los Angeles *improv* group composed of paid professionals and tuition-paying students at various levels of talent and experience. The word *improv* is short for "improvisational." In improv comedy, individual performers are given a situation or character and then expected to create comic dilemmas onstage without any rehearsal or written script. This spontaneous form of comedy requires quick thinking and a wide range of talent. The Groundlings offered classes for beginners, as well as advanced opportunities for actors and comedians who passed an audition. Ferrell passed the audition and began working with the advanced classes.

> —— " ——
>
> *"I grew up around the entertainment industry and it took away all my illusions,"* he recalled. *"I didn't want to do the same as my dad. I realized it was a month-to-month existence, with no real security."*
>
> —— " ——

Before joining The Groundlings, Ferrell tried standup comedy, the type of comedy performed in front of an audience using a microphone. He had no success and decided that he was unsuited for standup. He has never really seen himself as a funny person: he could not draw upon an unusual appearance or a dark past for comic material. Improv offered a solution. It allowed Ferrell to *inhabit a character,* someone other than himself, and to act in ways that fit the character.

Ferrell discovered that he liked to do impressions of famous people. One of the first was baseball radio announcer Harry Caray. Now deceased and enshrined in the Baseball Hall of Fame, Caray was quite famous for his unique on-air style. Ferrell began to mimic his voice patterns and unbridled enthusiasm. Then he put his "Harry Caray" character into odd situations, such as auditioning for a play. This material worked well when Ferrell performed it at The Groundlings classes.

Ferrell also began to create original characters. With fellow Groundlings member Chris Kattan he began an ongoing routine about the fictitious

Butabi brothers, a pair of losers who go out to dance clubs to try to meet women, only to be rejected time after time.

During the three years when he was learning improv, Ferrell needed part-time work in order to pay his bills. A friend of his, Viveca Paulin, helped him land a job at the auction house where she worked. The job gave Ferrell enough flexibility to attend auditions and to rehearse with The Groundlings. Gradually he began to get more and more paid work as an actor. He made guest appearances on television situation comedies like "Grace under Fire" and "Living Single," as well as commercials and low-budget comedy films, including *Bucket of Blood*. Even so he had to serve as a mall Santa Claus one winter. Little by little, however, Ferrell made progress. In 1994 he won a spot with The Groundlings' top professional group. Important show business executives came to watch his work, eventually leading to his move to "Saturday Night Live."

## Auditioning for "Saturday Night Live"

"Saturday Night Live" began its run on late-night television in October 1975. More than 30 years later the show is still on the air, with a weekly live show featuring sketch comedy appearing late on Saturday nights. Its edgy brand of rehearsed but spontaneous-looking comic skits has launched the film and TV careers of dozens of actors and actresses, including Dan Ackroyd, John Belushi, Chevy Chase, Billy Crystal, Jane Curtin, Tina Fey, Eddie Murphy, Bill Murray, Mike Myers, Chris Rock, Adam Sandler, and Molly Shannon. Each show includes short comedy sketches performed by cast members alongside the week's host, with musical numbers by a featured performer, usually one of the hottest acts around.

Just as "Saturday Night Live" has served as a proving ground for future movie stars, The Groundlings has served as a proving ground for "Saturday Night Live." Ferrell had been in The Groundlings' top performance group for only 10 months when a producer for "Saturday Night Live" came to see a performance. At that point "SNL" had fallen in popularity, and its production staff was eager to sign some new talent for the 1995 season. On the basis of his performance, Ferrell was invited to New York City to audition for "SNL" in front of its main producer, Lorne Michaels. Two fellow performers at The Groundlings, Chris Kattan and Cheri Oteri, were also asked to audition.

Onstage before Michaels, Ferrell launched into some of his best routines, including his take on Harry Caray and a one-man sketch in which a macho middle-class man becomes unhinged while simultaneously barbecuing meat and arguing with his children. Michaels invited Ferrell back for a business meeting to discuss adding him to the show. Ferrell did not quite know how to approach this meeting. He wondered if he should bring a comic twist to it, or simply play it straight. Finally he decided to stuff a briefcase with fake money and to pretend that *he* was trying to hire Lorne Michaels. The meeting turned out to be very serious, strictly business, and Ferrell never opened his briefcase. Then he was told to return for another meeting. Again he brought the briefcase, and again it stayed closed. When Michaels asked Ferrell to join the cast of "Saturday Night Live," the two men sealed the deal with a handshake. The unused briefcase full of fake cash became a memento that Ferrell has saved.

## Becoming a Star on "SNL"

Ferrell started on "Saturday Night Live" in 1995. Just before he went on the air in his first appearance, he expressed some anxiety. "I never got a sense of why they picked me," he admitted. "I'm either very talented or they're in trouble." While he didn't have a strong first season, he soon became an audience favorite. He and Kattan performed some of their Groundlings material, including their Butabi brothers routine. And as the writers for the show began to notice Ferrell's ability to mimic famous people, they started writing sketches especially for him. He often lampooned such national figures as former Attorney General Janet Reno, "Jeopardy" host Alex Trebec, and singer Robert Goulet.

> "I'm at play every time I get to act," Ferrell once said. "That never leaves me. It comes through more in the characters with eternal optimism. Whether it's joy, or cockiness, it's fun to play attitude to the nth degree."

Ferrell came into his own, however, when he began to impersonate George W. Bush. The comedian first appeared as Bush even before Bush became president in 2000. After the election, he regularly spoofed President Bush. Ferrell managed to mimic Bush's mannerisms and speech patterns even though the comedian looked nothing like the president. Ferrell also offered a level of satire that clearly criticized the president's ability to run the country. As Marc Peyser wrote in *Newsweek,* "Ferrell hasn't been shy about criticizing his alter ego."

Ratings for "Saturday Night Live" improved during the seven seasons that Ferrell appeared on the show. Despite his early anxiety about whether he

Some of Ferrell's early films: Dick *(top)*, A Night at the Roxbury *(center)*, and Zoolander *(bottom)*.

had enough talent for "SNL," he was nominated for an Emmy Award in 2001. Lorne Michaels even declared that Ferrell was "the center pillar" on the show for much of his seven-year run.

## Starting a Film Career

Despite this success with "Saturday Night Live," Ferrell worried that he might not be able to advance his career beyond television if he stayed on the show for too long. So while continuing to appear on "SNL," he took small roles in movies when it wasn't taping. He appeared in *Austin Powers: International Man of Mystery* (1997), a parody of 1960s spy movies, especially the James Bond series. Mike Myers starred as the super-spy Austin Powers, and Ferrell appeared in a small role as Mustafa, one of Dr. Evil's henchmen. He reprised his role as Mustafa in the follow-up film, *Austin Powers: The Spy Who Shagged Me* (1999).

Ferrell's first starring role came in *A Night at the Roxbury* (1998), in which he co-starred with Chris Kattan, with whom he also wrote the script. The movie was based on the characters Steve and Doug Butabi, which they had first created for The Groundlings and then continued to develop on "Saturday Night Live." Steve and Doug Butabi are pathetic but lovable brothers. During the day they work at their father's fake plant store; at night they prowl music clubs, dressed in their matching polyester suits, bobbing their heads together in time to the music, and trying to meet women. Reviews of the movie were mixed, as many felt that what worked as short sketch was a bit belabored as a full-length movie.

Ferrell had small parts in several additional movies while continuing to appear on "Saturday Night Live." In *Superstar* (1999), also based on an "SNL" skit, Molly Shannon starred as a nerdy Catholic schoolgirl, Mary Katherine Gallagher, who dreams of being famous. Ferrell played Sky Corrigan, on whom she has a crush. In *Dick* (1999), Ferrell played renowned investigative reporter Bob Woodward. He and fellow *Washington Post* journalist Carl Bernstein were pivotal in uncovering the Watergate scandal that became the downfall of President Richard Nixon. But *Dick* provides a fairly silly version of this serious historical event. It centers around two teen girls, played by Michelle Williams and Kirsten Dunst, who become embroiled in the scandal. In *Zoolander* (2001), a send up of the modeling world starring Ben Stiller and Owen Wilson as vacuous male models, Ferrell played the evil fashion mogul Jacobim Mugatu, who plans to assassinate the prime minister of Malaysia to ensure cheap labor for the fashion industry.

*Two of the movies that made
Ferrell a star:* Old School *and* Elf.

### Old School **and** Elf

In 2002, after seven seasons on "Saturday Night Live," Ferrell announced that he would retire from the show so he could spend more time making movies. That proved to be a turning point in his career, as he went on to appear in his second starring vehicle, *Old School* (2003). This comedy features Ferrell, Vince Vaughn, and Luke Wilson as a trio of aging men who decide to return to their glory days as college fraternity brothers. Ferrell is "Frank the Tank," the leader and most outrageous member of the gang. In one scene he convinces his friends to streak down a street and winds up sprinting naked all on his own—the other two chicken out.

*Old School* quickly became an audience favorite. Ferrell's many fans loved the film's raucous humor, as explained by David Denby. "It's party time, and the movie is wild and crude without being mean—it's a comedy of infantile regression, *Animal House* for grownups," Denby wrote. "The humor is hit or miss, but each of the three men is funny in his own way. Will Ferrell, of 'Saturday Night Live,' has a roly-poly childishness that reaches full flower in a sequence devoted to college athletics in which he waves a long red ribbon in graceful circles and assumes a crouching pose of artistic Olympian virtue." Reaction to the movie from critics was mixed, however, as in this comment by Robert Abele in a review of the movie for the *Los Angeles Times*. Abele wrote that Ferrell "expertly mines the humor in a man slipping backward down the evolutionary scale."

> "It's party time, and the movie [Old School] is wild and crude without being mean," wrote reviewer David Denby. "[Ferrell] has a roly-poly childishness that reaches full flower in a sequence devoted to college athletics in which he waves a long red ribbon in graceful circles and assumes a crouching pose of artistic Olympian virtue."

In Ferrell's next film, *Elf* (2003), he stars as Buddy, who was a baby when he crawled into Santa's bag one Christmas Eve and then was raised at the North Pole by Santa Claus (Ed Asner) and the elves. Like the elves and animated talking animals in his world, Buddy is happy and completely obsessed with Christmas. He knows he is different from the other elves, though. He towers over his friends and adopted father, and he cannot work as quickly as the other toymakers. When Buddy's North Pole father tells him he is adopted, Buddy decides to set out for New York City to find his real dad. Dressed in his outlandish elf clothing, brimming with high spirits, Buddy walks into Manhattan and into the life of his biological father (James Caan) and his skeptical 10-year-old half-brother. Faced with the cynicism of his family and other New Yorkers, he becomes determined to restore the true meaning of Christmas.

Ferrell liked the *Elf* script because it allowed him to clown, but also to show a range of endearing emotions. "I'm at play every time I get to act," he once said. "That never leaves me. It comes through more in the characters with eternal optimism. Whether it's joy, or cockiness, it's fun to play attitude to the nth degree." The film's director, Jon Favreau, had a slightly different take on his approach to acting. "His humor has a real vulnerability to it," said Favreau. "He was really sweet and nice and quiet. It was hard to evaluate his energy on that set, though, because he was always naked."

———— " ————

*"Anchorman is slyer than most other dumb comedies out there without ever making the mistake of taking itself too seriously," said critic Leah Rozen. "How could it when its hero, talking himself up to a prospective date, announces in his most sepulchral tone, 'I'm very important. I have many leather-bound books.' It's this kind of goofy line, and scene, that makes* Anchorman *a breezy hoot."*

———— " ————

*Elf* proved to be a big hit with critics, as in this comment from Lisa Schwarzbaum. "The disarming comedic tone—silly and novel in its lack of cynicism—is driven by the fearless, cheerful unself-consciousness of Will Ferrell, a big man last seen streaking (all too unself-consciously) through *Old School*. Now wearing lime green polar couture and a humiliation-proof grin, he's a sight for dour eyes." Audiences loved the movie as well. *Elf* grossed $31 million at the box office the weekend it opened in November of 2003. Since then it has earned more than $175 million in theaters and DVD rentals. *Old School* enjoyed similar financial success. Made for $24 million, it has earned more than $145 million and has become a huge hit on DVD. The combination of these two totals crowned Ferrell as "the comic lead that everyone in Hollywood wants to cast," explained analyst Sharon Waxman. Despite all this success, Ferrell still felt uneasy about his chosen career. "I always think of alternative careers, in case this thing doesn't work out," he said in 2004—after *Old School* and *Elf* had established him as a star.

### Anchorman and Talladega Nights

Ferrell's next big success came in the movie *Anchorman: The Legend of Ron Burgundy* (2004). Long before he scored the dual successes of *Old School*

*Ferrell as the title character Ron Burgundy in* Anchorman.

and *Elf*, Ferrell had been co-writing a screenplay with Adam McKay, a co-worker from "Saturday Night Live." That movie, *Anchorman,* pokes fun at the macho, all-male realm of television broadcasting in the 1970s. Ferrell appears as the title character, Ron Burgundy, a sexist anchorman in San Diego who believes that all women adore him and that women don't belong in the newsroom. He has to deal with this prejudice when a pretty, ambitious young woman (Christina Applegate) lands a position at his TV station.

*Anchorman* found favor with a variety of audiences and performed well at the box office, with reviewers pointing to Ferrell's performance. "[Ferrell] does a variation on his specialty—the completely unjustified egomaniac," wrote Owen Gleiberman. "Ron is a homegrown Austin Powers. He's blind entitlement wrapped around a core of utter dimness." Leah Rozen had this praise for the movie. "With little on its mind besides poking fun at egotistical TV-news Twinkies, *Anchorman* is slyer than most other dumb comedies out there without ever making the mistake of taking itself too seriously. How could it when its hero, talking himself up to a prospective date, announces in his most sepulchral tone, 'I'm very important. I have many leather-bound books.' It's this kind of goofy line, and scene, that makes *Anchorman* a breezy hoot."

Ferrell appeared in several films in 2005. He starred in the serious Woody Allen movie *Melinda and Melinda* and the family comedy *Kicking and Screaming*, a satire about the competitive nature of amateur soccer coaches in pee wee leagues. *Kicking and Screaming* features Ferrell as a coach with a grudge against his father, played by veteran actor Robert Duvall. As part of their feud, the two characters coach rival teams, using every trick to win games against one another. Although the film did not perform as well as *Elf*, *Kicking and Screaming* found its supporters. *Chicago Tribune* columnist Robert K. Elder called Ferrell "a mow-you-down comic engine" in his review of the movie.

*"Ricky Bobby is at once a creature of pure, extravagant absurdity and a curiously vulnerable, sympathetic figure," wrote reviewer A. O. Scott. "This movie is the real thing."*

Also in 2005 Ferrell appeared in *Bewitched* with Nicole Kidman. Based on a 1960s-era television show, *Bewitched* tells the story of a down-and-out actor (Ferrell) who attempts to revive his career by appearing in a movie version of the TV show. His co-star (Kidman) proves to have true magical powers, helping them both to shine—and to fall in love. Topping off a busy year, Ferrell took the role of the hapless Nazi playwright Franz Liebkind in the movie version of the Broadway musical *The Producers*. Somehow, in addition to all those major features, he managed to offer his voice to the animated comedy *Curious George* and to complete cameo roles in *Starsky & Hutch* and *The Wedding Crashers*.

Ferrell again teamed with Adam McKay to write the 2006 hit *Talladega Nights: The Ballad of Ricky Bobby*. McKay also directed the film. *Talladega Nights* satirizes one of America's favorite sports—NASCAR racing. It lampoons the sport's constant use of product advertising and its egotistical stars, all without offending its many fans. None too intelligent but brimming with personality, Ricky Bobby, as played by Ferrell, traces his addiction to speedy cars to his birth in the back of a souped-up Chevrolet. His father is a race car driver, so naturally Ricky follows his dad into the sport and becomes a huge success. But that success sometimes comes at the expense of his best friend, fellow driver Cal Naughton, Jr. (played by John C. Reilly). Hailing from North Carolina, Ricky sports a Southern accent and is devoted to his beautiful but cunning wife (Leslie Bibb). A rival driver from France named Jean Girard invades Ricky's ideal

*Ferrell (right) and John C. Reilly (left) in* Talladega Nights.

life and provides bitter competition. The Frenchman, performed by Sacha Baron Cohen, sips espresso and otherwise challenges the all-American macho image of NASCAR.

*Talladega Nights* was one of the most successful summer movies of 2006, becoming a hit with audiences and critics alike. "Ricky Bobby is at once a creature of pure, extravagant absurdity and a curiously vulnerable, sympathetic figure," wrote reviewer A. O. Scott. "This movie is the real thing." According to Kenneth Turan, "There is a real sincerity to Ferrell's characterization . . . an ability to take silly things so completely seriously that laughter inevitably results."

## Recent Projects

After a string of comedies, Ferrell appeared in a more serious movie late in 2006. In *Stranger than Fiction*, he played Harold Crick, a dull Internal Revenue Service agent who suddenly hears a women's voice in his head narrating the details of his life. Crick discovers that he has become the main character in a novel and that the author of the novel plans to end the book with his death. Desperate to save himself, Crick launches a search for the author, played by Emma Thompson. Ferrell said of the film, "I think it's the best thing I've done, with some amazing actors. Forget about me, it's really an amazing film just by itself."

*Ferrell in a scene from* Stranger than Fiction.

Next up for Ferrell was *Blades of Glory*, released in 2007. This comedy about the first male figure-skating pair features Ferrell and Jon Heder (from *Napoleon Dynamite*). They're opposed in the Olympics by another duo, played by Amy Poehler and Will Arnett. The idea of a male figure-skating pair creates some funny possibilities, particularly the skating routines. "When those guys lifted their legs, it was a beautiful move," said Poehler. "But they had some chafing problems." *People* magazine described it as "Think *Chariots of Fire* meets the Ice Capades meets *Talladega Nights*, and you've got *Blades of Glory*."

## MARRIAGE AND FAMILY

Ferrell married his longtime friend Viveca Paulin in August 2000. They have two sons: Magnus, who was born in March 2004, and Mattias, who was born in December 2006. Ferrell and his family live in Los Angeles. When he is working on location outside California, his wife and sons travel with him as often as they can.

## HOBBIES AND OTHER INTERESTS

Ferrell's busy work schedule leaves him little time to indulge in hobbies. He acts, writes, and serves as an executive producer on his major films.

Nevertheless, he has found an outside interest—distance running. He and his wife both compete occasionally in marathons. In 2003 he was featured on the cover of *Runner's World* magazine. Ferrell sees his interest in running as a natural outcome of his athletic youth. "If anything," he said, "it's given me more energy, more of a focus and drive in other areas of my life."

## SELECTED TELEVISION AND MOVIE CREDITS

*Bucket of Blood,* 1995
"Saturday Night Live," 1995-2002
*Austin Powers: International Man of Mystery,* 1997
*Men Seeking Women,* 1997
*A Night at the Roxbury,* 1998 (co-writer, with Chris Kattan)
*Dick,* 1999
*The Suburbans,* 1999
*Superstar,* 1999
*Austin Powers: The Spy Who Shagged Me,* 1999
*Drowning Mona,* 2000
*The Ladies Man,* 2000
*Jay and Silent Bob Strike Back,* 2001
"The Oblongs," 2001
*Zoolander,* 2001
*Elf,* 2003
*Old School,* 2003
*Anchorman: The Legend of Ron Burgundy,* 2004 (co-writer, with Adam McKay)
*Starsky & Hutch,* 2004
*Bewitched,* 2005
*Curious George,* 2005 (voice for animation)
*Kicking and Screaming,* 2005
*Melinda and Melinda,* 2005
*The Producers,* 2005
*The Wedding Crashers,* 2005
*Stranger than Fiction,* 2006
*Talladega Nights: The Ballad of Ricky Bobby,* 2006 (co-writer, with Adam McKay)
*Blades of Glory,* 2007

## HONORS AND AWARDS

American Comedy Award: 2001, Funniest Male Performer in a TV Special, for "Saturday Night Live-Presidential Bash 2000"

Teen Choice Awards: 2007, Choice Movie Actor-Comedy, for *Talladega Nights: The Ballad of Ricky Bobby* and *Blades of Glory*

## FURTHER READING

### Books

Epstein, Dwayne. *Will Ferrell,* 2005 (juvenile)
Miller, James A., and Tom Shales. *Live From New York: An Uncensored History of Saturday Night Live, as Told By Its Stars, Writers, and Guests,* 2003

### Periodicals

*Chicago Tribune,* Oct. 5, 2006, p.C1
*Current Biography Yearbook,* 2003
*Esquire,* Dec. 2003, p.162
*GQ,* Dec. 2006, p.296
*Los Angeles Times,* May 7, 2002, Calendar, p.1
*New York Times,* Jan. 25, 2001, p. E1; May 9, 2004, p.A2; Aug. 4, 2006, p.E1
*Newsweek,* Feb. 19, 2001, p.56; July 12, 2004, p.58
*People,* Apr. 6, 1998, p.143; Nov. 24, 2003, p.71; Nov. 20, 2006, p.83
*Time,* Nov. 10, 2003, p.90
*Variety,* Oct. 5, 1998, p.68

### Online Databases

*Biography Resource Center Online,* 2007

## ADDRESS

Will Ferrell
Creative Artists Agency
9830 Wilshire Blvd.
Beverly Hills, CA 90212

## WORLD WIDE WEB SITES

http://www.nbc.com/Saturday_Night_Live/bios/Will_Ferrell.shtml
http://www.oldschool-themovie.com
http://www.elfmovie.com
http://www.anchorman-themovie.com
http://www.sonypictures.com/movies/talladeganights

## America Ferrera 1984-

American Actress
Star of the TV Series "Ugly Betty" and the Movie
*The Sisterhood of the Traveling Pants*

### BIRTH

America Georgine Ferrera was born on April 18, 1984, in Los Angeles, California. Although her parents were born in Honduras, Ferrera and her five older siblings (four sisters and a brother) were raised by their mother in Woodland Hills, a district of Los Angeles located in the San Fernando Valley. "My mother decided to come to this country," she revealed, "for the sole purpose that my siblings and I could get an education, could have every opportunity in the business world, and whatever we wanted to pursue would be at our fingertips."

When America was seven, her parents divorced and her father returned to Honduras. Her mother raised her six children as a single mother, working as a director of housekeeping for the Hilton Hotels. "No matter how much a single mother makes, six mouths is a lot to feed," Ferrera said in praise of her mother, who is also named America. "And then to find time to raise them? I don't know how she did it. She's amazing."

## YOUTH

Ferrera spent much of her early life feeling like an outsider. She grew up in Woodland Hills, a predominantly white area with a large number of Jewish residents. Many of her friends held bar and bat mitzvahs, the Jewish coming-of-age celebration that takes place when a girl turns 12 or a boy turns 13. "Where I grew up, I went to tons of bar and bat mitzvahs, and I've never been to a single quinceañera," she recalled, referring to the traditional Hispanic celebration when a girl turns 15. Still, Ferrera felt a deep connection to her cultural heritage. "When you are first-generation anything, you have your past, which is these roots, and it's a part of you because you're so deeply connected to your relatives," she explained. "But then you have the society that you're supposed to blend into." Her mother spoke Spanish at home, but Ferrera and her siblings would usually respond to her in English. "I understand Spanish and I can speak it, but not fluently," she admitted.

As a child, Ferrera never felt like she fit in with the Latino community, primarily due to where she lived. "All of my friends were white Jewish kids," she recalled. "So the Latino kids thought I was this white girl." At the same time, she felt distant from the other children at school. "As early as second grade I remember feeling really different and isolated," she said. "I had the hugest crush on a boy, and my best friend had a crush on him too. One day he said to me, 'I like your best friend more because she's paler and she has freckles.' And it was right then that I began to feel like, 'Oh wow, I'm different.'" Although she experienced feelings of loneliness at school, she was close with her siblings. "Growing up, I never had a ton of friends. I always had two or three, but when you have four sisters and a brother all a year apart, you don't really need anyone else to play with," she stated.

While her mother worked, Ferrera spent her time watching television and movies, developing an interest in acting from an early age. "As a child I knew acting was what I wanted to pursue. Being able to interpret a role and communicating what I feel is very satisfying to me." She began taking roles in school plays, and she also performed in local community theater groups. "My first play was *Romeo and Juliet*. I was in third grade, but I went to a junior high school and auditioned for the play," Ferrera remarked. "They gave me the part of the Apothecary, the druggist who gives Romeo the drugs to kill himself." Later, in the fifth grade, she played the role of the Artful Dodger in the school production of *Oliver*. At the age of 15, she enrolled in acting classes, which she paid for by waiting tables and babysitting. In addition to her interest in theater, she also became an avid reader, identifying with the Latino lives portrayed in the works of such authors as Sandra Cisneros and Julia Álvarez.

## EDUCATION

At El Camino High School, Ferrera excelled in academics. She graduated in 2002 with a 4.3 grade point average and was named valedictorian, the student with the highest grade point average in her graduating class. Despite this success, she does not have fond memories of her experience at El Camino High School. "My high school days were definitely *not* the best days of my life," said Ferrera. "It was about hiding all the things that made me different and trying to fit in somewhere. I didn't know who I was."

*"My high school days were definitely not the best days of my life," said Ferrera. "It was about hiding all the things that made me different and trying to fit in somewhere. I didn't know who I was."*

Ferrera entered the University of Southern California on a presidential scholarship, deciding to pursue a double major in theater and international relations. "Acting is something I knew I wanted to do long term," she declared. "But not going to college was not an option. I think it probably helped me as an actress as well, because actresses need real-life experiences to draw from." While attending college, she also continued to act professionally. Her college career was interrupted by the success of her TV show, "Ugly Betty." Ferrera is currently one semester shy of earning her degree, having taken the 2006-07 school year off to concentrate on the show. She plans to complete her education soon. "Once doing the show becomes more routine, I hope to fit in a class at a time and just slowly work toward my degree. I've come too far to quit one semester before graduation."

## FIRST JOBS

According to Ferrera, her mother was reluctant to encourage her daughter to pursue acting professionally. "Acting was not something that they [my parents] came to this country to have me do," she said. "I don't think her fears came from thinking that I couldn't do it; she knew I had a passion and I really wanted to act. I think her fears came from her not being sure that I could make it in such a cruel business. . . . [She] wants security for me; she wants me to have a good life, and what I have had to do is prove to her that this is what the [good] life is for me." Despite her mother's skepticism about professional acting, her mother also counseled her on the importance of being proactive, advice which Ferrera has followed. "My mom told me that you have to be a go-getter. You have to go after what you want in life."

*"I never turned on the TV and saw a Latina woman with an average body," Ferrera revealed. "I thought, 'I'll never be a Charlie's Angel, because I can't fit into size zero leather pants.'"*

Ferrera began attending auditions for acting parts while she was still in high school. But these first auditions were not successful, prompting her mother to suggest that she reconsider her career choice. "I said, 'You need to change your mind. You're short. You're Latino. You're not blond. You don't have blue eyes. You won't get into this business,'" her mother remembered. "She [America] said, 'You don't understand. I want to do this like a doctor wants to be a doctor, like a teacher wants to be a teacher.'" While she was still attending El Camino High School, Ferrera was signed by a small talent agency. After a year of rejections for commercial auditions, she landed a role in the 2002 Disney Channel television movie *Gotta Kick It Up!*

## CAREER HIGHLIGHTS

While attending drama camp as a 16-year-old at Northwestern University in Chicago, Illinois, Ferrera shot a videotaped audition for a part in the 2002 independent film *Real Women Have Curves*. "I sent in the tape and then didn't think twice about it," Ferrera explained. "I just went back to enjoying my summer in Chicago." But the audition soon led to a part in what became her first major critical success.

*Ferrera in a scene from* Real Women Have Curves.

### Real Women Have Curves

*Real Women Have Curves* was adapted from the play by Josefina Lopez and starred veteran Hispanic actors Lupe Ontiveros and George Lopez. Ferrera was cast as Ana, a first-generation Mexican American teenager living in East Los Angeles with her mother, Carmen, played by Ontiveros. Ana is torn between accepting a scholarship to Columbia University and working with her family at a garment factory.

The title of the film, which refers to Ana's acceptance of her physique, served as a source of identification for Ferrera as well. Speaking of her own self-image, she stated: "I never turned on the TV and saw a Latina woman with an average body and I thought, 'I'll never be a Charlie's Angel, because I can't fit into size zero leather pants.'" She had to overcome her insecurities for a scene in which Ana strips down to her underclothes in an act of defiance against her mother. "It was weird at first," Ferrera confessed. "It was like a room with 20 men, the crew. I had to be really confident for that scene. I had to forget about my own feelings." The theme of pride and confidence in oneself runs throughout the film. "You leave this movie feeling happy about who you are. And that's something we're all hungry for," she maintained.

Originally filmed for HBO, *Real Women Have Curves* caused a sensation at the Sundance Film Festival. Critics lauded Ferrera's performance, nominating her for an Independent Spirit Award for Best Debut Performance and a Young Artist Award for Best Performance in a Feature Film—Leading Young Actress, both in 2003. Along with costar Ontiveros, Ferrera won the Special Jury Prize for acting at the 2002 Sundance Film Festival. The movie was released in theaters in 2002.

After the movie came out, Ferrera had conflicting feelings about pursuing an acting career. But then an influential professor changed her perspective: "I couldn't see how it could be important in a world with so much war and hatred, where people are starving to death and dying. So I went to my favorite college professor for advice. He told me about how he mentored a young Latina girl who asked him to watch my movie *Real Women Have Curves* because she felt like the story reflected her life. She had always felt invisible in the world, but the movie changed her life by giving her a voice and a better understanding of herself. That made me feel so much better about what I do."

### Plainsong

Ferrera got a chance to expand her range as an actress in the 2004 Hallmark Hall of Fame television movie *Plainsong*. Based on the best-selling

*Ferrera with castmates from* The Sisterhood of the Traveling Pants *(left to right): Blake Lively, Amber Tamblyn, and Alexis Bledel.*

novel by Kent Haruf, *Plainsong* revolves around the lives of simple towns-folk living in rural Colorado. The film features such notable actors as Aidan Quinn and Rachel Griffith. The character played by Ferrera, Victoria Roubideaux, is a pregnant teenager who has been kicked out of her mother's house. She is taken in by two kindly brothers who live alone on their farm. The movie contains a scene in which Victoria gives birth. "I wanted to make that as real as possible and I spent the most time trying to make that authentic," Ferrera explained. "I watched a lot of birthing videos, which were painful to watch." The experience made Ferrera think cautiously about her own life. "I told my mom she never has to worry about me getting pregnant," she added.

### The Sisterhood of the Traveling Pants

In 2005, Ferrera landed one of the main roles in *The Sisterhood of the Traveling Pants.* The movie was adapted from the best-selling young adult novel

179

of the same name by Ann Brashares, the first of several books in a series about a group of friends. *The Sisterhood of the Traveling Pants* stars Ferrera, Alexis Bledel, Blake Lively, and Amber Tamblyn as four teenage best friends. The group finds a pair of jeans in a thrift shop that magically fits them all despite differences in size and body type. In an effort to remain connected during a summer spent apart, each of the girls spends a week wearing the jeans, and then mails them to the next girl. Although the movie has a light touch, it deals with serious issues like divorce, death, and the loss of virginity. Ferrera's character, Carmen, is spending time with her father, who left her and her mother when she was a child. For her performance in the film, Ferrera was nominated for a 2006 ALMA Award for Outstanding Actress in a Motion Picture and a Teen Choice Award for Choice Movie Breakout Performance—Female.

> "What is special about it is Betty is just a regular girl that appeals to all different races and all kinds of audiences—and she just happens to be Latina. And for a Latina character to be out there in a mainstream way and without a banner on her head is a true success and a step forward."

Ken Kwapis, the director of *The Sisterhood of the Traveling Pants*, spoke admiringly of Ferrera's performance. "For me, what's amazing about America's character, Carmen, is that she's the most verbally expressive of the four girls and yet her entire story is about not being able to say something. And it takes the better part of the picture for her to finally step up and tell her father how much her parents' divorce has hurt her. One of the beautiful things about America's work is that she's able to be completely expressive and yet you understand how on this one point she can't open up. In any case, her rawness is a major contribution to the film." Kwapis encouraged the young actresses to form a bond in real life that would mirror the friendship of their characters. "He gave us $75 each, Canadian dollars," Ferrera recounted, "and dropped us off at a vintage shop. This was our rehearsal. 'I want you guys to shop together.' We were like, we feel good as far as chemistry goes, but if you want to send us shopping we will go."

## "Ugly Betty"

Ferrera's biggest success to date came with the starring role on the hit ABC television program "Ugly Betty." The series is based on "Yo soy Betty la fea," a popular Columbian telenovela, a type of Latin American TV show that is similar to a soap opera. One of the producers of "Ugly Betty" is the Mexican actress Salma Hayek, who appears on the show. The cast also features Eric Mabius, Ana Ortiz, Tony Plana, Rebecca Romijn, and Vanessa Williams.

Ferrera plays Betty Suarez, the assistant to an editor at a prominent fashion magazine. Everyone else at the magazine is gorgeous, perfect in their fashion sense and physical appearance. Betty's poor sense of style and distinct appearance (she has braces, oversized glasses, and thick eyebrows) make her an unlikely candidate for such a job. But her good humor and positive outlook help her boss improve his performance in the company, and "ugly" Betty is shown to be much more intrinsically beautiful than her perfect co-workers.

> *"When I'm in character and in Betty's costumes, I feel beautiful. I never feel as beautiful and confident in my real life. There's a light that shines from within. I love, love, love being her."*

The show's enthusiastic response from audiences all over the world has been lauded as a milestone for Latin American women in popular media. "The fact that she's not blonde-haired and blue-eyed is, by itself, very much a big deal," San Francisco State University professor Melissa Camacho stated. "We've been waiting a long time for a TV character who looks like her and has her voice." Ferrera also sees the character of Betty in this unique light. "What is special about it is Betty is just a regular girl that appeals to all different races and all kinds of audiences—and she just happens to be Latina," she claimed. "And for a Latina character to be out there in a mainstream way and without a banner on her head is a true success and a step forward rather than have a token Latin show for Latinos by Latinos."

Ferrera has said that she wholeheartedly enjoys her work on the show and has expressed her admiration for the character of Betty. "When I'm in character and in Betty's costumes, I feel beautiful. I never feel as beautiful and confident in my real life. There's a light that shines from within. I love, love, love being her." Tony Plana, the actor who plays Betty's father, considers her a natural fit for the role. "Acting for America is like breathing," he said. "She's naturally layered and complex." Critics agreed. In 2007, Ferrera was honored with a host of awards for her performance in "Ugly Betty": the Golden Globe Award from the Hollywood

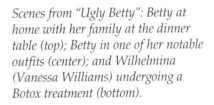

*Scenes from "Ugly Betty": Betty at home with her family at the dinner table (top); Betty in one of her notable outfits (center); and Wilhelmina (Vanessa Williams) undergoing a Botox treatment (bottom).*

Foreign Press Association for Best Performance by an Actress in a Television Series; the Actor Award from the Screen Actors Guild for Outstanding Performance by a Female Actor in a Comedy Series; the Teen Choice Award for Choice TV Breakout Star; the Alma Award from the American Latino Media Arts Awards for Outstanding Actress in a Television Series; and the Emmy Award for Outstanding Lead Actress in a Comedy Series. It was a very impressive first season for Ferrera on "Ugly Betty."

## Other Television, Film, and Theater Work

In 2005 Ferrera had a small part in the 1970s skateboarding film *Lords of Dogtown*, which dramatizes the true story of three teenage surfers from Venice Beach, California, who take an interest in skateboarding and subsequently create a new subculture. The three friends, known as the Z-Boys, are credited with developing a new style of skateboarding in the mid-1970s that transformed the sport and became a worldwide phenomenon. Ferrera played "Thunder Monkey," a skating groupie and the girlfriend of Sid, one of the skaters' close friends. Her performance has been cited by critics as one of the film's highlights. She also appeared in the family drama *How the Garcia Girls Spent Their Summer*, which was screened at the 2005 Sundance Film Festival. In this film, which explores the lives of three generations of Mexican-American women, Ferrera played Blanca, a 17-year-old on the verge of womanhood. Fed up with the boys in her neighborhood on the Arizona border, Blanca finds romance with an older boy from another town.

Ferrera then starred in the short film *3:52*, which won the Audience Award at the 2006 San Diego Women Film Festival, and the 2006 feature *Steel City*, which garnered nominations at the Independent Spirit Awards and the Sundance Film Festival. In 2007 she starred in the film *La Misma luna*, directed by Patricia Riggen. She also appeared as Sally in the off-Broadway production *Dog Sees God: Confessions of a Teenage Blockhead*, a take-off on the Charles Schulz comic strip *Peanuts*.

Recently, Ferrera starred in and executive produced the crime thriller *Towards Darkness*, which premiered at the Tribeca Film Festival in May 2007. Written and directed by José Antonio Negret, *Towards Darkness* is a Spanish-language drama concerning kidnapping in Colombia. The movie is based on Negret's 2004 short film *Darkness Minus Twelve*, in which Ferrera was also featured. Notably, the picture is the first in which she acts entirely in Spanish, which she found nerve-wracking. "I practiced with a dialogue coach . . . I knew that I could fool people who didn't speak Spanish, but a Spanish-speaking audience, I'm afraid they might know [that I'm not a native speaker]." She plans to film the sequel to *Sisterhood of the Traveling Pants* in sum-

*Ferrera was thrilled to win the Golden Globe Award for Best Performance by an Actress in a TV Series.*

mer 2007 before beginning work on season two of "Ugly Betty."

## Being a Role Model

Ferrera's work has been praised for representing men and women of Latin American descent in a realistic and positive light. For example, California Representative Hilda L. Solis addressed her accomplishments on the floor of Congress, stating: "Through her work, Ms. Ferrera is breaking down barriers for Latinos in prime-time television." Ferrera has frequently commented on the response that she has gotten from her fans. "Just last weekend, I read a letter from a young girl. I did the cover of *CosmoGIRL!*, and she was thanking the magazine for putting me on the cover, because, 'When I watched "Ugly Betty," it was the first time in my life that I felt beautiful.' That was overwhelming for me. All you can ever hope to do in this business is touch one person, and yet I'm sure there were others."

Ferrera has received attention in the media for her healthy body image and the positive example she sets for young women about the issue of weight and physical appearance: "I don't think your jean size is what makes you a person. It's about the persistence inside of you, and you want tons of that with you at all times. . . . Caring about your appearance is universal. I know 45-year-old women who still hate their bodies. There are no magazines that say 'love who you are on the inside first, and worry about the outside later.'"

Ferrera's character on "Ugly Betty" has been embraced as a role model by a number of different groups, including adolescent girls, the gay community, Latinas, and the fashion crowd. Remarking on the character's universal appeal, she stated: "Anyone who's ever felt like an outsider can see themselves in her and feel represented. And who hasn't, at some point in their life, felt like they didn't belong?" Although being a role model can be a heavy responsibility for a young actress, she has remained positive. "I don't mind being the spokesperson for things as long as I believe in them."

## HOME AND FAMILY

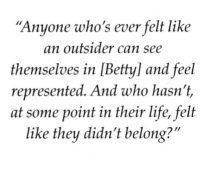

Ferrera lives in Los Angeles with her boyfriend, Ryan Piers Williams, and their pet golden retriever, Buddy. Ferrera met him at the University of Southern California while working on his student film project. Williams is an aspiring filmmaker from Texas who currently works for director Steven Soderbergh. She has adamantly denied rumors that she is engaged to be married. "It's totally not true!" she has insisted. "And his mom called me and my sisters were calling me, and I was like, 'Are you kidding? Did you not think I would tell you first?'" Although she is not presently planning a wedding, she has stated that she wants a large family someday.

*"Anyone who's ever felt like an outsider can see themselves in [Betty] and feel represented. And who hasn't, at some point in their life, felt like they didn't belong?"*

## HOBBIES AND OTHER INTERESTS

Ferrera has taken time out from her busy schedule to support young independent filmmakers. She made an appearance at the 14th annual San Diego Latino Film Festival in early 2007 in support of *Muertas*, a short film by her boyfriend, Ryan Piers Williams. She spoke to the crowd at the festival, complimenting the filmmakers for their vision: "I think this event is a testament to what you can do. You find stories you believe in, and you do what you can to tell them," she said. She also served as an executive producer on the project, in which she has a brief cameo. "She really believes in the film and she's really supportive," Williams told the *San Diego Union-Tribune*.

Ferrera enjoys spending time with her family and loved ones, including her dog. She loves to dance and considers taking her mom to see "Dancing with the Stars" as one of the highlights of being a celebrity. She prefers to keep busy and finds enjoyment in her work: "When there's a film I want to do, sleep doesn't matter," she explained. "Part of me would love to be sitting in the sun in Italy, but I'd be crazy by day four." She admits that she struggles to control her natural drive for achievement. "The hardest part of this year has been learning to enjoy it. It's almost like a full-time job reminding myself to live in the moment and not look for more, more, more," she remarked. Still, she has learned an important lesson about finding contentment: "Happiness is something that you have to decide to have in your life," she said. "No amount of accolades can make you a happy person, and learning that as young as I did was a gift."

## SELECTED CREDITS

### Television

*Gotta Kick It Up!*, 2002 (movie)
*Plainsong*, 2004 (movie)
"Ugly Betty," 2006- (series)

### Films

*Real Women Have Curves*, 2002
*How the Garcia Girls Spent Their Summer*, 2005
*Lords of Dogtown*, 2005
*The Sisterhood of the Traveling Pants*, 2005
*Steel City*, 2006
*La Misma luna*, 2007
*Towards Darkness*, 2007 (also executive producer)

## HONORS AND AWARDS

Special Jury Prize for Acting (Sundance Film Festival): 2002, for *Real Women Have Curves* (with Lupe Ontiveros)
The Actor Award (Screen Actors Guild): 2007, Outstanding Performance by a Female Actor in a Comedy Series, for "Ugly Betty"
Alma Award (American Latino Media Arts Awards, National Council of La Raza): 2007, Outstanding Actress—Television Series, Mini-Series or Television Movie, for "Ugly Betty"
Emmy Award (Academy of Television Arts and Sciences): 2007, Outstanding Lead Actress in a Comedy Series, for "Ugly Betty"
Golden Globe Award (Hollywood Foreign Press Association): 2007, Best Performance by an Actress in a Television Series—Musical or Comedy, for "Ugly Betty"
Teen Choice Awards: 2007, Choice TV Breakout Star, for "Ugly Betty"
The *Time* 100—The People Who Shape Our World: 2007

## FURTHER READING

### Periodicals

*America*, Feb. 12, 2007, p.18

*CosmoGIRL!*, Feb. 2007, p.84

*Entertainment Weekly*, Sep. 8, 2006, p.108; Mar. 16, 2007, p.28

*Los Angeles Times*, May 8, 2005, p.E4; Sep. 17, 2006, p.8E; Nov. 8, 2006, p.E1;
    Jan. 29, 2007, p.E1

*People*, Oct. 2, 2006, p.146; Feb. 5, 2007, p.132

*Teen People*, Sep. 1, 2002, p.160

*USA Today*, Oct. 18, 2002, p.E2; Nov. 16, 2006, p.D1

*Variety*, Sep. 25, 2006, p.68

## Online Articles

http://www.abcnews.go.com
    (*ABC News*, Good Morning America, "America Ferrera Makes 'Ugly'
    Beautiful," Jan. 8, 2007)

http://www.cosmogirl.com
    (*CosmoGIRL!*, "Miss America!," Feb. 2007)

http://www.ew.com
    (*Entertainment Weekly*, "America's Journey," May 8, 2007)

http://www.splicedonline.com
    (*SPLICEDwire: Film Reviews, News & Interviews*, "All American Girl,"
    Sep. 18, 2002)

http://www.time.com
    (*Time*, "The Time 100: America Ferrera," undated)

http://www.variety.com
    (*Variety*, "10 Actors to Watch: TV Class," Sep. 28, 2006)

http://www.style.com
    (*W Magazine*, "Hot Betty," May 2007)

## ADDRESS

America Ferrera
"Ugly Betty"
ABC TV
77 West 66th Street
New York, NY 10023

## WORLD WIDE WEB SITE

http://abc.go.com/primetime/uglybetty

# June Foray 1917-

American Voice Actor
The Voice behind Rocket J. Squirrel on "The
Bullwinkle Show" and Hundreds of Other Popular
Animated Characters in Cartoons and Films

## BIRTH

June Foray was born on September 18, 1917, in Springfield,
Massachusetts. Her mother was a semiprofessional pianist
and singer. Her father was an engineer.

## YOUTH

Though she would eventually become an actress, acting was not Foray's first dream for a show business career. She first considered a career in dance, after seeing the fame and talent of Eleanor Powell, a tap dancing star who had grown up in Springfield. But Foray abandoned her plans after a prolonged bout of pneumonia. Her mother, a talented pianist, encouraged her to develop her musical talents. But Foray didn't share her mother's enthusiasm for music, and when she broke her finger playing basketball she happily gave up her piano lessons.

By age six, Foray announced that she would become an actress. She traced the beginning of her life as an actress to the Springfield Public Library. "I would memorize the classics, and walk around the neighborhood, pretending to be all those wonderful characters," she recalled. Her parents supported her dream, taking her to movies, the theater, and opera performances. She soaked up all that she saw and recalled that she would "impersonate everybody" when she returned home. Her love of acting led her to a part in "just about every school play that was put on," she said. "But I'm only 4 feet 11. I wanted to be on stage, but what are you going to do when you're this short? So I went into radio."

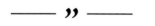

> *As a teen, Foray's love of acting led her to a part in "just about every school play that was put on," she said. "But I'm only 4 feet 11. I wanted to be on stage, but what are you going to do when you're this short? So I went into radio."*

Foray's life in radio began at age 12, when she appeared on a local radio program that was produced by her school drama teacher. Within three years she had joined the WBZA Players, a repertoire company in Springfield, and contributed regularly to local radio plays. When Foray was 17 her family moved to Los Angeles. Soon after her arrival, the ambitious young actress landed roles on Hollywood-produced national programs such as *The Jimmy Durante Show, The Danny Thomas Show,* and the *Lux Radio Theatre.*

Foray's talent attracted the attention of producers throughout the entertainment industry, and by the end of her teens she was appearing on two or three radio programs a day. At age 19 Foray was given her own children's radio program, *Lady Makebelieve.* This program, in which Foray read her own children's stories over the airwaves, was broadcast by the Los Angeles Board of Education into district classrooms for three years.

## EDUCATION

Foray attended elementary school in the Springfield public school system, and she split her high school years between Massachusetts and California. Foray's acting career started before she finished high school. Sources suggest that she completed high school, but the date of her graduation is unknown.

## CAREER HIGHLIGHTS

Starting work at such a young age, Foray developed most of her expertise on the job. "Radio was the greatest training ground," she said. "You had to be very quick and you had to be very versatile." Foray was both. Comedian and radio star Stan Freberg declared that Foray was "quite simply, the best in the business. I could write anything, confident in the knowledge that whatever the age, whatever the accent, June could do it."

During the 1940s Foray became known for her voice work on Jerry Fairbanks' *Speaking of Animals* short films, in which she was the voice of a filmed animal with an animated mouth. She also began recording children's records for Capitol Records with Stan Freberg, Daws Butler, and Mel Blanc.

Neither Foray nor Blanc knew it, but this collaboration came at a time when both actors were just beginning to emerge as the two leading providers of many of America's most beloved cartoon voices. Blanc became a dominant figure in animated films and television shows over the next several decades, providing the voices of such memorable characters as Bugs Bunny, Elmer Fudd, Foghorn Leghorn, and Daffy Duck. Foray, meanwhile, became the most famous female voice-over actor. Her status prompted some people to call her "the female Mel Blanc." But Chuck Jones, Foray's friend and employer and one of the giants of American animation, asserted that "June Foray is not the female Mel Blanc. Mel Blanc was the male June Foray."

### Working for Disney

Foray's work with Capitol Records brought her to the attention of Disney Studios. In 1950 she left radio for animated film for the first time, providing the vocals for Lucifer the Cat in the Disney film *Cinderella*. Next she played the voice of Witch Hazel in the short animated film *Trick or Treat*. Foray's voice for Witch Hazel became the standard from which almost every subsequent witch voice has been patterned. "I did so many witches I should have a wart out of my nose," Foray said of her many variations on Witch Hazel. She then created the voices for an Indian squaw and a mermaid in the 1953 animated feature *Peter Pan*.

That same year Foray unveiled one of her most famous and enduring voices: that of Granny, the owner of Tweety Pie the canary and Sylvester the cat. She first brought Granny to life in *A Streetcat Named Sylvester,* produced by Warner Brothers. Foray then continued to supply the voice of Granny in Sylvester and Tweety Pie cartoons for the next 15 years. She also provided Granny's voice in the late 1990s, when the WB Network broadcast a new cartoon series, "The Sylvester and Tweety Mysteries."

## The Voice of Rocky

In 1958 Jay Ward, the creator of the first animated television series, "Crusader Rabbit," approached Foray with an interesting job offer. He asked Foray to provide the voice of Rocket J. Squirrel, a spunky squirrel in a pilot for an animated series called "Rocky and His Friends." Ward's idea was to create a type of animated variety show that would satirize contemporary American life. He especially wanted to comment on the "Cold War." The Cold War began at the end of World War II and finally came to an end with the collapse of the Soviet Union in 1991. The term Cold War refers to a period of political, military, and economic rivalry between the United States and the Soviet Union and their respective allies. It was marked by deep distrust, continuing hostility, and sometimes open conflict among many nations in the world.

Foray happily signed up for the role of Rocky, which would become the most famous of her entire career. She recalls that when she asked Ward what sort of voice he would like for Rocky, he responded that he "just wanted Rocky to be a little, All-American boy." Foray responded by actually using her own voice for the little squirrel. Her decision proved to be a wise one.

The show, which starred Rocky the flying squirrel and his devoted, dimwitted friend Bullwinkle J. Moose, was an immediate hit. Children and parents alike loved watching the duo match wits with Mr. Big, an evil midget, and his spies from the fictional Pottsylvania, Boris Badenov and Natasha Fatale. Another popular aspect of the show was its use of short animated segments. These included "Fractured Fairy Tales," which parodied traditional children's stories; "Adventures of Dudley Do-Right," which followed

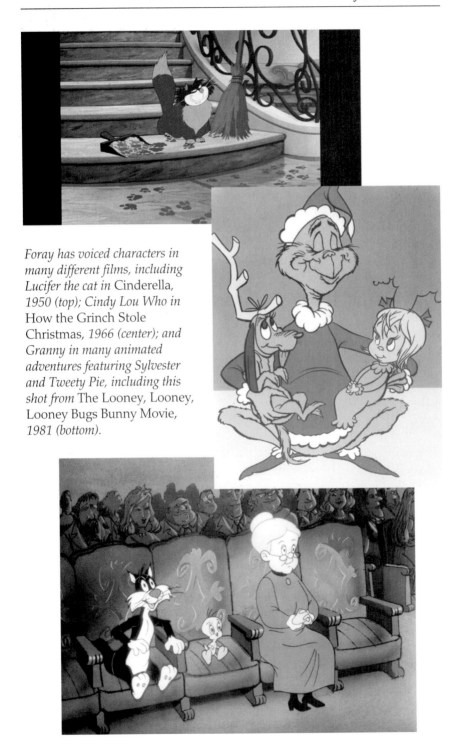

*Foray has voiced characters in many different films, including Lucifer the cat in* Cinderella, *1950 (top); Cindy Lou Who in* How the Grinch Stole Christmas, *1966 (center); and Granny in many animated adventures featuring Sylvester and Tweety Pie, including this shot from* The Looney, Looney, Looney Bugs Bunny Movie, *1981 (bottom).*

Canadian Mountie Dudley Do-Right's battles against the evil Snidely Whiplash; and "Peabody's Improbable History," which followed an intelligent talking dog and a young boy name Sherman as they traveled back in time to various historical eras.

ABC broadcast "Rocky and His Friends" from 1959 to 1961. During this time, Foray not only provided the voice of Rocky, but also of Natasha Fatale, Nell Fenwick—the innocent object of Canadian Mountie Dudley Do-Right's affections—and many other characters. The show then moved to NBC, where it became the first prime-time animated series in network television history. The show, which was renamed "The Bullwinkle Show" when it moved to NBC, ran until 1964.

---

## A Show for Everyone

Rocky and Bullwinkle's enduring popularity stemmed from the ability of their creators to combine adult-friendly humorous commentary about the Cold War and other current events with goofy hijinks that appealed to young children. "The children enjoyed it because of the humorous look of the characters and the sounds of the voices," confirmed Foray. "The adults find it so inventive because of the puns, the satire. . . . It was a show that was different from everything that came before it or after it."

> "The children enjoyed [Rocky and Bullwinkle] because of the humorous look of the characters and the sounds of the voices," said Foray. "The adults find it so inventive because of the puns, the satire. . . . It was a show that was different from everything that came before it or after it."

The writers wrote to amuse themselves, poking fun at everyone and everything. "We offended everybody, of course—presidents, congressmen, actors," remembered Foray. "We spared no one." Not surprisingly, many people in the animation business expressed great admiration for the show and its approach. As the legendary animator Chuck Jones said in the *New York Times*, "Bugs, Daffy Duck, Wile E. Coyote . . . were character actors, funny for what they did. Rocky and Bullwinkle were stand-up comics, funny for what they said." The clever humor convinced viewers to overlook the show's terrible soundtrack and budget-conscious animation. "Sometimes Boris had only half a mustache," Foray remembered.

*Rocky J. Squirrel, Bullwinkle J. Moose, Natasha Fatale,
and Boris Badenov from "Rocky and His Friends."*

Foray has many fond memories of those Rocky and Bullwinkle years. She recalls that for each show, the actors would assemble in Ward's studio, read the script once before recording, and tape it in one sitting. "The only time we ever did it over was when we'd go too long, or I'd laugh too much," Foray related. She also enjoyed the challenge of instantly switching voices between Rocky and Natasha when they were placed in scenes together. "Rocky would say, 'Hokey smoke, haven't I seen you before?' And then I'd say, 'No, dahling,' in the same breath," she said. "I had to have different colored pencils so I would know what part was coming up."

The task of delivering multiple voices was even greater for Foray in some of the "Fractured Fairy Tales" segments. In a few of these pieces, Foray would deliver lines from princesses, fairy godmothers, and witches, all one after another in quick succession. Years later, she recalled her work on those shows with great affection. "It was like working in a beautiful insane asylum," Foray remembered. "The scripts were brilliant satire and mordantly witty."

More than four decades after Rocky the squirrel made his debut, it is that voice that is most closely associated with Foray. In fact, she claims that complete strangers sometimes identify her as the voice of Rocky when she is out shopping. But her career continued long after the creators stopped making new Rocky and Bullwinkle adventures. She did voice work well into her eighties, playing hundreds of different animated characters. Her most recent high-profile job was as the voice of Grandmother Fa in the 1998 Disney film *Mulan*.

## Inspired by Literature

Throughout her long and distinguished career, Foray has often claimed that her love of reading was an essential factor in her success. She says that literature provided the inspiration she needed to develop such believable characters. Foray based her "little old lady" voice, for instance, on her reading of James M. Barrie's *The Old Woman Shows Her Medals*: "I used to memorize all of her speeches, and all the speeches of Lady Bracknell in *The Importance of Being Earnest*. That's what I do."

*To be a good voice-over actor, Foray once said, "you have to be an actress first and a voice technician second. It's not just a matter of changing your voice. You have to become the creation, to assume the attitude. Otherwise it's just one-dimensional."*

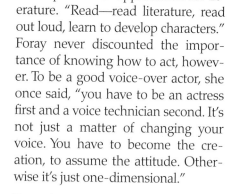

Foray has encouraged young actors to develop a similar appreciation for literature. "Read—read literature, read out loud, learn to develop characters." Foray never discounted the importance of knowing how to act, however. To be a good voice-over actor, she once said, "you have to be an actress first and a voice technician second. It's not just a matter of changing your voice. You have to become the creation, to assume the attitude. Otherwise it's just one-dimensional."

Foray has complained over the years that a lot of the animated children's television shows have become "simplistic and condescending." But she also appreciates some of the work done by men and women in the industry. To honor those individuals, Foray founded the Annie Awards in 1972 through her membership in the Association Internationale du Film d'Animation (ASIFA). Each year, the Annie Awards honor the top achievements in the art of animated films. In the 1990s, Foray's contributions to the world of animation inspired ASIFA-Hollywood, the organization's U.S. chapter, to create the June Foray Award to honor individuals who significantly and benevolently impact the art and industry of animation. She re-

**W**e want to cover the people *you* want to know about in *Biography Today*. Use this card to list the people you want to see in *Biography Today*. If we include someone you suggest, your library wins a free issue, and you get one to keep with our thanks.

## People I'd like to see in BIOGRAPHY TODAY:

_____

_____

_____

_____

_____

Name _____

Institution _____

Address _____

City _____

State, Zip _____

## www.omnigraphics.com

ceived the first June Foray Award in 1995. In 2000, in a testimony to her enduring popularity, Foray was honored with a star on the Hollywood Walk of Fame in Hollywood, California.

## MARRIAGE AND FAMILY

Foray married the writer Hobart Donovan in 1954. The couple had no children. Donovan died in 1976.

## SELECTED CREDITS

### As Voice of Rocket J. Squirrel

"Rocky and His Friends," voice of Rocky and other characters, 1959-61 (TV series)

"The Bullwinkle Show," voice of Rocky and other characters, 1961-62 (TV series)

*Of Moose and Men*, 1991 (film)

*The Adventures of Rocky & Bullwinkle*, 2000 (film)

### As Voice of Witch Hazel

*Trick or Treat*, 1952 (short film)

*Broom-Stick Bunny*, 1956 (short film)

*A Witch's Tangled Hare*, 1959 (short film)

"The Bugs Bunny Show," 1960-68 (TV series)

*A-Haunting We Will Go*, 1966 (short film)

### As Voice of Granny

*A Streetcat Named Sylvester*, 1953 (short film)

*This Is a Life?* 1955 (short film)

*Red Riding Hoodwinked*, 1955 (short film)

*A Bird in a Bonnet*, 1958 (short film)

*A Pizza Tweety Pie*, 1958 (short film)

"The Bugs Bunny Show," 1960-68 (TV series)

*The Looney, Looney, Looney Bugs Bunny Movie,* 1981 (film)

"The Sylvester & Tweety Mysteries," 1995-2000 (TV series)

*Space Jam*, 1996 (film)

*Tweety's High Flying Adventure,* 2000 (film)

### Other Character Voices

*Cinderella,* voice of Lucifer the cat, 1950 (film)

"The Flintstones," voice of Betty Rubble, 1964 (TV pilot)

*Frosty the Snowman,* multiple voices, 1969 (film)

*How the Grinch Stole Christmas!* voice of Cindy Lou Who, 1966 (film)

"The Tom and Jerry Show," voice of Jerry, 1966-72 (TV series)
*The Phantom Tollbooth*, multiple voices, 1970 (film)
*Rikki-Tikki-Tavi,* voice of Mother, 1975 (film)
"The Smurfs," voices of Jokey Smurf and Mother Nature, 1981-90 (TV series)
"The Gummi Bears," voice of Grammi Gummi, 1985-89 (TV series)
*Who Framed Roger Rabbit?,* multiple voices, 1988 (film)
*Mulan,* voice of Grandmother Fa, 1998 (film)

## HONORS AND AWARDS

June Foray Award (Association Internationale du Film d'Animation): 1995

## FURTHER READING

### Books

Scott, Keith. *The Moose that Roared: The Story of Jay Ward, Bill Scott, a Flying Squirrel and a Talking Moose,* 2000

### Periodicals

*Advertising Age,* Dec. 1, 1986, p.57
*Back Stage West,* July 20, 2000, p.25
*Los Angeles Daily News,* June 29, 2000, pp.L3, L6
*Los Angeles Times,* May 3, 1985, p.1; Nov. 13, 1988, p.6; June 20, 1994, p.F6;
    June 29, 2000, p.F22
*People,* May 20, 1991, p.75
*Seattle Times,* June 29, 2000, p.D4

### Online Articles

http://www.awn.com/mag/issue5.03/5.03pages/evanierforay.php3
    (*Animation World Magazine,* "The Remarkable June Foray," June 2000)
http://starbulletin.com/96/07/11/features/story3.html
    (*Honolulu Star-Bulletin,* "Women Find Place in Humor's Boys' Club," July
    11, 1996)
http://movies2.nytimes.com/gst/movies/filmography.html?p_id=24175
    (*New York Times,* "June Foray," undated)

## ADDRESS

June Foray
Don Pitts Voices
11365 Ventura Blvd., Suite 100
Studio City, CA 91604

## WORLD WIDE WEB SITE

http://www.annieawards.com/juneforayaward.htm

## Sarah Blaffer Hrdy 1946-

American Anthropologist and Primatologist
Pioneer in the Scientific Study of Motherhood

### BIRTH

Sarah Blaffer Hrdy (rhymes with "birdie") was born on July 11, 1946, in Dallas, Texas. Her parents were both members of prominent Texas families. Her father, John H. Blaffer, was heir to an oil fortune, while her mother, Camilla Davis, came from a Dallas banking family. Sarah was the third of four daughters born to the Blaffers before they had their fifth and last child, a son.

## YOUTH

Sarah Blaffer grew up in an atmosphere of privilege. Her parents were wealthy enough to afford a nanny for their large family, and their children were able to attend the best private schools. Still, it was an era in which many experts believed that children should not be coddled. "My mother's idea of good management was that if a child became too attached to a nanny, it was time to hire a new one, lest maternal control be diminished," Hrdy recalled. "This meant I was reared by a succession of governesses." Still, she added, "No one ever doubted that my mother loved her five children."

Hrdy also credits her mother with supporting her intellectual curiosity and deep love of learning. This encouragement may have stemmed in part from her mother's own youthful experiences. Camilla Davis had graduated from college with the hope of attending law school. Instead, she had returned to Dallas society and married, as her family expected. Young Sarah grew up in this same "high society" environment, one in which a young woman's debut at a society ball was widely regarded as one of the most important moments in her life. Sarah, however, was more concerned with intellectual pursuits, and "in the social environment in which I grew up, that was not acceptable," she recalled.

> "My mother's idea of good management was that if a child became too attached to a nanny, it was time to hire a new one, lest maternal control be diminished," Hrdy recalled. "This meant I was reared by a succession of governesses."

As the third-oldest sister, however, Sarah enjoyed a greater level of freedom than her older sisters. "I was the heiress to spare, and that left me a lot of freedom," she said. When at 16 she was given the chance to attend an academically challenging boarding school, she enrolled with her mother's blessing.

## EDUCATION

After graduating from high school in the early 1960s, Hrdy entered her mother's old school, Wellesley College. She transferred to Radcliffe College, formerly the women's college of Harvard University, when Harvard was segregated by sex. Hrdy graduated summa cum laude ("with highest honors") with a bachelor's degree in 1969. Her senior thesis, on the Mayan myth of the bat demon, was published in 1972 as *The Black-Man of Zinacantan: A Central American Legend.* That same year she married Daniel B. Hrdy, a fellow student at Harvard.

Hrdy then briefly studied filmmaking at Stanford University in hopes of making educational films for people in underdeveloped countries. She lost interest, though, when it became clear that her film classes were primarily concerned with Hollywood and popular moviemaking. Around this same time, a biology seminar at Stanford inspired her to pursue a doctorate in anthropology, the scientific study of human origins and behavior. She returned to Harvard University and earned her doctoral degree or doctorate (PhD) in anthropology in 1975.

## CAREER HIGHLIGHTS

### Pioneering Observations of Langurs

Earning a doctoral degree, or PhD, usually includes doing significant intellectual research and then writing it up in a book-length paper called a dissertation. For her doctoral research, Hrdy decided to study the Hanuman langur monkeys of Mount Abu in Rajasthan, India. Hanuman langurs are sacred to local residents, who feed them and protect them from

*Hrdy watching langur monkeys in India.*

harm whenever possible. But many observers believed that these attitudes were contributing to the species' increasing problems with overpopulation in the region. Hrdy's decision to study the Hanuman langur monkeys also stemmed in part from reports that male langurs in the region were killing infant monkeys. Some scholars speculated that this troubling behavior was a reaction to the increasingly overcrowded conditions in the monkeys' territory.

Hrdy spent almost 1,500 hours between 1971 and 1975 observing Hanuman langurs in their natural environment. She documented that under normal conditions, adult male langurs seemed very tolerant of infants. But she discovered that when a new male took over leadership of a langur tribe, he would attack infants sired by other males. Hrdy realized that although the practice of "infanticide" (baby-killing) by the Hanuman langur males was shocking, there was actually a biological motive behind it: without a baby to nurse, females would be ready to mate sooner, ensuring the new "alpha" (dominant) male could produce more of his own offspring.

Hrdy detailed her observations and conclusions in her 1977 book *The Langurs of Abu: Female and Male Strategies of Reproduction.* In addition to explaining the reasons for male infanticide, she noted that langur females had their own methods for dealing with this behavior. When a new alpha male came into the tribe, females with infants would pretend to be fertile and have sex with the male. He would then believe that any new babies might be his, and leave them alone.

When Hrdy first published her study, many fellow scientists dismissed her conclusions. They suggested that the monkeys she studied were abnormal or that she had used flawed methods of observation. In the decades since she first proposed her theories about infanticide, however, scientists have observed similar behavior in a wide range of species including mice, wasps, fish, foxes, deer, bears, and lions, as well as several other species of monkeys.

## Challenging Conventional Wisdom

Despite the controversial nature of her thesis work, Hrdy's academic career soared. After completing her PhD, she worked as a lecturer in biological anthropology at Harvard from 1975 to 1976, and then earned a postdoctoral fellowship in Harvard's biology department from 1977 to 1978. She continued doing field research on the Mount Abu langurs until 1979, when the tense political climate in the region and the needs of her toddler daughter, born in 1977, convinced her to stop. "Field work is incompatible with having children," she noted. "You compromise to have a family, but you don't give everything up."

Hrdy became an associate in biological anthropology at Harvard's Peabody Museum in 1979. She also spent time teaching at the American Institute of Indian Studies in New Delhi, India, and at Rice University in Houston, Texas. Throughout this period, Hrdy found that working in a male-dominated field of research carried special challenges for a woman. Some fellow scholars dismissed her research and conclusions simply because of her gender. "I was blown away," she remembered. "All my life I had felt guilty for being overprivileged, and all of a sudden people were discriminating against *me*."

Undaunted by this hostility, Hrdy pressed on with her research. "It was painful at the time, but I think it was probably very fruitful," she admitted. "I started to challenge conventional wisdom, which is a good thing to do."

She turned from studying infanticide to exploring the female role in mating practices. The result was her 1981 work *The Woman That Never Evolved,* which the *New York Times Book Review* named a Notable Book of the Year in Science and Social Science.

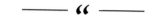

*"All my life I had felt guilty for being over-privileged, and all of a sudden people were discriminating against* me,*" remembered Hrdy.*

In *The Woman That Never Evolved,* Hrdy challenged the idea put forth by Charles Darwin, pioneer of evolutionary theory, that females play a passive role in sexual selection of mates. The 19th-century culture in which Darwin lived had always thought of women as faithful creatures who were uninterested in sex, but Hrdy wanted to test this belief. By studying primates (humans and their closest relatives, apes and monkeys), she hoped to discover "why some current notions of what it means to be female depict natures that never did, and never could have, evolved within the primate lineage."

Hrdy's book detailed many different patterns of behavior in primate females. She pointed out that some have one mate for life, while others take many mates; some have limited breeding seasons, while others can breed throughout the year; some display signs of being fertile, while others do not; some only have sex when fertile, while others have sex at other times. By exploring the many variations in female primate behavior, Hrdy "clearly demonstrates that there cannot be any generally ordained role for fe-

# Mother Nature

A History of Mothers,
Infants, and
Natural Selection

Sarah Blaffer Hrdy

*In her book* Mother Nature, *Hrdy uses her research into primate behavior to explore the bond between human mothers and their babies.*

males," Paul A. Colinvaux noted in the *New York Times*. The book was also warmly received by feminist activists who hailed it for pointing out the complexity of female sexuality. For her part, Hrdy called her work "an effort to expand the range of attributes encompassed by a term like *female nature.* . . . Rather than reducing female nature to any single set of stereotypes, we talk about a whole range of possibilities."

## Exploring the Nature of Motherhood

Hrdy was gratified by the response to her work and the greater acceptance that her theories were receiving. At the same time, though, she noted that "I found myself torn between my work and an admittedly adorable but insatiably demanding human baby." When a dismissive colleague told her to "devote more time and study and thought to raising a healthy daughter," the remark hit upon a secret guilt—but it also inspired her to think about the nature of motherhood. Were all mothers really the selfless, giving creatures of popular myth? Hrdy decided to explore the subject, "to understand not just who I am, but how creatures like me came to be."

In 1984 Hrdy took a post as professor of anthropology at the University of California, Davis, where she increasingly focused her research on the subject of motherhood. In 1987 she received a Guggenheim fellowship, a prestigious financial grant, to write a book on the subject. Nine years later she retired as professor emeritus from the University of California to focus more time on her project and her family. In all, she spent almost 15 years researching and writing *Mother Nature: A History of Mothers, Infants, and Natural Selection,* which was published in 1999.

In *Mother Nature,* Hrdy examined the numerous primate methods of mothering as well as the ways in which various human cultures throughout history have raised children. Again, she discovered there was no single strategy that was "natural" to mothers. Instead, their methods ranged "from total commitment to absence of caring," she stated. "The way any given mother responds will vary with her circumstances—how old she is, her physical condition, how much social support she can anticipate." For instance, in ancient Rome babies were often abandoned on roadsides. A similar phenomenon occurred in 18th-century Europe, where orphanages became badly overcrowded with thousands of children abandoned by impoverished parents. Hrdy further documented how concepts of parenthood vary in modern cultures. She noted, for instance, that some cultures place a higher value on one gender over another.

Hrdy's work emphasized that successfully raising a child requires enormous expenditures of time and effort from parents in general and mothers in particular. Given this reality, Hrdy suggests in *Mother Nature* that humans evolved as cooperative breeders. Mothers are "resourceful opportunists who elicit help from a range of different parties," Hrdy noted. These assistants, whom she calls "allomothers" (from the Greek "allo," meaning "other than"), can include the mother's mates, mother, brothers and sisters, and older children. Unrelated females from the same tribe can also help out.

> *In her book* Mother Nature, *Hrdy wanted to explore "our preconceptions about women—yes, they're nurturing; yes, they're cooperative; but they're also competitive, destructive, ambitious and creative. The same goes for mothers."*

Hrdy also asserted that women who are ambitious and career-oriented are in some ways actually well-equipped for motherhood; after all, successful, high-status females have more power and resources to spend on their children. It is only "because jobs, status and resource defense occur in separate domains from child-rearing" that women face a conflict between work and parenting, she explained. In *Mother Nature* she hopes to expand "our preconceptions about women—yes, they're nurturing; yes, they're cooperative; but they're also competitive, destructive, ambitious and creative. The same goes for mothers."

*Mother Nature* garnered a lot of attention when it was published. *Library Journal* and *Publishers Weekly* both named the book to their Best Books of 1999 lists, and it was a finalist for the PEN USA West Literary Award for Research Nonfiction in 2000. In 2001 Hrdy's peers in the American Anthropological Association awarded the book the Howells Prize for Outstanding Contribution to Biological Anthropology. In the London *Independent,* Daniel Britten called *Mother Nature* "a splendidly thought-provoking book. . . . With one great stride Blaffer Hrdy has carried the debate about parenting to a higher stage of adaptation. It should be required reading for parents, feminists, and evolutionary scientists alike."

*Scientists need to go beyond simple data collection and theorize and imagine how things might work, Hrdy believes. "You're trying to model what might be true and to generate the hypotheses that you want to look at," she noted. "Then you have the actual collection of data and all the methodologies that go into that. Imaginary worlds have a place in science."*

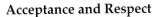

## Acceptance and Respect

Hrdy's early struggles with her male colleagues have vanished. The quality of her research and insights into human behavior finally forced her peers to give her the respect and praise that she deserved. She was elected to the National Academy of Sciences and became a fellow of Animal Behavior Society in 1990. Two years later she was invited to become a fellow of the American Academy of Arts and Sciences. In addition, she has served on editorial boards for several scholarly journals in the fields of primatology, anthropology, and evolution.

During this same period, Hrdy became known for her efforts to make science understandable to general audiences. She created the 1988 episode "Monkeys of Abu" for the TV series "National Geographic Explorer" and consulted on the 1990 series "Human Nature" for the British Broadcasting Corporation (BBC) and the 2001 series "Evolution" for the Public Broadcasting System (PBS). She also is a regular contributor to such popular magazines as *Natural History.*

Hrdy's enthusiasm and curiosity about anthropology remains undiminished. In recent years she has devoted much of her efforts to the study of genetic inheritance patterns. She is also considering writing what she calls a "history of the human family." But Hrdy admits that she has great concerns about the health and vitality of human families of the future. "Now, women are conceiving when they don't have the kind of social supports needed for offspring," she said. "And [the offspring] are surviving in large

*In this shot of Hrdy in India, it's unclear who is watching whom.*

numbers. This is new. . . . The creatures down the line may not be recognizably human. They may be smart, they may be bipedal, they may have language. But how nice are they going to be?"

Hrdy believes that thinking about such issues is vitally important to science. She asserts that scientists need to go beyond simple data collection and theorize and imagine how things might work: "You're trying to model what might be true and to generate the hypotheses that you want to look at," she noted. "Then you have the actual collection of data and all the methodologies that go into that. Imaginary worlds have a place in science."

## MARRIAGE AND FAMILY

Sarah Blaffer met fellow student Daniel B. Hrdy in an undergraduate anthropology class at Harvard. She claims that she fell in love with the future physician and professor of infectious diseases "almost from the moment I first set eyes on him." In 1972 they married in Kathmandu, Nepal, during a break from their doctoral research. They have three children: Catherine (known as "Katrinka"), born in 1977; a second daughter, Sasha, born in 1982; and son Niko, born in 1986. The Hrdys live on a 1,000-acre walnut farm in Winters, California.

## HOBBIES AND OTHER INTERESTS

Hrdy and her husband harvest almost 300 tons of walnuts every year on their farm. They allow flocks of wild turkeys to roam the farm, giving them and nearby students a chance to observe the birds' natural behavior. Hrdy also owns several Rhodesian Ridgebacks, a breed of large hunting dog with African origins. She enjoys listening to "books on tape" when she travels, especially works by such classic authors as George Eliot—the pseudonym of Mary Ann Evans, an early British feminist.

## SELECTED WRITINGS

*The Black-Man of Zinacantan: A Central American Legend,* 1972
*The Langurs of Abu: Female and Male Strategies of Reproduction,* 1977
*The Woman That Never Evolved,* 1981
*Infanticide: Comparative and Evolutionary Perspectives,* 1984 (editor, with
  Glenn Hausfater)
*Mother Nature: A History of Mothers, Infants and Natural Selection,* 1999

## HONORS AND AWARDS

Member, National Academy of Sciences: 1990
Fellow, Animal Behavior Society: 1990
Fellow, American Academy of Arts and Sciences: 1992
Howells Prize for Outstanding Contribution to Biological Anthropology
  (American Anthropological Association): 2001, for *Mother Nature: A History of Mothers, Infants and Natural Selection*

## FURTHER READING

### Books

Hrdy, Sarah Blaffer. *The Woman That Never Evolved,* 1981
Hrdy, Sarah Blaffer. *Mother Nature,* 1999

### Periodicals

*Current Biography Yearbook,* 2000
*Discover,* Sep. 1996, p.72; Mar. 2003, p.40
*Houston Chronicle,* Oct. 31, 1999, Lifestyle p.3
*Independent* (London), Nov. 14, 1999, p.10
*New Scientist,* Mar. 24, 2003, p.46; Apr. 8, 2006, p.50
*New York Times,* Nov. 15, 1981, sec.7, p.9; Feb. 8, 2000, p.F1
*Omni,* June 1988, p.91
*Radcliffe Quarterly,* Summer 2000

## Online Databases

*Biography Resource Center Online,* 2007, article from *Contemporary Authors Online,* 2004

## ADDRESS

Sarah Blaffer Hrdy
Professor Emeritus
Department of Anthropology
212 Young Hall
University of California
Davis, CA 95616

## WORLD WIDE WEB SITES

http://www.citrona.com

# Alicia Keys 1981-

American Singer, Composer, and Pianist
Winner of Nine Grammy Awards

## BIRTH

Alicia Keys was born Alicia Augello Cook on January 25, 1981, in Manhattan, New York. Her mother, Terri Augello, a paralegal and part-time actress, is white. Her father, Craig Cook, a flight attendant, is black. Her father, though, was not around for most of her childhood. "He didn't live with me, he didn't raise me, I don't call him Dad," she said. Keys has a younger half-brother, Cole, on her father's side, but they did not grow up together.

Keys has said that she loves both sides of her heritage. "I grew up in New York, and thank God, I never had to go through that in regards to 'you're not black enough, you're not white enough, the whole kind of white/black mixture thing,'" she said. "I never had to go through that. I went through prejudices and all, surely. But I never had to battle with those two parts of me. . . New York is so diverse and there are so many different types of people. People couldn't care less what you are."

## YOUTH

Keys grew up with her mother in a small, one-bedroom apartment in "Hell's Kitchen," a tough Manhattan neighborhood that had long been riddled by crime and poverty. (In recent years, this area has seen many improvements.) Her mother struggled to support herself and her daughter, often working two or three jobs a day. "My mom is definitely my rock," Keys said. "Growing up, we didn't have anybody but each other to survive in the city. She really helped me to become the person I am; the strongmindedness that I have is all because of her."

Keys also credits her mother for inspiring her love of music. She remembers waking up on Sunday mornings to the sounds of her mother's jazz recordings, especially the music of Ella Fitzgerald, Billie Holiday, and Thelonious Monk. "I've had a deep love for music since I was four," Keys recalled. "Music came before everything, everything, everything." Keys discovered her singing talent in kindergarten, when her teacher chose her to play the starring role of Dorothy in a class production of the *Wizard of Oz*. "I shocked myself because I didn't realize I could sing," Keys said. "I was terrified to get on the stage. When I did, I felt free! Ms. Hazel [the teacher] is still around. I speak to her."

Keys began playing the piano when she was seven years old. "A friend was getting rid of this old, brown upright piano she rarely played, and she agreed to let us have it if we'd move it from her apartment," Keys said. "We used the piano as a divider between our living room and my bedroom. That gift is one of the main reasons I'm playing today." Keys took piano lessons for the next several years, learning classical pieces by composers such as Mozart, Beethoven, and Chopin. She practiced up to six hours a day. "I'm not going to sit here and lie and tell you I was happy practicing the scales every day when my friends were outside playing," she said, "My mom just wasn't having it, though. She was serious about my practicing first, then playing. And now, of course, I appreciate that."

Keys wrote her first song, "I'm All Alone," when she was 11. She wrote it after seeing the movie *Philadelphia,* which starred Denzel Washington as a lawyer who defends another lawyer, played by Tom Hanks, who is fired from his job after contracting AIDS. "I had just lost my grandfather and that movie made me reflect on what it was to lose somebody," Keys remembered. "I went home and sat down at the piano—it was so natural. I hadn't really allowed myself to feel that he had passed. I felt better to express that sadness." Keys never recorded the song in a studio, but she admits that a home recording of that song—and many others she wrote as a young girl—are stored in her New York apartment. "Some of it is very embarrassing," she admits with a laugh.

As Keys grew older, she became aware that the expense of her piano and dance lessons stretched her mother's already tight budget. She recalls that she repeatedly offered to quit. "But my mom would tell me, 'Quit what you like, but you're not quitting piano.' She didn't care what it cost," Keys said. Meanwhile, she received fascinating glimpses into the world of show business on days when her mother, unable to find a babysitter, brought her to theatre rehearsals. Watching all the actors work on a play was fascinating to Keys. "I'd take in how they'd transformed from when they first came in to when it was actually showtime," she said. "It was very inspiring. I was able to see the dream side—anything's possible. But I was also able to see the broken-dream side, the people who would never make it, and the way they had to survive as hookers on the streets of my neighborhood."

> "
>
> *"My mom is definitely my rock," Keys said. "Growing up, we didn't have anybody but each other to survive in the city. She really helped me to become the person I am; the strong-mindedness that I have is all because of her."*
>
> "

Keys has admitted that such grim surroundings made growing up more challenging for her. "Sure, there were times when I could have ended up in trouble," she said. "It's easy at that age to get caught up with people who are not necessarily doing the right thing and there were those people all around, but I had just enough sense to realize when things were getting over the top. I'm also lucky because my mother is such a strong woman, and she raised me to be strong and independent."

## EDUCATION

When Keys was 12, she was accepted into the Professional Performing Arts School, a junior/senior public high school in New York City that was the setting for the 1980 movie and subsequent television series *Fame*. The students at this unique school go to academic classes in the mornings and then receive performing arts instruction at professional studios in the afternoons. Famous alumni of the school include the singer Britney Spears and the actress Claire Danes.

———— " ————

*Music industry manager Jeff Robinson first saw Keys perform when she was 15. "I could see right away that she had a lot of soul as a singer, but there are lots of singers with that street twang," he recalled. "What really convinced me was when she sat down at a beat-up piano and began singing her own songs. I couldn't believe someone that young could be so fully developed musically."*

———— " ————

Keys developed a special bond with her music teacher, Linda Miller, during her years at the school. "She was eccentric, with beads and wooden bangles," Keys recalled. "We learned classical [music]. But she also wrote R&B [Rhythm and Blues] songs which she co-ordinated into the curriculum. She was the person who made me fall in love with harmonies. I surely loved them before then, but she fine-tuned my ear."

An excellent student, Keys graduated from high school as her class valedictorian in 1995, when she was only 16. She then accepted a scholarship to attend Columbia University in New York City. It was around this same time that she changed her last name from Cook to Keys. The inspiration for the new name came from "lots of places," she explained. "Keys to opening doors, doors that have never been opened before. Keys to opportunity. Keys to life. And keys to the piano." She attended classes at Columbia briefly before leaving to devote all her energies to her singing career.

## CAREER HIGHLIGHTS

Around age 14, Keys began a transition from playing classical piano to jazz and rhythm and blues. Around this same time, she began frequenting jazz clubs in Harlem, a primarily African-American neighborhood in Manhattan with a rich musical history. She also joined the girl's choir at the Police Athletic League Community Center in Harlem, practicing after school with vocal coach Conrad Robinson. Keys and a couple of other girls

*Keys performing in 2001.*

formed a group called EmBishion. Their repertoire included two songs written by Keys, "The Life" and "Butterflyz." Versions of both of these songs were later included on her first album, *Songs in A Minor.*

Conrad Robinson told his brother, Jeff, a music-industry manager, about the talented young performer. Jeff Robinson first heard Keys sing at the community center when she was 15 years old. "I could see right away that she had a lot of soul as a singer, but there are lots of singers with that street twang," Jeff Robinson recalled. "What really convinced me was when she sat down at a beat-up piano and began singing her own songs. I couldn't believe someone that young could be so fully developed musically. She was the complete package. That's not something you see a lot these days."

Jeff Robinson encouraged Keys to pursue a career as a solo artist. Soon afterward, he signed her on as a client. He began booking her at music-industry shows, where influential people could hear her accompany herself on the piano. This period of travel and performing was made even more challenging by the heavy school load Keys was carrying. But Keys juggled her busy schedule without stumbling on stage or in the classroom.

One showcase performance, delivered without backup singers or an accompanying band for music-label executives, proved especially important to the young singer. The assembled executives were dazzled by her voice

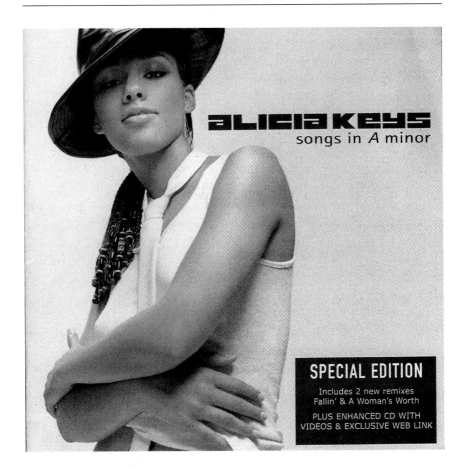

and piano playing. A bidding war ensued as industry executives competed to sign Keys to a recording contract. She ultimately decided to sign with Columbia Records, in part because the label included a baby grand piano for Keys in the contract.

Keys was ecstatic about her good fortune. But she soon discovered that juggling her recording career with the workload from her first semester at Columbia University was a daunting task. "I was always good at school . . . but Columbia is a whole other ball game!" she recalled. "I was coming in from the studio at four in the morning and getting up at eight to try and do my homework on the train to my classes—no way! I was the worst student ever at that point in my life, and I was so stressed." As a result, Keys dropped out of college four weeks into the first semester.

Keys hoped that this decision would help her music career, but as the weeks passed she repeatedly clashed with her music producers over her singing style and song selection. They also wanted to mold her image in a way that made Keys uncomfortable. "I felt that they wanted me to be a clone of Mariah [Carey] or Whitney [Houston] and I couldn't do that," she said. "I'm not the sequined dress type, or the high-heeled type, or the all-cleavage type," Keys said.

Robinson tried to intercede on her behalf, but the Columbia producers were determined to do things their way. The stalemate ended in 1998, when Keys performed for Clive Davis, the famous head of Arista Records. Davis had been instrumental in advancing the careers of such artists as Bruce Springsteen and Whitney Houston. He was bowled over by the young singer's talent and her beauty. Afterwards, he made a point of contacting Keys. "Clive was the only executive that ever asked me, how do I see myself, how do I see my career," she said. "When he asked me that question, I knew immediately that's where I had to be . . . What he sees for me, I see for myself." Davis quickly bought out her contract with Columbia and signed her with Arista.

### Songs in A Minor

At Arista, Keys was finally able to record her album the way she wanted. She sat with producers and studio engineers to learn the process of recording music. "I knew the only way it would sound like anything I would be remotely proud of is if I did it," she said. "I already knew my way around a keyboard, so that was an advantage."

Meanwhile, the 17-year-old Keys left her mother's apartment and got her own place in Harlem. Soon after moving in, she installed a recording studio so that she could easily work on her music whenever the spirit moved her. "[Moving out] was necessary for my sanity," she said. "I was confused and all over the place. And I remember going to my mother's house, because that was where my only real piano was, and I wrote a song that was really a conversation with God. . . . I came back to Harlem and started to work on it, starting with the piano and building up with all the little things I was learning, and it became 'Troubles.' That's when the album started coming together. Finally, I knew how to structure my feelings into something that made sense, something that can translate to people. My confidence was up, way up." Soon afterward she wrote "Fallin'," a soulful love ballad that later became a breakout hit.

Keys was very happy with how her debut album, which she had decided to call *Songs in A Minor*, was coming along. But just as it was nearing completion, Davis was forced out of Arista in an ugly battle for control of the label.

217

The legendary executive subsequently formed his own label, J Records, and Keys signed on as one of the label's first artists. She admits that the delay in the release of her album due to the label switch "built my character and tested my confidence." But the wait proved to be worth it. In June 2001, *Songs in A Minor* was released on the J Records label. To the young singer's amazement, the 16-song album (including 14 songs written or co-written by Keys) debuted at number one on the charts.

## Sudden Stardom

Most reviewers were quite impressed with Keys's combination of R&B, jazz, hip-hop, and gospel music. In a review for the *Los Angeles Times*, Robert Hilburn called Keys "a singer-songwriter-pianist of immense potential." Hilburn added: "The reason for all the excitement is the 20-year-old New Yorker's remarkable range. She moves convincingly in the album from the Janet Jackson school of youthful Top 40 attitude in 'Girlfriend' to the funky sensuality of Prince's 'How Come U Don't Call Me Anymore' to the neo-soul vitality of Macy Gray and Jill Scott in 'Fallin.'"

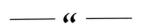

*"I thought I did good work and I hoped people would like [Songs in A Minor], but it's been crazy, the attention I've been getting," Keys said. "I'm like, 'Are you sure they want me on Leno?' or 'You're sure Prince wants to meet me?' It's bonkers."*

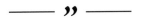

Keys gave an additional boost to the album with various television appearances. She shot a popular music video for "Fallin'" that portrayed her as a broken-hearted young woman visiting her boyfriend in prison. At around the same time that the video aired on MTV, Davis arranged television appearances for Keys on "The Oprah Winfrey Show" and "The Tonight Show." This publicity further boosted record sales, and within a year of its release, six million copies of *Songs in A Minor* had been sold. The sudden fame and fortune was initially overwhelming for Keys. "It took off and it just didn't stop," she said. "I thought I did good work and I hoped people would like it, but it's been crazy, the attention I've been getting. I'm like, 'Are you sure they want me on Leno?' or 'You're sure Prince wants to meet me?' It's bonkers."

Keys also launched her first national tour in 2001, performing to enthusiastic audiences across the United States. She also appeared on a televised benefit concert for the families of the victims of the September 11, 2001,

terror attacks, singing a moving rendition of Donny Hathaway's song "Someday We'll All Be Free." In January 2002 Keys won an American Music Award for favorite new artist in both the pop/rock and rhythm and blues categories. The following month, she captured five of the six Grammy Awards for which she had been nominated, including song of the year for "Fallin,'" best new artist, and best R&B album for *Songs in A Minor*. She seemed stunned by all the accolades she received. "You don't know how much this humbles me," she said in one of her acceptance speeches.

### The Diary of Alicia Keys

After the Grammy Awards, Keys resumed a busy touring schedule in the United States and Europe. Between concerts, she often wrote songs on a keyboard on her private tour bus or in her hotel room. Many of the songs appeared on her second album, *The Diary of Alicia Keys*, which was released in December 2003. The album sold more than 600,000 copies in its first week to vault to the top of the music charts.

Several guest artists accompany Keys on the album, including Kanye West, Harold Lilly, and Tim Mosley. A top-ten single from the *Diary*, "You Don't Know My Name," was called "gorgeous," and the "album's centerpiece," by Steve Jones in a four-star review of the album in *USA Today*. Keys's rendition of the song is "vulnerable yet in control as she makes a move on the object of her infatuation," Jones added. "It's a position she's often in as she covers a broad range of emotions." Other popular songs on the album include "Karma," "Heartburn," Dragon Days," and "Samsonite Man."

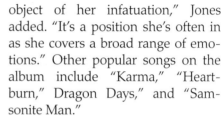

*Keys enjoyed her 2004 "First Ladies Tour" with Beyonce Knowles and Missy Elliott. "I think we all really respect each other and we really respect the work that each one does and we really have an admiration for each other," she said.*

Keys's second album was also a big hit with critics and her fellow musicians. At the 2005 Grammy Awards, *The Diary of Alicia Keys* won three Grammies: best R&B album; best R&B song for "You Don't Know My Name" with Harold Lilly and Kanye West; and best female R&B vocal performance for "If I Ain't Got You." Keys also won a Grammy for "My Boo," a duet she recorded with Usher in 2004.

The release of *The Diary of Alicia Keys* also took the young star back on tour. In March and April of 2004, Keys teamed up with the singers Beyonce Knowles and Missy Elliott for what they called the "First Ladies Tour." The three Grammy-winning artists sang to sold-out crowds in 26 U.S. cities, making it one of the most successful tours of the year. According to Keys, there was no competition between the three stars. "I think we all really respect each other and we really respect the work that each one does and we really have an admiration for each other," she said.

In 2005 Keys unveiled *Alicia Keys Unplugged*, her first live album. The album, which was recorded before an audience at the Brooklyn Academy of Music in New York, included many of her biggest hits, including "Fallin'" and "You Don't Know My Name." Other highlights included "Intro A Capella," a prayer-like ballad that Keys sings without accompaniment; covers of the Prince songs "Heartburn" and "How Come You Don't

*Keys performing at the 2005 Grammy Awards.*

Know Me"; as well as a gospel-inspired version of "Every Little Bit Hurts." Guest artists include the hip-hop artists Mos Def and Common, reggae star Damian Marley, and Maroon 5 singer Adam Levine. In a review for the *Boston Globe*, Renee Graham wrote that *Unplugged* proves why "the singer-songwriter-pianist is one of the greatest talents of her generation."

*Unplugged* brought Keys yet another wave of Grammy Awards in 2006. She received a total of five nominations, including best R&B album for *Unplugged* and best R&B song for "Unbreakable." For the first time in her career, though, she did not win any of the awards for which she was nominated.

## Branching Out

Keys has kept a journal for years in which she has recorded her thoughts and feelings about her life and the world around her. Her journal also includes poetry, and in 2005 she combined several of these poems with lyrics to some of her songs in a book called *Tears for Water*. Many fans of her music embraced the book. But *Tears for Water* was not as well received by critics. Several reviewers commented that without her vibrant voice and accompanying music, the poems were of average quality. "These poems read like what they are—journal entries from a young woman—and they don't have great insight or clever wordplay," Jamie Watson wrote in *School Library Journal*. "Even her song lyrics, so powerful when accompanied with lush piano arrangements, come across as banal when unadorned with instrumentation. However, both their creator and their subject matter will give these simple selections immense appeal with a teen audience. The writer talks about insecurities, personal growth, loneliness, and love—good, bad, long distance, and unrequited."

Writing a poetry book is just one of the ways that Keys has been diversifying her career. She has also begun a career as a film actress. "I grew up around the theater, my mother was an actress," she explained. "It's always been my destiny." She plays a major role, as an assassin, in the action-comedy *Smokin' Aces* (scheduled for release in 2007). Keys is excited about the film, which features an all-star cast that includes Ben Affleck, Don Cheadle, Jeremy Piven, and Andy Garcia. But she has also expressed some concern about how her part in the film will be received. "I think I have to put out a public service announcement for all my fans who are under 18," Keys said. "This role is that crazy. I get to deal with emotions that most people have to suppress, like extreme anger and rage."

> *Keys has expressed great excitement about branching out into acting. "I grew up around the theater, my mother was an actress," Keys explained. "It's always been my destiny."*

Keys has also signed on to star in *Composition in Black and White*, a film about the pianist and composer Philippa Schuyler. She was hand-picked to play Schuyler by the actress Halle Berry, who is producing the movie. Like Keys, Schulyer was a musical prodigy and the daughter of a mixed-race couple. Born 50 years earlier than Keys, in 1931, Schuyler struggled against racial and gender prejudice throughout her career.

## HOME AND FAMILY

Alicia Keys lives in New York City, although she travels widely for her career and charity work. A very private person, Keys refuses to answer questions about her personal life. She acknowledges, though, that one of the first things she did after becoming successful was to buy her mother her own apartment in New York City. "That was really exciting to be able to decorate it," she recalled. "And she brought the oldest stereo. Before I was born she had this stereo. I said, 'What is this doing here? Get a new stereo!'"

## HOBBIES AND OTHER INTERESTS

Keys likes to swim, read, and listen to music in her spare time. Her favorite musicians include Nina Simone, Duke Ellington, Miles Davis, Prince, Curtis Mayfield, Stevie Wonder, Carole King, Scott Joplin, and Marvin Gaye. "I like the old stuff," she remarked. She also likes coloring books. "I love those complex geometric books where I can sit on planes and just . . . color!" she said.

Keys has become active in charity work to benefit children. She supports Keep a Child Alive, an organization that provides medicine for children with AIDS. Her work with this organization led her to contribute the centerpiece essay to *How Can I Keep from Singing: Transforming the Lives of African Children and Families Affected by AIDS,* a 2006 photographic book that also features contributions from former U.S. President Bill Clinton and First Lady of South Africa Graça Machel.

She also is involved with a group called "Frum Tha Ground Up," which works to give teenagers the skills and opportunities to be successful. "Everything I do stems from something personal, not just because it will look good on paper or be a tax write-off," Keys said. "Camps are great, and I want to do one, but I want to be involved, hands-on. These possibilities give my life meaning, and they give me something other than the red carpet to look forward to."

## SELECTED WORKS

### Recordings

*Songs in A Minor,* 2001
*The Diary of Alicia Keys,* 2003
*Alicia Keys Unplugged,* 2005

### Writings

*Tears for Water: Songbook of Poems & Lyrics,* 2004
*How Can I Keep from Singing: Transforming the Lives of African Children and Families Affected by AIDS,* 2006

## SELECTED HONORS AND AWARDS

MTV Video Music Awards: 2001, Best New Artist in a Video, for "Fallin'"; 2004, Best R&B Video, for "If I Ain't Got You"; 2005, Best R&B Video, for "Karma"

American Music Awards: 2002, Favorite New Artist—Pop or Rock n'Roll; Favorite New Artist—Soul/Rhythm and Blues; 2004, Favorite Artist—Soul/Rhythm and Blues

Grammy Awards (National Academy of Recording Arts and Sciences): 2002, Song of the Year, for " Fallin'"; Best New Artist; Best Female R&B Vocal Performance, for "Fallin'"; Best R&B song, for "Fallin'"; Best R&B Album, for *Songs in A Minor*; 2005, Best R&B Song, for "You Don't Know My Name"; Best R&B Album, for *The Diary of Alicia Keys*; Best Female R&B Vocal Performance, for "If I Ain't Got You"; Best R&B Performance by a Duo or Group with Vocals, for "My Boo" (with Usher)

NAACP Image Awards (National Association for the Advancement of Colored People): 2002, Outstanding New Artist; Outstanding Female Artist; 2004, Outstanding Female Artist; 2005, Outstanding Music Video, for "If I Ain't Got You"; Outstanding Song, for "If I Ain't Got You"; 2006, Outstanding Female Artist; Outstanding Song, for "Unbreakable"; Outstanding Music Video, for "Unbreakable"

Songwriter of the Year Award (American Society of Composers, Authors and Publishers): 2005, for rhythm and blues

## FURTHER READING

### Books

Bankston, John. *Alicia Keys,* 2004 (juvenile)
Horn, Geoffrey. *Alicia Keys,* 2005 (juvenile)
Keys, Alicia. *Tears for Water: Songbook of Poems & Lyrics*, 2004
Keys, Alicia. *How Can I Keep from Singing: Transforming the Lives of African Children and Families Affected by AIDS,* 2006
*Who's Who in America*, 2006

### Periodicals

*Current Biography Yearbook,* 2001
*Daily Telegraph* (London, Aug. 2, 2001, p.20; Oct. 8, 2005, Arts , p.4
*Ebony*, Jan. 2004, p.134
*Los Angeles Times*, June 24, 2001, p. 62
*New York Times*, Jan. 27, 2002, Arts and Leisure, p.1
*O, The Oprah Magazine*, Sept. 2004, p.256
*Observer* (London), Mar. 21, 2004, Music Magazine, p.32
*Orlando Sentinel*, Feb. 15, 2002, Visitor Guide, p.1
*People*, Oct. 17, 2005, p.93
*Rolling Stone*, Nov. 8, 2001, p. 82; Feb. 24, 2005, p.28
*USA Today*, Dec. 1, 2003, p.D5

## Online Databases

*Biography Resource Center Online*, 2006, articles from *Contemporary Black Biography*, 2002, and *Notable Black American Women*, 2002

## ADDRESS

Alicia Keys
c/o J Records
745 Fifth Avenue
New York, NY 10151

## WORLD WIDE WEB SITE

http://www.aliciakeys.net

# Cheyenne Kimball 1990-

American Singer and Songwriter
Star of the MTV Reality Series "Cheyenne"

### BIRTH

Cheyenne Nichole Kimball was born on July 27, 1990, in Jacksonville, North Carolina. She grew up in Frisco, Texas, with her older sister Brittany. Her father, Brett, is a personal fitness trainer who has worked with celebrities, including the singer Avril Lavigne and members of the bands Sum 41 and Velvet Revolver. Cheyenne's mother, Shannon, has worked as a personal trainer and advertising executive, but now serves as Cheyenne's road manager.

## YOUTH

Cheyenne has loved music for as long as she can remember. Her favorite childhood band was Blind Melon. "I remember very clearly the first time I heard [the song] "No Rain," she recalled on her website, www.cheyennemusic.com. "It came on the radio—it had to be a few years after the record was out—and I was hooked. I just had to learn how to make those sounds." She was helped in that regard by a friend who gave her a guitar when she was seven years old. She quickly taught herself to play left-handed, and at age eight she wrote her first song, "All I Want is You." Cheyenne composed the song after being sent to her room for making a mean remark to her sister. "I remember writing it and hoping it would get me out of trouble," she admitted. "I haven't stopped writing songs or getting into trouble since."

> "
>
> *Cheyenne wrote her first song, "All I Want is You," after being sent to her room for making a mean remark to her sister. "I remember writing it and hoping it would get me out of trouble," she admitted. "I haven't stopped writing songs or getting into trouble since."*
>
> "

Once she could play the guitar, Cheyenne kept asking her parents for permission to sing on street corners because she had heard that the Dixie Chicks started their career that way. Her parents always refused, but she remained undaunted. When nine-year-old Cheyenne entered herself in a talent night at a local club, her parents relented and let her perform. "I told my husband that because Cheyenne had never sung in a microphone or been in front of a crowd, we should let her do it and get it out of her system," Shannon Kimball recalled. To her parents' great surprise, though, Cheyenne sang with gusto and poise. "I turned and looked at my husband and we both knew she was born for this," said Cheyenne's mother. Cheyenne won second place in the contest.

After the contest, Cheyenne began singing at clubs and coffee shops throughout Texas, accompanied by her mother. At age 12, armed with nearly 200 songs she had written herself, Cheyenne learned that auditions for the television show "America's Most Talented Kid" were being held in Dallas, Texas. Cheyenne's audition was successful, and she was booked on the series, which ran in 2003.

"America's Most Talented Kid," which originally aired on NBC, was hosted by the actor Mario Lopez. Children appearing on the show displayed different skills and talents, including singing, dancing, and magic tricks. There were three age groups in the competition: four to seven years old; eight to 12 years old; and 13 to 15 years old. Each performer was judged by the pop singer Lance Bass and two other guest judges. A winner was eventually decided in each age category and then an overall winner was crowned.

When Cheyenne's moment in the spotlight arrived, she selected the Sheryl Crow song "A Change Will Do You Good." Her strong singing and guitar playing vaulted her to first place in her age category (8 to 12 years). As the contest continued, she performed some of her own songs, impressing the judges with every performance. In the season finale, the judges crowned her the overall "Most Talented Kid" winner, which came with a $50,000 prize. "I always really wanted to be a performer and the show really just kind of made it a reality, which was great," she remarked. "I figured I wouldn't get started until I was 16, but I got a little bit of a head start."

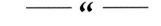

*"I don't really know what [high school] is supposed to be like," Cheyenne said. "I feel like everything is balanced out. Even though I am going to miss out on my prom or I am going to miss out on walking across the stage to accept my diploma, that's okay to me because I know I will have other perks in life."*

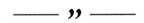

## EDUCATION

Cheyenne was wrapping up middle school around the same time as her "Most Talented Kid" triumph. But her new-found fame got in the way of her studies. "She was hounded by students at her school to the point where she went from being a straight 'A' student, head cheerleader and class mediator to someone who didn't want to go," her mother explained. "We wound up home schooling which, as it turns out, was a good move."

Shannon Kimball served as Cheyenne's tutor until she began filming her television show *Cheyenne*. At that point executives at MTV hired a professional tutor for her. As a result, Cheyenne has never attended high school. "I don't really know what it [high school] is supposed to be like," she said. "I've seen movies and stuff. Even that is different than what normal high school is. I feel like everything is balanced out. Even though I am going to miss out on my prom or I am going to miss out on walking across the stage to accept my diploma, that's okay to me because I know I will have other perks in life."

## CAREER HIGHLIGHTS

During the "America's Most Talented Kid" competition, Cheyenne appeared on NBC's "The Today Show," a morning television show. "Sony's head of global A & R, David Massey, saw me on the 'Today' show giving an interview before I had even won," she recalled. "He had no idea I was a musician. He was on the treadmill, watching TV on mute and he just saw how poised I was for 12 and was like, 'I need to find that girl!'"

Soon afterward, when Cheyenne was 13, she signed a multi-record deal with Sony/Epic Records and began working on her first album. Although she had already written hundreds of songs, Cheyenne wanted new material. She collaborated on some songs with several veteran songwriters, including Billy Mann (who has worked with Joss Stone and Teddy Geiger) and Kara DioGuardi (who has worked with Ashlee Simpson and Lindsay Lohan). "I started completely fresh," she said. "My lyrics are not age based. If anything, I write a lot older than my age. Maybe I could outgrow them when I'm more mature, but they are always going to be the songs that introduced me to the world."

### The Day Has Come

Cheyenne spent the next three years working on her debut album while still maintaining a challenging touring schedule. This period included six months in a California recording studio with bassist Brad Smith and guitarist Christopher Thorn, former members of Blind Melon, Cheyenne's favorite band. "When I was working on [the song] 'Everything to Lose' with the guys, I started to feel more confident than I ever had," she recalled on her website. "I can never thank them enough for helping me open up as a songwriter and teaching me how to let the music flow organically. I cried the day I left their studio because it felt like I was leaving home."

Cheyenne recorded more than 50 songs for the album, which she decided to call *The Day Has Come*. But there was only room for 12 songs on the album. The songs the young singer selected were more mature than her mother had expected. "People always think that I write Cheyenne's songs because they don't know how a girl that young could write about love," she said. She even joked that she occasionally looked under Cheyenne's bed to try and find the 30-year-old who was providing song lyrics to her daughter.

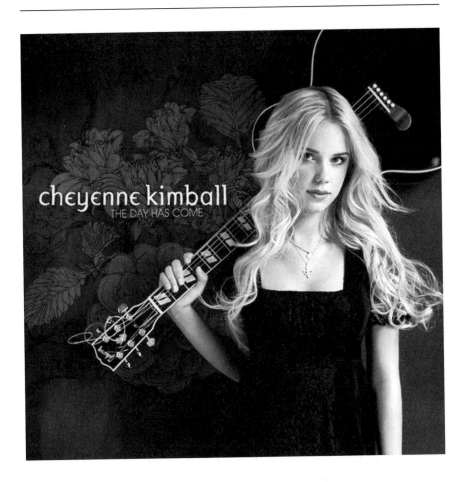

The signature piece of *The Day Has Come* was "Hanging On," which later became a hit single (and the theme song of her MTV series, *Cheyenne*). "It's a song about following your dreams and never letting things stand in your way; basically what I've been doing all my life," Cheyenne explained. "The song was really important to me because it kept reminding me to be patient, which is something that I'm not very good at." The song "Four Walls" also has special significance to Cheyenne because she recorded it while her father was hospitalized with a severe infection. "What you hear of that song is not a performance," she said. "The emotion is coming from a very real and honest place."

### "Cheyenne," the Television Series

About midway through the recording of *The Day Has Come,* Cheyenne and her parents were approached by MTV executives about doing a television show based on her daily life. The idea for the show was to have a camera crew film Cheyenne for weeks at a time as she pursued her music career. An agreement was reached and a MTV camera crew started filming in June of 2005.

MTV management was very excited about the show, called "Cheyenne" after its star. "The MTV audience will have a front-row seat to all the struggles and triumphs faced by Cheyenne in her quest to be music's next big star," declared Lois Curren, executive vice-president for MTV Series Entertainment. Cheyenne was seen as a natural fit for the MTV audience because in addition to her career ambitions, she still shares most teenage experiences. "She loves to shop, she's boy crazy, whines about how strict her parents are, hates homework, and is counting the days until she gets her driver's license," Curren said.

> ———— " ————
>
> *Cheyenne admits that it was "weird" having a film crew around all the time, but "you get used to it after a while. They're like family now, so it's better. I feel more comfortable. But, at first, it's kind of awkward. The first day they were filming, I was really stressed out."*
>
> ———— " ————

The show has no script, other than the prepared narration Cheyenne reads as a voice-over. Cheyenne admits that it was "weird" having the crew around all the time, but "you get used to it after a while. They're like family now, so it's better. I feel more comfortable. But, at first, it's kind of awkward. The first day they were filming, I was really stressed out." The cameras kept running even during family arguments. "My mom and I argue a lot," Cheyenne remarked. "My mom's my manager, my teacher and, of course, my mother. So I guess it gets hard sometimes because we're always around each other."

The first episode, which aired on May 24, 2006, began with Cheyenne celebrating her 15th birthday the summer before with some Texas friends whom she had not seen for a while. After a trip to New York City to talk to record executives, Cheyenne traveled to Los Angeles for a concert, where she battled a sore throat and a bad case of nerves. Subsequent episodes showed Cheyenne breaking up with a boyfriend, moving to California with her parents, going on tour, getting a new boyfriend, shooting a music video, and performing with her musical idol, Sheryl Crow.

When Cheyenne watches the show, she admits that she sometimes has to pinch herself in excitement to relive all that has happened to her. "I'll have one of those,'oh, my gosh, that's hysterical, that's me' moments," she said. Other times, she winces in embarrassment at the TV screen. In one episode, for instance, "I'm picking a wedgie," she said. "I could change it if I really wanted to, if I was like 'please don't put that in there,' and they wouldn't, or we would compromise, but I know that it's reality and I know that they're trying to be real, so I have to accept the fact that they're going to use that kind of stuff."

## On the *Billboard* Charts

The popularity of Cheyenne's MTV television series assured that *The Day Has Come* would receive a fair amount of attention from music fans and critics alike when it was finally released in July 2006. In the first week of its release, *The Day Has Come* appeared on the Billboard 200 list of top-selling albums at number 15. In addition, the song "Hanging On" came in at number 53 on the Billboard Hot 100 singles list. "I feel like I just graduated songwriting school so maybe this album is my diploma," Cheyenne remarked. "I hear a lot of people say that albums are like snapshots in time, but I think my album feels more like a movie because I see myself growing up in these songs."

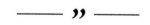

> Cheyenne's song "Hanging On" became a hit single. "It's a song about following your dreams and never letting things stand in your way; basically what I've been doing all my life," she explained. "The song was really important to me because it kept reminding me to be patient, which is something that I'm not very good at."

*The Day Has Come* was embraced by fans of Cheyenne's television show. But music critics gave it mixed reviews. Some reviewers admitted that Cheyenne displayed talent, but they also asserted that the album was bland and uninspired. Other reviewers, including Stephen Thomas Erlewine of the website allmusic.com, had a more positive assessment. "[Cheyenne] still sounds like a teen, but that's the good thing about *The Day Has Come*: it has the musical scope of somebody in their early twenties, but the freshness and spunk of a teenager, which is quite remarkable," wrote Erlewine. "So maybe she did get an unfair advantage by being plastered all over MTV prior to the release of her debut, but this record is good

*Cheyenne performing at a party for her debut album,* The Day Has Come, *2006.*

enough to provide a compelling reason why Epic and MTV have staked so much on Cheyenne Kimball: based on this very good debut, she certainly does seem the star she's positioned to be."

Cheyenne's popularity with American teens has led several companies to approach her about endorsing their products. Cheyenne has appeared in a series of television and print advertisements with the 1980s rock star Pat Benatar for a special vintage collection of the Candie's brand of apparel, footwear, and fashion accessories. Cheyenne has also signed on to represent the Sephora cosmetic company in advertisements for its line of "Pii-ink" makeup.

## HOME AND FAMILY

When she is not on tour, Cheyenne lives with her parents in Los Angeles. Her mother travels with Cheyenne and aims to keep her "in my sight at all times. . . . to protect her from this business. She calls the shots but also she's still a 16-year-old who was only allowed to start dating this year, isn't going to be allowed to play bars until she's of age and gets grounded with no computer access frequently." Cheyenne has two black teacup chihuahuas that are named Olivia and Priscilla. "They are very spoiled!" she said.

## HOBBIES AND OTHER INTERESTS

Cheyenne has a blog on MySpace.com, which she updates frequently to keep her fans up to date on her touring schedule and other activities. In her spare time, she also enjoys shopping and reading (her favorite books are the "Gossip Girls" series). To keep herself in shape, Cheyenne tries to work out five times a week.

## SELECTED CREDITS

### Recordings

*The Day Has Come*, 2006

### Television

"Cheyenne," 2006-

## FURTHER READING

### Periodicals

*Boston Herald*, May 29, 2006, p.O24
*Dallas Morning News*, Jan. 2, 2006, p.B1
*Fresno (CA) Bee*, June 22, 2006, p.E1
*Girls' Life*, June/July 2006, p.36; Oct./Nov. 2006, p.38
*Hartford (CT) Courant*, Aug. 17, 2006, Calendar p.11
*New Jersey Star-Ledger*, Aug. 9, 2006, p.34
*Toronto Sun*, June 25, 2005, p.S20

### Online Articles

http://www.ellegirl.com/article/article.do?articleId=5230
   (*ELLEgirl*, "Cheyenne Kimball: On the Verge," Aug. 20, 2006)
http://bellaonline.com/ArticlesP/art42310.asp
   (*BellaOnline*, "Cheyenne Kimball Interview," undated)
http://www.billboard.com/bbcom/search/google/article_display.jsp?vnu_
   content_id=1002877080
   (*Billboard*, "Cheyenne Kimball," July 20, 2006)
http://www.teenmag.com/celeb/babe/articles/0,,639409_688920,00.html
   (*Teenmag*, "Getting to Know: Cheyenne," undated)

## ADDRESS

Cheyenne Kimball
Epic Records
Sony BMG Music Entertainment
550 Madison Avenue
New York, NY 10022-3211

## WORLD WIDE WEB SITES

http://www.cheyennemusic.com
http://www.mtv.com/ontv/dyn/cheyenne/series.jhtml

# Keira Knightley 1985-

British Actress
Star of *Bend It Like Beckham, Pride and Prejudice,* and
*Pirates of the Caribbean*

## BIRTH

Kiera Christina Knightley (pronounced "KEE-ra") was born
on March 26, 1985, in the southwest London suburb of Teddington, England. She later changed the spelling of her first
name from Kiera to Keira to make it easier for international
audiences to pronounce. She was the second child of Will
Knightley, a stage actor, and Sharman Macdonald, a playwright who once worked as an actress. Keira has one older

brother, Caleb, who was born in 1979. He is also involved in the performing arts, having worked as a musician, sound engineer, and television studio manager.

Keira's birth was the result of a bet between her parents. Jobs in the theater were hard to find, and money was so tight that they were uncertain they could afford to have a second child. "My mum was desperate for another child, and my dad told her that the only way they could afford to have one was if she sold a play." Apparently his suggestion worked. In 1984 Macdonald's first play, *When I Was a Girl, I Used to Scream and Shout,* was staged in London. It won an Evening Standard Award and ran for eight years. Its success gave the couple the financial stability they needed to have a second child. Soon after its sale, Keira joined older brother Caleb.

## YOUTH

Knightley was three years old the first time she asked her parents for an agent, even though she didn't know what an agent was. (An agent manages artists' careers by helping them find work.) She had heard her parents talking on the phone with their agents, so she wanted one of her own. Her parents refused. They wanted her to focus on her schoolwork, especially when they later discovered young Keira was having trouble learning to read. Although she was never formally diagnosed, she believes she had dyslexia, a learning disorder in which people have trouble recognizing and decoding words, which can make reading and spelling difficult. People with dyslexia often have trouble with reading comprehension. When Keira still wouldn't drop the idea of an agent, her mother made a bargain with her: if she would spend a summer reading for an hour every day, they would find her an agent. She fulfilled her end of the deal and got her first agent at the age of six.

Knightley's parents knew how difficult it could be to make a living as an actor and wanted to be sensible about their daughter's career. She was allowed to act only during school vacations, and only if she kept her grades up. Despite these restrictions, young Keira got her first job at age seven. She started out in a couple of commercials and earned some small television parts. Her first role was in a 1993 TV movie, *Royal Celebration,* billed as "Little Girl." She soon followed with a part in her first film, *A Village Affair* (1994). Knightley noted that these early roles had her "running into the picture saying 'Mummy' and 'Daddy' a lot and then running out of it again." She also earned roles as the younger version of adult characters in the films *Innocent Lies* (1995) and *Coming Home* (1998), and she played a princess in the TV movie *Treasure Seekers* (1996). Although she enjoyed acting, she had no idea what kind of success, if any, lay ahead of her.

## EDUCATION

Knightley attended her local secondary school, Teddington School. Through hard work she overcame her reading difficulties and finished with top grades. She then was faced with a decision about what to do next. In England, compulsory secondary school ends at age 16. After that, some students leave school, but those who want further education can attend school for an additional two years before taking university entrance exams and then going on to university. This additional two years of schooling is referred to as "sixth form." Knightley began taking her sixth form at nearby Esher College, focusing on liberal arts such as art, history, and English literature. Because her acting career was taking off, however, she dropped out during her first year to work full-time; she also turned down a place at the London Academy of Music and Drama.

Knightley has often said she regrets not finishing college, but notes that "not having letters after my name won't define me as a person." She intends to pursue some kind of continuing education, explaining that "there's never an excuse to stop learning."

## CAREER HIGHLIGHTS

### Early Television and Film Roles

As a teenager Knightley began earning larger and more prominent parts. In 1998, she appeared in the TV miniseries of Charles Dickens's *Oliver Twist*. Her supporting role as Rose, a girl who assists the title character, was secondary but important. The miniseries was broadcast on both sides of the Atlantic, making it her first appearance on American television.

Her next role was in a film eagerly awaited by audiences all over the world: *Star Wars: Episode I—The Phantom Menace* (1999). Only sharp-eyed viewers noticed her in the film, though. She played Sabé, a servant who acts as a stand-in for Queen Amidala, played by actress Natalie Portman. When the two actresses were wearing their makeup, they looked so similar that their own mothers had trouble telling them apart. No wonder, then, that many viewers didn't notice Knightley and believed that Portman was playing both parts. Because the existence of Knightley's character Sabé as a decoy for Queen Amidala was a key plot twist, her part in the film wasn't publicized. She received little notice for the film, but it did give her valuable experience acting in a major Hollywood blockbuster.

At age 16 Knightley earned her first starring role, as the title character in the American TV movie *Princess of Thieves* (2001). Knightley trained for several weeks in archery, sword fighting, and horse riding for her role as

Gwyn, the daughter of Robin Hood and Maid Marian. In the film her character disguises herself as a boy to battle her father's old enemy, the Sheriff of Nottingham. That same year Knightley also appeared in *The Hole,* a psychological thriller. She plays snobbish, shallow Frankie, one of four teenagers who hide in an underground bunker to avoid a school field trip. They get locked in and two weeks later, only one of the four emerges alive. While the film was only a modest success, it was a chance for the actress to take a more mature role.

*Even though Knightley had captained her school's soccer team, "I still had to learn to play for* Beckham, *because my version of playing soccer was being fast and kicking people in the shins."*

Knightley continued to find more challenging roles in 2002. In the film *Pure,* she starred as a pregnant, teenaged heroin addict who has already had one child taken from her by social services. It was only a supporting role in a small, independent film, but it enabled her to demonstrate her acting range. In 2002 she also earned her first adult starring role in the TV miniseries of *Dr. Zhivago,* based on the classic novel by Boris Pasternak. The story is set in Russia during the early 20th century and focuses on the doomed romance between the title character and the beautiful nurse Lara. As Lara, Knightley had to portray the character from ages 16 to 32. The role was a major challenge, but the young actress was up to the task. Her passionate portrayal of Lara brought her to the attention of TV audiences in both Britain and the United States.

### Bend It Like Beckham

Knightley's first big movie success came in *Bend It Like Beckham* (2002). While still in school she had played a role in what was expected to be a small British movie about women's football (as soccer is called outside the U.S.). Knightley played Jules (short for Juliet), a British girl who is dedicated to her women's soccer team. Parminder Nagra played Jess, a girl of Indian descent who wants to play soccer, although her traditional parents push her to focus on school and marriage. Jules sees Jess messing around with a soccer ball and convinces her to join the local team. For both Jules and Jess, playing soccer means defying the wishes of their parents and dealing with the hard feelings that creates. The film's title, *Bend It Like Beckham,* refers to how British soccer superstar David Beckham can kick a ball so that it curves into the goal.

*Above:* Bend It Like Beckham *was the first film to bring Knightley widespread attention and success.*

*Below: Knightley with Orlando Bloom in* Pirates of the Caribbean: The Curse of the Black Pearl.

Preparing for the role required Knightley to train intensively for several weeks. Even though she had captained her school's soccer team, "I still had to learn to play for *Beckham,* because my version of playing soccer was being fast and kicking people in the shins." When the film debuted in Britain in spring 2002, it became a surprise success. In 2003 the movie was released in the U.S., where reaction to the movie was very strong, especially among young female athletes. The film earned a respectable $32.5 million in America. Much of its success was due to the chemistry between Knightley and Nagra, whose believable friendship was at the center of this coming-of-age story.

### Pirates of the Caribbean: The Curse of the Black Pearl

> *In* Pirates, *Knightley was drawn to the feisty spirit of Elizabeth Swann. "[The character] fights back and gives as good as she gets,"* Knightley said. *"Why would you want to be the simpering maiden in the corner when you could be hitting people in the head?"*

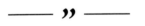

Knightley's next prominent role came in the Disney blockbuster *Pirates of the Caribbean: The Curse of the Black Pearl* (2003). Knightley beat out 75 other young actresses for the part of Elizabeth Swann, who is kidnapped by a gang of pirates because of the magical medallion she possesses. Elizabeth's secret admirer, young blacksmith Will Turner (played by Orlando Bloom), enlists the assistance of pirate Captain Jack Sparrow (played by Johnny Depp) to rescue her. But instead, Elizabeth ends up rescuing Will. Knightley remarked that 20 years ago, "my character would have been a damsel in distress, . . . probably tied up a couple of times and get rescued by the boys. . . . [This character] fights back and gives as good as she gets." Indeed, that feisty spirit is why the character appealed to her. "Why would you want to be the simpering maiden in the corner when you could be hitting people in the head?"

*Pirates* was a big-budget Hollywood film, but expectations were modest before it debuted in July 2003. It was based on a Disney theme-park ride and was competing for moviegoers' attention against installments in several successful film franchises, including *Charlie's Angels, Legally Blonde, The Matrix, The Terminator,* and *X-Men.* In addition, pirate movies had been box-office disappointments for the past 20 years. Even the actors were un-

*Knightley as Guinevere in* King Arthur.

certain about how it would do in theaters. "We all thought it was going to . . . tank," Knightley said about the wildly successful film. "I remember sitting at a screening with Orlando, going, 'Just smile through it. United front. It's gonna be all right.'"

*Pirates of the Caribbean: Curse of the Black Pearl* surprised critics and audiences, however, with its inventive action, sense of fun, and appealing lead actors, especially the antics of Johnny Depp as Captain Jack Sparrow. It earned over $300 million in the U.S. and $653 million worldwide, making it one of the top three films of the year, and one of the top 30 films of all time. It also made Knightley into an international star.

The actress finished off 2003 with a part in the successful British ensemble romantic comedy *Love Actually.* The film starred many of Britain's most famous actors—including Knightley's childhood idol, Oscar-winner Emma Thompson—and followed several romances between loosely connected characters. Knightley played a young bride who discovers her husband's best friend is unfriendly not because he dislikes her, but because he is in love with her. The R-rated film earned $62.5 million in Britain alone, and $245 million worldwide. At the end of this breakout year, Knightley was only 18 years old, yet her films had taken in almost $1 billion worldwide.

Although Knightley was now an undeniable star, many critics still reserved judgment on whether she was more than just a pretty face. The young actress responded by taking on a wide variety of roles to show her acting skills. In *King Arthur* (2004), she was cast as the title character's love interest, Guinevere. In more familiar versions of this legend, Guinevere is merely one side of a love triangle between King Arthur and his best friend Lancelot. In this film, however, Guinevere is a warrior princess who battles to save her British homeland against Saxon invasion in the fifth century. Knightley trained in boxing, fighting, horseback riding, and archery four days a week for three months before filming started. She worked so hard she didn't need a stunt double. As a result, "Knightley has little trouble persuading one to accept the spirited future queen as an action heroine," according to *Variety* reviewer Todd McCarthy. He added that she "rivets the attention whenever she's on-screen, showing every sign of a real star in the making."

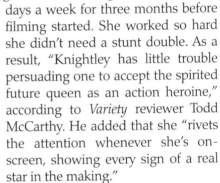

*"What I love about acting is moving on quite quickly. It's ships passing in the night, this profession, which is kind of romantic. I became an actress to change as much as possible, that's what makes it fun."*

Knightley had a smaller role in her next film, the psychological thriller *The Jacket* (2005). She co-starred with Oscar-winner Adrian Brody, who played a Gulf War veteran who seems to travel through time. Knightley played a struggling waitress whom Brody's character first encounters as a little girl. Although the director was hesitant to cast her, she won him over with a believable American accent—and her desperation to play a part in something other than a costume drama. "I'm not good when people go, 'You're amazing, you're perfect for this role.' I think you've really got to fight for stuff." Although the film was only a modest success at the box office and earned middling reviews, several critics praised Knightley's performance as a believable stretch from her old roles.

## Pride and Prejudice

Knightley next appeared in another costume drama, *Pride and Prejudice* (2005), based on the beloved 19th-century novel of the same name by Jane Austen. Knightley had loved the book since she was seven years old; she even bought a dollhouse of the hero's mansion with one of her first acting paychecks. In this story of the five Bennet sisters, Knightley

*Knightley as Elizabeth in* Pride and Prejudice.

played Elizabeth. The story follows the lively, quick-witted Elizabeth's growing relationship with the rich but proud Mr. Darcy, even as misunderstandings seem to destroy their chance for happiness together. "The beauty of Elizabeth is that every woman who ever reads the book seems to recognize herself, with all her faults and imperfections," Knightley said. With that kind of part, "if you give an actress who is even remotely good the chance to play a fantastic character like that, they are going to revel in it."

Knightley still wasn't sure if she was that kind of "remotely good" actress in *Pride and Prejudice.* Seeing herself play Elizabeth on screen, "I can pick it apart completely. The way I speak, the way I look, the way I move, anything." Most critics, however, warmly praised her performance. *Entertainment Weekly* reviewer Owen Gleiberman called it a "witty, vibrant, altogether superb performance," explaining that Knightley makes Elizabeth's relationship with Darcy believable by playing her "not [as] a feminist but [as] a confused, ardent girl charting her destiny without a map."

Knightley earned a Golden Globe nomination for Best Actress in a comedy or musical and an Academy Award (Oscar) nomination for best actress for her work in *Pride and Prejudice.* At age 20, she was the third youngest actress ever nominated for the best actress Oscar. While she didn't win either award (Reese Witherspoon's performance in *Walk the Line* earned both trophies), the nominations were reward enough. For all the critics who thought she was just a pretty face, she said, "at least [the nominations] shut them up for a while."

After finishing *Pride and Prejudice,* Knightley had only four days' rest before she began filming her next movie, *Domino* (2005). In this fictionalized biography she played the title character, a female bounty hunter named Domino Harvey. She is the daughter of a British film star and a fashion model who has turned her back on the Hollywood lifestyle to involve herself in the criminal underbelly of Los Angeles. To prepare for the role, Knightley trained for an hour a day during *Pride and Prejudice,* focusing on martial arts. Using guns was a different issue, however. "I thought I liked them, because I enjoyed doing things with swords and knives on *Arthur* and *Pirates.* . . . The reality of guns, and knowing how easy it was to pick one up and shoot somebody dead, really freaked me out." While director Tony Scott cast Knightley for her combination of beauty and toughness, critics were not entirely convinced by her performance, and the film performed poorly at the box office.

> "The beauty of Elizabeth [Bennet] is that every woman who ever reads the book seems to recognize herself, with all her faults and imperfections," Knightley said about **Pride and Prejudice**. *"[If] you give an actress who is even remotely good the chance to play a fantastic character like that, they are going to revel in it."*

### Returning to *Pirates of the Caribbean*

Her next film put Knightley back in the Hollywood spotlight. After the first *Pirates* film proved box office gold, she had agreed to reprise her role as Elizabeth Swann in two sequels. In the second installment, the 2006 blockbuster *Pirates of the Caribbean: Dead Man's Chest,* Elizabeth is about to marry sweetheart Will Turner when they are arrested and imprisoned for treason, for aiding the escape of the swaggering Captain Jack Sparrow. They face execution unless they locate Sparrow and his magical compass, which leads to a buried treasure chest. This task is made more difficult by the sinister and ghostly Davy Jones, a monstrous blend of man and squid, and his ghoulish followers.

When writing about the new movie, many critics faulted its two-and-a-half-hour running time as too long, its plot as overly convoluted, its special

*Scenes from*
Pirates of the Caribbean:
Dead Man's Chest.

effects as excessive, its gags as repetitive, and Depp's performance as over the top. But audiences couldn't get enough. *Dead Man's Chest* earned $135.6 million in its first weekend alone—a record in the U.S.—on its way to taking in over $420 million total from American audiences. Worldwide, the film earned just over $1 billion, making it the third highest-grossing film of all time (behind *Titanic* and *Lord of the Rings: Return of the King*).

Fans around the world eagerly await the third installment of the series, *Pirates of the Caribbean: At World's End,* which is scheduled to be released in May 2007. According to director Gore Verbinski, the final film will bring the unfolding romantic drama between Will and Elizabeth to a climax. "They realize love is something that hurts," Verbinski said, "and there are things they have to overcome if the relationship is to last."

> " 
>
> *According to director Gore Verbinski, the final* **Pirates** *film will bring the unfolding romantic drama between Will and Elizabeth to a climax. "They realize love is something that hurts,"* Verbinski said, "and there are things they have to overcome if the relationship is to last."
>
> "

Filming the two *Pirates* sequels took up much of Knightley's time in 2005 and 2006. Still, the actress found time to complete two other movies for release in 2007. One is the historical drama *Silk,* based on the bestseller by Italian novelist Alessandro Baricco. The film focuses on a 19th-century silk merchant who travels from France to Japan and embarks on a forbidden affair. Knightley plays the merchant's wife, who gradually becomes aware of her husband's romantic obsession. She is also scheduled to appear in *Atonement,* based on Ian McEwan's novel set in Britain during the 1930s and 1940s. Knightley plays Celia, a girl whose relationship with a young servant leads to tragedy when her younger sister misinterprets it. The actress also has plans to star in *The Best Time of Our Lives,* a script written by her mother, Sharman Macdonald. The story is set in the mid-20th century and deals with the complex relationship between Welsh poet Dylan Thomas and his childhood friend, Vera Phillips, the role Knightley is slated to play. Knightley has said that acting in one of her mother's works will fulfill a longtime dream.

Knightley has been in the acting business for more than a decade and shows no signs of slowing down. Part of that is due to her parents. "I'm the daughter of a theater actor and a playwright and I know this is a job that blows down even quicker than it blows up. All you can do is ride the wave while it's there and enjoy it." She expects that some day "the work is going to dry up, and people will get bored of me. That's not bitterness, just the truth." Nevertheless, she hopes to keep working as an actress. "What I love about acting is moving on quite quickly. It's ships passing in the night, this profession, which is kind of romantic. I became an actress to change as much as possible, that's what makes it fun." If she can make films that move people, that would be the best reward. When she was growing up, "there was a sense that my parents' work was important and that it could change the world in a way. That's an amazing thing to be around. It's inspiring. It makes you want to be great."

## HOBBIES AND OTHER INTERESTS

Knightley's busy filming schedule leaves her little spare time, but when she is home she enjoys cooking. She roots for West Ham United, a soccer team in the English Premier League. When she goes out, she enjoys art galleries and shopping, with shoes being her favorite indulgence. She also likes experimenting with creative arts such as drawing, painting, and photography.

> "You can't make yourself anything you're not. If you're going to be thin, that's fine. But if you're not, that's fine. Celebrate whatever shape you are."

Knightley's striking good looks and acting success have brought her endorsement deals with British luxury jeweler Asprey and Chanel's Coco Mademoiselle fragrance. But she also uses her image to benefit charities. In 2005, she posed for publicity photos on behalf of WaterAid, a charity dedicated to providing safe drinking water and sanitation in Africa and Asia. She also lent her image to the American Library Association's "Read" campaign, appearing in a poster connected to *Pride and Prejudice.*

Knightley's physical appearance has certainly won her many admirers, but it has also made her the focus of some controversy. As she has become more popular, she has become a regular feature in fan magazines, where photographs show that she has gotten noticeably slimmer. The actress has admitted that her grandmother and great-grandmother struggled with anorexia, but she has denied rumors that she has an eating disorder. She attributes her slender figure to genetics and a healthy diet and tries not to obsess over it. "You can't make yourself anything you're not. If you're going to be thin, that's fine. But if you're not, that's fine. Celebrate whatever shape you are." Still, after photographs were widely published in which she appeared to be dangerously thin, many have become concerned about her weight and her health.

## HOME AND FAMILY

Knightley owns an apartment in London, which she sometimes shares with friends and her brother Caleb. Despite her success, she doesn't have a personal manager or assistant. As a young adult, she explains, "you're meant to be growing up and handling things on your own." The actress gets advice from her family instead: "They're fantastically supportive but also highly critical. I prefer that to somebody completely [sucking up to] me." When she films far away from home, her mother sometimes joins her on location.

Knightley, who is single, has said that that her busy work schedule leaves her little time for relationships. The actress refuses to comment on her personal life, except to say that she does not get involved in on-set romances with co-stars. Occasionally some of her on-set friendships have developed into romances after shooting ended, and she has been linked with young actors from England and Ireland.

## SELECTED ROLES

### Television Films

*Royal Celebration,* 1993
*Treasure Seekers,* 1996
*Coming Home,* 1998
*Oliver Twist,* 1998 (miniseries)
*Princess of Thieves,* 2001
*Doctor Zhivago,* 2002 (miniseries)

### Movies

*A Village Affair,* 1994
*Innocent Lies,* 1995
*Star Wars: Episode I—The Phantom Menace,* 1999
*The Hole,* 2001
*Bend It Like Beckham,* 2002
*Pure,* 2002
*Love Actually,* 2003
*Pirates of the Caribbean: The Curse of the Black Pearl,* 2003
*King Arthur,* 2004
*Domino,* 2005
*The Jacket,* 2005

*Pride and Prejudice,* 2005
*Pirates of the Caribbean: Dead Man's Chest,* 2006

## HONORS AND AWARDS

Best Newcomer Award (London Critics Circle): 2003, for *Bend It Like Beckham*
Best International Actress Award (Irish Film and Television Festival): 2004
Breakthrough Award (Hollywood Film Festival): 2004
Variety UK Personality of the Year (British Independent Film Awards): 2005
Teen Choice Award: 2007, Choice Movie Actress—Action Adventure, for *Pirates of the Caribbean: At World's End*

## FURTHER READING

### Books

*Contemporary Theatre, Film, and Television,* Vol. 38, 2002
Hurst, Brandon. *Keira Knightley,* 2006

### Periodicals

*Biography Magazine,* Dec. 2003
*Boston Globe,* Nov. 6, 2005, p.N13
*Elle,* Aug. 2006
*Entertainment Weekly,* Nov. 18, 2005, p.102
*CosmoGIRL!,* Aug. 2006, p.128
*Cosmopolitan,* Aug. 2004, p.44
*Current Biography International Yearbook,* 2005
*Los Angeles Times,* July 6, 2003, part 5, p.12; Mar. 5, 2006, p.E7
*Sunday Times* (London), Oct. 2, 2005, Features p.4
*Time,* July 5, 2004, p.84
*Times* (London), Sep. 10, 2005, p.22
*USA Today,* July 4, 2003, p.D2
*Vanity Fair,* April, 2004, p.314
*Variety,* July 6, 2004, p.4; Nov. 21, 2005, p.C2
*Vogue,* Dec. 2005, p.318; May 2006, p.222

### Online Articles

http://www.elle.com/coverstory/9029/keira-knightley.html
   (Elle Magazine, "Shining Knightley," July 18, 2006)
http://www.wateraid.org/international/about_us/newsroom/3060.asp
   (WaterAid, "Keira Knightley Takes the Plunge for WaterAid," Jan. 15, 2005)

**Online Databases**

*Biography Resource Center Online,* 2007, article from *Contemporary Theatre, Film, and Television*

## ADDRESS

Keira Knightley
Endeavor Agency
9601 Wilshire Boulevard
Beverly Hills, CA 90201

## WORLD WIDE WEB SITES

http://www.foxsearchlight.com/benditlikebeckham
http://disney.go.com/disneyvideos/liveaction/pirates/main_site/main.html
http://www.prideandprejudicemovie.net/splash.html
http://disney.go.com/disneypictures/pirates

## Wendy Kopp 1967-

American Education Activist
President and Founder of Teach for America

### BIRTH

Wendy Kopp was born in Austin, Texas, on June 29, 1967. Her parents, Jay D. and Mary Pat Kopp, were the owners of a company called Convention Guides, Inc., which published guidebooks for travelers. She has a brother, David, who is two years younger.

### YOUTH

Kopp was raised near Dallas, Texas, in the wealthy suburb of University Park. She went to Highland Park High School, a public school near her home, and graduated in 1985.

Kopp was always a high achiever. She was editor of the student newspaper, took part in theater productions, and was a member of the debate team. She was also her class valedictorian, the student with the highest grade point average in her graduating class. In addition, she had a part-time job at a crafts store and helped out at her parents' business. She and her friends liked to go for long walks and have "very intense, very engaging conversations about big, abstract issues like 'Does God Exist?'" remembered Neeta Vallab, one of her friends from the debate team. "I think we probably thought of ourselves as the cooler smart kids."

## EDUCATION

After graduating from high school, Kopp went to Princeton University in Princeton, New Jersey. There, she majored in public policy, the study of how public authorities can deal with society's problems. Her roommate during her freshman year was a woman from the South Bronx in New York City. She came from a low-income area where most families are poor and schools struggle with intractable social and economic problems. Kopp saw that her roommate was "absolutely brilliant," yet she struggled to keep up with her basic coursework because her school had not prepared her for college.

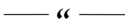

> *Kopp and her friends liked to go for long walks and have "very intense, very engaging conversations about big, abstract issues like 'Does God Exist?'" remembered Neeta Vallab, a friend from the debate team. "I think we probably thought of ourselves as the cooler smart kids."*

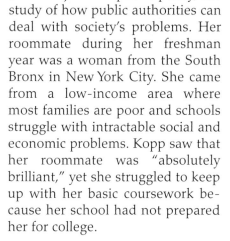

In theory, public education is supposed to give all American citizens an equal opportunity to achieve. But in reality, Kopp soon learned, being born in an affluent area with good schools gives a person a much better chance to excel than being born in an under-funded area with struggling schools. Many studies have documented this. For example, one study showed that children who live in low-income neighborhoods are seven times less likely to earn a college degree than those from wealthier neighborhoods. Nine-year-old children in low-income schools are, on average, three to four reading levels behind nine-year-olds who attend schools in higher-income districts.

*Teach for America participant Joseph Leslie-Bernard helps his students work through math problems at a school in the Bronx in New York City.*

## Hard Work Brings Success

At Princeton, Kopp kept up the busy pace she had set for herself in high school. She worked for the Foundation for Student Communication (FSC), an organization that runs a yearly conference where students and business leaders meet. The foundation also publishes the magazine *Business Today*. Kopp got started with the FSC doing some writing for *Business Today*, and within two months, she was the publication's associate editor. Issues of *Business Today* usually had 32 pages, and the magazine's yearly revenue was about $300,000. This was not considered successful. "We couldn't sell ads and couldn't publish some issues," Kopp recalled. "There was a whole group of us who really worked to turn things around. We totally did. It became a complete obsession. We built it up to the point where it made $1.4 million. At one point, we put out a 140-page magazine."

That increased success didn't come easily. Kopp often worked 70 hours per week at the FSC, but her dedication paid off. She was president of the organization during her senior year at Princeton. By that time, she was managing a budget of $1.5 million dollars, nearly five times as much as the annual budget had been when she first became involved with the FSC.

### An Ambitious Senior Project

During the fall of her senior term, Kopp organized an FSC conference about education reform. One of the topics covered there was the critical shortage of qualified teachers in low-income communities. There are many reasons for this problem, but Kopp felt that one of them is the image of teaching as a profession. Top graduates from the best schools are aggressively recruited to work for banking and investment firms, as well as other corporations, and the financial rewards for employment with those companies can be great. Teachers, on the other hand, are not recruited in the same way, and teaching is not viewed as a profession with high potential for career advancement. Kopp began to think about how this problem could be addressed.

— " —

*"My generation was dubbed the 'Me Generation.' People thought all we wanted to do was focus on ourselves and make a lot of money. But that didn't strike me as right. I felt as if thousands of us talented, driven graduating seniors were searching for a way to make a social impact."*

— " —

Then an idea came to her: Why not have a national teacher corps that would aggressively recruit top graduates, just as the banking and investment firms do? Inspired by the thought, she wrote a letter about it to George H.W. Bush, who was then president of the United States. In response, she received a standard job-rejection letter. Undaunted, Kopp began to outline her idea as part of her senior project at Princeton. She called her thesis "A Plan and Argument for the Creation of a National Teacher Corps." In it, she proposed starting up a nonprofit organization that would recruit the top college students in America, give them eight weeks of intensive training, and place them in six of the nation's most troubled school districts for a period of two years. She proposed doing this with a budget of $2.5 million, to be funded through donations from big businesses and foundations.

Kopp's idea was very ambitious. She wanted not just to bring additional teachers into the schools for short-term help, but also to fundamentally change the school system and the image of teaching. She knew top students were very competitive about getting into public service programs—in part because service in the Peace Corps and other programs looks great on a resume when looking for another job. She wanted her teacher corps to have the same kind of selective, high-minded image.

"We're not going to have a first-class education system as long as the public views teaching as downwardly mobile," Kopp reasoned. "We want to try to change that, to show the public that outstanding individuals compete to enter this profession and that they find it incredibly challenging and rewarding." She also believed that people who had worked for a national teacher corps would feel inspired to keep trying to improve the quality of American education, even long after they finished their service with the corps. If she were able to recruit high-achieving students, they would probably continue to lend their involvement and financial support after they went on to take over important positions in business and government.

Kopp's advisor considered her plan noble, but unrealistic. Knowing how hard it can be to raise even a few thousand dollars, he suggested starting with just 50 teachers and working in one test location. But Kopp refused to alter her plan: she believed that if she downscaled her operation, it would never really work. Full of enthusiasm, she revised her senior thesis into a working business proposal. In 1989, Kopp graduated from Princeton with her Bachelor of Arts (BA) degree in public policy. She had applied for jobs at several top business firms, but she failed to get any of those positions. So she got to work making her senior thesis a reality.

## CAREER HIGHLIGHTS

Kopp faced significant challenges in implementing her idea. Many people doubted that she would be able to get students to sign on. After all, their pay would be minimal, and they would have to go into some depressed, troubled areas to tackle tough, long-standing problems. "My generation was dubbed the 'Me Generation.' People thought all we wanted to do was focus on ourselves and make a lot of money," Kopp later said. "But that didn't strike me as right. I felt as if thousands of us talented, driven graduating seniors were searching for a way to make a social impact but simply couldn't find the opportunity to do so." She felt if she could make her idea a reality, "it would make a huge difference in kids' lives, and that ultimately it could change the very consciousness of our country, by influencing the thinking and career paths of a generation of leaders."

Kopp wanted to "surround teaching with many of the same factors surrounding investment banking and management consulting: Create an aura of service and status and selectivity. Recruit college students aggressively. Make teaching accessible to people who did not major in education. And make it a two-year commitment, on the theory that the experience will shape their interests and that a lot of them will continue in education."

*Megan Nix helps her students with an in-class
English assignment at a school in New Orleans.*

The teaching recruits wouldn't only be drawn from the ranks of education majors, but from all fields. They would be people who had demonstrated strong leadership qualities. Kopp believed that these energetic people would bring inspiration and new ideas to depressed areas. She hoped that their example would inspire their students to work for positive change in their own lives and in their communities, too.

### Founding Teach for America

Kopp decided to call her teacher corps Teach for America. After writing her business plan, her next job was to raise enough start-up money. She has described herself as shy, but she had learned how to communicate effectively with business leaders during her time with the FCS. The need for funds for Teach for America (TFA) gave her the courage to start phoning every major business and foundation she could think of to solicit funds. She sent her proposal and a request for funding to the chief executive officers of 30 major corporations.

In June 1989, the month that she graduated from Princeton, she received her first response, a letter from the Mobil Corporation offering her $26,000 to help get TFA started. She used that money to travel, meeting with representatives from various school districts and corporations. At the same time, she and her team were recruiting students at many of the best colleges in the country, using such simple methods as sliding flyers about the program under doorways in dormitories.

One year after her graduation, Kopp had the $2.5 million she had envisioned in her plan. In addition to the first donation from Mobil, she had obtained funds from the Chrysler Corporation, the pharmaceutical giant Merck, and other large companies. Union Carbide, another major corporation, had donated the use of office space in New York City. Texas billionaire Ross Perot had agreed to provide matching funds with the first $500,000 Kopp collected. In addition to funding, she had applications from 2,600 undergraduate students who wanted to join the TFA program.

Kopp has said that her lack of experience helped her to achieve her goals. "My very greatest asset in reaching this point was that I simply did not understand what was impossible. I would soon learn the value of experience, but Teach for America would not exist today were it not for my naivete," she remarked. She believed something similar happens with the students and teachers in her program: "I see this same phenomenon every day as I watch 23-year-olds walking into classrooms and setting goals for themselves and their students that most people believe to be entirely unrealistic." Like Kopp, many of those teachers and students go on to meet or exceed their own lofty goals.

——— " ———

*Reflecting on TFA's first year, Kopp said, "There were many times when I wasn't sure I was going to make it. There was a lot of failure and there were many mistakes, just as there were successes."*

——— " ———

## A Strong Start

In fall 1990, after attending their intensive training workshops, the first TFA recruits went into schools in some of the poorest areas in the United States. Their destinations included such urban locations as New Orleans, Houston, Los Angeles, and New York City, as well as rural areas in the South and Southwest. TFA recruits went into public schools, where teachers are required to meet certain standards. These vary by state but virtually all include a college degree in education or a related field plus certification by the state. But TFA recruits came from all fields of study and did not necessarily have any college credits in the field of education. Since the schools in which they taught were already experiencing serious teacher shortages, these schools were allowed to hire substitutes who had no teaching credentials or experience.

In that first year, there were a lot of challenges to meet and lessons to learn. Some studies say that it takes at least two years of classroom experience to become an effective teacher. Kopp and her staff learned firsthand that it was difficult to train people and equip them to go into the classroom in just eight weeks. Added to that difficulty was the fact that many of the students in the schools served by TFA struggled with hunger, drugs, and crime in their daily lives.

Not all educators supported TFA. In fact, recruits sometimes faced resentment from long-term teachers. Some teachers believed these inexperienced newcomers lacked the knowledge and skill to handle a tough classroom. They also worried the TFA recruits came to shake things up, only to leave two years later. Some recruits couldn't handle the cultural differences they faced in the communities where they had been assigned and left their positions, but most of them stuck it out. Many went on to see their students meet and even exceed the goals they had set, dramatically improving their test scores, working many extra hours in the classroom, and becoming strong learners. Reflecting on TFA's first year, Kopp said, "There were many times when I wasn't sure I was going to make it. There was a lot of failure and there were many mistakes, just as there were successes."

## Criticism, Setbacks, and Recovery

By 1992, TFA had 1,200 teachers at work and had raised more than $12 million. But just two years later, the foundation suffered a serious setback. Linda Darling-Hammond, a highly respected professor of education and co-director of the National Center for Restructuring Education, Schools, and Teaching, published a lengthy article titled, "Who Will Speak for the Children? How 'Teach for America' Hurts Urban Schools and Students." Darling-Hammond argued that TFA encouraged an overly simple approach to teaching, created staffing disruptions and morale problems in the schools where the program was allowed, and produced ineffective teachers. She concluded that TFA was bad both for children and for the teaching profession.

Kopp countered those claims by pointing out a report in which more than 90 percent of school principals who had hired TFA teachers said they considered them an asset to their schools, gave them very favorable evaluations, and felt they would definitely hire from TFA again. She also showed that about 60 percent of TFA alumni remain involved with education in some way after their term of service was up, and almost all of them report that working for the foundation gave them a strong sense of social responsibility.

TFA had also been criticized as "elitist" for sending many white teachers into minority neighborhoods, but Kopp argued that TFA had a much higher percentage of minority teachers than the teaching profession as a whole. As for charges that TFA teachers were unfairly bypassing normal requirements for certification, Kopp argued that the schools that hired them were already forced to hire unaccredited individuals as teachers because there were no qualified applicants. TFA's defenders also stressed that Darling-Hammond strongly defended the existing system. But that system included many students who were failing, which demonstrated that there were many ongoing, serious problems that she failed to address.

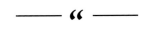

Even though Kopp disputed her critics, some key supporters of TFA chose to withdraw their funding following the publication of Darling-Hammond's article. Faced with having to shut TFA down completely due to lack of money, Kopp personally phoned all her contacts to ask for emergency donations to keep the foundation afloat. She managed to avoid a complete shutdown, but by 1996, she had been forced to slash TFA's budget almost in half in order to survive. She also had to cut 60 jobs from the staff.

*"Your idealism can enable you to pursue noble aims, but it takes hard work and personal growth and a kind of determined patience to see them actually come to be."*

By 2000, things seemed to be looking up. Don Fisher, the founder of the Gap chain of clothing stores, offered TFA an $8.3 million challenge grant that year. If Kopp could raise that much from other sources, he would match the amount. Within four months, TFA had raised $25 million. Furthermore, U.S. President George W. Bush seemed to take a strong interest in TFA. He met with its staff, mentioned it in speeches as an example of an admirable service organization, and designated it as a program that would get special attention from First Lady Laura Bush. Later, however, TFA learned that the promised support from the government had been cut.

### A Leader with Vision

In good times and bad, Kopp has remained a strong leader, willing to work hard to make her ideas become reality. After sleeping just four or five

*Sen. Edward Kennedy giving Kopp the John F. Kennedy
New Frontier Award for her commitment to public service.*

hours a night, she gets up at about 3:00 or 4:00 in the morning, spends a little time on her computer, then goes for a five-mile run. Then she is ready to start her 15-hour workday. Kopp is not known as a "people person," but she is a hard worker and good organizer. She has shown confidence in her own way of doing things. During TFA's low point, some of the staff threatened to quit if she didn't start making her decisions more democratically. She didn't agree to their demands, but no one quit.

In 2001, Kopp published a memoir about her experiences with TFA titled *One Day, All Children...: The Unlikely Triumph of Teach for America and What I Learned Along the Way*. The book was recommended by a reviewer for *Publishers Weekly*: "Kopp has brought a fresh approach to the educational process that has proved effective; her inspiring story will challenge schools and professional educators to take notice, while motivating college seniors and recent graduates to join her team."

Some critics have questioned Kopp's lack of background in education. But she has argued that she is not trying to use TFA as a means to fix all the problems within the American educational system. Instead, she is trying to build up interest in educational issues and to encourage fresh thinking. She has described the foundation as a social-justice organization, not a model for teacher training. "We don't feel that we have the answers at all. The challenge is to remember that there's always a better way. That's the responsibility of the leaders of an organization," she said. As for her own qualifications, she admitted, "I think Teach for America has suffered from the fact that I did not teach, in a major way." But she also said that "I also think if I had taught, I wouldn't have started Teach for America."

Kopp has realized her dream of recruiting talented college students just as well as any investment firm or large corporation. TFA is now one of the largest hirers of college seniors. In 2006, 19,000 college seniors applied to TFA, including a full 10 percent of the graduating class of Yale University. Of those 19,000 applicants, only one in eight will be asked to join the corps. That year, her organization had a budget of $70 million and could claim that it had served 2.5 million students in 1,000 schools, located in 25 different communities. In 2006, the New York City public schools hired 8 percent of their new teachers from TFA, and in Newark, New Jersey, about 30 percent of new teachers were hired from TFA.

Over the years, Kopp has won a variety of awards for her service to TFA, including the 2003 Clinton Center Award for Leadership and National Service from the Democratic Leadership Council, the 2003 Outstanding Social Entrepreneur Award from the Schwab Foundation, and the 2004 John F. Kennedy New Frontier Award from the John F. Kennedy Library Foundation and the Institute of Politics at the Kennedy School of Government, Harvard University. In 2006, Kopp's achievements were recognized with the Austin College Leadership Award. She was chosen over several other contenders, including U2's Bono, television journalist Bill Moyers, and New Mexico governor Bill Richardson. The honor included a $100,000 prize, which she donated directly to TFA.

Looking back on all the roadblocks TFA has had to overcome, Kopp said, "Luckily, I don't worry all that much. . . . I really have this attitude that things will work out. All those little obstacles that people think will stop everything—you can get around anything." She doesn't pretend that success can come merely through positive thinking, however. "Your idealism can enable you to pursue noble aims, but it takes hard work and personal growth and a kind of determined patience to see them actually come to be."

## MARRIAGE AND FAMILY

Wendy Kopp married Richard Barth Jr. in New York City on February 7, 1998. Barth is a former TFA staff member and is the chief executive officer of the Knowledge is Power Program (KIPP), another organization dedicated to improving the quality of America's schools. They live in New York City with their three sons, Benjamin, Francis, and Haddon.

## HOBBIES AND OTHER INTERESTS

In 1997, Kopp also founded the New Teacher Project, an organization that works in a variety of ways to improve teacher quality and to recruit new, high-quality teachers into high-need schools. Rather than drawing from the pool of recent college graduates, the New Teacher Project recruits professionals who are in the middle of their careers. She has remained on the Board of Directors of this organization and is also on the board of the Learning Project, another association that seeks to launch and maintain quality schools for children in high-need areas. She has also served on advisory boards of the Center for Public Leadership at Harvard University's Kennedy School of Government, and the National Council on Teacher Quality.

## WRITINGS

*One Day, All Children...: The Unlikely Triumph of Teach for America and What I Learned along the Way*, 2001

## HONORS AND AWARDS

Citizen Activist Award (Gleitsman Foundation): 1994
Voice of Conscience Award (Aetna Foundation): 1994
Clinton Center Award for Leadership and National Service (Democratic Leadership Council): 2003
Outstanding Social Entrepreneur Award (Schwab Foundation): 2003
John F. Kennedy New Frontier Award (John F. Kennedy Library Foundation and the Institute of Politics at the Kennedy School of Government, Harvard University): 2004
Austin College Leadership Award: 2006

## FURTHER READING

### Books

Kopp, Wendy. *One Day, All Children...: The Unlikely Triumph of Teach for America and What I Learned along the Way*, 2001

## Periodicals

*Christian Science Monitor,* Mar. 20, 2001, p.3
*Current Biography Yearbook,* 2003
*Forbes,* Oct. 14, 1991, p.S22
*Fortune,* Nov. 27, 2006, p.87
*New York Times,* June 20, 1990, p.A1; Jan. 7, 1996, Education Life Supplement, sec.4A, p.26; Nov. 12, 2000, Education Life Supplement, sec.4A, p.23
*People,* May 28, 2001, p.131
*Time,* Aug. 25, 2004, p.23

## Online Articles

http://www.unc.edu
(University of North Carolina at Chapel Hill, transcript of commencement address given by Wendy Kopp, May 14, 2006)

## ADDRESS

Wendy Kopp
Teach for America
315 West 36th Street
7th Floor
New York, NY 10018

## WORLD WIDE WEB SITE

http://www.teachforamerica.com

# Sofia Mulanovich 1983-
Peruvian Surfer
2004 World Champion Female Surfer

### BIRTH

Sofia Mulanovich was born on June 24, 1983, in Lima, Peru. Her father, Herbert Mulanovich Barreda, is a seafood exporter. Her mother, Ines Aljavin de Mulanovich, is a restaurant owner. Sofia is the second of three siblings. Her brother Herbert, Jr., is four years older than Sofia and is a national surfing champion. Matias is three years younger than Sofia and is also pursuing a career in competitive surfing.

### YOUTH

Mulanovich grew up in the small coastal village of Punta Hermosa, located about 30 miles outside Lima, the nation's capital. She describes Peru as "a beautiful country in South America. We have the mountains where it rains a lot and it is super cold. But it is full of really amazing things to see, such as Machu Picchu which is an old temple built by the ancient

Incas. There is another region of Peru which is all jungle and extremely hot all year long and full of native people and mysteries."

Mulanovich is also proud of Peru's rich cultural heritage, including its status as the possible birthplace of the sport of surfing. Pottery that was made in the region more than 1,500 years ago depicts surfers. Some historians believe that this evidence suggests that the sport may have originated in Peru rather than Hawaii, the area that is usually most identified with surfing. Scholars also note that in the mid-20th century, a wealthy Peruvian named Carlos Dogny played an important role in popularizing surfing beyond the Hawaiian Islands. Dogny founded the elite Waikiki Surf Club in Lima in 1942, and another surf club in Biarritz, France, a short time later. Dogny's clubs not only helped make the sport a worldwide one, but also influenced generations of the Mulanovich family. Sofia Mulanovich's grandfather and her father were both members of the prestigious Waikiki Club.

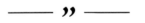

*"I just loved it," Mulanovich said of her early years of surfing. "It was easy for me. [The surf] was right there in front of the house. I open one eye and I see the waves."*

Living on the coast and growing up in a family that was so enthusiastic about surfing, Mulanovich learned how to handle herself in the water at a very early age. She began swimming when she was just three years old. By the age of five she was using a bodyboard—a small foam board that can be ridden on waves while kneeling, lying down, or standing up. By the age of nine, she had graduated to a small surfboard known as a shortboard. The size of these boards makes it hard to catch big waves, but they are considered easier to maneuver than a standard board, so they are ideal for beginners.

When Mulanovich first started surfing, she was informally coached by Roberto Meza, one of Peru's top surfers. Meza took her to a beach called Cerro Azul to get her started. "She tried to stand up but fell the first few times," Meza recalled. "But before the day was over, she stood up and went for a long ride. Not many can do that on their first day."

"I just loved it," Mulanovich said of her early years of surfing. "It was easy for me. [The surf] was right there in front of the house. I open one eye and I see the waves." At the time, Mulanovich was one of few females hitting the waves, but she did not mind that. She routinely tagged along with her older brother and other boys who surfed, building her own skills by watching them and informally competing against them. When she was not out in the ocean riding waves, she spent much of her free time studying surf videos for inspiration and technical insight.

## Ocean Provides Refuge from Violence

Mulanovich's parents encouraged her interest in surfing. They knew their daughter was safer riding the waves with her brothers and her friends than she would have been nearly anywhere else. Peru was a dangerous place in the early 1990s, boiling with political problems and related violence. Kidnappings, bombings, and murders happened nearly every day in Lima and other large cities. "We were really frightened to go anywhere, to the bank, to the malls, the movies and restaurants," remembered Sofia's mother, Ines Mulanovich. "People were killed every day."

Fortunately, Mulanovich's parents had the financial resources to protect their family in ways that poorer families could not. For example, Mulanovich and her brothers attended expensive private schools in Lima rather than the dangerous public schools, and they were transported to and from their home in bulletproof vehicles. "Sofia was very young at that time," recalled Ines Mulanovich, "and fortunately it was not very shocking for her as it was for us adults."

Insulated from the violence swirling around her, Mulanovich was able to focus on her dream of a career in professional surfing. "When I first stood on a surfboard I knew I wanted to be a pro surfer," she remembered. Roberto Meza continued to be one of her mentors, and as her skills developed, she was coached by another Peruvian surfing great, Magoo de la Rosa. Their guidance helped her make a big splash in amateur surfing competitions, which had no separate categories for girls and women. "I actually loved surfing against the boys," she remembered. "They were funny when I beat them."

Even though there were many fine surfers in Peru, however, there was no surf industry to support and sponsor them. "Peru is a really poor country and there is not much support or organization in any sport besides soccer," Mulanovich explained. "We try to improve it, but it is really hard to make things happen when the country's economy is so bad." This knowledge convinced her parents to allow her to go to Guadalupe, Mexico, at age 12 to attend a major Pan American surfing competition. She was there merely to observe and get the feel of high-level competition, but Mulanovich also impressed onlookers with her aggressive, fluid, powerful moves in the water.

## EDUCATION

During her youth in Lima, Mulanovich attended a British-run, private school for girls called the San Silvestre School. "Peru is a poor country, but it is divided into sectors. The lower sector kids go to public schools which have terrible education because they don't have money enough to pay good teachers. The other sector has private schools which are really expensive but they give you an insane education," she explained. Of the San Silvestre School, Mulanovich said that "the worst part was that it was only for girls! It was a nightmare sometimes, but now I am thankful because I had great teachers and I can say that I learned a lot of things."

## CAREER HIGHLIGHTS

Mulanovich's surfing career began in earnest in 1996, when the 13-year-old sensation was recommended for a place on the Peruvian surfing team by Roberto Meza and Magoo de la Rosa. Later that year, she made her debut at the top level of surfing competition at the U.S. Open at Huntington Beach, California. She even faced the reigning women's world champion, Layne Beachley, in one of her first heats. Mulanovich made it all the way to the quarterfinals before being eliminated. (For more information on Beachley, see *Biography Today Sports*, Vol. 9.)

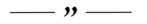

*"I actually loved surfing against the boys,"* Mulanovich remembered. *"They were funny when I beat them."*

One year later, Mulanovich represented her country at the Pan American competition, held in the Caribbean. Geoff Moysa, a member of the United States team at that time, remembered watching the newcomer surf and said, "We were all tripping on this tiny little girl who was just ripping—tons of speed and really aggressive. Everyone knew right away she was the real deal." After competing in the U.S. Open again that year, Mulanovich complained about having to leave the competition in order to get back to school in Lima: "I'm not looking forward to that," she said. "I want to stay and surf. It's so cool here."

### Teen Surf Star

In 1998 Mulanovich won the Pan American championship in Brazil at the stunningly young age of 15. Her growing stardom received another boost after the release of a surf documentary called *Blue Crush*. The film, produced by Bill Ballard (not to be confused with the 2002 Hollywood surf movie *Blue Crush*), was a showcase for talented female surfers, including Mulanovich, Keala Kennelly, Kate Skarratt, Rochelle Ballard, and Sanoe Lake. *Blue Crush* eventually became one of the best-selling surf documentaries of all time. It was featured in five film festivals and sold in more than 45 countries. Although Mulanovich was only a teenager, her power and style were evident in the film.

Analyzing her own style, Mulanovich notes that she is what surfers call a "regular footer," meaning she rides with her left foot forward (someone who rides with their right food forward is known as a "goofy foot"). "My body is what makes me a good surfer," she adds. "Being short . . . I have a low center of gravity, which helps me drive power through my legs and initiate turns faster. Feeling my legs and abs tightening and the board turning in response—that's the best feeling for sure, because it reminds me how strong I am. I've watched my body become more powerful as I've surfed; it's adapted to what I have to do. As an athlete, I use my body to express myself. Without surfing, I wouldn't be me!"

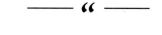

*"My body is what makes me a good surfer," said Mulanovich. "I've watched my body become more powerful as I've surfed; it's adapted to what I have to do. As an athlete, I use my body to express myself. Without surfing, I wouldn't be me!"*

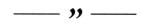

Mulanovich acknowledges, though, that despite her fast and powerful surfing style, the greater body strength of men naturally allows them to achieve more in surfing than most women can hope to do. "I love watching the boys surf but we will never be as good as them. . . . Men are men and women are women and the boys are always going to surf better and that's a fact."

### Surfing on the World Championship Tour

Mulanovich ranked as Peru's female national surfing champion from 1999 to 2002. During this time, she was increasingly treated as a national hero, someone that Peruvians could feel good about after so many years of trouble and violence in their country. Her success also brought her a wave of new endorsement deals. In 2001, for example, she reached a deal with Roxy, the womenswear division of sportswear manufacturer Quiksilver.

*Mulanovich at the World Championship Tour
Roxy Pro competition in Hawaii, 2001.*

This endorsement deal gave her the funding she needed to enter the World Qualifying Series (WQS) for the first time.

The WQS is the doorway to the World Championship Tour (WCT), the highest level of surfing competition, sanctioned by the Association of Surfing Professionals (ASP). In the WCT, the 18 top surfers travel around the world for 10 months of the year, living and surfing together and competing against one another for the world championship. In her first year in the WQS competition, Mulanovich finished second overall and missed qualifying for the WCT by only one position.

In 2002 Mulanovich remained with the WQS but took advantage of several opportunities to compete in wildcard slots in WCT events. The first was the World Championship Tour Roxy Pro competition on Australia's Gold Coast. She had won the chance to surf there by defeating 15 rivals at a trial competition. According to one writer for the *Gold Coast Bulletin*, Mulanovich performed at the trials "with a style and savagery rarely seen in women's surfing." Mulanovich also won two other wildcard spots in WCT events that year. She then closed out the 2002 season with a third-place finish at the WQS Turtle Bay Resort Women's Pro event in Hawaii. This performance, combined with her record for the rest of the season, qualified her to surf as a regular with the WCT in 2003.

## Hungry and Humble

By 2003 Mulanovich was well-known to even the top competitors of the world surfing community. Surfing legend Layne Beachley, for example, commented that she was "typical of the young guns around the tour now. Most of them have the power to pull off men's moves. They also have nothing to lose and are unpredictable, which can make them more daunting to surf against than the seasoned competitors."

Other members of the tour described Mulanovich as a humble, kind person as well as an incredibly talented athlete. "Sofia is always looking for ways not to stand out," said Megan Abubo of Hawaii. "If she wins a contest, she just wants to be part of the gang and hang with her friends. She is so cool. She never makes you feel bad if she wins and you lose, and she never says anything bad about anyone." Mulanovich became particularly close friends with Chelsea Georgeson, a surfer from Australia's Gold Coast who is the same age.

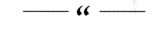

*"Traveling with friends, surfing contests, and surfing good waves is great. I'm having the times of my life right now," Mulanovich said. "Traveling has its ups and downs but everything is like that, so I have to always keep positive and never lose focus."*

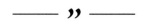

Mulanovich surfed well in 2003, her rookie season on the WCT tour. She turned in her best performance at the November Roxy Pro in Hawaii, the first of three contests in the so-called women's triple crown of surfing. She was the first Peruvian ever to win this prestigious event. On her first wave she scored a 7.0 out of a possible 10, turning five times on a left-handed wave. Next, she earned a score of 8.0 for performing three top-to-bottom carves on a four-foot wave. "She was killing it," said competitor Melanie Bartels, who placed second that day. "I would watch her when I was sitting out there and she was throwing big chunks [of water]. Real impressive."

The 2003 season was a dream come true for Mulanovich. "Traveling with friends, surfing contests, and surfing good waves is great. I'm having the times of my life right now," she said. "Traveling has its ups and downs but everything is like that, so I have to always keep positive and never lose focus. I have felt lonely many times because in a way I am different from everybody else on tour; different language, culture, and sometimes beliefs. Yet in many ways, we are all the same; we love surfing and we have the

*Mulanovich at the World Championship Tour*
*Roxy Pro competition in Australia, 2002.*

same dreams and ambitions. It is hard to be far away from family and my country but I love what I am doing and I am conquering new experiences and feel good about life."

## World Champion

In 2004, at the age of 21, Mulanovich realized her lifelong dream. She took the gold at the 2004 World Surfing Games in Salinas, Ecuador, won the Fiji Roxy Pro in April, and racked up more wins at events in Tahiti, France, and the United States. By the end of the tour, she had triumphed over Layne Beachley, who had held the world champion title for six consecutive years. Mulanovich was crowned the 2004 World Champion female surfer, the first ever to come from Latin America.

Not surprisingly, Mulanovich's victory boosted her celebrity status in her native Peru to even greater heights. Billboards around the country displayed pictures of the star surfer, huge crowds greeted her when she made public appearances, and a monument was erected in front of the National Stadium to honor her. Yet despite the adoration from her fellow Peruvians, Mulanovich remained as humble and unpretentious as ever. "Sofia's popularity is due not only to her success as a world champion, but to her simplicity, naturalness and modesty that she always carries with her," declared her press agent, Hans Firbas. "She is one of us, and the people admire her for it."

In 2005 Mulanovich faced a new challenge—defending her world championship. Her keenest competition came from her best friend, Chelsea Georgeson. The rivalry between the two was intense throughout the 2005 season, with each winning key victories. In the end, Georgeson triumphed over Mulanovich by a narrow margin, taking the world championship from her friend. Mulanovich was unable to reclaim the championship crown in 2006, but she did win the U.S. Open at Huntington Beach for the first time in her career.

Mulanovich remains one of the world's top surfers, and she is confident that she can reclaim her former spot at the top of her sport. She has said that her future plans are to "keep surfing, try to improve myself as a surfer and a human and just enjoy the ride." She reflected that achieving those goals also requires a commitment to taking good care of herself: "I never forget that I have a goal in life and whatever I do I have to make sure it is not ruining my mind nor my body because I will need both in order to follow my path."

———— **"** ————

*"Sofia is always looking for ways not to stand out,"* said fellow surfer Megan Abubo. *"If she wins a contest, she just wants to be part of the gang and hang with her friends. She is so cool. She never makes you feel bad if she wins and you lose, and she never says anything bad about anyone."*

———— **"** ————

In 2006 Mulanovich's career became the subject of an award-winning documentary film titled *Sofia: A Documentary.* It explores the background of terrorism and political violence in Peru, chronicles her rise to surf star, and looks at her influence on the surfing industry and on Peru in general. Mulanovich has also been featured in the surf documentaries *Peel: The Peru Project, Shimmer, Modus Mix,* and *MUVI 2,* which was made by Mulanovich herself.

## HOME AND FAMILY LIFE

Mulanovich is single and travels with the WCT for 10 months of the year, but has her own condominium at Punta Hermosa in Peru, a short distance from her family's home. She remains close to her parents and her brothers.

*Mulanovich at the World Championship Tour*
*Roxy Pro competition in Hawaii, 2006.*

## HOBBIES AND OTHER INTERESTS

Mulanovich is a big music fan who counts Bob Marley, UB40, The Doors, and Carlos Vives as particular favorites. She also enjoys surf videos and documentaries so much that she has begun to explore film-making herself. Other interests include backgammon, jogging, dancing, and playing tennis. "It is really good to keep your mind and body active all the time," she explained. "I also watch what I eat because I want to be loose on my board and super fast. I like salads and fish and I hate junk food."

## SELECTED HONORS AND AWARDS

ASP Rookie of the Year (Association of Surfing Professionals): 2003
*Surfer* Magazine Video Award for Best Wipeout: 2003
WCT Champion Female Surfer (World Championship Tour): 2004
ESPY Award for Best Female Action Sports Athlete (ESPN): 2005
Teen Choice Awards: 2006, Choice Action Sports-Female

## FURTHER READING

### Books

*Current Biography International Yearbook*, 2004

## Periodicals

*Los Angeles Times,* Aug. 5, 1997, p.C8; Feb. 28, 2005, p. D1; Oct.7, 2005, p. D11
*Miami Herald,* Nov. 1, 2004, p.A13
*Teen People,* Mar. 1, 2006, p.110

## Online Articles

http://www.surflifeforwomen.com/
    (*Surf Life,* "Pro-File, Sofia Mulanovich," 2003)
http://www.transworldsurf.com/surf/
    (*SURF Magazine,* "Girls Gone Wild: Sofia Mulanovich," Sep. 23, 2004)

## ADDRESS

Sofia Mulanovich
Mosaic Sports Management
2033 San Elijo Avenue, # 102
Cardiff-by-the-Sea, CA 92007

## WORLD WIDE WEB SITES

http://sofiamulanovich.com
http://www.aspworldtour.com

# Barack Obama 1961-

American Political Leader
U.S. Senator from Illinois

## BIRTH

Barack Obama, known in childhood as Barry, was born on
August 4, 1961, in Honolulu, Hawaii. His mother was Stanley
Ann Dunham, a teacher and anthropologist. She was given
her unusual first name by her father, who had hoped for a
son; she eventually dropped the name Stanley and was
known simply as Ann. Obama is named after his father,
Barack Obama Sr., who was a Kenyan government official.
Obama has eight half-siblings, including one half-sister from

his mother's second marriage and seven half-brothers and half-sisters from his father's first and third marriages.

## YOUTH

Obama's father came to the United States on an education scholarship from a small village in Kenya, a country located on the eastern coast of Africa. The Kenyan government sponsored Obama Sr.'s college education in America in exchange for a promise that he return to Kenya and work for the government after completing his studies. Obama Sr. left his Kenyan wife and children behind and traveled to Hawaii in 1958, where he became the first African to attend the University of Hawaii in Honolulu. It was there that he met Obama's mother, Ann Dunham.

———— " ————

*"It was women," Obama wrote, "who provided the ballast in my life—my grandmother, whose dogged practicality kept the family afloat, and my mother, whose love and clarity of spirit kept my sister's and my world centered."*

———— " ————

Despite their different backgrounds, Obama Sr. and Dunham quickly fell in love and decided to marry. Marriage between a white woman and a black man, however, was not socially accepted in the late 1950s—an era in which many white Americans openly embraced racial segregation and bigoted views. In fact, marriage between people of different races was a felony crime in many states; some state laws called for extended jail sentences or even death for people convicted of such an offense. These feelings and discriminatory laws were especially common in the Deep South, but they existed throughout the country.

Hawaii, though, was different. Its society was made up of people from many different races, including native Hawaiians, Asians, Filipinos, Portuguese, African-Americans, and whites. People living in Hawaii were generally more accepting of racial differences than residents of other parts of the United States. This environment made it easier for Obama's parents to marry.

When Obama was born, the new family lived together with Ann's parents, Stanley and Madelyn Dunham, in a small apartment near the university. Obama's grandparents often cared for him while his parents attended classes. In 1963, when he was two years old, his father left Hawaii to continue his studies at Harvard University in Cambridge, Massachusetts. Obama and his mother stayed in Hawaii because the scholarship provided to Obama Sr. did not include enough money to support the whole family. They divorced a short time later. Obama's father then returned to Kenya and took a government position, fulfilling his obligation to the Kenyan government that had paid for his education.

Obama thus grew up without his father. He notes that as he grew older, his mother remained in regular contact with his father, and older men such as a stepfather and his maternal grandfather gave him guidance and affection. But as he wrote in *The Audacity of Hope*, "it was women . . . who provided the ballast in my life—my grandmother, whose dogged practicality kept the family afloat, and my mother, whose love and clarity of spirit kept my sister's and my world centered."

## From Hawaii to Indonesia

Obama spent his early childhood in a Hawaiian paradise, exploring beautiful beaches, learning to swim and body surf in the ocean, and going on excursions with his grandfather. He was exposed to all different cultures during visits with his grandfather's friends. He learned to enjoy traditional Hawaiian poi (a sticky grayish-purple pudding made from pounded taro, a root plant related to the potato), sashimi (thinly sliced raw fish), and rice candy with edible wrappers. His mother and grandparents often told stories about his father so that Obama would know about him.

When Obama was six years old, his life changed dramatically. His mother married an Indonesian man named Lolo, another foreign student whom she met at the University of Hawaii. In 1967 Obama and his mother moved to Jakarta, Indonesia, an island nation in Southeast Asia. Trading Honolulu city life and the ocean for an open-walled house on the edge of the jungle, Obama soon adapted to his new life. He had a large ape named

> "It left a very strong mark on me living [in Jakarta] because you got a real sense of just how poor folks can get," Obama recalled. "You'd have some army general with 24 cars and if he drove one once then eight servants would come around and wash it right away. But on the next block, you'd have children with distended bellies who just couldn't eat."

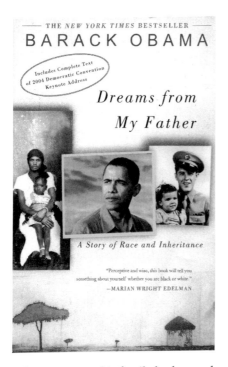

Obama recounts his family background
and his early life in his memoir,
Dreams from My Father.

Tata for a pet, along with a big yellow dog. The household also included large colorful tropical birds, including a white cockatoo and two birds of paradise, chickens and ducks that wandered freely outside the house, and two baby crocodiles that lived in a pond in a corner of the yard.

Lolo taught Obama how to box, and the youngster learned to eat native foods like raw green chili peppers, dog meat, snake meat, and roasted grasshopper, which Obama later remembered only as "crunchy." Obama slept under a mosquito net, falling asleep to the sounds of the jungle each night. In his autobiography *Dreams from My Father*, he described these years as "one long adventure, the bounty of a young boy's life."

During his years in Jakarta, however, Obama also became aware of poverty and human despair for the first time. Most Indonesians in the area were farmers who were at the mercy of the weather, which was notoriously severe and unpredictable in that part of the world. Sometimes it rained so much that crops were washed away in rivers of mud, while other times drought conditions would turn the fields as hard as stone. Many people struggled just to survive from day to day, and beggars frequently came to his house asking for help, food, or money. "It left a very strong mark on me living there because you got a real sense of just how poor folks can get," Obama recalled. "You'd have some army general with 24 cars and if he drove one once then eight servants would come around and wash it right away. But on the next block, you'd have children with distended bellies who just couldn't eat."

Obama also had his first realizations about race and racial differences in Jakarta. When he was about seven years old, he was waiting at his mother's office for her to get out of a meeting. Idly paging through a magazine, he found a story about African-American people who had tried to bleach their skin in order to appear white. The results of the bleaching procedure were terrible, and the photos showed strange-looking people who seemed very sad. Obama recalled feeling angry and confused by the pictures. "I remember that was the first time when I thought about race not in terms of me being darker than somebody else, but in terms of thinking, 'You know, there's something about race that's not a good thing.' I didn't think of it in terms of being about my own race necessarily, but it struck me that there was this sickness out there that would cause somebody to feel they had to bleach their skin."

Up until that point, Obama had not thought much about race, or the idea that he might be different somehow from his mother and grandparents. The magazine pictures disturbed him so deeply that he felt unable to talk to anyone about how he felt. It would be many years before he was able to make any sense of the swirl of emotions he felt on that day.

### Returning to Hawaii

Many Americans living in Jakarta were business executives or government officials. Most of them enrolled their children in an international school in the city. Obama, though, attended a school with mostly Indonesian students. His mother supplemented his education with lessons at home. She woke Obama at four o'clock each morning for several hours of study before school.

When Obama was ten years old, his mother decided that she could better prepare him for the future by enrolling him in a school back in the United States. She thus sent him back to Hawaii to live with his grandparents while she remained in Jakarta. In 1971 he enrolled in Punahou Academy, a prestigious school that began with fifth grade and continued through high school.

Obama recalled his early days at Punahou as "a ten-year-old's nightmare." Because life in Hawaii was so drastically different from the village in Jakarta, Obama was unprepared for traditional schooling. His clothes were old-fashioned and dowdy, he did not know how to play football or ride a skateboard like the other kids, and none of them knew how to play soccer, badminton, or chess. He was also one of only a few African-American students in the whole school, and he began to be painfully conscious of his race. Other students teased him about his name, his hair, and his African heritage.

Desperate to defend himself from this harassment, Obama made up stories about his background to impress the other kids. He claimed that his father was an African prince and the chief of his tribe, and that he himself would one day become the chief when the time was right. These tales, combined with Obama's winning smile and charisma, brought an end to the teasing. By the time he entered high school, he was actually one of the more popular students in his class.

Obama's first year back in Hawaii was also highlighted by a month-long visit from his father. He found his father to be both intimidating and fascinating. He was especially interested in his father's descriptions of his own childhood and of African culture in general. The month passed quickly, and Obama's father then returned to Kenya. The two never saw each other again.

———— " ————

*"I learned to slip back and forth between my black and white worlds," Obama said. "Sometimes I lashed out at white people and sometimes I lashed out at black people. I knew there had to be a different way for me to understand myself as a black man and yet not reject the love and values given to me by my mother and her parents."*

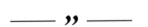

### Searching for Identity

By the time that Obama entered high school at Punahou, his mother had separated from Lolo. She returned to Honolulu and began studying for a master's degree in anthropology. Obama left his grandparents' apartment and went to live nearby with his mother and his half-sister Maya. He joined the high school basketball team, made fairly good grades, and took part-time jobs to make extra money.

During this time, though, Obama struggled privately with issues of race and his own biracial background. He loved the white family members that surrounded him at home, and he established strong friendships with a few African-American friends at school, but Obama felt like an outsider in both communities. Many fellow African-American students at the school believed that all whites were racist, and when he challenged these claims he was ridiculed. Although he had always enjoyed support and love from his family, Obama stopped telling people that his mother was white.

As a teenage boy trying to find his place in the world, Obama says that he "learned to slip back and forth between my black and white worlds. . . . Sometimes I lashed out at white people and sometimes I lashed out at

*Obama with his paternal grandmother in Kenya.*

black people. I knew there had to be a different way for me to understand myself as a black man and yet not reject the love and values given to me by my mother and her parents. I had to reconcile that I could be proud of my African-American heritage and yet not be limited by it."

During this time, Obama began to read works by such African-American authors as James Baldwin, Toni Morrison, Malcolm X, Ralph Ellison, Langston Hughes, W.E.B. DuBois, and Richard Wright. He gained some understanding of race relations and self-identity from studying these writers, but still felt caught in the middle of two opposing communities. By the late 1970s, though, he reached a greater level of comfort with his heritage. During this time, Obama realized that no matter what his racial background was, he would always be seen as African American. "If I was an armed robber and they flashed my face on television, they'd have no problem labeling me as a black man," he said. "So if that's my identity when something bad happens, then that's my identity when something good happens as well."

Eventually much of Obama's frustration, confusion, and self-doubt subsided, although he still felt like an outsider among other African Americans.

## EDUCATION

Obama's first few years of schooling were at a public school in Jakarta, but at age 10 he was sent to Hawaii so that he could receive his education in an American school. He attended Punahou Academy in Honolulu and earned his high school diploma in 1979. Later that same year, Obama enrolled in Occidental College in Los Angeles, California, where he studied international law, economics, and social issues.

At Occidental, Obama became part of a larger African-American community for the first time. He was active in the Black Students Association, and spent many hours discussing philosophy and literature with his friends. Around this time he stopped telling people his name was Barry, and began using Barack, his full name.

## Becoming a Political Activist

Obama also participated in student demonstrations and rallies on a variety of issues during his time on the Occidental campus. He worked particularly hard on the issue of apartheid in South Africa, a country located at the southernmost tip of the continent of Africa. Apartheid, meaning "apartness" in the South African Afrikaans language, was a social and political policy of racial segregation and discrimination that was enforced by white minority governments in South Africa from 1948 to 1994. During the 1980s, the South African government came under tremendous pressure to end apartheid. This unrelenting pressure from student activists, human rights organizations, and governments around the world forced South Africa to officially abolish apartheid in 1994.

Obama's political activism on the apartheid issue sparked his interest in tackling problems in American society as well. He soon discovered that he was a gifted speaker in his own right and that people listened attentively whenever he spoke at a rally or demonstration. "I noticed that people had begun to listen to my opinions," he recalled in *Dreams from My Father.* "It was a discovery that made me hungry for words. Not words to hide behind but words that could carry a message, support an idea."

## Living in New York City

In 1981 Obama took advantage of a college transfer program and enrolled at Columbia University in New York City. He wanted to experience life in what he considered to be a "true city, with black neighborhoods in close proximity." Obama spent all his free time walking the city streets, exploring and observing the exciting world around him. "Manhattan was humming, new developments cropping up everywhere," he recalled. "The beauty, the filth, the noise, and the excess, all of it dazzled my senses; there seemed no constraints on originality of lifestyles." But although Obama enjoyed New York, his studies at Columbia were marred in 1982 by the news that his birth father had died in an automobile accident in Kenya.

Obama graduated from Columbia University in 1983, earning a bachelor's degree in political science. After graduating from college, Obama wanted to work as a community organizer with a nonprofit organization or an African-American elected official. This desire was driven by his belief that the best way to address social problems was to work with local communities. When no one replied to his inquiries, though, he decided to take a more conventional job while he continued his search for the right community work. He worked as a research assistant and financial writer in New York for a consulting firm that served multinational corporations. But when he became concerned that he was drifting away from his dream of community work, Obama quit his job and took a series of positions with various political campaigns in New York and surrounding areas.

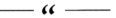

"I noticed that people had begun to listen to my opinions," Obama recalled. "It was a discovery that made me hungry for words. Not words to hide behind but words that could carry a message, support an idea."

Most of these jobs were volunteer positions, or paid very little money. Obama paid for his living expenses out of the money he had saved. By 1985 his savings were almost gone and he was reluctantly considering a return to the corporate world. At that time, though, he was offered a job with an organization in Chicago. He accepted the position, which set him on a new and exciting path in his life.

## Moving to Chicago

As a community organizer for Chicago's Developing Communities Project, Obama worked with some of the poorest neighborhoods on the south side of Chicago. "I took a chance and it paid off," he said. "It was probably the best education I've ever had." He led a coalition of ministers and volunteers who pushed for improved living conditions in neighborhoods that were plagued by crime and high unemployment. He also helped to form a tenants' rights group in some of Chicago's poorest housing projects, and he established a job training program to help unemployed people in the area.

Obama then decided that studying the law would help him understand how to implement social change on a larger scale. He wanted to learn about "power's currency," things like economics, legislation, business and financial regulations, and real estate. Believing that deep knowledge of these topics would help him to be more effective at helping others, Obama left Chicago to attend Harvard Law School in Cambridge, Massachusetts. Besides being one of the most prestigious universities in the country, it was also the school that his father had attended many years earlier.

> "One of the luxuries of going to Harvard Law School is it means you can take risks in your life," Obama said. "You can try to do things to improve society and still land on your feet. That's what a Harvard education should buy—enough confidence and security to pursue your dreams and give something back."

Before starting classes at Harvard, though, Obama made his first journey to Kenya, where he met his extended family from his father's side for the first time. As he traveled from Nairobi to the surrounding villages, Obama learned more about his father and his African heritage. This trip allowed Obama to explore a side of himself from which he had always felt disconnected. He was also able to resolve the feelings of abandonment that had been with him since he was a young boy. Being welcomed into his father's family gave Obama the sense of belonging that he had been looking for his whole life.

## Making Waves at Harvard

Obama entered Harvard in 1988. At the end of his first year there, he won a place on the *Harvard Law Review*, a legal journal run entirely by students. The *Harvard Law Review* is considered to be the most prestigious of all law reviews in the country, and election to its staff is the highest honor for law students. Obama was one of 80 student editors who prepared articles for

*Obama as a law student at Harvard in 1990,*
*shortly after being elected president of Harvard Law Review.*

the monthly journal. After only one year on the staff, Obama was elected by all the other editors as president of the *Review* in 1990. He was the first African American to receive this honor in the 120-year history of the *Harvard Law Review*.

The presidency of the *Harvard Law Review* assured that Obama would have his choice of high-profile jobs after graduation. Many law review presidents go on to highly sought-after clerkships with the U.S. Supreme Court, or else they can choose from multiple offers to work at law firms across the country. Obama chose neither of these options. After graduation, he planned to work for a corporate law firm for a short time, return to community work, and then explore a life in politics. "One of the luxuries of going to Harvard Law School is it means you can take risks in your life," Obama said. "You can try to do things to improve society and still land on your feet. That's what a Harvard education should buy—enough confidence and security to pursue your dreams and give something back."

Many of the students and faculty members at Harvard had no doubt that Obama would be successful in politics. Professor Laurence Tribe, one of the country's best-known attorneys, taught Obama constitutional law and chose him as a research assistant. He was dazzled by Obama's potential.

*Obama filing petitions with the State Board of Elections to get on the ballot for the race for a seat in the U.S. Senate.*

"I've known senators, presidents," he told *Time* magazine. "I've never known anyone with what seems to me more raw political talent."

The summer before he graduated, Obama returned to Chicago to work as a clerk in a large law firm. Although he came to dislike the corporate environment of the firm, he realized during that summer that Chicago was his home. He decided to return to Chicago after completing his law degree. Obama graduated from Harvard Law School in 1991 with highest honors.

## CAREER HIGHLIGHTS

Obama's first work in Chicago after graduating was as a lawyer specializing in civil rights. In 1992 he directed Illinois Project Vote, which registered 150,000 new voters. One year later, he began teaching constitutional law at the University of Chicago. In his spare time, Obama began writing his autobiography. He recognized that he was really only just beginning his career and rather young to be writing his life story, but he felt that he had some valuable things to say. "By writing about my mistakes, I was trying to show how I was vulnerable to the same pitfalls as American youth everywhere." *Dreams from My Father* was published in 1995.

## Entering Politics

In 1996 Obama ran for a seat in the Illinois state legislature as a member of the Democratic Party and won the election. Four years later, his bid for a seat in the U.S. House of Representatives was turned back in the primary election by Democratic incumbent Bobby Rush. But this defeat did not deter Obama. Instead, he returned to Illinois state government and compiled an impressive record of legislative success. In 2003, for example, he successfully pushed for a new Illinois state law that required law enforcement agencies to make recordings of police interrogations and confessions in homicide cases. Overall, Obama ushered 26 bills through the Illinois state legislature, including a large tax credit for the working poor and expanded health care benefits for uninsured children and adults. He also cosponsored legislation to prevent racial profiling by requiring all Illinois police departments to report the race of every person stopped for questioning for any reason.

In 2004 Obama launched a campaign for the Democratic nomination for an open seat in the U.S. Senate representing Illinois. Obama secured the nomination, partly because of his charisma and thoughtful analysis of the issues, and partly because of damaging revelations about the personal life of his leading opponent. After his victory in the primary election, Obama said, "I think it is fair to say the conventional wisdom was we could not win. We didn't have enough money. We didn't have enough organization. There was no way that a skinny guy from the South Side with a funny name like Barack Obama could ever win a statewide race. Sixteen months later we are there."

> ————— **"** —————
>
> *"There's not a liberal America and a conservative America, there is the United States of America," Obama declared in his famous 2004 Democratic Convention address. "There's not a black American and a white America and Latino America and Asian America, there is the United States of America."*
>
> ————— **"** —————

But winning the primary meant that Obama's work was only just beginning. He still had to run a successful campaign against Republican candidate Jack Ryan to win the Senate seat. In a remarkable turn of events, though, Ryan was forced to withdraw from the race due to a public scandal. It took the Republican Party nearly four months of valuable campaign

291

time to find a replacement candidate. During this time, meanwhile, Obama connected with Illinois voters who were inspired by his hopeful and patriotic campaign themes.

## Speaking at the Democratic National Convention

By the summer of 2004, Obama's soaring popularity had caught the attention of national Democratic leaders. Eager to showcase the exciting young politician, they asked him to give the keynote address at the 2004 Democratic National Convention in Boston, Massachusetts. The keynote speech is an honor usually reserved for the most respected and seasoned politicians, so it was highly unusual to select a state legislator who had not yet been elected to Congress for the role. Undaunted by any of this, Obama accepted the invitation and wrote his speech during two nights in hotel rooms while he was traveling for his own campaign. The eloquent speech he delivered at the convention has been called one of the greatest convention speeches of all time.

> "People may look different, talk different, and live in different places, but they've got some core values that they all care about and they all believe in," Obama declared. "If you can speak to those values, people will respond—even if you have a funny name."

Obama's address was both humble and inspiring. It praised America as truly a land of opportunity, declaring that "I stand here knowing that my story is part of the larger American story, that I owe a debt to all those who came before me, and that, in no other country on earth, is my story even possible." But he observed that America would never achieve its fullest potential if it was unable to overcome the distrust and prejudices that divide many Americans. "There's not a liberal America and a conservative America, there is the United States of America. There's not a black America and a white America and Latino America and Asian America, there is the United States of America. . . . Go to any inner city neighborhood, and folks will tell you that government alone can't teach our kids to learn—they know that parents have to teach, that children can't achieve unless we raise their expectation and turn off the television sets and eradicate the slander that says a black youth with a book is acting white."

Obama put into words what many people had been thinking and feeling, and his remarks resonated with the convention crowd and television view-

*Obama giving the keynote speech at the 2004 Democratic National Convention.*

ers alike. By the next morning, he had become an instant celebrity, the political equivalent of a rock star. Requests for interviews, talk show appearances, and speaking engagements flooded into his office. Reflecting on his
newfound fame, Obama acknowledged that "the news coverage was very
flattering. But the best sign came when we were walking down the street
in Boston and the hotel doormen and the cops and the bus drivers were
saying, 'Good speech.' It's when you know you've gone beyond the political insiders. . . . I didn't realize then that the speech would strike the chord
that it did. I think part of it is that people are hungry for a sense of authenticity. All I was really trying to do was describe what I was hearing on the
campaign trail, the stories of the hopes, fears, and struggles of what ordinary people are going through every day."

Obama went on to win the election with an amazing 70 percent of the
vote, the widest victory margin for a U.S. Senate seat in Illinois history. He
won a majority of votes from virtually every key demographic group. He
even won a significant number of votes from Republicans. "I debunked
this notion that whites won't vote for blacks," he said. "Or suburbanites
won't vote for city people. . . . People may look different, talk different, and
live in different places, but they've got some core values that they all care
about and they all believe in. If you can speak to those values, people will
respond—even if you have a funny name."

*Sen. Obama testifies alongside Sen. John McCain
during a 2006 meeting of the Senate Homeland Security Committee.*

### Becoming a U.S. Senator

With his election triumph, Obama became the only African American serving in the U.S. Senate, the third in the last 100 years, and the fifth ever in the history of the U.S. Congress. The national media referred to these facts repeatedly, but Obama was careful to note that the people of Illinois had elected a senator, not a celebrity. "Given all the hype surrounding my election, I hope people have gotten a sense that I am here to do work and not just chase cameras," he said.

As Obama settled into his new role as a U.S. senator, he set ambitious goals for himself. "I want to make real the American ideal that every child in this country has a shot at life. Right now that's not true.... So many kids have the odds stacked so high against them. The odds don't have to be that high. ... There are things we can afford to do that will make a difference." He also restated his intentions to try to tear down walls of distrust and animosity between ethnic, religious, and social groups in America. "I'm well situated to help the country understand how we can both celebrate our diversity in all its complexity and still affirm our common bonds," he said. "We have to build a society on the belief that you are more like me than different from me. That you know your fears, your hopes, your love for your child are the same as what I feel. Maybe I can help with that because I've got so many different pieces in me."

Obama's popularity extended to Kenya, where he is welcomed as a native son. When he visited Kenya in 2006 as part of a tour of several African countries, he was greeted by crowds everywhere he went. Thousands of people lined the streets to watch his motorcade pass by. Across Kenya, schools, roads, and even babies have been named after him. Obama took maximum advantage of his celebrity status. For example, he repeatedly spoke out on the issue of AIDS, which has devastated many Kenyan communities and families. At one point he even went to a public clinic and submitted to an AIDS test himself as a way of raising public awareness and encouraging Kenyans to be tested for the AIDS virus.

### The Audacity of Hope

In 2006 Obama published his second book, *The Audacity of Hope: Thoughts on Reclaiming the American Dream.* His purpose in writing this work, he explained, was to help Americans reclaim a sense of pride, duty, solidarity, and shared sacrifice—things that he worries are being lost in a sea of political ruthlessness, economic uncertainty, and fears about the future. "I offer no unifying theory of American government," he wrote. "Instead what I offer is something more modest: personal reflections on those values and ideals that have led me to public life, some thoughts on the ways that our current political discourse unnecessarily divides us, and my own best assessment—based on my experience as a senator and lawyer, husband and father, Christian and skeptic—of the ways we can ground our politics in the notion of a common good."

Obama's hopeful and encouraging message resonated with American readers, who quickly pushed the book to the top of bestseller lists around the country. It also was warmly received by many reviewers.

### Running for President of the United States

In his first years as a senator, Obama's talents as a powerful speaker remained in high demand. He spent a significant amount of time campaigning for other Democratic candidates who were running for various offices, and he made appearances all over the country whenever his schedule permitted. Obama saw these opportunities as another way that he could work to create unity and bring about change. "I feel confident that if you put me in a room with anybody-black, white, Hispanic, Republican, Democrat— give me half an hour and I will walk out with the votes of most of the folks.

. . . I don't feel constrained by race, geography, or background in terms of making a connection with people."

After Obama was elected to the U.S. Senate, his future became the subject of much public commentary and discussion. Although he had spent relatively few years in national politics, many political analysts predicted that he could become the first African-American U.S. President. They pointed to his popularity and his unique ability to gain support from all kinds of people as evidence that he might one day occupy the White House.

In February 2007, Obama announced that he was running for president of the United States. He made the announcement in Springfield, Illinois, where he had served in the Illinois state legislature. He exhorted those in attendance—his campaign supporters—with these words:

"This campaign can't only be about me. It must be about us—it must be about what we can do together. This campaign must be the occasion, the vehicle, of your hopes, and your dreams. It will take your time, your energy, and your advice—to push us forward when we're doing right, and to let us know when we're not. This campaign has to be about reclaiming the meaning of citizenship, restoring our sense of common purpose, and realizing that few obstacles can withstand the power of millions of voices calling for change. . . . If you feel destiny calling, and see as I see, a future of endless possibility stretching before us; if you sense, as I sense, that the time is now to shake off our slumber, and slough off our fear, and make good on the debt we owe past and future generations, then I'm ready to take up the cause, and march with you, and work with you. Together, starting today, let us finish the work that needs to be done, and usher in a new birth of freedom on this Earth."

In his campaign appearances, Obama has identified several major areas of concern and has spoken frequently on these issues: planning the end of the war in Iraq; strengthening the U.S. overseas; developing a health care system that works; creating a comprehensive energy policy; cleaning up the environment; addressing issues that affect senior citizens; improving schools; tackling immigration issues and border security; addressing voting rights issues and election reform; and many others.

In his bid for the Democratic nomination for the presidency, Obama faces some formidable challengers. The other Democratic candidates include U.S. Senators Joseph Biden, Hillary Clinton, and Christopher Dodd; former U.S. Senator John Edwards; U.S. Representative Dennis Kucinich; and New Mexico Governor Bill Richardson. In late 2007, Hillary Clinton appeared to be the frontrunner among the Democrats, with Obama a close second. But

a run for the presidency is a long campaign, often with surprises along the way, and the outcome won't be clear until the election in 2008.

## MAJOR INFLUENCES

Obama is inspired by such heroes as Abraham Lincoln, Martin Luther King Jr., Indian political and spiritual leader Mahatma Ghandi, and Mexican-American labor leader Cesar Chavez. Although each worked on different causes, in different places and times, they all believed in bringing about change through peaceful means. Obama described them as "people who struggled not only with right vs. wrong but right vs. right. They struggled with values that are difficult and contradictory. . . . They didn't just practice politics. They changed how people thought about themselves and each other. . . . They dug really deep into the culture and wrestled with it." These are the ideals that Obama has kept in mind for his own work.

## MARRIAGE AND FAMILY

Obama met his wife Michelle Robinson in Chicago. They married in 1992 and have two daughters, Malia Ann (born 1999) and Natasha (born 2002). Michelle works as an executive in the University of Chicago Hospital system.

Obama divides his time between Washington DC and Chicago. He works during the week in Washington and returns to Chicago each weekend to be with his family. "The hardest thing about the work I do is the strain it puts on Michelle, and not being around enough for the kids," he said. When he is home, he strives to lead a normal life. In his free time, he likes to read, take walks, and go to the movies. His household chores include taking out the garbage and grocery shopping.

## WRITINGS

*Dreams from My Father*, 1995
*The Audacity of Hope: Thoughts on Reclaiming the American Dream*, 2006

## HONORS AND AWARDS

Newsmaker of the Year (National Newspaper Publishers Association): 2004
One of the Fifty Most Intriguing Blacks of 2004 (*Ebony*): 2004
Grammy Award: 2005, Best Spoken Word Album for *Dreams from My Father*
Image Awards (NAACP): 2005 (two awards), Fight for Freedom Award, Chairman's Award
One of the 100 Most Influential People (*Time*): 2005

## FURTHER READING

### Books

Brill, Marlene Targ. *Barack Obama: Working to Make a Difference,* 2006
*Contemporary Black Biography,* Vol. 49, 2005
Obama, Barack. *Dreams from My Father,* 1995
Obama, Barack. *The Audacity of Hope,* 2006

### Periodicals

*American Prospect,* Feb. 2006, p.22
*Black Enterprise,* Oct. 2004, p.88
*Chicago Tribune,* Mar. 20, 2005, p.C1; June 30, 2005
*Current Biography Yearbook,* 2005
*Ebony,* Nov. 2004, p.196
*Jet,* Aug. 16, 2004, p.4; Apr. 11, 2005, p.30
*Nation,* June 26, 2006
*National Journal,* Mar. 18, 2006, p.18
*New York Times,* Oct. 25, 2004, p.A4
*New Yorker,* May 31, 2004
*Newsweek,* Dec. 27, 2004, p.74; Sep. 11, 2006, p.26
*O: The Oprah Magazine,* Nov. 2004, p.248
*Rolling Stone,* Dec. 30, 2004, p.88
*Time,* Nov. 15, 2004, p.74; Oct. 23, 2006, p.44
*USA Today,* Mar. 6. 2006, p.A1

### Online Databases

*Biography Resource Center Online,* 2006, article from *Contemporary Authors Online,* 2006

## ADDRESS

Sen. Barack Obama
713 Hart Senate Office Building
Washington, DC 20510

## WORLD WIDE WEB SITES

http://obama.senate.gov
http://www.barackobama.com

# Soledad O'Brien 1966-
American Journalist
Co-Host of the CNN Daily News Program
"American Morning"

## BIRTH

Maria de la Soledad Teresa O'Brien was born on September 19, 1966. She grew up in St. James, New York, a small suburban town on the north shore of Long Island. Her full first name is a common one among Hispanic Catholic families. It translates as "Our Lady of Solitude," a title honoring the Virgin Mary. Even as a small child, however, she answered to the shortened version, "Soledad," and the nickname "Solly."

Her father, Edward O'Brien, is a professor of mechanical engineering at the State University of New York at Stony Brook. Her mother, Estella, worked as a high school teacher for many years before retiring. Soledad was the fifth of six siblings. Her eldest sister, Maria, was born in 1961; Cecilia followed in 1962; older brother Tony was born in 1963, followed by another sister, Estela, in 1964. Soledad also has a younger brother, Orestes, who was born in 1968.

## YOUTH

O'Brien's parents met in the late 1950s as students at Johns Hopkins University in Baltimore, Maryland. Her father was from Toowoomba, Australia, and had an Irish background, while her mother was from Cuba and of African and Spanish descent. When the two decided to marry, they had to go to Washington DC to do so, because marriage between people of different races was illegal in Maryland at that time.

After marrying, the O'Briens moved to St. James, New York, in hopes of finding a more tolerant atmosphere in which to raise their children. They found what they were looking for, but even so, "when you are the only Cuban black family in town it is strange," Soledad said. "You stick out." O'Brien insists that she never felt traumatized by the ethnic differences between her family and the rest of the community. But she also grew up convinced she would "never date anybody in high school. Nobody wants to date somebody who looks different," she recalled.

## EDUCATION

Soledad and her siblings were all energetic, competitive students who loved school. Their parents, both educators, strongly encouraged their children to learn and made it clear that college was a top priority. All six of the O'Brien children eventually attended Harvard University in Cambridge, Massachusetts, either as undergraduates or in graduate school. From there they pursued rewarding careers in business, medicine, and law. Soledad was successful as well, but her education choices prepared her for a different career path.

After graduating from Smithtown High School East in St. James, New York, O'Brien enrolled at Harvard. "I met a lot of international students and people with ideas from A to Z," she remembered. "I felt comfortable in my skin, seeing that everybody did what they wanted to do and were happy." O'Brien knew that she wanted to get into a profession that would help people, so she first explored a career in the field of medicine. Her struggles with an organic chemistry course, however, convinced her that she did not really have the makings of a true scientist. Rather, she found that she was more interested in the human side of medicine, such as the ways in which individuals and families grappled with health problems or triumphed over life-threatening diseases and other health crises.

During her junior year at Harvard, O'Brien was offered an internship at WBZ, a large Boston television station that was affiliated with the NBC network. "The day I stuck my foot into the newsroom was the day I knew that I was going to be in the business," O'Brien recalled. "It just was one of those moments where you know it's exactly the perfect fit."

Exhilarated by the fast pace and excitement of a big-city newsroom, O'Brien eagerly carried out each task she was asked to do, whether it involved fetching coffee for people or pulling staples out of the wall. "Within about 30 seconds of meeting her, I hoped she would come into television," recalled Jeanne Blake, a producer and medical reporter with the station. "She is one of the brightest people that I have ever met and had almost an instant understanding of the media. Plus she is hysterically funny." For her part, O'Brien says that Blake was an important mentor, one who taught her "to be really obsessed with accuracy, obsessed with detail."

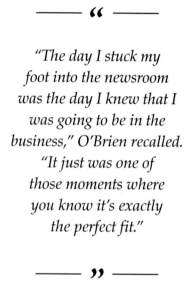

*"The day I stuck my foot into the newsroom was the day I knew that I was going to be in the business," O'Brien recalled. "It just was one of those moments where you know it's exactly the perfect fit."*

As it turned out, O'Brien's career path interrupted her studies for several years in the 1990s, when she left school to start work. She later returned to college. In 2000, she received a bachelor's degree in English and American Studies from Harvard.

## FIRST JOBS

O'Brien started her first job in television in 1989, when she left behind her studies at Harvard to take a position at WBZ as associate producer and newswriter. She further supplemented her income as the producer of the radio program "Second Opinion" and the creator and host of "Health Week in Review," both of which aired on the Boston radio station KISS-FM.

In 1991 O'Brien was hired by NBC headquarters in New York City to work as a researcher and field producer for Robert Bazell, the network's medical correspondent. The job gave her valuable experience behind the cameras, but network executives urged her to explore on-air opportunities. In 1993 she relocated from New York to San Francisco to work as a reporter at KRON-TV, the NBC affiliate in that city. Her first live reporting assignment was to cover a major victory by the city's baseball team, the Giants, from a sports bar full of rowdy fans. Just as the cameras rolled, someone from the crowd lunged at her. "[He] grabbed my butt," she explained. "I just stopped talking. Time stopped. The cameraman was going, 'Talk! Talk!'" she recalled. "To this day it makes my skin crawl." When O'Brien was unable to pull her report together, the station cut away to a taped segment.

> *O'Brien acknowledges that prejudice remains a problem in America, and that it is always painful to encounter. But she believes that the best thing to do when faced with it is to "move on. You can debate the issues until the cows come home or keep your eyes on the prize."*

Unnerved by the incident, O'Brien struggled through her next live appearances. But the station's producers were patient with her, and before long she was delivering live news reports like a seasoned pro. Her assured reporting and likeable screen presence convinced KRON management to promote her to chief of the East Bay news bureau. While employed by the station, she also worked on a Discovery Channel program titled "The Know Zone," winning a local Emmy Award for her contributions to the show. Her personal life, meanwhile, thrived as well. In 1995 she married Bradley Raymond, an investment banker.

During these early years in the television business, O'Brien occasionally was criticized for not being "black enough." In other words, some people felt she should play up the African-American aspect of her background in order to appeal more strongly to African-American viewers. She was even advised to change her name and her appearance, but she never seriously considered following any of this advice. O'Brien's attitude about race and prejudice was formed by her parents. As a biracial couple during the 1950s and 1960s, they often encountered racism and bigotry, but they never let these incidents discourage them from pursuing their dreams.

O'Brien acknowledges that prejudice remains a problem in America, and that it is always painful to encounter. But she believes that the best thing to do when faced with it is to "move on. You can debate the issues until the

*O'Brien on the set of "The Site," the MSNBC daily show on technology, 1996.*

cows come home or keep your eyes on the prize." Although proud of the African, Hispanic, and Caucasian elements in her background, she ultimately feels that "definitions are important to other people; they make no difference to my life."

## CAREER HIGHLIGHTS

O'Brien's career continued to blossom during the mid-1990s, when technological developments were transforming American business and culture in a multitude of ways. The Internet was rapidly evolving from an obscure scientific research tool into a communications network used every day by millions of people and businesses. The technology boom also prompted new business and investment strategies across the United States, including a merger between the Microsoft Corporation and the NBC television network. The new MSNBC cable television network and its partner Web site, msnbc.com, were aimed at young adults who were comfortable with computers and technology and eager to stay on the cutting edge of the latest innovations. O'Brien knew she would fit in well with the new network, and in 1996 she left KRON to work for MSNBC.

O'Brien was first slated to host "The Site." One of the first programs planned by MSNBC, it offered the latest in technology news, product reviews, and human interest features for a tech-savvy audience. O'Brien felt she was ideally suited to host this show. Her viewpoint would be the same as that of her viewers—she did not feel threatened by technology, but she was not an expert either. Network executives agreed that she was ideally suited to make the show's tech-heavy subject matter more accessible to a general audience.

O'Brien took the show's subjects seriously, but she also infused the show with a relaxed, humorous quality. When one viewer wrote asking for recommendations on software to make his computer work as an alarm clock, she showed her special brand of lighthearted sarcasm when she told him to "buy an eight-dollar clock at Walgreen's for heaven's sake!" "The Site" and O'Brien quickly gained such a loyal following among technology enthusiasts that she acquired the nickname "Goddess of the Geeks."

## Stepping into National News

In 1997 "The Site" was canceled by MSNBC executives who were still looking for the right programming mix for the young network. O'Brien's career was still on the rise, however. She was assigned to host "Morning Blend," a two-hour, weekend news and talk program on MSNBC. Around this same time, she began filling in as co-host on NBC's "Weekend Today" and filing news reports for "NBC Nightly News." She also began making regular appearances on the popular "Today" morning show, either as a substitute host or reporter on breaking news events. "My career has been a history of running with the ball and taking advantage of opportunities," she noted.

O'Brien covered a number of notable news events during this time, including the plane crash that took the life of John F. Kennedy, Jr.; school shootings in Littleton, Colorado and Springfield, Oregon; and the disaster that befell the space shuttle *Columbia*. But not all of the stories she covered were tragic in nature. For example, in 1998 she traveled with Pope John Paul II to Cuba, a Communist country that had never before welcomed a Pope to its shores.

The assignment in Cuba gave O'Brien her first opportunity to visit the country where her mother had been born, and where much of her extended family still lived. She enjoyed meeting her relatives and found the country a beautiful place in some ways, but she was also deeply disturbed by the country's widespread poverty and political repression. "It was a great opportunity. But when I left I got very depressed," she said later. O'Brien nevertheless valued the experience and the insights she gained from it.

"Any time you talk about your roots and family, you learn a lot about yourself," she reflected.

In July 1999 O'Brien was named the permanent co-host of "Weekend Today." Her first co-anchor was Jack Ford, who praised his colleague's warmth and professionalism. "With early morning TV, you have to make sure the viewer feels really comfortable with you; Soledad immediately reached a comfort level [with audiences,]" Ford said. After Ford departed the show to work at another network, O'Brien quickly established a good working relationship with his replacement, David Bloom.

Over the next year, O'Brien somehow managed to continue her anchoring duties in New York City while also completing her studies at Harvard. She did so by commuting to her sister's Boston home each Monday, Tuesday, and Wednesday, then returning to New York for work. Moreover, she carried out this hectic, demanding schedule while she was pregnant with her first child. "I'd walk around Harvard Yard thinking, I would pay one of these undergraduates $20 if I could just lie down in her bed for 20 minutes!" she remembered.

*"[Visiting Cuba] was a great opportunity. But when I left I got very depressed," O'Brien said. Still, she valued the experience and the insights she gained from it. "Any time you talk about your roots and family, you learn a lot about yourself."*

### Weekday News Anchor at CNN

In April 2003, O'Brien's "Weekend Today" co-anchor, David Bloom, unexpectedly died of a pulmonary embolism (a blood clot affecting the lungs) while on assignment in Iraq. He was just 39 years old. "I had looked to David as a role model in many ways," O'Brien said. After he died, she felt that "Weekend Today" ceased to be a team. "The bottom fell out emotionally," she admitted.

O'Brien recognized that it would be easy to remain in what had become a comfortable job and await the designation of a new co-host. But O'Brien said that her colleague's sudden death reminded her that "life is short and if you have a dream, go out and accomplish it." Accordingly, in July 2003 she accepted an offer from the CNN television news network to co-anchor their weekday morning news show, "American Morning." "I felt like I

*O'Brien on the set of the CNN show "American Morning."*

learned from the best in the business at 'Weekend Today'—Katie Couric and Matt Lauer. I grew. You can't help but grow. But I also learned when to take the next challenge," O'Brien explained.

O'Brien's move to CNN represented a clear step up in her career. It gave her more exposure, more travel opportunities, and more high-profile guests to interview. It also made her more financially secure; her four-year contract with CNN was said to include a salary of approximately $750,000 a year.

Over the next few years, O'Brien's assignments took her all over the world. During these travels, she reported on a fascinating parade of events and people. In the fall of 2003, O'Brien was the only broadcast journalist permitted to accompany Laura Bush when the First Lady traveled to Paris and Moscow. In November 2004, she traveled to Columbus, Ohio, to report on disputes over votes cast there in the presidential election. In December of that year she reported from Thailand on the aftermath of the devastating tsunami that took the lives of more than 155,000 people across Southeast Asia. She and her team won the Alfred I. duPont Award for their coverage of that disaster. In July 2005, she reported from London on the terrorist attacks in that city. Later that summer, she went to New Orleans in the wake of Hurricane Katrina to give viewers the story of the storm and the devastating flood that followed it.

O'Brien says that covering these and other world events has given her a global perspective that she wants to pass on to her children. "You just learn so much," she said. "I get to sit there and talk to somebody and be inspired by them. I love to be moved and impressed by people . . . who do remarkable things."

## Covering Katrina

O'Brien is frequently characterized as attractive, pleasant, and non-threatening. She has proved her toughness and professionalism, however, on several reporting assignments. In the wake of Katrina, for example, thousands of New Orleans residents were left for days without food, water, medical attention, or adequate police protection. O'Brien seemed to channel the outrage many Americans felt when they saw images of the suffering survivors on television.

In one televised interview, O'Brien confronted Michael Brown, the head of the Federal Emergency Management Agency (FEMA), about the

——— " ———

*"Do you look at the pictures that are coming out of New Orleans?" O'Brien demanded in an interview with FEMA Director Michael Brown. "And do you say, I'm proud of the job that FEMA is doing on the ground there in a tough situation? Or do you look at these pictures and you say, this is a mess and we've dropped the ball."*

——— " ———

agency's poor response to the disaster. Brown defended himself and FEMA by saying that he had only recently become aware of certain aspects of the situation and stating that communication and travel were difficult in the area. O'Brien promptly challenged these claims: "How is it possible that we're getting better intel [intelligence] than you're getting? We had a crew in the air. We were showing live pictures of the people outside the Convention Center. . . . And also, we've been reporting that officials have been telling people to go to the Convention Center if they want any hope of relief. I don't understand how FEMA cannot have this information." She continued to grill Brown, asking why four days had passed without any

*O'Brien reporting from New Orleans after Katrina.*

massive airdrop of food or water to those who were trapped in the Super-dome and at the city's Convention Center. "Do you look at the pictures that are coming out of New Orleans?" she demanded. "And do you say, I'm proud of the job that FEMA is doing on the ground there in a tough situation? Or do you look at these pictures and you say, this is a mess and we've dropped the ball."

O'Brien's passion and dedication in covering this story were officially rec-ognized when she and her teammates at CNN were given the George Foster Peabody Award for their reporting on Katrina and the flood in New Orleans. Reflecting on her job and the place of media in society, she stated: "We get to tell people what is happening in the world and be a part of their lives. It is an important mandate and something very valuable."

## MARRIAGE AND FAMILY

O'Brien married Bradley Raymond, an investment banker, in 1995. Their first child, Sofia Elizabeth, was born on October 23, 2000; another daughter, Cecilia, followed on March 20, 2002; and the couple welcomed twin boys, Charlie and Jackson, on August 30, 2004. Just as her parents and siblings were very important to her in childhood, so are her husband and children vitally important to her adult life. Working the early morning shift at CNN allows her to be home in time to be involved with her children's daytime activities and at mealtime.

O'Brien's commitment to parenting and strong family bonds is reflected in a bimonthly column she contributes to the magazine *USA Weekend.* Asked about one of the most important things she learned from her own parents about raising children, she said that "it's okay to be strict. That kids, as much as they fight against the rules, they really want them and need them. It takes a lot more time and effort to teach children good manners, but in the long run it is really worth it."

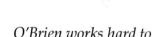

O'Brien is often asked how she manages to balance work with family demands. She says that her secret is "not to strive for real balance. I set a low bar on the things that don't matter, and I set a high bar for the things that do matter—spending lots of time with my kids and husband. It's about

*O'Brien works hard to balance work and home responsibilities. "Sometimes there's a tsunami and you have to fly to Thailand," she said. "Sometimes the first day of school is a priority and you make pancakes and take everyone to school."*

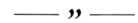

being flexible and understanding that we are all human and make mistakes and there are limits to what we can accomplish in 24 hours. Get off your own back!"

O'Brien credits her mother and her three older sisters with showing her that a woman can juggle a fulfilling career and a happy family. The keys, she claims, are learning to prioritize on a daily basis, letting go of the things that are not really essential, and accepting the fact that life doesn't always run smoothly. "Sometimes there's a tsunami and you have to fly to Thailand. Sometimes the first day of school is a priority and you make pancakes and take everyone to school," she said.

## HOBBIES AND OTHER INTERESTS

O'Brien likes to hike, swim, and run to stay in shape. She enjoys writing and is working on a book about family and child-raising, as well as a novel loosely based on her mother's life. She also sits on the board of directors of the Harlem School for the Arts.

## TELEVISION PROGRAMS

"The Know Zone," 1995
"The Site," 1996-97
"Morning Blend," 1998
"Weekend Today," 1999-2003
"American Morning," 2003-

## HONORS AND AWARDS

Hispanic Achievement Award in Communications: 1997
Hispanic Heritage Vision Award (Hispanic Heritage Foundation): 2005
National Association of Minorities in Cable Vision Award: 2006
Women of Power Award (National Urban League): 2006

## FURTHER READING

### Books

*Contemporary Hispanic Biography,* Vol.1, 2002
*Who's Who in America,* 2006

### Periodicals

*Arizona Republic,* Apr. 14, 2006, p.3
*Ebony,* Dec. 2004, p.8
*Electronic Media,* June 30, 1997, p.16
*Good Housekeeping,* Jan. 2006, p.148
*Hispanic Outlook in Higher Education,* May 17, 2004, p.9
*Houston Chronicle,* June 17, 2003, p.6
*Jet,* Dec. 20, 2004, p.26
*Latino Leaders,* May 1, 2006, p.32
*Newsday,* June 23, 2005, p.B12
*People,* June 16, 1997, p.108; May 8, 2000, p.148
*Redbook,* May 2005, p.29
*Runner's World,* June 2003, p.18
*San Francisco Chronicle,* Apr. 15, 1997, p.B1

### Online Articles

http://www.hispaniconline.com
   *Hispanic Magazine,* "And Now the News," June 2001; "Running with the News," June 2005)

http://modernmom.com
   (*Modern Mom,* "Modern Mom Profiles . . . CNN's Soledad O'Brien," undated)

## Online Databases

*Biography Resource Center Online,* 2006, article from *Contemporary Hispanic
   Biography,* 2002

## ADDRESS

Soledad O'Brien
CNN
One Time Warner Center
New York, NY 10019

## WORLD WIDE WEB SITE

http://www.cnn.com

## Jamie Oliver 1975-

British Chef and Cookbook Author
Star of TV Cooking Shows and School
Nutrition Activist

### BIRTH

Jamie Trevor Oliver was born on May 27, 1975, in Clavering, a
small village in Essex, England. His parents, Sally and Trevor
Oliver, own a pub-restaurant in Clavering called The Cricketers. Sally manages the business end of their establishment,
while Trevor runs the kitchen. Oliver has one younger sister,
Anna-Marie.

## YOUTH

Throughout his early life, Oliver was surrounded by cooking and restaurants. He grew up above the family pub, and his first job there was cleaning up and taking out the garbage. He began peeling potatoes and shelling peas when he was about seven or eight. His mother remembered his enthusiasm for cooking at an early age: "We used to stand him on a chair so that he could reach the work surface and obviously he used to get into a real mess—he still uses his hands for everything when he's cooking!"

> "I remember being fascinated by what went on in the kitchen. It just seemed such a cool place, everyone working together to make this lovely stuff and having a laugh doing it. . . . A lot of the boys at school thought that cooking was a girlie thing. I didn't really care."

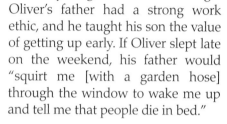

Oliver's father had a strong work ethic, and he taught his son the value of getting up early. If Oliver slept late on the weekend, his father would "squirt me [with a garden hose] through the window to wake me up and tell me that people die in bed."

For Oliver, one incentive for working for his parents was the pocket change he earned. He knew that some people—his friends included—thought cooking was women's work, but he considered himself one of the boys in the kitchen, working with the male chefs his parents employed. "I remember being fascinated by what went on in the kitchen. It just seemed such a cool place, everyone working together to make this lovely stuff and having a laugh doing it. . . . A lot of the boys at school thought that cooking was a girlie thing. I didn't really care, especially as I could buy the coolest trainers [tennis shoes] with what I'd earned from working at the weekend."

Oliver experienced a lot of early success in the kitchen. At age 13, he was sent by his father to work part time at Starr, a finer restaurant than The Cricketers. Oliver hadn't had any formal training in cooking yet. Within a few weeks, he replaced a 26-year-old chef who couldn't prepare the appetizers as well as he could. According to Oliver, hearing his dad tell him he was proud of him left him feeling "all tingly and funny."

Another episode in Oliver's early life inspired him to keep cooking. He and his friends would take sandwiches with them on escapades into the countryside on summer days. Oliver prepared smoked salmon sandwiches one day, and a friend who only ate jam on bread reluctantly took a bite of the fancier fare. "He really didn't want to eat it, and then, when he did, he wouldn't eat anything else all summer," Oliver said. "That's when I understood how powerful food can be."

## EDUCATION

Oliver was popular in school, but he struggled academically. He has dyslexia, a learning disability that is an inherited neurological condition. People with dyslexia have trouble recognizing and decoding words, which can make reading, writing, and spelling difficult. People with dyslexia often have trouble with reading comprehension.

At the age of 16, Oliver was accepted at Westminster Catering College in London. Having done poorly in local schools until then, going to cooking school brought him long-awaited academic success. "The course was a perfect mix of practical and theory, which suited the type of person I am. I can pretty much take anything in as long as I can see it. We didn't just sit there reading out of a book, which is basically why I failed at school. Even when it was pretty hardcore science, like growing bacteria and learning how it affects kitchens, it was fine because it related straight to cooking."

## FIRST JOBS

After finishing his studies at Westminster Catering College, Oliver spent several years trying different experiences and jobs to learn all about cooking. First he went to France to learn about French cooking. Then he returned to London to work as the head pastry chef at The Neal Street Restaurant, a renowned establishment where he became fascinated with Italian food. After reading a cookbook by Rose Gray and Ruth Rogers, Oliver sought out a job at their London restaurant, the critically acclaimed River Café. He spent over three years there, learning more about Italian food from the proprietors. "Those two ladies taught me all about the time and effort that goes into creating the freshest, most honest, totally delicious food."

## CAREER HIGHLIGHTS

### "The Naked Chef"

One night while Oliver was working at the River Café, a film crew from the TV network the British Broadcasting Corporation (BBC) showed up at the restaurant to film a documentary. Without even trying, Oliver stole the show. "I didn't even know they were filming me in particular. We were all

*Oliver in a shot from his TV show "The Naked Chef," squeezing lemon on his food.*

working, and I was just doing my thing. Because it was so busy . . . there wasn't even any room to be polite to them, much less perform for the camera," he recalled. Still, his "performance" impressed many in the television industry, and five different production companies called him when the documentary aired. All wanted to develop a cooking show for him. Oliver was surprised: "I couldn't believe it and thought it was my mates winding me up!"

It took some convincing before Oliver agreed to do a cooking show. "Being a restaurant chef, my industry feeling was TV chefs are idiots and cheesy geezer cop-outs," he declared, "and my dream is to open my own restaurant." Being an active participant in the development of his own show made the decision easier—and so did adding a rock and roll soundtrack. The show was called "The Naked Chef," although Oliver didn't like the title. "I was worried about what my nanny (grandma) would think—like I was a bloody porn star or something!" The title of the show actually referred to his philosophy of cooking good food with high quality ingredients and basic techniques. "The idea behind 'The Naked Chef' was to strip food down to its bare essentials—to prove that you didn't need to dress up ingredients or buy a load of fancy gadgets to make something really tasty."

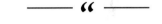

*"The idea behind 'The Naked Chef' was to strip food down to its bare essentials—to prove that you didn't need to dress up ingredients or buy a load of fancy gadgets to make something really tasty."*

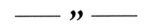

Oliver's enthusiasm and skill made for popular television when "The Naked Chef" first aired in 1999. As a critic for the *Observer* noted, "Jamie Oliver was a breath of fresh air. Within months he was one of the most popular personalities in the country." The show had Oliver riding his scooter around London, searching for ingredients and sharing his passion for food with shop owners and fishmongers. He could hardly contain his excitement as he cooked, jumping about the kitchen and sliding down a banister to let in his friends for his on-air dinner parties.

The success of "The Naked Chef" as a TV show prompted Oliver to write a cookbook of the same name. "I always wanted to write a book, though I doubt my old English teacher would believe it!" His success inspired two more series and accompanying cookbooks. The TV shows "Return of the Naked Chef" and "Happy Days with the Naked Chef," along with the cookbooks of the same names, made Oliver a rich and busy chef. Since

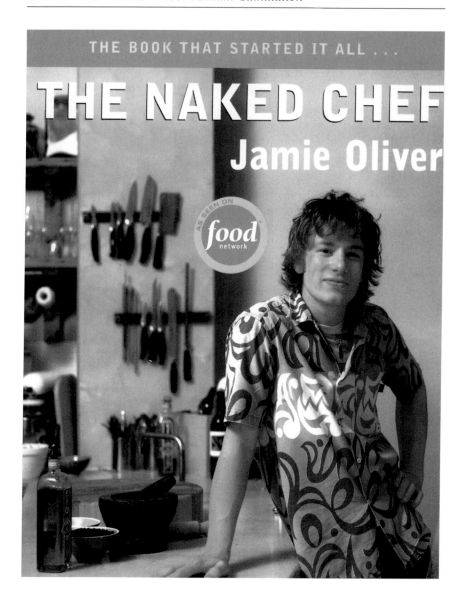

then, he's gone on to do a number of other cookbooks based on his experiences in the kitchen.

### Fifteen Underprivileged Youngsters

In 2002, Oliver started a new project: he came up with a plan to train 15 troubled teens how to cook. Using his own money, he developed a course for these kids and, along with many of his friends and colleagues, set about teaching them everything about the cooking and catering business. Once they completed the class, the 15 graduates were responsible for running Oliver's new restaurant, aptly named Fifteen. Most of his students had no chef's training, and some had never eaten in a restaurant. Oliver explained, "Essentially, the trainees are unemployed but most of them are also coming from the same classes I did at school—not academic. The course is about second chances. Half the kids who had attitude problems didn't have steady families and have experienced drug or alcohol abuse. How do you expect these kids to get a break if no one offers them one?"

Oliver felt that the 15 teens he chose for his program needed something positive to focus on, and what better than food? His own passion for cooking was something he wanted to share. "For me, cooking is like breathing," he said. "I look forward to breakfast when I go to bed, I look forward to lunch, I look forward to dinner, I look forward to a dinner party in two weeks' time. I honestly, truly, truly think cooking is an integral part of life, of having fun. I don't eat to live, I live to eat."

"Jamie's Kitchen," a TV miniseries about the London group's experience, revealed both successes and failures when it aired in 2002. Several students lost interest, while a few others were asked to leave the program due to disciplinary or attendance problems. Many support programs were available to the students, including mentoring, counseling, and a ten-year plan with provisional backing for a business once they'd gotten that far. But some could not step up to the challenge of long hours and demanding instructors.

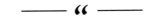

> "For me, cooking is like breathing. I look forward to breakfast when I go to bed, I look forward to lunch, I look forward to dinner, I look forward to a dinner party in two weeks' time. I honestly, truly, truly think cooking is an integral part of life, of having fun. I don't eat to live, I live to eat."

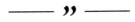

Despite the failure of some of the kids, Oliver recruited a second group to train. "Early on," he admitted, "I think I was a bit too careful not to offend anyone and I had this optimistic belief that the kids would all be all right in the end. I probably needed to be harder on them. I am harder on them now!" During the second course, he learned more about being a mentor and relished the difference he was making in his trainees' lives. "I'm perfectly happy. I get my pleasure out of the students. That's becoming a stronger part of why I do it.'Fifteen' is not some airy-fairy TV show. It's for life."

The London restaurant Fifteen is still in operation. It's owned by the Fifteen Foundation, a not-for-profit group for which Oliver is a trustee. The foundation has established Fifteen restaurants in Amsterdam, Cornwall, and Melbourne. Profits from the restaurants go back to the foundation to fund development.

> "Everyone now is looking round schools talking about the food in the kitchen, and that alone keeps schools on their toes," Oliver said. "But I'm worried that sufficient money hasn't filtered through to our glorious dinner ladies, who are the grass roots of the whole thing. Deep down, I don't know how much better off they are a year later."

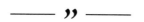

## Improving School Food

Oliver's charitable attention turned next toward British schoolchildren and what they were eating at school. He was concerned about the low nutritional value of school lunches and thought that kids would change their eating habits if they learned more about good food and fresh ingredients. He knew that dietary changes could help children lead healthier lives, especially important given that obesity rates had drastically increased over recent years. "Basically, I wanted to get rid of the junk," Oliver said.

The "Feed Me Better" campaign began in one school district in Greenwich, England. The district fed 15,000 children every day at dinner (lunch in the U.S.). Oliver gathered the head dinner ladies and taught them the basics of fresh food preparation. Previously the dinner ladies had been simply heating up prepared foods that arrived at the schools in bags, cartons, and cans.

The kids did not react well at first. The healthier fare tasted strange and they longed for the comfort of their familiar crisps (potato chips) and fizzy drinks (soda). The *New York Times* reported on student reactions: "'It looks disgusting and it smells disgusting,' said one student, confronted by Mr. Oliver's chicken tagine (stew). Another little boy, tasting what he said was his first-ever vegetable, threw up on the table." But the program was ultimately a winner: most children eventually grew to like the new cuisine,

*Oliver's efforts to improve the eating habits of British schoolchildren
were captured in a 2005 TV documentary.*

teachers reported a rise in academic performance and concentration, and parents commented on their children's improved behavior. To help some of the younger kids along, Oliver donned a corn-on-the-cob costume, sang a tune about vegetables, and handed out stickers.

Oliver filmed a TV documentary called "Jamie's School Dinners" showing the trials of the dinner ladies and the reactions of the schoolchildren in Greenwich. Once the documentary aired in 2005, an impressive number of people signed his petition to the government for better nutrition in British schools. Oliver argued for several important changes in his "Feed Me Better Campaign": guaranteeing that children receive nutritionally balanced meals; introducing nutritional standards and banning junk food from schools; supporting dinner ladies by giving them better kitchens, more work time, and more training; teaching kids about food and nutrition; and committing long-term funding to improve school food. Oliver's campaign was a great success. Prime Minister Tony Blair set up a School Food Trust and pledged over $500 million to improve school meals. New standards were put in place for school food, and school junk food sales were banned. Oliver called it "20 years too late. . . . [The government should be] bloody embarrassed that London has some of the most unhealthy children in Europe."

*Oliver putting the finishing touch on a dessert.*

A 2006 follow-up documentary, "Jamie's Return to School Dinners," showed Oliver in various parts of the country, checking up on schools and the changes that had been made. While many schools had made drastic improvements, others continued to struggle with outdated kitchen facilities and limited funds for cafeteria operations. "The subliminal ripples, especially through the middle class, have been fantastic," Oliver reported. "Everyone now is looking round schools talking about the food in the kitchen, and that alone keeps schools on their toes. But I'm worried that sufficient money hasn't filtered through to our glorious dinner ladies, who are the grass roots of the whole thing. Deep down, I don't know how much better off they are a year later."

## Recent Projects

Oliver has continued to tackle a wide range of projects related to food and cooking. In summer 2005 he had the opportunity to explore one of his long-time passions. He has been enamored of Italian food for most of his career, so he set off across Italy to uncover the secrets of authentic Italian cooks. He drove an old Volkswagen bus, which broke down repeatedly, and had a camera crew follow him on his adventure. "Jamie's Great Italian Escape" was a six-part miniseries that showcased Oliver's passion for food, its preparation, and the people who appreciate it. He recalled the journey on his website: "I had a great time exploring the delights of the busy night markets in Palermo, entering pasta making competitions with the mammas in the small mountain community in Le Marche and injecting some enthusiasm into cooking for the Benedictine community north of Rome." Oliver's tribute to Italy was his cookbook *Jamie's Italy*, published after his experience.

Oliver returned to the original group of 15 student chefs from "Jamie's Kitchen" in "Jamie's Chef," a TV miniseries that aired in 2007. After the original experience, he had hoped that one of his students would open their own restaurant. Oliver decided to give them that chance. He invited the group to a competition, where each presented their best dishes to a panel of judges from the foundation. The judges picked four chefs, who had to prove themselves in the kitchens of some of London's best restaurants. It was a grueling experience, but one lucky and talented winner will get the opportunity to open his or her own restaurant.

> "People who press olive oil, grow tomatoes, dive for scallops, pig farmers who breed rare pigs and feed them on chestnuts and herbs and produce the most amazing pork . . . these people are all fantastically brilliant," Oliver raved. "I accredit all of my success to these people for giving me the inspiration for what I do."

## MARRIAGE AND FAMILY

Oliver married Jools (Juliette) Norton, his childhood sweetheart, in 2000. They have two daughters, Poppy Honey and Daisy Boo. As Oliver's family has grown, so has press fascination with his private life. When their first daughter was born and they were getting ready to leave the hospital, Oliver and Jools realized they could either embrace the waiting hordes of photographers or flee, and they chose to face the press. "The hospital offered to smuggle us out the back, but we knew that as well as all the mob out front, there were already five paparazzi outside our house with long lenses that could see in through the windows. . . . So we said, OK, we'll be out around 3:30 tomorrow. And when we came out, they were the politest I'd ever seen them—they kept saying, 'Congratulations!'"

## MAJOR INFLUENCES

Oliver is appreciative of and inspired by the people who provide the food he cooks. "People who press olive oil, grow tomatoes, dive for scallops, pig farmers who breed rare pigs and feed them on chestnuts and herbs and produce the most amazing pork," he asserted. "These people are all fantastically brilliant and, whether you like it or not, it's infectious. I accredit all of my success to these people for giving me the inspiration for what I do."

## SELECTED CREDITS

### Television

"The Naked Chef," 1999 (series)
"Return of the Naked Chef," 2000 (series)
"Happy Days with the Naked Chef," 2001 (series)
"Jamie's Kitchen," 2002 (miniseries)
"Oliver's Twist," 2002-2003 (series)
"Jamie's Great Italian Escape," 2005 (miniseries)
"Jamie's School Dinners," 2005 (documentary)
"Jamie's Return to School Dinners," 2006 (documentary)
"Jamie's Chef," 2007 (miniseries)

### Writings

*The Naked Chef,* 1999
*The Return of the Naked Chef,* 2000
*Happy Days with the Naked Chef,* 2001
*Jamie's Kitchen,* 2002
*Jamie's Dinners,* 2004
*Jamie's Italy,* 2005
*Cook with Jamie,* 2006

### Videos

"The Naked Chef," 2000
"Pukka Tukka," 2000
"The Naked Chef—Volume Two," 2001
"Happy Days Tour Live!," 2002
"Oliver's Twist," 2003
"Jamie's Kitchen," 2004
"Oliver's Twist—Volume Two," 2005

"Jamie's School Dinners," 2005
"Jamie's Christmas," 2005
"The Naked Chef, Series 1-3," 2006 (boxed set)

## HONORS AND AWARDS

Best Chef of the Year *(GQ):* 2000
Man of the Year *(GQ):* 2000
BAFTA (British Academy of Film and Television Arts): 2001, for "The Naked Chef"
Member of the British Empire (MBE): 2003
National Television Awards: 2005 (two awards), Most Popular Factual Programme for "Jamie's School Dinners" and Special Recognition Award

## FURTHER READING

### Books

*Current Biography International Yearbook,* 2005

### Periodicals

*Caterer & Hotelkeeper,* Nov. 27, 2003, p.22
*Daily Telegraph* (London), May 13, 2006, p.1 (Weekend section)
*Guardian* (London), Sep. 24, 2005, p.18
*New York Times,* Apr. 23, 2005, p.A4
*Observer* (London), Apr. 14, 2002; Mar. 26, 2006, p.22; Aug. 22, 2006, p.1 (Features section)
*People,* Nov. 13, 2000, p.107
*USA Today,* Apr. 2, 2001, p.D1
*Vogue,* May 2006, p.260

### Online Articles

http://www.bbc.co.uk/food/food_matters/schoolmeals.shtml
(British Broadcasting Corporation, "School Dinners," Sep. 2006)

### Online Databases

*Biography Resource Center Online,* 2007

## ADDRESS

Jamie Oliver; Enquiries
PO Box 51372
London N1 7WX
England

## WORLD WIDE WEB SITES

http://www.jamieoliver.com
http://www.fifteenrestaurant.com
http://www.foodnetwork.com/food/jamie_oliver

## Skip Palenik 1947-

American Forensic Microscope Scientist
World-Renowned Expert in Analysis of
Microscopic Material

### BIRTH

Samuel James Palenik III was born in 1947 in Chicago, Illinois.
Palenik was named after his father, who worked as a truck driver, but he has been known by the nickname "Skip" since
early childhood. Palenik's mother was a homemaker. He has
one brother and one sister.

### YOUTH

Even as a young boy, Palenik was fascinated by microscopes
and the invisible world they revealed. "The idea of taking a

piece of dust and seeing what others do not see has always intrigued me," he said. "Ever since I was a kid, I've thought there is a whole world of things regular people don't look at."

Palenik's parents encouraged this interest, buying him his first micro-scope when he was eight years old. "I had wanted it for some time before that, but for Christmas, I got my first one, a Gilbert microscope," he recalled. This microscope could magnify objects up to 400 times their size, and it opened up a whole new world for the inquisitive youngster. Soon he was using the device for hours at a time, studying common items found around the home such as dirt, cooking spices, swatches of clothing, and water.

> "I learned how to detect spices from the kitchen, talcum powder from the bathroom, and hairs that belonged to Mom or Dad or my brother or sister," recalled Palenik. "I was hooked. I read everything I could on crime investigation, microscopy, and science. . . . Things just took off from there."

Palenik also performed all of the experiments outlined in the microscope's instruction manual, which he says may be the most influential book he's ever read. "In the instruction manual, there was a chapter called 'The Vacuum Cleaner Detective,' which was about science and crime detection," he recalled. "It explained how you could take apart your mother's vacuum cleaner bag and decipher all of the components in the dust. I learned how to detect spices from the kitchen, talcum powder from the bathroom, and hairs that belonged to Mom or Dad or my brother or sister. I was hooked. I read everything I could on crime investigation, microscopy, and science. . . . Things just took off from there."

## Exploring Laboratory Science

By the time Palenik was 12 years old, his father had built a laboratory for his two sons in the basement of the family's home. Working with his brother Mark, Palenik used the lab to conduct a wide range of scientific experiments. They studied chemical reactions and examined all sorts of household materials, taking samples that would fit under the microscope's lens. The boys also explored basic criminal investigation techniques, such as making marks on sheets of metal with different types of tools in order to

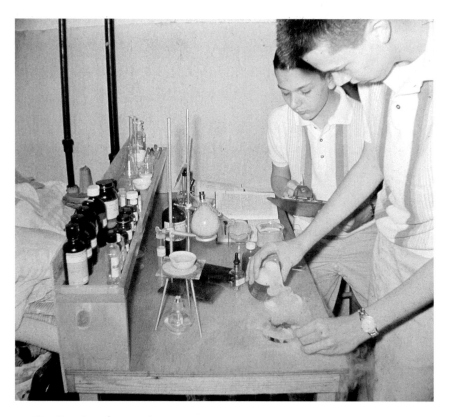

*Skip (front) and Mark (rear) in one of their earliest laboratories, about 1955.*

study the distinctive marks made by each tool. "We worked through every experiment that I could get supplies for," Palenik said.

The Palenik brothers' experiments led them to make regular trips to the local library and drug store, as well as other places that fed their curiosity. "Our big Saturdays, about once a month, my brother Mark and I would take the Archer Express [train] downtown," Palenik remembered. "There were three stops we would make. The first stop was the Chicago Library reading room. . . . If you got there early, you'd get a seat at those beautiful big tables. We'd sit there all day reading—well, not quite all day, because Mark didn't like that part too much. Then we'd drop off our chemical order at Sargent's Drug Store on Wabash Avenue. A big order for us was $5. We'd saved to get that much to order chemicals for our lab at home. . . . Then we'd go to Kroch's & Brentano's [book store]. I found copies of Charnot and Mason's *Handbook of Chemical Microscopy* in two volumes, and this really opened possibilities. I thought I could do every form of microanalysis with it. Then we'd go to Walgreen's or Woolworth's, where they had a basement cafeteria, and we'd eat lunch. Other Saturdays, we'd do normal kid stuff—go to movies, play ball, or work in our labs."

## EDUCATION

Palenik attended elementary and high school in the Chicago area. He recalls that after earning his high school diploma, "I couldn't wait to get to college to study chemistry." But he became discouraged soon after arriving at the University of Illinois at Chicago. His professors tried to steer him away from studying the techniques in which he was most interested. For example, his instructors urged him to reconsider his interest in forensic microscopy, the scientific use of microscopes to examine physical evidence for criminal investigation and other purposes. At the time, researchers had concluded that using microscopes in this way was outdated and would be a useless skill to possess within a matter of a few years. Palenik recalled that one of his professors told him, "This is all very nice, but nobody does this anymore."

*"I went back to school for chemistry and was a much better student this time," said Palenik. "I still had my lab, but I paid attention in class more!"*

Disheartened by these developments, Palenik drifted away from his classes and launched his own course of study at the university library. Palenik eventually left school and was drafted by the Army in 1966. He served three years in the Army as an intelligence analyst. After completing his military service, Palenik returned to the University of Illinois at Chicago to finish his degree. "I went back to school for chemistry and was a much better student this time. I still had my lab, but I paid attention in class more!" he said. During this time he also worked in various laboratories at the university. Palenik first worked as a research assistant for the Department of Chemistry (1970-1972), then moved on to the Department of Criminal Justice (1972-1974). In 1974, Palenik received his Bachelor of Science (BS) degree in chemistry with an emphasis on analytical methods.

## CAREER HIGHLIGHTS

Immediately after graduating from college, Palenik went to work for the McCrone Research Institute in Chicago, a leading research company for law enforcement and criminal investigation agencies around the country.

*Walter McCrone at the microchemical bench in his lab, about 1975.*

The institute was founded by Walter McCrone, a forensic microscopist who had been one of Palenik's childhood heroes. Palenik had actually contacted McCrone before he had even earned his degree, and it was at that time that the two began a long friendship based on their shared enthusiasm for microscopic science. During the mid-1970s, McCrone was one of the only scientists in the world who remained dedicated to the use of microscopes for investigation and analysis of materials. He became Palenik's mentor, teaching him many advanced research techniques. Under McCrone's tutelage, Palenik declared, "I learned what a real scientist is."

Palenik claims that McCrone deserves special credit for helping him develop and sharpen his skills in logical deduction. In addition to their regular work assignments, the researchers at the McCrone Institute played a never-ending game called "UFO." "You would come into the laboratory in the morning and on your microscope would be a microscope slide, and in a Sharpie pen it said, 'UFO,'" recalled Palenik. "And it could be anything in the world on it. And so we had such things—residue from the bottom of a bag of pistachio nuts . . . combustion products from a cogged railway . . . hops from beer making."

331

The goal of the game was to correctly identify the material on the slide. Palenik and other lab players would do this by using different microscopes to analyze the material's characteristics, then match those characteristics to a known substance. "Most people think dust is dust," Palenik said. "Well, it's not. It all comes from someplace. It comes from the pollen grains in the air. It comes from fibers. It comes from the asphalt and tire rubber on the roads. Each is a clue to its origin . . . only a microscopist knows what it's like. Dust and debris and stains are our business." The UFO game became Palenik's specialty, and it was valuable in helping him develop his expertise in identifying unknown materials.

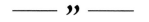

*"Most people think dust is dust," Palenik said. "Well, it's not. It all comes from some place. It comes from the pollen grains in the air. It comes from fibers. It comes from the asphalt and tire rubber on the roads. Each is a clue to its origin . . . only a microscopist knows what it's like. Dust and debris and stains are our business."*

### Founding Microtrace

When McCrone retired in 1993, Palenik founded his own laboratory called Microtrace. "I always wanted to open my own lab, so people wouldn't touch my stuff," he joked. The Microtrace collection of microscopes can magnify objects up to 70,000 times, using beams of light or streams of electrons to reveal the specific molecular composition of objects. Palenik has also assembled a reference collection of samples of more than 10,000 various materials to use for comparison matching. The collection includes many samples of dust created from drilling, sawing, and crushing different materials. It also includes thousands of different man-made fibers, human and animal hair, pollen, spices, grains, starches, soil, sand, and so on. The Microtrace facility also houses Palenik's large library of books, journals, and specialized encyclopedias. All of these tools are used to characterize and identify unknown materials that are brought to Microtrace for analysis.

At Microtrace, Palenik and the other forensic scientists use many different types of microscopes to analyze materials. For example, a comparison microscope is used to compare two materials under exactly the same conditions. A hot stage microscope has a compartment that is temperature controlled by a computer. The temperature can be varied to show the melting point of a particle or fiber. A fluorescence microscope uses an ultraviolet light source instead of visible light commonly used in light microscopes. The ultraviolet radiation is absorbed by certain compounds, which re-emit light in the visible wavelength in a process known as fluorescence. This can identify the presence of optical brighteners, dyes, and other organic materials.

Other microscopes in Palenik's investigative arsenal include a reflected light microscope, which is used to study opaque particles. A light source above the specimen focuses on the surface of a sample (like a metallic particle such as lead from a bullet). This can show how light is reflected off the material to reveal striations, cracks, or other markings that give clues about an unknown particle's identity or origin. A scanning electron microscope uses electrons instead of light to create an image. Because an electron has a much shorter wavelength than light in the visible region of the spectrum, a scanning electron microscope sometimes reveals valuable information that is undetectable with a light microscope. Taken together, the results of tests from all these microscopes can reveal many different features of an unknown particle.

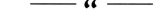

*"We try to solve problems by establishing facts from the physical evidence we are given," said Palenik. "And usually that evidence is quite small—a grain of sand, a speck of dust. You could probably fit all the material I've been asked to analyze in the last 30 years into a couple of tablespoons."*

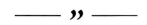

### Crime Scene Investigator

Throughout his career, Palenik has worked on many highly publicized cases on behalf of various clients in the world of law enforcement. He analyzed materials related to the 1993 World Trade Center bombing in New York City and the 1995 bombing of the Alfred P. Murrah Federal Building in Oklahoma City, Oklahoma. Palenik has also helped to determine the source of explosives used in aircraft bombings in Ireland and Japan. He also has participated in the investigation of many serial crimes, including the "Unabomber" mail bombing attacks that claimed three lives and wounded 29 others (Ted Kaczynski was eventually convicted for these bombings, which took place from the late 1970s through the early 1990s) and a series of child murders that terrorized Atlanta from 1979 to 1981 (Wayne Williams was captured and convicted for these crimes in 1982). Palenik also participated in investigations

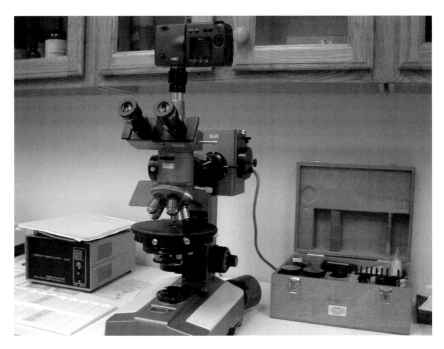

*The fluorescence microscope uses ultraviolet (UV) light,
which is absorbed and re-emitted in a process known as fluorescence.
It's used in particle analysis and in the study of biological material.*

of the terrorist aircraft hijackings and destruction of the World Trade Center towers on September 11, 2001.

Palenik has even lent his expertise to the investigation of crimes of yesteryear. For example, he assisted with a re-investigation of the 1968 assassination of civil rights leader Martin Luther King Jr. This investigation confirmed that King had been shot by only one gunman, contradicting various conspiracy theories.

Palenik's talents have drawn the attention of overseas law enforcement agencies as well. The Royal Canadian Mounted Police, England's famed Scotland Yard criminal investigation agency, and the International Criminal Police Organization known as Interpol have all enlisted his help on various cases over the years.

### The Search for Truth

Palenik has been hired by both prosecutors and defense attorneys during his long career, but he says that he does not work exclusively for one side or the other. In most cases, in fact, he does not even follow the trial to learn the verdict after he has concluded his research and reported his findings. He simply works to discover, understand, and explain the facts about the material he is asked to analyze. He does recall one time when he happened to hear a news report of a verdict for a trial he'd worked on. "I was real excited," he admitted. "But not for the reason people think, because we caught a killer. It was the intellectual joy a scientist gets from knowing his theory is right. . . . My role is to establish facts. We pick up these little particles, isolate them, analyze them, and finally try and establish what the material is. From there we must take the next step and apply some controlled imagination and interpret these findings in the light of the situation. That's justified as long as people know what the facts are and what you are basing your conclusions on. . . . The scientist's role is to establish facts. The jury has to decide who did it."

Even at a time when criminal investigators and courts are increasingly reliant on DNA evidence, cases still arise in which DNA evidence is unavailable. Those are the cases where Palenik's brand of research is most valuable. "We aren't traditional detectives, in that we don't interview suspects and witnesses. Instead, we are true scientific investigators who work in a laboratory with microscopes and chemicals," he observed. "We try to solve problems by establishing facts from the physical evidence we are given," he said. "And usually that evidence is quite small—a grain of sand, a speck of dust. You could probably fit all the material I've been asked to analyze in the last 30 years into a couple of tablespoons."

Palenik pointed to one particular case to show how the smallest piece of evidence can result in an arrest and conviction. His company was called in to investigate an aircraft bombing after other investigators were unable to determine the composition of the bomb, where it came from, or who was responsible for the attack. "We found one particle of cocoa shell dust—used as filler for dynamite—in the bottom of a bag and were able to identify the exact kind of dynamite and trace it back to the suspect's apartment," Palenik recalled. With successes like that, Palenik earned a worldwide reputation as an expert in his field.

Palenik has rejected comparisons to the crime scene investigators featured on the popular television show "CSI," however. "This kind of work isn't what people imagine," he said. "We get facts and go to the library and try to figure out what they mean. Things don't pop out of an instrument. It's not like 'CSI.' . . . If you really want to learn about solving crimes you don't watch 'CSI'—you read Edgar Allan Poe. Anybody who comes to work for me has to read the Poe stories, especially 'The Murders in the Rue Morgue.'

They show how to use reason to solve a crime. That's what we do. But to reason you have to have facts. Our laboratory gives you facts."

## A Thriving Business

Today, Palenik's skills are in such high demand that he works six or seven days a week. The workload also convinced him to recruit his brother Mark, who joined Microtrace in 2004, and his son Chris, who joined Microtrace one year later. In addition to laboratory research, Palenik sometimes testifies in court in order to explain his findings to the judge, attorneys, and the jury. He is considered an excellent expert witness because his work is thorough and accurate and he is able to communicate facts very well. "You'd think with the work [Palenik] does, he'd be difficult to understand," said Assistant Hennepin County Attorney Mike Furnstahl to the *Chicago Daily Herald*. "But he takes that into account and gives an elementary description. It's not just his expertise, it's the complete lack of bias." That view was echoed by Edward Rhodes of the San Diego police department. "He manages to put things into terms that people who don't have his sophisticated knowledge are able to understand," Rhodes confirmed in an interview with the *Chicago Tribune*.

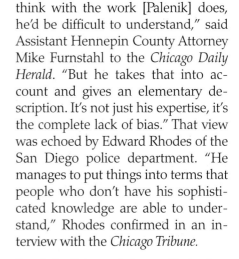

*"You'd think with the work [Palenik] does, he'd be difficult to understand," said Assistant Hennepin County Attorney Mike Furnstahl. "But he takes that into account and gives an elementary description. It's not just his expertise, it's the complete lack of bias."*

But Palenik's work is not limited to criminal investigation. He has analyzed art objects and historical documents for scholars and collectors to confirm authenticity and date of creation. He has also performed research for manufacturers of items as varied as beverages, cosmetics, and tobacco products. Sometimes manufacturing companies hire him to analyze the ingredients in a product made by their competitors, and sometimes they want him to look at their own products. Palenik's work has been featured on several programs produced by cable television's History Channel and Discovery Channel, and he has also appeared on the *Oprah* television talk show to explain his analysis of the ingredients used in popular beauty products.

Palenik revealed that one of his favorite challenges was to analyze Yoo-Hoo, a bottled chocolate drink, to determine why black specks were appearing in their products. Samples had already been analyzed twice, by two different teams of scientists, but they had been unable to agree on what the specks were. One team said the problem was caused by burned milk while the other team insisted that burned sugar was the culprit. Palenik was then called in to investigate. "They thought it was some type of charred material . . . so they sent the sample to me. First, I isolated the specks by chipping away the charred part with microscopic scalpels. Then I tested to see if the particles were a protein or a carbohydrate. . . . Finally, I identified the amino acid that was most prominent—tryptophan, which is highly present in milk but not at all in sugar." Palenik thus confirmed the conclusion that the specks were being caused by burned milk during the production process.

*The phase contrast microscope is modified from a normal light microscope to enhance the contrast observed in an image. It's used by biologists and is also used in particle analysis when studying small particles.*

In addition to performing microscopic analysis of materials for clients all over the world, Palenik has provided training in his areas of expertise. He has instructed other researchers and law enforcement investigators in microchemical analysis, forensic fiber microscopy, identification of animal hair, and vegetable fiber analysis. Palenik has given classes at the McCrone Institute, where he is a member of the board of directors. He also has taught courses at the Illinois Institute of Technology as well as the University of Illinois at Chicago's School of Pharmacy and Department of Criminal Justice.

Palenik is now recognized as one of only about 24 forensic microscopy experts in the world. He is a member of numerous scientific organizations, including the American Academy of Forensic Sciences, the Canadian Society of Forensic Scientists, and even the International Sand Collectors Society—a valuable source of reference samples for his tests. "I've been looking through a microscope almost every day of my life since I was eight years old," Palenik stated. "I'm one of those people who ended up doing exactly what he always wanted to do. I like to look at something someone has looked at before and see things they've never seen . . . I love it. I am one of the lucky few who is actually doing as an adult what he dreamed about doing as a child. And the job never gets boring."

## MAJOR INFLUENCES

Palenik attributes much of his success to the scientists who pioneered the field of forensic microscopy and to the teachers who helped him develop the skills he now uses. In addition to his mentor Walter McCrone, Palenik says that a scientist named Edmond Locard was also very influential. Locard was one of the first forensic microscopists, and he formulated what is now known as the exchange principle: whenever two objects come into contact, there is always a transfer of material. Every person and every object comes into contact with thousands of particles in the course of a day, and microscopic traces of those contacts leave behind a road map of all the places they have been. The science of forensic microscopy is based on Locard's exchange principle, and Palenik is an expert in applying it to form logical, fact-based conclusions.

*"I've been looking through a microscope almost every day of my life since I was eight years old," Palenik stated. "I'm one of those people who ended up doing exactly what he always wanted to do. . . . I am one of the lucky few who is actually doing as an adult what he dreamed about doing as a child. And the job never gets boring."*

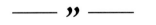

Palenik's list of heroes also includes the fictional 19th century detective Sherlock Holmes. Holmes is the main character in numerous books and short stories written by Sir Arthur Conan Doyle. Palenik said that he developed a love of Sherlock Holmes stories when he was a young boy, around the same time he became interested in microscopy. Holmes is known for his encyclopedic memory and skills in logical deduction. Like Holmes, Palenik uses scientific reasoning and deduction to make connections and draw conclusions that other investigators might overlook. In fact, Palenik is sometimes compared to his boyhood hero. Peter De Forest, professor of criminalistics at John Jay College of Criminal Justice at the City

University of New York, commented in the *Chicago Tribune*, "[Palenik] is the only real-world epitome of Sherlock Holmes. He's a stellar scientist, the kind of guy that Doyle would be writing about if he were writing today. [Palenik] is probably the premier practitioner. He's a top-notch microscopist and problem-solver."

## MARRIAGE AND FAMILY

Palenik's wife Peggy is a second-grade teacher. They have two sons, Christopher and Jeffrey. They live in Elgin, Illinois, a suburb of Chicago.

## HOBBIES AND OTHER INTERESTS

Palenik has devoted his life to his work, and he has few other interests. His hobbies are collecting, reading, and studying antique books and manuscripts related to microscopic science and microchemistry. His enthusiasm for microscopy has not diminished since he was a boy; in fact, he has admitted that whenever he returns home from a trip, he vacuums his clothes just for fun. He then tries to identify all the particles he finds, working in a custom-built laboratory in the basement of his home. "I stay clear of the lab," said his wife, Peggy. "He doesn't like anyone to touch anything. When you're working with small particles, everything has to be dust free, so you try to keep as few people as possible in the area."

## WRITINGS

*The Particle Atlas*, 1973-1979 (co-author)

## FURTHER READING

### Periodicals

*Chicago*, Mar. 2005, p.44
*Chicago Tribune*, Apr. 7, 1988, p.4; Sep. 6, 1992, p.1, p.6; Dec. 30, 1993, p.3; Apr. 6, 2003, p.10
*Los Angeles Times*, May 14, 1986, p.4
*Odyssey*, Jan. 2004, p.35
*Reader's Digest*, Jan. 2003, p.135

### Online Articles

http://www.popsci.com/popsci/crimeseen/982e9aa138b84010vgnvcm 1000004eecbccdrcrd.html
(*Popular Science*, "Crime Seen," undated)

## ADDRESS

Skip Palenik
Microtrace
1750 Grandstand Place
Elgin, IL 60123-4900

## WORLD WIDE WEB SITE

http://www.microtracescientific.com

## Nancy Pelosi 1940-

American Political Leader
First Woman to Serve as Speaker of the United
States House of Representatives

### BIRTH

Nancy Pelosi was born Nancy Patricia D'Alesandro on March
26, 1940, in Baltimore, Maryland. Her father was Thomas
D'Alesandro Jr. and her mother was Annunciata "Nancy"
Lombardi D'Alesandro. The youngest of six children, Pelosi
has five older brothers: Thomas III, Nicholas, Hector, Joseph,
and Franklin.

Pelosi's father served as the mayor of Baltimore from 1947-1959, beginning when she was seven years old. A born political leader, D'Alesandro had previously held seats in the Maryland legislature, the Baltimore City Council, and the United States Congress. Nancy's mother helped her husband in his political aspirations. A member of the Democratic Women's Club, her mother dropped out of law school to focus on her family. "My father was more the centerpiece," explained Pelosi's oldest brother, Thomas III. "We all rallied around him and his career, and none rallied more than my mother. But as successful as my father was, we all knew my mother was the strength of the family."

## YOUTH

Pelosi's family lived on Albemarle Street in the Little Italy section of Baltimore. Like most of the children in her Italian-American neighborhood, "Little Nancy" spent time playing on the front stoops of the row houses on her block and visiting the local candy store.

> "Our whole lives were politics," Pelosi said about her childhood. "If you entered the house, it was always campaign time, and if you went into the living room, it was always constituent time."

The Pelosi family's three-story brick home was used as her father's political headquarters, and city residents frequently visited their home to voice complaints or discuss issues of concern. "People would come to the door and they wanted help," she remembered. "My father always knew how to refer to people. And they'd end up having dinner at our house, because they were hungry." She sometimes sat behind a desk at the front door, greeting visitors and directing them to various city departments. "Our whole lives were politics," she explained. "If you entered the house, it was always campaign time, and if you went into the living room, it was always constituent time." Being the mayor's daughter had its perks. In 1957, she accompanied her father to a formal dinner where she was seated next to future U.S president John F. Kennedy.

Her father and the Democratic leaders of his time helped inform Pelosi's growing political awareness. "It was always about the progressive economic agenda for a fair economy, where many Americans, all Americans, could participate in the economic success of our country," she said. Faith was also an important component of the D'Alesandro

*Pelosi as a young girl with her family.*

household. "I was raised . . . in a very strict upbringing in a Catholic home where we respected people, were observant, [and where] the fundamental belief was that God gave us all a free will and we were accountable for that, each of us," she explained. "We were all christened into the Roman Catholic Church and the Democratic Party." Overall, these experiences growing up prepared her for the future. According to Representative Anna G. Eshoo, "Nancy's life was a dress rehearsal for what she's doing now."

## EDUCATION

Pelosi attended St. Leo's Catholic school, a few blocks from her house. When her father was elected mayor, he received a car and driver, and seven-year-old Nancy began to be chauffeured to school, though she insisted on walking the last block to avoid embarrassment. After graduating from the Institute of Notre Dame, an all-girls Catholic high school, she attended Trinity College, a small women's college in Washington DC. She graduated in 1962 with a Bachelor of Arts (BA) degree in political science.

## MARRIAGE AND FAMILY

Pelosi met her husband, Paul, while she was attending Trinity College and he was enrolled at nearby Georgetown University. They married in 1963, shortly after she graduated from college. They soon moved to New York City, where Paul pursued a career as an investment banker. In 1969, the couple settled in his hometown, San Francisco. While she stayed home to raise their five children—Nancy Corinne, Christine, Jacqueline, Paul, and Alexandra—her husband became a successful businessman in the fields of computer technology and real estate.

For Pelosi, being a stay-at-home mom was a full-time job. "When you raise five children born six years apart, you do most of the work yourself. You can't attract a good deal of people to help out," she joked. Being a devoted mother taught her skills that would later help her in her political career. "It trains you to anticipate, to be organized, and to be flexible," she noted. "To me, the center of my life will always be raising my family. It is the complete joy of my life. To me, working in Congress is a continuation of that."

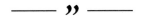

> "[Being a mother] trains you to anticipate, to be organized, and to be flexible," Pelosi noted. "To me, the center of my life will always be raising my family. It is the complete joy of my life. To me, working in Congress is a continuation of that."

## FIRST JOBS

While raising a family in San Francisco, Pelosi did volunteer work during the early 1970s for the city's Democratic Party. Some of those efforts were to support the governor of California, Jerry Brown, who was also a childhood friend of Paul Pelosi. Brown soon became involved in national politics as well.

In 1976 the Democrats were looking for a strong candidate to run for president against the Republican incumbent, President Gerald Ford. Jimmy Carter, the former governor of Georgia, seemed to be the Democratic favorite. Despite Carter's lead, Jerry Brown decided to enter the presidential race and compete in the Maryland primary. Primary elections are held throughout the country by both the Democratic and Republican parties; they are used to determine who will become the Democratic and the Republican candidates in the presidential election. Brown wanted to beat Carter for the Democratic candidacy. Brown recruited Pelosi to help him in

*Pelosi at the headquarters of her first*
*congressional campaign on the night of the election, 1987.*

the race because she still had strong family and political ties to Maryland. Against all odds, Brown managed to get more votes than Carter in Maryland, although Carter would eventually win both the Democratic candidacy and the presidential election. But Pelosi's invaluable help with this small victory did not go unnoticed. She was soon elected chair of the Northern California branch of the Democratic Party, subsequently becoming the head of the party for the entire state.

After the election, Pelosi continued raising her children and volunteering in Democratic politics. Her efforts were soon rewarded. San Francisco Congresswoman Sala Burton became ill with cancer in 1987, and she chose Pelosi to run for her seat in the U.S. Congress in the upcoming election. Though Pelosi had always put her children before her political aspirations, she decided that they were now old enough that she could give up her duties as a full-time mother.

Pelosi's opponent was Harry Britt, a San Francisco City Supervisor who was openly gay, which made him very popular among the members of San

Francisco's large homosexual community. She relied on the fundraising skills that she learned during the Brown campaign and accumulated one million dollars in less than two months. In the end, she defeated Britt by a small margin. Fred Ross Jr., who helped organize her campaign, attested to her political skills. "She has an organizer's instinct. An organizer has to have imagination, has to have a very strategic mind about how to think about a campaign, how to organize a campaign and how to win it. What are the vulnerabilities of the other side? What are the resources you can amass? She understands all of that."

## CAREER HIGHLIGHTS

Since 1987, Pelosi has been a member of the United States House of Representatives. During this time, she has become well known as a champion of liberal causes. She has been active in the areas of human rights, particularly in China, as well as gay and lesbian rights. She has worked for gun control and sponsored the Brady Bill, which called for background checks for persons attempting to buy guns. This bill was signed into law in 1993. Additionally, she has been a vocal opponent of the federal death penalty, has rejected proposals to drill for oil in Alaska, and has advocated the legalization of medical marijuana.

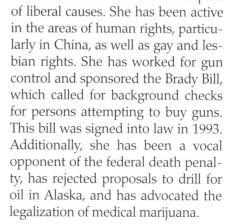

—————— " ——————

*"I will fight discrimination of any form, including gays and lesbians," Pelosi emphasized. "If that makes me unacceptable to some people, that is very fundamental to me and everyone should know it from the start."*

—————— " ——————

Pelosi also strongly endorsed the Challenge America program, a branch of the National Endowment for the Arts (NEA) designed to fund the arts in small towns and urban areas. In 2001 her support paid off when Congress voted to fund the program. On the floor of the House of Representatives, she claimed that "today's vote by the House to increase funding for the NEA . . . is a victory of imagination over ideology. In recent years, we have worried a great deal about the digital divide—a lack of access to technology that could limit opportunity to lower-income Americans. We should be equally concerned about a creativity crisis."

### Criticism of the Chinese Government

Pelosi has paid special attention to issues related to the Chinese government and their approach to human rights. One contributing factor occurred in

1989. Approximately 100,000 Chinese students staged a protest in Beijing's Tiananmen Square against their Communist government. The protest lasted for two months, until the military took deadly action against the students. Hundreds of protesters are thought to have been killed. In 1991, Pelosi was one of three members of Congress to travel to China. Along with her colleagues, she made a visit to Tiananmen Square during their trip. They held up a banner that read: "To those who died for democracy in China." As the press gathered to cover the event, the Chinese police closed in. "I started running," she recalled. "My colleagues, some of them got a little roughed up. The press got treated worse because they had cameras, and they were detained."

Throughout the 1990s, Pelosi protested the meetings between Chinese officials and members of the U.S. Congress. She opposed President Bill Clinton's 1998 diplomatic trip to China and decried the International Olympic Committee's decision to hold the 2008 Summer Olympic Games in China. To this day, she keeps a picture of herself holding up the banner in Tiananmen Square and continues to speak out against the oppression of the Chinese people by their government.

## AIDS and Gay Rights

AIDS and gay rights are also significant issues for Pelosi. During her time in Congress, she has supported funding for research into the AIDS epidemic. Because of the large population of gay men afflicted with AIDS in and around San Francisco, this issue is close to her heart. Prior to her arrival in the House of Representatives, the U.S. government had taken no significant action toward dealing with AIDS. Once elected, she became involved in the creation of the Housing Opportunities for Persons with AIDS program. This initiative supplies federal housing aid to victims of the disease and their families. She also backed legislation that extends Medicaid (a federal program that helps pay medical bills) to men and women with AIDS.

Pelosi's work for gay rights has been widely recognized in the gay community. According to *The Advocate*, a national gay and lesbian magazine, "[Pelosi] is considered one of the House's staunchest supporters of gay rights and a leader on AIDS issues since she arrived on Capitol Hill in 1987." Furthermore, Pelosi has pushed for the legalization of same-sex marriages and promoted the rights of gay couples to adopt children in Washington DC. She remains steadfast in her dedication to issues of gay rights. "I will fight discrimination of any form, including gays and lesbians," she emphasized. "If that makes me unacceptable to some people, that is very fundamental to me and everyone should know it from the start."

*Congresswoman Pelosi on the floor of the U.S. House with her grandchildren.*

### Becoming the Democratic Whip

In 1999 Pelosi began campaigning for the position of Democratic whip, a leadership position in the U.S. House of Representatives. The leadership roles in the House of Representatives are tied to the status of the major parties. Many important benefits are tied to being the majority party, the party with the most members in the House. And with elections for the House of Representatives held every two years, the majority and minority parties can switch frequently.

The House of Representatives is led by the speaker of the house, who is elected by the majority party. The next level of leadership is the party leader—one for each party—who is referred to as the majority leader or the minority leader. Below that is the whip, the position Pelosi was seeking. The job of the whip—the majority and minority whip, one for each party—is to make sure that the members of his or her party are working together as a group and are voting along the same lines.

Beginning in 1994, the Democrats became the minority party in the House of Representatives. At that time, Democrat Bill Clinton was president, and

Al Gore was vice president. The Democrats were expecting Clinton to win a second term as president in the 1996 election, and they expected Al Gore to win the presidential election in 2000. Democrats also assumed that if the voters were going to elect a Democrat president, then the voters would also elect more Democrats to the House of Representatives. In that case, the Democrats would become the majority party. If that were to happen, then Democrat Richard A. Gephardt, who was then the House minority leader, would become the speaker of the house. This would allow the Democratic whip to become the new majority leader. Pelosi saw this as an excellent opportunity to advance in the ranks of the Democratic leadership, and she started campaigning early for the position of minority whip.

The presidential election of 2000 turned out to be far more complicated than anyone expected. Al Gore lost the election to George W. Bush after a lengthy legal dispute involving the counting of ballots in Florida. Similarly, the Democrats failed to secure enough new seats to become the majority party in the House. Despite the blow to her party, Pelosi successfully defeated fellow Democratic Representative Steny Hoyer for the position of minority whip in 2001. This victory made her the first woman in United States history to hold the position of whip in the House of Representatives.

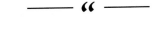

*According to her brother, Thomas III, "The day Nancy was sworn in [as Democratic whip] was one of the happiest days of my mother's life. [Nancy] was the reincarnation of my mother's ambition."*

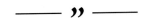

"I think there was a glass ceiling for women in politics," Pelosi stated. "I think I did break that. I think my election as House Democratic whip sent a very clear message. . . . It took some getting used to for people to think that I will now move into the Capitol with my offices there, to have the additional staff and opportunity that a woman hasn't had before in the House or in the Senate. And that I will have influence over how our party goes forward and hopefully on public policy. My candidacy was not about me. It was about showcasing the tremendous talent in the Democratic Party." Even Tom DeLay, the Republican majority whip, praised her victory. "She's a worthy opponent," he admitted. "I've always sort of liked her. But, obviously, I want to beat her at every turn."

While Pelosi was pleased with her new position, she couldn't help but notice that women still had many obstacles to overcome in Washington DC.

*As the head Democrat on the House Intelligence Committee,*
*Pelosi was deeply involved in hearings on the terrorist attacks of 9/11.*
*Here she is shown with Rep. Jan Harman and Rep. James Clyburn.*

"Shortly after my election, the top congressional leaders were invited to the White House for a meeting with the president to talk about the agenda for the next session of Congress," she recounted. "I'd been there on many occasions, so I wasn't particularly apprehensive. But when the door closed behind us, I saw that there were very few other people at the table with the president, and of course they were all men. It occurred to me that this was unlike any meeting that I'd ever attended at the White House. In fact, because a woman was there as a top elected leader and not as staff, it was unlike any meeting ever held at the White House."

Pelosi's appointment as whip was a historic moment for women in the United States, and it resonated back home in Baltimore as well. According to her brother, Thomas III, "The day Nancy was sworn in was one of the happiest days of my mother's life. [Nancy] was the reincarnation of my mother's ambition."

## Investigating 9/11

On September 11, 2001, terrorists hijacked four commercial airplanes in the United States and crashed them into the World Trade Center towers in New York City and the Pentagon in Washington DC; one plane crashed in a field in Pennsylvania. Almost 3,000 people died. The citizens of America were devastated and wondered what could have been done to prevent this horrifying incident. Congress created a House-Senate Joint Inquiry to investigate the events leading up to the terrorist attack.

As the head Democrat on the House Intelligence Committee, Pelosi played a large role in these hearings. In particular, the committee wanted to understand how the intelligence community (the FBI and CIA) processed the information that they had been gathering. "There was a report in August (2001) . . . [that said the terrorists] were planning a strike imminently in the U.S. but again, we didn't have a time and place. So we have to see where the breakdown was in the system," Pelosi stated. The committee was also interested in the lack of enforcement of immigration laws that allowed the hijackers into the county. "Was it a breakdown in communication with the Immigration and Naturalization Service," she asked. "I hope that we will have a review of all of the federal agencies which had a responsibility, which could have prevented what happened on September 11."

One agency that did not allow the committee access to all of its information was the National Security Council. The NSC consists of the president, vice president, secretary of state, and the foreign-policy experts who regularly meet with the president. Pelosi was angered by what she saw as a lack of cooperation. "If we're going to have a real and complete investigation, if we are going to get the job done for the families and for the country and protect the American people into the future, the National Security Council records must be available to the committee and the public," she asserted.

Although the Bush administration eventually provided some information to the National Commission on Terrorist Attacks in 2003, Pelosi argued that they were still protecting the government of Saudi Arabia. Many of the September 11 terrorists were from Saudi Arabia, but the Saudi government is one of the few American allies in the Middle East. The Bush administration explained that they were merely maintaining a diplomatic relationship with the Saudis and did not want to offend them. Pelosi countered by saying, "Classification should protect sources and methods, ongoing investigations, and our national security interests. It is not intended to protect reputations of people or countries."

## Opposing the War in Iraq

A year after the terrorist attacks of September, 11, 2001, Congress was scheduled to vote on whether or not to endorse an invasion of Iraq. President George W. Bush insisted that the leader of Iraq, Saddam Hussein, was hiding weapons of mass destruction. During the 2001 State of the Union Address, President Bush asserted: "U.S. intelligence indicates that Saddam Hussein had upwards of 30,000 munitions capable of delivering chemical agents. Inspectors recently turned up 16 of them, despite Iraq's recent declaration denying their existence. Saddam Hussein has not accounted for the remaining 29,984 of these prohibited munitions. He has given no evidence that he has destroyed them." Republican whip Tom DeLay added, "Saddam Hussein is seeking the means to murder millions in just a single moment. He's trying to extend that grip of fear beyond his own borders and he is consumed with hatred for America." Consequently, many Democrats, including House minority leader Gephardt and Senate majority leader Tom Daschle, supported the use of military force against Iraq. "I believe it is important for America to speak with one voice," Daschle said at the time.

> "Becoming the first woman speaker will send a message to young girls and women across the country that anything is possible for them, that women can achieve power, wield power, and breathe the air at that altitude. As the first woman speaker of the House, I will work to make certain that I will not be the last."

This made it all the more uncomfortable for Pelosi to speak out against the war. During the debate leading up to the vote, she claimed that military conflict with Iraq "poses a risk to the war on terrorism. It will unravel the coalition [of Muslim allies in the Middle East]. It will make Arab countries that are friendly to our cause now shaky." Furthermore, her role as whip would normally force her to convince Democrats to vote along the same lines as their minority leader, Gephardt. But she insisted that the members of the House listen to their conscience. Although Congress eventually voted to back the war, less than half of the Democrats in the House of Representatives sided with Gephardt.

Shortly afterwards, the Republicans claimed even more seats in the House and Senate during the Congressional elections of 2002. The Democrats began to question Gephardt's leadership capabilities as House minority

*Pelosi holds the speaker's gavel during opening day ceremonies, after being sworn in as the first female speaker of the U.S. House.*

leader. Sensing the discontent within his party, Gephardt resigned from his position. Pelosi was elected to take his place, making her the first woman to hold the position of minority leader in Congress. "It was a very powerful vote of confidence," she acknowledged. "It was quite stunning, I have to admit myself. What it says is a recognition of what I can do as a leader to take us to victory." This new position only strengthened her resolve to speak out against the Iraq war, and she has continued to be one of the leading voices of Congressional opposition on this front.

## Becoming Speaker of the U.S. House of Representatives

When Pelosi became the Democratic minority leader, many Republicans hoped that her left wing, or liberal, stances would actually hurt her party.

*When the president addresses the House and Senate, as in this scene from the 2007 State of the Union address, he is flanked by the vice president and the speaker of the house. Here, President George W. Bush is shown with Vice President Dick Cheney and Speaker of the House Nancy Pelosi.*

"If she is true to her past and her district," claimed Ohio Representative Deborah Pryce, "the Democratic caucus will be far too liberal for the country." Others were not so sure, including Porter J. Goss, a Republican representative who worked with her on the 9/11 inquiry. "Does she have the ability to go beyond representing the left wing of her party? The answer is clearly yes," Goss said. "While it's true she does represent the left wing of the [Democratic] party, it's equally true that if you say that's all she's going to do, you would be underestimating her badly."

In the November 2006 Congressional election, the Democrats gained the majority of the seats in both the Senate and the House of Representatives. This victory for the Democrats gave them control of Congress for the first time in 12 years. It also allowed the Democrats to vote for a new speaker of the house. They elected Pelosi. This was especially significant because the speaker of the house is second in line (after the vice president) to the presidency.

Just as she had been the first female congressional leader, Pelosi was now the first female speaker of the house. "When my colleagues elect me as speaker on January 4, we will not just break through a glass ceiling, we will break through a marble ceiling," she proclaimed. "In more than 200 years of history, there was an established pecking order and I cut in line." She added, "Becoming the first woman speaker will send a message to young girls and women across the country that anything is possible for them, that women can achieve power, wield power, and breathe the air at that altitude. As the first woman speaker of the House, I will work to make certain that I will not be the last."

When Pelosi was sworn in as the speaker of the house in early 2007, she was accompanied by her six grandchildren. "For our daughters and granddaughters," she proclaimed during her speech on the floor of the House of Representatives, "today we have broken the marble ceiling." President Bush acknowledged the historical relevance of her new position during the State of the Union Address that took place soon afterward. The president announced, "Tonight I have the high privilege and distinct honor of my own as the first president to begin the State of the Union Message with these words:'Madam Speaker.'"

## The First 100 Hours and Beyond

As Pelosi settled in as the speaker of the house for the 110th session of Congress, she pledged to focus on six legislative initiatives during the first 100 hours. These goals, which the Democratic Party had developed during the 2006 campaign year, were dubbed the "Six for '06": "We will make America safer by implementing the recommendations of the 9/11 Commission [a bipartisan plan to handle the escalating violence in Iraq with diplomacy]. We will make our economy fairer by raising the minimum wage. We will promote stem cell research to offer hope to the millions of American families who suffer from devastating diseases. We will improve health care by requiring Medicare to negotiate for lower prescription drug prices. We will make college more affordable by cutting interest rates on student loans. We will take the first step toward achieving energy independence by repealing subsidies to Big Oil and investing the savings in renewable energy." Yet some Republicans were skeptical of this plan and doubted that many of these goals would be achieved.

Meanwhile, the war in Iraq continued to spark heated debate. In January 2007, President Bush announced his plan to deploy more than 20,000 additional troops to Iraq in an effort to stop the increasing bloodshed. Pelosi voiced her opposition to this plan on the floor of the House in February 2007. "Let us be clear on one fundamental principle: we all support the troops," she emphasized. "Four previous troop escalations have resulted in escalating levels of violence. In light of the facts, President Bush's escalation proposal will not make America safer, will not make our military stronger, and will not make the region more stable, and it will not have my support."

## HOBBIES AND OTHER INTERESTS

Pelosi is a self-admitted chocoholic and has professed a particular weakness for chocolate mousse. Her favorite television show is "The Daily Show with Jon Stewart," which she watches avidly, and she is also a devoted fan of "Jeopardy." Her favorite band is the Grateful Dead, and she enjoys doing the *New York Times* crossword puzzle. Although she hates to shop (her husband chooses her clothes), she is recognized as a stylish dresser and is fond of Armani suits.

## HONORS AND AWARDS

Distinguished Citizens Award (Commonwealth Club of California): 2002
Alan Cranston Peace Award (The Global Security Institute): 2003
Cesar Chavez Legacy Award (Cesar E. Chavez Foundation): 2003
Millard E. Tydings Award for Courage and Leadership in American Politics (University of Maryland's Center for American Politics and Citizenship): 2003
"Unsung Hero" Award (The American Legion): 2004
Community Service Award (The University of California, San Francisco): 2005
Congressional Leadership Award (Minority Business RoundTable): 2006
Excellence in Leadership Award (The Mexican American Legal Defense and Educational Fund): 2007
Peace Award (The American Ireland Fund): 2007

## FURTHER READING

### Books

*Encyclopedia of World Biography Supplement,* 2005
Marcovitz, Hal. *Nancy Pelosi,* 2004

### Periodicals

*Baltimore Sun,* Nov. 14, 2002, p.A1
*Boston Globe,* Feb. 5, 2003, p.D1
*Christian Century,* Feb. 6, 2007, p.8
*Economist,* Feb. 24, 2007, p.42
*Los Angeles Times,* Jan. 4, 2007, p.A1; Jan. 5, 2007, p.A11; Jan. 11, 2007, p.A10; Feb. 9, 2007, p.A14; Mar. 16, 2007, p.A1
*Los Angeles Times Magazine,* Jan. 26, 2003, p.12
*National Catholic Reporter,* Jan. 24, 2003, p.3
*New Scientist,* Jan. 6, 2007, p.8
*Newsweek,* Nov. 20, 2006, p.50
*O, The Oprah Magazine,* Apr. 2004, p.66
*People,* Dec. 2, 2002, p.217
*Time,* Nov. 20, 2006, p.40; Nov. 27, 2006, p.30
*Washington Post,* Nov. 19, 2002, p.A25; Nov. 10, 2006, p.C1

## Online Articles

http://abcnews.go.com
  (*ABC News*, "Pelosi Conveys Israeli Peace Message to Syria," Apr. 4, 2007)
http://www.cbsnews.com
  (*CBS News*, "Nancy Pelosi: Two Heartbeats Away," Oct. 22, 2006; "Pelosi: No Blank Check for Bush In Iraq," Jan. 7, 2007)
http://www.cnn.com
  (*CNN*, "Pelosi Becomes First Woman House Speaker," Jan. 5, 2007)
http://www.nytimes.com
  (*New York Times*, "A Shift in Power, Starting with 'Madam Speaker,'" Jan. 24, 2007)
http://www.trinitydc.edu/admissions/profile_pelosi.php
  (Trinity University, "Making History, Making Progress," undated)
http://usatoday.com
  (*USA Today*, "Pelosi To Be the First Woman to Lead Congress," Nov. 9, 2006)
http://www.washingtonpost.com
  (Washington Post, "Democrats Won't Try To Impeach President," May 12, 2006)

## Online Databases

*Biography Resource Center Online*, 2007, article from *Encyclopedia of World Biography Supplement*, 2005

## ADDRESS

Nancy Pelosi
Office of the Speaker
H-232, US Capitol
Washington, DC 20515

## WORLD WIDE WEB SITES

http://www.house.gov/pelosi
http://www.speaker.gov

## Jack Prelutsky 1940-
American Children's Poet
First U.S. Children's Poet Laureate

*[Editor's Note: Jack Prelutsky was originally featured in* Biography Today Authors, *Vol. 2. In honor of his selection by the Poetry Foundation as the first Children's Poet Laureate, the entry has been expanded and updated to include his most recent accomplishments.]*

### BIRTH

Jack Prelutsky was born on September 8, 1940, in Brooklyn, New York, to Charles and Dorothea Prelutsky. Charles was an electrician and Dorothea was a homemaker.

## YOUTH

While still a baby, Prelutsky was saved from a fire at his family's apartment building in Brooklyn. He was pulled from the flames by his Uncle Charlie, a stand-up comic who played the Borscht Belt (a predominantly Jewish resort area in New York State). Prelutsky has credited his uncle with giving him an appreciation of language as well. "He used to tell me these stupid jokes," Prelutsky remembered, "but they really made me realize what language was about."

Prelutsky grew up in a tough neighborhood in the Bronx, a borough of New York City. "It consisted mainly of Jewish, Irish, and Italian families," he explained. "My father, mother, younger brother and I lived in an apartment house where everyone knew everyone else, just like in a small town. The older people sat on milk crates on the sidewalk and socialized, while the kids played stickball and other street games." The family was poor and Prelutsky never owned a bicycle while growing up. He was often targeted by tougher boys. "I was a sensitive kid in a working-class neighborhood. I got beat up a lot. I was a skinny kid with a big mouth. A bad combination."

> "I was an imaginative kid and I would dream of having pets like unicorns and tiny elephants. One of my dreams was that I had my own dragon . . . a small one, of course, that I could manage and train."

Although he loved animals, Prelutsky could not have any pets in the house because his mother suffered from asthma. So he dreamed of animals he could have for his own. "I was an imaginative kid and I would dream of having pets like unicorns and tiny elephants. One of my dreams was that I had my own dragon . . . a small one, of course, that I could manage and train."

## EARLY MEMORIES

"I remembered that my mother used to threaten me with the bogeyman when I would misbehave," Prelutsky once wrote. "My mother would say, 'Wash your hands,' and I would say, 'No.' My mother would say it again and I would say 'No.' She'd say, 'You're making me mad at you,' and I would say, 'I don't care,' and she would say, 'Wash your hands or the bogeyman will get you.' So I washed my hands."

*Prelutsky spends a lot of time with his readers,*
*as in this visit to a children's bookstore in Seattle.*

## EDUCATION

Prelutsky attended the local public schools in the Bronx and hated it. He was bored in class. Although he enjoyed playing word games like Hangman, doing crossword puzzles, and inventing puns, he did not like poetry. "Sometime in elementary school I had a teacher who, in retrospect, did not like poetry herself. She was determined to inflict her views on her captives. The syllabus told her she had to recite a poem once a week. She would pick a boring poem from a boring book and read it in a boring voice, looking bored while she was doing it."

When Prelutsky was in his early teens, his teachers discovered that he had musical talent and suggested that he attend a special high school for the arts. At the High School of Music and Art, he was finally happy. He had a beautiful singing voice and began to take part in high school musical performances. After graduating in 1958, he attended Hunter College for two years. He studied "philosophy, psychology, and a couple of other things," Prelutsky remembered. He flunked English three times before dropping out.

## BECOMING A WRITER

Prelutsky had many different jobs before becoming a professional writer. He drove a cab, moved furniture, and worked as a busboy, a potter, a woodworker, and a door-to-door salesman. By the late 1960s, he was working in a bookstore in the Greenwich Village neighborhood in New York City and singing in coffeehouses in his spare time. While working as a singer, he met Bob Dylan. They became friends and admired each other. In fact, Dylan once said that Prelutsky sounded "like a cross between Woody Guthrie and Enrico Caruso."

> "Sometime in elementary school I had a teacher who, in retrospect, did not like poetry herself. She was determined to inflict her views on her captives. . . . She would pick a boring poem from a boring book and read it in a boring voice, looking bored while she was doing it."

Prelutsky also liked to draw, creating ink drawings of imaginary animals. A friend encouraged him to take his drawings to a New York publishing house. At the last minute, he wrote poems to go with the drawings. Susan Hirshman, the editor, liked his work. He remembered that she said, "You have talent. You should be published." "You like my drawings?" he asked. "Are you kidding?" she said. So the drawings that had taken Prelutsky six months to do were rejected, but the poems he had written in two hours were accepted. He was just 24 at the time. The poems appeared in 1967 in his first book, *A Gopher in the Garden and Other Animal Poems*. "The editor told me I was a natural poet," Prelutsky recalls, "and encouraged me greatly to keep writing. She published my first book, and remained my editor for 37 years, until she retired."

## CAREER HIGHLIGHTS

Since that time, Prelutsky has become one of the nation's most beloved poets for young readers. Over a career spanning some four decades, he has sold over a million copies of his books. One of the reasons he has become so popular is because he writes about topics that inspire and fascinate children. Homework, bad meatloaf, and bullies are just some of the topics he has tackled. "Children are flesh and blood. They're just like us, only smaller," he explained. "I write about the things kids care about." In fact, he writes the kinds of poems he would have wanted to read as a kid. Traditional children's poetry, he once said, is full of "hills and daffodils." But when he was a kid, "we didn't care about that. If I wanted to hear poems, and I wasn't sure I did, I wanted them to be about the cop on the corner, the butcher, the guys in the neighborhood, food fights, dinosaurs, monsters, outer space."

Prelutsky has spent a lot of time with his readers over the years. "Little by little, I got to visiting with children and found out what they liked and didn't like," he recalled. "And I tried to write about the things I wish I had heard about when I was a kid: sibling rivalry, food fights, monsters, dragons, and all that good stuff." He regularly visits schools, libraries, and bookstores where he often sings his poetry to kids, accompanying himself on guitar.

Prelutsky gets ideas for his poems everywhere: from his readers, from his daily life, and from experiences in his past. "Sometimes I take things from my childhood," he said. "My mother was not a particularly good cook. She was a lovely person, but I have never eaten such bad meat loaf." From this experience came the poem "My Mother Made a Meat Loaf," where the meat loaf is so tough it cannot be cut with a cleaver or a drill and must finally be used as bricks to build houses. This type of humor is a large part of what has made his poetry so popular with kids.

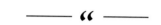

*"Little by little, I got to visiting with children and found out what they liked and didn't like," he recalled. "And I tried to write about the things I wish I had heard about when I was a kid: sibling rivalry, food fights, monsters, dragons, and all that good stuff."*

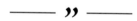

Prelutsky uses language that is full of word play, puns, and all around fun words. His simple and direct language is influenced by the lyrics of folk music. "In folk music, the words are written the way people actually talk, and the melodies are simple and accessible," he says. In choosing his word, Prelutsky explains that he "never talks down" to his readers. "If a $50 word works better than five $10 words, I use the $50 word. I do use words like 'mucilaginous' and 'gelatinous' because children love those words and will find out what they mean."

## Silly Poems

Many of Prelutsky's favorite poems are on the silly side. *The Queen of Eene* features poems about people who eat such odd things as cars and

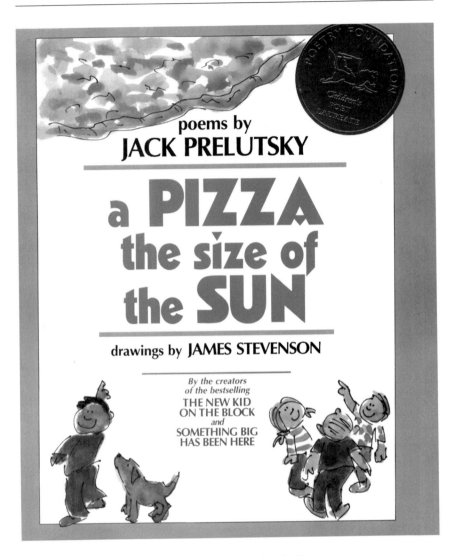

*One of Prelutsky's many books of silly poems.*

basketballs. In *The Sheriff of Rottenshot,* one poem tells of a catfish that is trying to find a mousefish to chase. *A Pizza the Size of the Sun: Poems* contains silly poems about a boy who hides his camel by using "camelflage," and another one about a salesman with strange goods: "Eyeballs for sale! / Fresh eyeballs for sale! / Delicious, nutritious, / not moldy or stale." *Scranimals* is about an island with unusual creatures that are half-vegetable and half-animal. Among the creatures are the hippopotamushroom, antelopetunia, and bananaconda. *Behold the Bold Umbrel-*

*laphant and Other Poems* carries the idea even farther, introducing the alarmadillo, the ballpoint penguin, and the clocktopus.

"Writing humorous verse is hard work," Prelutsky has admitted. "For the humor to succeed, every part of the poem must be just right: It requires delicacy. If the poet uses too heavy a hand, the poem goes beyond being funny and turns into something disquieting or even grotesque. Conversely, if the poet doesn't push the idea far enough, the incongruities that are supposed to make the poem funny bypass the reader."

## Scary Poems

Some of Prelutsky's poems are considered so scary that they have been restricted by librarians, especially those from *Nightmares: Poems to Trouble Your Sleep*. That book was even banned in the school district where he lived. "I believe certain things are inappropriate for children," he allowed. "But I don't believe in shielding children from reality." But Prelutsky's scary poems often provide both chills and chuckles. Many of the poems feature characters from horror stories but in a humorous way. One poem tells of a barber who caters to werewolves; another poem is about a giant's dentist. Despite some librarians' qualms about its subject matter, *Nightmares: Poems to Trouble Your Sleep* was named Best of the Best Books by the *School Library Journal*.

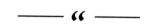

*"Writing humorous verse is hard work," Prelutsky has admitted. "For the humor to succeed, every part of the poem must be just right: It requires delicacy. If the poet uses too heavy a hand, the poem goes beyond being funny and turns into something disquieting or even grotesque."*

More of Prelutsky's spooky verse appears in *The Headless Horseman Rides Tonight: More Poems to Trouble Your Sleep* and *The Gargoyle on the Roof.* The poems often warn the reader of dangerous creatures: A bogeyman will "crumple your bones" or a ghoul might eat you like he has eaten other children. But many of these poems are chilling in a comical way. One poem from *The Gargoyle on the Roof* is about a vampire grooming himself: "When I look into the mirror / My reflection's never there. / So I always stare at nothing / As I shave and comb my hair." *The Headless Horseman Rides Tonight* was named a *New York Times* Outstanding Book and a *School Library Journal* Best Book.

*One of Prelutsky's most acclaimed books of scary poems.*

### Earning Acclaim from Readers and Others

Every week, Prelutsky receives about 100 letters from kids who have enjoyed his books. He replies to them in verse: "Thank you for your letter,

I'm delighted that you wrote, And very glad to answer you by sending you this note." "I have a talent: I can make anything rhyme," Prelutsky maintained. "The trick was to take the thing I do and work at it—become not just adept, but professional. Just because you can make things rhyme doesn't mean you have anything to say."

Despite the deluge of fan mail, Prelutsky seems to be modest about his talents. "Real poets kind of look down on me," he once said, "though I don't care." But others would disagree. His work has been widely admired by readers, reviewers, and other poets, as in this comment from poet Karen Glenn. "He knows how to have fun and makes boatloads of puns, but Prelutsky is more than a tall, clever child. He is a real poet who knows as much about form, rhythm, and rhyme as he does about burned meatloaf, umbrellaphants, and preposterpusses. He also knows about feelings and, for lack of a better word, soul. . . . He writes real poetry, both formal and informal. He's got rhythm. He's got rhyme. He's even got onomatopoeia, as curious creatures 'honk and quack and squawk.' This is not pretend poetry, gutted of its elements. It's the real thing, filled with alliteration and music. . . . He knows all about form. He writes rhyming couplets. He follows strict rhyme schemes. He writes sonnets—not that kids would ever know it! His poetry is not like spinach, but like chocolate cream pie."

Indeed, Prelutsky's poetic skill is so celebrated that in 1997 he was asked to finish a manuscript that Dr. Seuss had left incomplete when died in 1991. It was an honor to be selected to work on Dr. Seuss's material. Prelutsky finished the story, working with illustrator Lane Smith, and *Hooray for Diffendoofer Day!* was published in 1998. It is the story of a special school where individuality and creative thinking are celebrated.

In 2006, Prelutsky was named the first Children's Poet Laureate by the Poetry Foundation. The laureateship lasts for two years, during which time he will give two major poetry readings and serve as an advisor to the Poetry Foundation on children's literature. The award also includes a $25,000 prize, some of which Prelutsky has said he plans to spend on writing contests for children. According to John Barr, the president of the foundation, "Generations of children have learned to love poetry through Jack Prelutsky's work. His extraordinary service to an important branch of literature makes him the perfect first recipient of the Children's Poet Laureate Award."

Prelutsky heard the news about winning the award while riding on a ferry boat in Seattle. He began jumping up and down and yelling. "I think they thought I was a security risk," he recalled. "I was just shocked and floored. I've never won anything in my life except a two-pound Polish ham in a Vivaldi radio contest, and that was more than 30 years ago."

―――― " ――――

*"He knows how to have fun and makes boatloads of puns, but Prelutsky is more than a tall, clever child. He is a real poet who knows as much about form, rhythm, and rhyme as he does about burned meatloaf, umbrellaphants, and preposterpusses. He also knows about feelings and, for lack of a better word, soul."*
— Karen Glenn

―――― " ――――

## MAJOR INFLUENCES

Prelutsky has listed Woody Allen, Groucho Marx, and Jimmy Durante as early influences on his work. He also called Dr. Seuss a "genius" and nonsense poet Ogden Nash "my poetic daddy."

## MARRIAGE AND FAMILY

Prelutsky married his wife, Carolynn, in 1979. He was on a book tour in Albuquerque, New Mexico. She was a children's librarian with the job of showing him around town. He claims it was love at first sight, and he asked her to marry him the day they met. Just as impetuous as Jack, Carolynn accepted. The couple has lived in Arizona, Boston, New York, and Olympia, Washington. They currently have a loft apartment in downtown Seattle and an apartment on nearby Bainbridge Island. They have no children.

## HOBBIES AND OTHER INTERESTS

"I enjoy photography, carpentry, and creating games, collages, and 'found object' sculpture," Prelutsky explained. "Lately I've been teaching myself to draw on the computer." He is also an avid collector of children's books, owning over 4,000 titles. He also collects toy frogs.

## SELECTED WRITINGS

*A Gopher in the Garden and Other Animal Poems,* 1967
*The Terrible Tiger,* 1970
*Toucans and Other Poems,* 1970
*Nightmares: Poems to Trouble Your Sleep,* 1976
*It's Halloween,* 1977

*The Mean Old Hyena*, 1978
*The Queen of Eene*, 1978
*The Headless Horseman Rides Tonight: More Poems to Trouble Your Sleep*, 1980
*Rolling Harvey Down the Hill*, 1980
*It's Christmas*, 1981
*The Baby Uggs Are Hatching*, 1982
*It's Thanksgiving*, 1982
*Kermit's Garden of Verses*, 1982
*The Sheriff of Rottenshot*, 1982
*It's Valentine's Day*, 1983
*Zoo Doings: Animal Poems*, 1983
*It's Snowing, It's Snowing!*, 1984
*The New Kid on the Block*, 1984
*Ride a Purple Pelican*, 1984
*Tyrannosaurus Was a Beast*, 1988
*Something Big Has Been Here*, 1990
*A. Nonny Mouse Writes Again*, 1993
*The Dragons Are Singing Tonight*, 1993
*Monday's Troll*, 1996
*A Pizza the Size of the Sun: Poems*, 1996
*The Beauty of the Beast: Poems*, 1997
*Hooray for Diffendoofer Day!*, 1998 (with Dr. Suess)
*Dog Days: Rhymes around the Year*, 1999
*The Gargoyle on the Roof*, 1999
*The 20th Century Children's Poetry Treasury*, 1999
*Awful Ogre's Awful Day*, 2000
*It's Raining Pigs and Noodles: Poems*, 2000
*The Frogs Wore Red Suspenders: Rhymes*, 2002
*Scranimals*, 2002
*If Not for the Cat*, 2004
*Behold the Bold Umbrellaphant and Other Poems*, 2006
*Good Sports: Rhymes about Running, Jumping, Throwing, and More*, 2007
*Me I Am!*, 2007

## SELECTED HONORS AND AWARDS

Best of the Best Books (*School Library Journal*): 1979, for *Nightmares: Poems to Trouble Your Sleep*
Best Books (*School Library Journal*): 1980, for *The Headless Horseman Rides Tonight*; 1981, for *The Wild Baby*; 1983, for *The Random House Book of Poetry for Children*; 1986, for *Read-Aloud Rhymes for the Very Young*
Outstanding Books (*New York Times*): 1980, for *The Headless Horseman Rides Tonight*

Book of the Year (Library of Congress): 1983, for *The Random House Book of Poetry for Children*

Children's Book of the Year (Child Study Association): 1983, for *The Random House Book of Poetry for Children*

Parents' Choice Award: 1986, for *The New Kid on the Block*

Editor's Choice (*Booklist*): 1990, for *Something Big Has Been Here*

Notable Book (Association for Library Services to Children): 1990, for *Something Big Has Been Here*

Best Book for Young Adults (American Library Association): 1998, for *The Beauty of the Beast*

Teachers' Choice Award (International Reading Association): 1998, for *The Beauty of the Beast*

National Parenting Publication Award: 2001, for *Awful Ogre's Awful Day*

Children's Poet Laureate Award (Poetry Foundation): 2006

## FURTHER READING

### Books

*Contemporary Authors New Revision Series*, Vol. 38, 1993
*Major Authors and Illustrators for Children and Young Adults*, 2002
*Something about the Author*, Vol. 66, 1991
*St. James Guide to Children's Writers*, 1999

### Periodicals

*Allentown (PA) Morning Call*, Oct. 4, 1999, p.D1
*Chicago Sun-Times*, Sep. 28, 2006, p.46
*Chicago Tribune*, Sep. 28, 2006, p.9
*Columbus Dispatch*, Jan. 28, 1993, p.B7
*Instructor*, Sep. 1993, p.81
*Publisher's Weekly*, Sep. 20, 1991, p.46
*San Francisco Chronicle*, Feb. 24, 1991, Sunday Review Section, p.10
*School Library Journal*, Nov. 2006, p. 7
*Seattle Post-Intelligencer*, Oct. 11, 1990, p.D3; Sep. 28, 2006, p.C1
*The Writer*, Nov. 1990, p.7

### Online Articles

http://www.wildewritingworks.com/int/prelutskyjack.htm
(*BookPage*, "Interview with Jack Prelutsky," 1993)

http://www.harpercollins.com/authors/13328/Jack_Prelutsky/index.aspx
(*HarperCollins*, "Author Interview: Jack Prelutsky on *It's Raining Pigs and Noodles*," undated)

http://www.poetryfoundation.org
(*Poetry Foundation*, "Foundation: Announcements," Sep. 2006)

http://www.poetryfoundation.org/features/feature.children.html?id=178694
   (*Poetry Foundation*, "Never Poke Your Uncle with a Fork: Jack Prelutsky, the Nation's First Children's Poet Laureate," undated)

## Online Databases

*Biography Resource Center Online*, 2006, articles from *Contemporary Authors Online*, 2006, *Major Authors and Illustrators for Children and Young Adults*, 2002, and *St. James Guide to Children's Writers*, 1999

*Wilson Web*, 2006, article from *Fifth Book of Junior Authors and Illustrators: Junior Authors Electronic*, 1999

## ADDRESS

Jack Prelutsky
Greenwillow Books / HarperCollins
10 East 53rd Street
New York, NY 10022

## WORLD WIDE WEB SITES

http://www.jackprelutsky.com
http://www.poetryfoundation.org

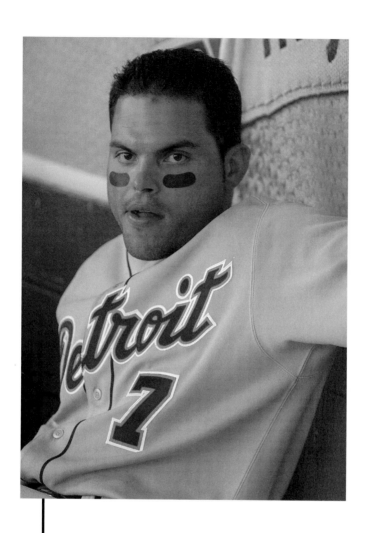

## Ivan "Pudge" Rodriguez 1971-

Puerto Rican Professional Baseball Player with the
Detroit Tigers
Record-Setting Catcher with 13 Gold Glove Awards
and 14 All-Star Game Appearances

### BIRTH

Ivan Rodriguez was born in Manati, Puerto Rico, on November 30, 1971 (some sources state November 27, 1971). He is
often known by his nickname, Pudge. His father, Jose

Rodriguez, was an electrical supervisor for an international construction company. His mother, Eva Torres, was a second-grade teacher, and later became a school principal. Though his parents divorced when he was 12, he has remained close with them both. Ivan has an older brother, Jose Rodriguez Jr., a factory worker and amateur baseball player.

## YOUTH

Rodriguez was raised in Vega Baja, Puerto Rico, a town located five miles south of the Atlantic Ocean and 18 miles west of San Juan. He lived in a small cinderblock house in the Algarrobo barrio, a poor neighborhood on the fringe of Vega Baja. At the age of seven, he joined the barrio's little league team and began practicing baseball drills with his father for two or three hours a session.

> *The local baseball field upon which Rodriguez played as a kid had an uneven infield full of pebbles and an outfield with bare patches in the grass. "The ball, it could bounce anywhere," recalled Rodriguez. "It could hit you right in the face. It taught you to be ready for anything."*

Rodriguez loved baseball, and he often dreamed of becoming a major league pitcher. After school and throughout the summer, he walked through the neighborhood with a bat and ball, looking for kids with whom he could play. The equipment he used was battered and worn, but he never let that bother him. He and his brother made baseballs by wrapping medical tape around a cork, and they often played a baseball-like game called "chapitas" using bottle caps and broomsticks. Rodriguez's passion for baseball was so great that he often wore his baseball glove when he was sitting around the house. Some evenings, he even went to bed in his little league uniform. "From the time he was 7, it's been baseball, baseball, baseball," said his mother.

Rodriguez pitched and covered third base for his little league team. During these early years on the diamond, he often found himself playing against Juan Gonzalez, who grew up to become a feared major league slugger—and Rodriguez's teammate on the Texas Rangers for several years. The local baseball field, which Rodriguez still visits regularly, had an uneven infield full of pebbles and an outfield with bare patches in the grass. "It made you always be ready," he recalled. "The ball, it could bounce anywhere. It could hit you right in the face. It taught you to be ready for anything."

It was on that field, surrounded by a rusty fence, graffiti-covered benches, and rickety wooden bleachers, that Rodriguez developed his talent. When he was eight years old, he pitched four no-hitters in one year. "Everybody was afraid to face me. . . . Nobody could hit my fastball," he remembered. "Even when I was little, I could throw a ball. I guess it was my gift." Adults in the neighborhood could tell that he was a special talent as well. "Since Ivan was nine or ten years old, in my mind, I knew he was a pro," his father said.

Despite his powerful pitching arm, Rodriguez was persuaded by his father to train as a catcher in little league. Jose Rodriguez feared that his son's short stature would prevent him from becoming a major-league pitcher, since most of them are at least six feet tall. "Everybody is small in the family," Rodriguez explained. "So my father says: 'Let's keep working the catching.'"

Rodriguez embraced the challenge of being a catcher. Big league catchers such as Johnny Bench of the Cincinnati Reds and Lance Parrish of the Detroit Tigers became his heroes, and Rodriguez practiced his catching and batting skills with his father on a regular basis. His father's instructions did not end on the playground either. His parents often sat behind the backstop during games so Rodriguez's father could talk to his son when he was catching or batting. Rodriguez said that his father was ordinarily a very quiet man, but during games he would shout out words of encouragement and advice: "'Think, Ivan! . . . Be aggressive! . . . Play hard!' I wanted to make him happy with me," Rodriguez acknowledged. "My father . . . made me what I am."

## An Exciting Prospect

Rodriguez played little league baseball in Vega Baja from age seven to 15. By his early teens he was on the roster of top teams that traveled throughout Latin America. During that time, one of his coaches nicknamed him "Pudge" because of his stocky build. Although Rodriguez disliked the name at first, he grew to accept it.

At age 15, Rodriguez joined the Mickey Mantle League. His performance in this top junior league attracted the attention of several major league scouts, including Luis Rosa and Manny Batista of the Texas Rangers. "He was very smart and aggressive at such a young age," recalled Batista. "It was difficult to find a catcher, at that age, who could do what Ivan did."

Rosa offered Rodriguez a contract as a minor-league professional baseball player in July 1988. Although Rodriguez was only 16 years old, Rosa was confident that the player was ready for the challenge. "Pudge was hard-nosed, even then," he explained. "He showed leadership at 16 that I'd seen in few kids. He knew where he was going."

Rodriguez admitted that when he left for spring training with the Texas Rangers at the young age of 16, he had very mixed feelings. "I'm still a little kid," he recalled. "My family is crying at the airport, because I leave for the first time alone." Though he was excited about the opportunity ahead, Rodriguez admitted harboring fears and doubts about leaving Puerto Rico. "I don't know how to speak the language at all," he explained. "I don't know how to say yes or no."

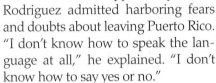

*Rodriguez was signed to a minor-league professional baseball contract at the young age of 16. "Pudge was hard-nosed, even then," explained a scout. "He showed leadership at 16 that I'd seen in few kids. He knew where he was going."*

## EDUCATION

Rodriguez attended Lino Padron Rivera High School in Vega Baja before being discovered by major league scouts. According to his mother, he was very shy in school. "[Ivan was] quiet in the extreme. Even when he was in grade school, teachers literally had to take the words out of his mouth," she said. His favorite subject was math, which came naturally to him, and he has said that he might have pursued a career in accounting if he had not become a professional athlete. Rodriguez left high school to play baseball before earning his diploma, but he often emphasizes the importance of education when he talks to young athletes.

## CAREER HIGHLIGHTS

In baseball, some players start their professional careers in the major leagues. But many more start playing for a team in the minor leagues, also called the farm system. The teams in the minor leagues are affiliated with those in the major leagues. There are a variety of minor leagues, which are ranked according to the level of competition. The top or best league is Class AAA (called Triple A), next is Class AA, then Class A, then below that are the rookie leagues. Players hope to move up through the system to a Class AAA team and then to the major leagues.

Rodriguez spent less than three years in the minor leagues before being called up to "The Show"—the major leagues. He started the 1990 season in the Class A Florida State League. His outstanding performance caught the attention of *Baseball America* magazine, which named him the league's best major league prospect. Rodriguez was promoted to Class AA in 1991 and joined the roster of the Tulsa Drillers. Rodriguez immediately earned a reputation for exceptional defensive skills, throwing out 23 of 39 base-stealers in the first two months of the season. "It's unbelievable how hard this kid wants to work," Drillers manager Bobby Jones raved. "Some kids you have to push. But this one comes up begging for it. His attitude and work ethic are outstanding."

*Rodriguez batting for the Texas Rangers in 1991.*

On June 20, 1991, Rodriguez was called up to the major leagues to make his debut as a Texas Ranger. Earlier that same day, Rodriguez married Maribel Rivera in Tulsa. In his first major-league appearance, Rodriguez threw out two players who attempted to steal second base and hit a two-run single as the Rangers coasted to a 7-3 victory. "It was a crazy day, in a positive way," Rodriguez recalled. "Getting married was wonderful, and I got a hit in the game. But throwing out two guys, that made the day unforgettable. I really felt proud." The 19-year-old was the youngest athlete in Major League Baseball at the time, a designation he held until the 1993 season. Rodriguez went on to lead all American League catchers in throwing out base-stealers for the 1991 season.

## Building a Career

Once he reached the big leagues, Rodriguez made it clear that he intended to stick around for a while. By midway through the 1992 campaign—only his second season in Major League Baseball—he was widely regarded as one of the game's fastest-rising stars. Tim Kurkjian of *Sports Illustrated* declared that he was "without a doubt, the best-throwing catcher in the American League," and he was named to the American League's All-Star team for the 1992 campaign. He also earned a Gold Glove Award for his exceptional defensive skills at season's end—the first of ten consecutive Gold Gloves for the rocket-armed catcher.

The mid-1990s brought continued success for Rodriguez. He earned the first of six consecutive Silver Slugger Awards (given annually to the best offensive player at each position in each of Major League Baseball's two leagues) in 1994. One year later, he led the Rangers in batting average, total bases, and doubles, and ranked second on the team in hits. His overall performance during the 1995 season prompted the Rangers to name him Player of the Year. At the end of each season, meanwhile, Rodriguez returned to his native Puerto Rico for three months of winter baseball in the Caguas Winter League.

> "Pudge has the best arm in baseball, maybe the best arm for a catcher ever," declared New York Yankee superstar Derek Jeter. "He's quick and he's accurate. The key is being accurate."

Rodriguez's terrific play made him a fan favorite in Texas. But his popularity also stemmed from his ability to connect with fans. During the final game of the 1995 season with the Texas Rangers, for example, he was introduced to a five-year-old boy with muscular dystrophy, a disease that causes the muscles in the body to weaken and eventually stop working. After talking with the boy for a little while, he invited the youngster to kiss his bat for good luck. Rodriguez then walked out to the plate and hit a home run on the first pitch, a moment he has described as "something out of a movie." As he rounded the bases, he pointed to the boy, who was smiling and clapping from his wheelchair. "After I touched the plate, I ran over to him and hugged him," Rodriguez remembered. "Then I gave him a high five." As Texas Rangers President Tom Schieffer told *Sports Illustrated*, "It's one of those stories that makes you love baseball. I still get a little catch in my throat every time I retell it. I got the feeling that Babe Ruth was up there somewhere and smiling."

During the 1996 campaign, Rodriguez was a key player in the club's rise from mediocrity to playoff contender. As usual, his powerful throwing arm kept opposing base runners from running wild on the base paths. But he also became a bigger force at the plate. His 19 home runs, 86 runs batted in (RBIs), 116 runs scored, and .300 batting average helped lift the

*With the bases loaded, Rodriguez manages a double play by tagging a runnner out at home and then throwing out the runner at first.*

Rangers to a 90-72 record and a playoff berth. Unfortunately, Texas lost in the first round of the playoffs to the heavily favored New York Yankees in four games.

The Rangers slumped in 1997, falling to 77-85. But Rodriguez continued to play at a high level. He pounded 20 home runs and registered 77 RBIs to go along with 98 runs scored and a sizzling .313 batting average. He was eligible for free agency at the end of the 1997 season, meaning his contract with the Rangers would end and he would be free to sign with another team. Rumors surfaced that the Major League Baseball Players Association wanted Rodriguez to become a free agent since he would likely command a high salary and thus raise the pay scale for catchers around the league. Rodriguez, however, wanted to stay with the Rangers. Much to the surprise of Rangers President Tom Schieffer, Rodriguez appeared at his office door one day and declared his desire to remain with the team. "I'm really worried about this," he confessed. "I don't want to be traded. I love playing here, and I want to stay here. I want to work out a deal." They agreed on a five-year contract worth $42 million.

"

*Rodriguez received the most votes by fans for the 2000 All-Star game. "It's an honor for me," he remarked. "I never expected in my career that would happen. . . . I don't consider myself the best catcher. I just consider myself another player in the game. . . . I'm just trying to do my best."*

"

### Best Catcher in Baseball

Rodriguez had his best season yet in 1998. His 21 home runs, 91 RBIs, and .321 batting average were all career bests, and they helped lift Texas to an 88-74 mark and a spot in the playoffs. The season ended in disappointment, though, when the team was swept in the first round by the New York Yankees.

In 1999 Rodriguez took his game to such a high level that he became the first catcher in over 20 years to win American League's Most Valuable Player Award from the Baseball Writers Association of America. He earned the honor by throwing out nearly 55 percent of base-stealers—a major league record—and hitting more home runs (35) than any other American League backstop in history. Additionally, he knocked in a career-best 113 runs, including a club record nine RBIs in one game, scored a whopping 116 runs, stole 25 bases himself, and hit at a blazing .332 clip. His exploits enabled the Rangers to compile a 95-67 record and earn a spot in the postseason. But once again, the Yankees dumped Texas in the first round to bring the season to a close for Rodriguez and his teammates.

By the end of the 1999 campaign, Rodriguez had also become the first catcher in major league history to hit at least 20 home runs and steal at least

20 bases in one season. Moreover, he had the highest batting average by a catcher in the American League since 1937. "He dominates his position, offensively and defensively. That's what a great player does," said long-time major league manager Jim Leyland. Fellow superstar Derek Jeter offered a similar assessment: "Pudge has the best arm in baseball, maybe the best arm for a catcher ever. He's quick and he's accurate. The key is being accurate." The media recognized his worth as well. Johnette Howard of *Sports Illustrated,* for example, remarked that Rodriguez's strong work ethic, willingness to learn, and passion for the game, combined with his technical abilities, had made him "the most irreplaceable player in baseball."

Following his record-breaking performance in 1999, Rodriguez's popularity rose to new heights. He received the most votes by fans for the 2000 All-Star game. "It's an honor for me," he remarked. "I never expected in my career that would happen." Rodriguez remained humble, despite the increase in attention. "I don't consider myself the best catcher. I just consider myself another player in the game. . . . I'm just trying to do my best."

Unfortunately, injuries put Rodriguez on the sidelines for extended periods of time in 2000—and the following two seasons as well. When he was healthy, he remained a top player; in 2000 he hit a career best .347, and the following year he threw out 35 of the 58 players who tried to steal a base against him. But from 2000 to 2002 he missed a total of 176 games, and with their team leader beset by injuries, the Rangers failed to reach 75 victories during any of those years.

The Rangers decided not to re-sign Rodriguez when his contract expired. Team management explained that it simply could not pay a top salary to a player with a recent history of injuries and declining productivity. At the time of his departure, Rodriguez held the ball club's record for all-time at-bats, hits, and doubles. He ranked second in games played, runs, and total bases, and third in home runs and RBIs. It was only fitting, then, that he received multiple standing ovations from the crowd during the last game of the 2002 campaign. Appearing before the home town fans for the final time in a Ranger uniform, Rodriguez hit a home run in the seventh inning, and doubled in the eighth to drive home a run. "[This last day is] something I'll remember . . . for the rest of my career," he affirmed.

### Leaving Texas for the Florida Marlins

Rodriguez was offered a one-year, $10-million contract with the Florida Marlins for the 2003 season. Mired in a five-year losing streak, the team's management believed that he could help the team's young pitching staff and give a much-needed boost to the offense. "We saw his injuries, but we

*Rodriguez celebrates with his Florida Marlins teammates, Derrek Lee (#25) and Alex Gonzales (#11), after beating the New York Yankees to win the 2003 World Series.*

didn't see them as major," Florida General Manager Larry Beinfest explained. Rodriguez accepted the offer, and within a matter of weeks he had become a trusted mentor to the team's young hurlers. "He's our captain," said Marlins pitcher Carl Pavano. We look to him for just about everything." Pitcher Chad Fox echoed Pavano, stating: "I've grown to trust him completely. . . . If he believes in me, I believe in myself."

At the start of the season, Rodriguez expressed confidence in his new team. "I think we're going to win a lot of games. I think the 2003 season is going to be the year of the Marlins," he said. His prediction was astoundingly accurate. Aided by his 16 home runs, 85 RBIs, and .297 average, the Marlins marched to a 91-71 regular season record and a playoff birth. Florida then knocked off the San Francisco Giants and the Chicago Cubs (in seven dramatic games) to earn a chance to face the New York Yankees—Rodriguez's old playoff nemesis—in the 2003 World Series. Rodriguez performed at a high level throughout the postseason, contributing 17 RBIs and three home runs. But many analysts claimed that his clubhouse leadership was even more important in helping the Marlins register a stunning triumph over the feared Yankees in six games.

Rodriguez has called the night of the Marlins' World Series victory one of the most memorable of his whole life. After the game, he fulfilled a pledge he had made to his 11-year-old son, Ivan Dereck. "If we win the World Series," Rodriguez had told his son prior to the playoffs, "we're going to walk around the bases, and we're going to get down on our knees and pray." Rodriguez—now a World Series champion—circled the infield of Yankee Stadium with his oldest son, kneeling down before each base. When they reached home plate, they kissed it and knelt together in prayer.

After the season, Rodriguez was named the Most Valuable Player (MVP) of the National League Championship Series and *Baseball Digest's* 2003 Player of the Year. Through effort and determination, he had proven that despite a few injury-filled years, he still had a lot of baseball left in him. "When you believe in yourself, work hard, and prepare yourself, anything is possible," he declared.

## Joining the Detroit Tigers

Armed with a World Series ring and many fond memories, Rodriguez left Florida and signed a four-year contract with the Detroit Tigers prior to the 2004 season. The Tigers had held the worst record in baseball in the 2003 season, but the club's decision to sign the veteran catcher showed players, fans, and sports reporters that it was serious about improving. "Once we got Pudge, we immediately became respectable," manager Alan Trammell said. "He's been the total package."

> *"Once we got Pudge, we immediately became respectable," said Detroit Tigers manager Alan Trammell. "He's been the total package."*

Once the 2004 season began, Rodriguez displayed leadership ability, drive, and a steadfast commitment to the game. He won his 11th Gold Glove award, the most by any catcher in history, and earned a record-tying seventh Silver Slugger Award on the strength of 19 homers, 86 RBIs, and a sizzling .334 batting average. His performance helped the Tigers win 29 games more than they had a season earlier. Rodriguez also reached several career milestones during the 2004 season. He knocked in his 1000th run, earned his 2000th career hit, and scored his 1000th career run. Baseball legend Al Kaline expressed pride in seeing Rodriguez meet these milestones as a Detroit Tiger: "To me, he has changed the whole face of this organization. He really has," he said.

Heartened by the Tigers' improvement in 2004, many Detroit fans expressed excitement about the approaching 2005 season. But just as the season began, retired major league slugger Jose Canseco, a former Pudge teammate, published a book in which he accused Rodriguez and several other star players of illegal steroid use. Rodriguez denied the allegations. "I'm in shock," he told the press. "[Canseco] is saying things that aren't true, and it hurts me a lot that he would say things like that because I've always had a lot of respect for him, and I've even helped him many times when things weren't going well for him."

*Rodriguez shows his superlative fielding skills as he charges out
from behind the plate while playing for the Detroit Tigers, 2006.*

Rodriguez had lost 22 pounds prior to the opening of the season. Though
he credited the weight loss to a change in diet and exercise, some critics
suspected a connection to Canseco's accusation of steroid use. Rodriguez
ignored the whispers, but the season was not a happy one for him. In addition to Canseco's allegations, Rodriguez had to deal with a painful divorce and multiple broken bones in his hands. In addition, the Tigers
stumbled to a disappointing 71-91 record. Even so, he remained the most
feared defensive catcher in the game. By season's end, he had thrown out
35 out of 58 runners who tried to steal a base on him.

## 2006 American League Champions

The 2006 season was one of hope and excitement for the Detroit Tigers. The team roared out of the gate to claim first place in its division. Armed with a stable of hot young pitchers and a tough batting order, the Tigers held the best record in baseball for much of the season. The team stumbled in the home stretch to lose the division crown, but its 95 victories still earned Detroit a spot in the postseason for the first time since 1987.

To the surprise of fans everywhere, the Tigers beat the New York Yankees in the first round of the playoffs, then swept the Oakland Athletics to win the American League Championship. Tiger fans were thrilled, and they talked openly about how sweet it would be to cap a "Cinderella" season with a World Series championship. Their dreams of victory were thwarted, however, when the St. Louis Cardinals defeated the Tigers to clinch the 2006 World Series title.

Rodriguez was disappointed that he fell short in his bid to earn a second World Series champion ring. But he expressed optimism about the future of the team and pride in the role he had played in turning around the Tigers franchise: "I feel very happy, because when I came here three years ago, Mr. Ilitch [the owner of the Tigers] was telling me he was going to put a winning team together. I was the first one to sign here as a free agent and then others came. . . . Now I'm sure there are a lot of players on the market that want to come to Detroit and play. And that for me makes myself very happy."

> "I feel very happy, because when I came here three years ago, Mr. Ilitch [the owner of the Tigers] was telling me he was going to put a winning team together," said Rodriguez. "I was the first one to sign here as a free agent and then others came. . . . Now I'm sure there are a lot of players on the market that want to come to Detroit and play. And that for me makes myself very happy."

## 2007 and Beyond

The following season proved to be a bit of a disappointment for Detroit Tigers fans, who were hoping for a replay of the preceding year. After an impressive start, the team fell behind in August, and they finished the season with a record of 85-72. Rodriguez once again made the All-Star team, although his batting average was a bit lower than some past years. He finished the season batting .280 (career average .302), with 11 home runs and 63 RBIs for the season. He also won his 13th Gold Glove Award. He achieved a personal milestone in September when he caught his 2,056th game, surpassing Gary Carter for third on the all-time list. Rodriguez has a ways to go before he reaches the top two catchers on the list: Bob Boone (2,225 games) and Carlton Fisk (2,226 games).

Rodriguez has said that he is not sure if he will end his career in Detroit. He has expressed an interest in returning to Texas to finish his career. "Every player's dream is to start and finish with the same team. I still have a couple of years left in me," he hinted. Wherever he concludes his career, Rodriguez has indicated that he plans to remain in baseball in some capacity for years to come. "I've loved to play this game since I was born," he said. "Baseball is going to be in my blood for life."

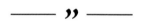

> "I'm a player who likes to learn every single day because I want to get better," Rodriguez said. "So my father tells me more about what I do wrong than right. The success of my career is because of my father."

## MARRIAGE AND FAMILY

Rodriguez wed Maribel Rivera on June 20, 1991, in Tulsa, Oklahoma. Rodriguez and Rivera have three children together: son Ivan Dereck, born June 5, 1992; daughter Amanda Christine, born June 21, 1995; and daughter Ivanna Sofia, born January 12, 2000. Their marriage ended in divorce in 2005.

During the baseball season, Rodriguez resides in Bloomfield Hills, Michigan. His permanent residence is a lavish, nine-bedroom home in Miami, Florida. He has also spent many winters in Rio Piedras, Puerto Rico, an exclusive community south of San Juan.

## MAJOR INFLUENCES

Rodriguez has discussed a number of influences on his life and career. Specifically, he has named power pitcher Nolan Ryan and Hall of Fame catcher Johnny Bench as professional inspirations. He also admires legendary outfielder Roberto Clemente, a native of Puerto Rico who helped the poor throughout Latin America before his life was cut short by a tragic plane crash in 1972. In Puerto Rico, Clemente is a symbol of perseverance, leadership, integrity, and charity. "Roberto spent a lot of his time with people. . . . It showed that he really cared. I want to do the same things," Rodriguez said. The Texas Rangers recognized Rodriguez's efforts to follow in Clemente's footsteps, twice naming him Roberto Clemente Man of the Year for his community achievements.

Rodriguez has always identified his father as the most significant influence on his life. "My father was there all the time for me," he emphasized. Jose Rodriguez was his son's first baseball coach, and years later, he continues to offer him guidance in his professional career. Rodriguez appreciates his father's honesty. "I'm a player who likes to learn every single day because I want to get better," he explained. "So my father tells me more about what I do wrong than right. The success of my career is because of my father."

## HOBBIES AND OTHER INTERESTS

Rodriguez has admitted that he is addicted to ESPN's "SportsCenter," but he also has various interests outside of the world of professional sports. He reads the Bible on a daily basis and enjoys many different kinds of music, from Elton John to JaRule. He is also a fan of salsa music. His athletic interests other than baseball include swimming, golf, and scuba diving. He also enjoys playing video games and watching professional wrestling.

Rodriguez also devotes a lot of time to the Ivan "Pudge" Rodriguez Foundation, which was founded in 1993. The organization assists the families of children suffering from cancer and other serious diseases. Though the foundation initially focused on helping families in Texas and Puerto Rico, he has recently established a fund at the Children's Hospital of Michigan to help kids in the Detroit area. "I love kids," Rodriguez said. "I always go into hospitals and talk to kids and try to make them happy." He also has hosted numerous baseball clinics for young athletes to help them learn hitting techniques and fielding skills. "I did the same thing when I was a little kid, seeing older superstars come and do clinics, I was one of those [kids] who sat down and listened to them," he stated. "As long as [the kids] are having fun, and they're smiling and they're happy, that's what I care about."

## HONORS AND AWARDS

American League All-Star Team (Major League Baseball): 1992-2001; 2004-07
Rawlings Gold Glove Award: 1992-2001; 2004, 2006-2007
Louisville Silver Slugger Award: 1994-99; 2004
Most Valuable Player Award, American League (Baseball Writers Association of America): 1999

Player of the Year (*Baseball Digest*): 1999; 2003
Most Valuable Player, National League Championship Series: 2003

## FURTHER READING

### Books

DeMarco, Tony. *Latinos in Baseball: Ivan Rodriguez,* 2000 (juvenile)
Wendel, Tim. *The New Face of Baseball: The One-Hundred Year Rise and Triumph of Latinos in America's Favorite Sport,* 2003
*Who's Who in America,* 2006

### Periodicals

*Baseball Digest,* July 1, 2001, p.32; Jan. 1, 2004, p.17; Dec. 1, 2004, p.52
*Dallas Morning News,* Mar. 30, 1997, p.E1; Aug. 21, 2005, p.C6
*Detroit Free Press,* Feb. 21, 2006, Sports section, p.5; Apr. 6, 2006, Sports section, p.7
*Detroit News,* July 11, 2006, p.D1; Aug. 15, 2006, p.D5
*Sporting News,* Jan. 5, 1998, p.56
*Sports Illustrated,* Aug. 11, 1997, p.40; Feb. 18, 2002, p.58; Oct. 31, 2003, p.12
*Sports Illustrated KIDS,* Aug. 1997, p.52; July 1999, p.6; June 2003, p.54
*Texas Monthly,* June 1998, p.114

### Online Articles

http://www.puertorico-herald.org
(*Puerto Rico Herald,* "Rangers' Rodriguez Tours Homeland," Mar. 30, 2001, Sports & Entertainment Category Archive, 2001)

### Online Databases

*Biography Resource Center,* 2006, article from *Marquis Who's Who,* 2006

## ADDRESS

Ivan "Pudge" Rodriguez
Detroit Tigers
Comerica Park
2100 Woodward Avenue
Detroit, MI 48201

## WORLD WIDE WEB SITES

http://detroit.tigers.mlb.com
http://sports.espn.go.com
http://sportsillustrated.cnn.com
http://www.pudge.org

# Michael Sessions 1987-

American Politician
Elected Mayor of Hillsdale, Michigan,
at the Age of 18

### BIRTH

Michael Sessions was born on September 22, 1987, in Goshen, Indiana. He lived the first six years of his life in Nappanee, Indiana, before moving to Hillsdale, Michigan, with his family. His father, Scott Sessions, is a medical technician, and his mother, Lorri Sessions, is a housekeeper for a sorority house at Hillsdale College. He has a younger sister, Sarah.

## YOUTH AND EDUCATION

Sessions attended Gier Elementary School and Davis Middle School in Hillsdale. He was an inquisitive and active youngster. "I think I was really hyper as a kid," he said. "I was always occupied with something."

While Sessions was growing up, current events and politics were frequent topics of conversation around the dinner table. "Dad always had an opinion and he always voiced it," he recalled. His early interest in politics was further sparked in the fourth grade, when his class took a field trip to the state capitol in Lansing. He was fascinated by the hustle and bustle of the lawmakers as they debated various measures and voted on important state business. By the end of the day, he decided that he wanted to learn more about how elected officials dealt with the problems and challenges of running a government.

Over the next several years, Sessions read about politics and even attended political rallies, including a local rally for then-presidential candidate George W. Bush in 2000. He also decided to study the local political scene in his hometown of Hillsdale, a community of 8,200 people located about 100 miles southwest of Detroit. "He would watch the town City Council meeting on TV every week," his mother said. "He'd try to get us to join him. He found the whole process fascinating."

Sessions attended Hillsdale High School, where he played football, ran cross country, and was a member of the track team. "I was an above average student," Sessions said, "in the A's and B's range." His favorite subject was history. In the afternoons, he often worked as a volunteer tutor at the middle school. Meanwhile, his interest in politics continued to grow. During his senior year, he ran for vice president of the student council and lost. Undaunted, Sessions turned his attention to a much bigger office—the mayorship of Hillsdale.

## CAREER HIGHLIGHTS

Sessions's keen interest in local politics was driven in large part by his belief that the city's elected officials had not done enough to attract and keep manufacturing businesses in the area. In 2003, for example, a local automobile manufacturing plant had closed and moved its operations to Mexico. Sessions's father, who had been a plant supervisor, was one of the local residents who found himself out of work as a result of the plant closure. Scott Sessions was unemployed for two years before he completed his retraining as a medical technician. The period of his father's joblessness was "horrible," Michael Sessions recalled. "It just hits the family hard—the lack of money. The lack of being able to do stuff like before. Coming home and figuring out, well what are we going to put on the table?"

In spring 2005 Sessions learned that the city's incumbent 51-year-old mayor, Douglas Ingles, was running unopposed in the upcoming November election for another four-year term. "I thought, 'you can't generate many new ideas for the city of Hillsdale without the whole campaign process,'" Sessions recalled. "So I decided to throw my name into the race.'"

## Throwing His Hat into the Ring

When Sessions called the city clerk and asked about filing papers for his candidacy, he was told that at 17, he was too young to be a legal candidate.

In September 2005, though, Sessions registered to vote on his 18th birthday. By that time, the deadline had passed for him to get his name on the ballot. Rather than give up, however, Sessions filed papers with the city clerk to become a write-in candidate for mayor. The position of mayor in Hillsdale is nonpartisan, which means the candidates do not run as a member of a political party. The position is a part-time one that comes with a $3,600 salary but no office or staff. The mayor's responsibilities include presiding over two City Council

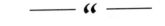

*"[Sessions] would watch the town City Council meeting on TV every week," his mother said. "He'd try to get us to join him. He found the whole process fascinating."*

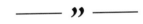

meetings a month, where policy and budget decisions are made. Day-to-day administration of the city's affairs is carried out by the city manager.

Sessions made the decision to run for mayor without talking to his family. When he told his parents of his candidacy, they were very surprised. "'You're crazy! You're crazy, Michael,'" he recalled them saying. "They weren't angry. They were skeptical as to what I was doing. [I told them] 'I really want to do this and I'm going to do it, Mom and Dad.'"

Once they saw how serious Sessions was about his candidacy, his parents firmly supported him. But it was up to Sessions to organize and finance his campaign himself. He used the $700 he had earned from a summer job working for a concessions company to purchase business cards, as well as window and lawn signs. Admitting that he was "not very good with slogans," he ordered simple signs that said: "Write in Michael Sessions for

*Sessions being sworn in as mayor of Hillsdale, Michigan.*

Mayor." He put the signs up all over the city and began knocking on doors to introduce himself. "Each day after school, he would pick an area and go door to door, telling people who he was and that he was running for mayor," recalled Lauren Beck, a friend who helped him with his campaign. "He'd talk about why he should be mayor, and had a sample of the ballot so he could show people where they had to write in his name."

Residents who found Sessions at their doorstep often asked how old he was. Most of them were startled to learn that the candidate was an 18-year-old high school senior. At first, many people thought that his candidacy was a hoax or a scheme to bolster his college application. But as Sessions persisted, many people expressed admiration for his spirit and sense of civic duty. Those who showed a willingness to hear what he had to say often came away impressed by his grasp of current events and his deep affection for Hillsdale. His teachers, meanwhile, expressed pride in his campaign. According to Peter Beck, the assistant principal of Hillsdale High School, "He's not our smartest kid. He's not our best athlete. He's just an ordinary kid with some big goals. He's a closer. He gets the job done."

Sessions organized town hall-style meetings at the Kiwanis Club, a record and coffee shop, and the local firehouse so residents could ask him questions. At each of these events he laid out his plan for the city, which included attracting more jobs, turning an old factory into a bio-diesel plant, and forming a stronger partnership with nearby Hillsdale College. His pledge of support for increasing the Hillsdale fire department from three to four full-time members earned him his first high-profile endorsement, from the Hillsdale City Fire Association.

In the weeks leading up to Election Day, Sessions kept up a demanding schedule of campaigning and school. But the pressure of being a full-time student and a candidate finally wore him down. Five days before the election, he came down with a severe case of bronchitis. His mother blamed his illness on long hours of campaigning outside in the cold. "I tried to tell him to wear a coat," she said, "but he wouldn't."

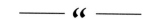

## Celebrity Mayor

The Hillsdale mayoral election took place on November 8, 2005. When the final votes were counted, Sessions was declared the winner, by a two-vote margin of 670 to 668. "It's amazing," he said after his victory had been officially recognized. "I'm so excited, I think I'm going to be ill."

The victory made Sessions one of the youngest mayors in the United States and sparked a flood of media interest in the young man and his community. Dozens of reporters flocked to Hillsdale to ask the mayor-elect about his triumph. He also

*"Each day after school, he would pick an area and go door to door, telling people who he was and that he was running for mayor," recalled Lauren Beck, a friend who helped Sessions with his campaign. "He'd talk about why he should be mayor, and had a sample of the ballot so he could show people where they had to write in his name."*

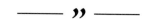

made appearances on several television shows, including "The Today Show," "Countdown with Keith Olbermann," and "Late Night With David Letterman." Sessions flew to New York City with his parents to appear on Letterman's show, where he participated in the show's famous "Top Ten" segment by reading a list prepared by the show's comedy writers called "The Top Ten Reasons to Be an 18-Year-Old Mayor." Two of Sessions's favorite jokes on the list were: "Every night, a different member of the town council does my homework," and "Parents try to tell me what to do, I raise their taxes."

*Sessions leading a city council meeting.*

Sessions's unlikely rise to mayor even attracted interest from foreign media outlets. More than 20 camera crews from as far away as Japan and Russia traveled to Hillsdale to record his swearing-in ceremony. Astounded by the coverage, Sessions asked a Japanese reporter why he was interested in him. The reporter answered that "age equals wisdom." Recalling that conversation in a speech to a youth group, Sessions remarked, "That's the thing about America. We don't necessarily believe that age equals wisdom. We think youth can make a difference."

Once the media interest in his victory subsided, Sessions was able to refocus on his high school studies and begin his mayoral duties. For the remainder of his senior year, his typical weekday began with high-school classes from 7:40 in the morning to 2:30 in the afternoon, followed by a meeting with Hillsdale's city manager to discuss various municipal business. He also made a point to get out in the community and meet with constituents and business owners. "I never want to call a business and find out they're leaving because the city wasn't listening," he explained. To make time for his new schedule, however, Sessions had to make some sacrifices. He reluctantly quit all after-school activities. "I am quite good with time management and managing my time, which you have to be in this situation," he said. "I really lay out what my priorities are and go and attack them."

Sessions earned his high school diploma in spring 2006, as scheduled. He then enrolled at Hillsdale College, where he is studying politics and economics. Even as he shouldered a college workload, though, he continued with all his mayoral duties. Sessions reserved most evenings for city-related business, including the bimonthly City Council meetings. Afterwards, he would head home to do his college work. He tried to get to bed before midnight, but his work often kept him up later than that.

## Facing Challenges

Sessions faced some challenges, both professional and personal, early in his term as mayor. First, he was involved in an internet prank that got him into legal trouble. After a disagreement with his campaign manager, who had also been his friend, Sessions broke into the computer network of a major university and tampered with his email and internet accounts. Sessions sent out disparaging emails about his former friend and also deleted his MySpace and Facebook accounts. Sessions pleaded no contest to a misdemeanor charge of malicious annoyance by writing; he had to pay a fine of $850 and do 40 hours of community service.

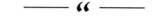

*"In government, everything starts locally," Sessions remarked. "Folks, there are a ton of things that can be done in your community. Whether it is washing windows in downtown or volunteering at the senior center. We as young people have the power to change the world and ourselves."*

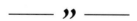

After that, Sessions became the target of a recall campaign by voters who wanted to oust him from his position as mayor. The recall petition said that the mayor should be recalled for his criminal activity, which constituted conduct unbecoming of a mayor and a city representative, according to Jeffrey Buchhop, a former city council member. "The mayor has consistently caused problems or done things that basically don't reflect well on the city," Buchhop said. "I just want the city to have the best leadership we can have. Something like this shows we don't have the best leadership." After a radio interview in which Sessions voiced his regret and issued a public apology, the recall campaign was dropped.

A more difficult challenge soon followed. After the recall campaign died down, Sessions learned that he had testicular cancer. He had two rounds of surgery, in July and September 2007. He didn't want to discuss it publicly, but he knew word would get around his small town. When asked to speak by the American Caner Society, he went public with his illness. "I wish it could have stayed private," he said. "But I didn't walk well. I didn't look well. People were asking. And I thought I could raise awareness. I've chosen to be mayor. I have to face the public life. But there are times when I wish it was different." It's been a difficult ordeal, but there has been one small advantage. "The obstacles and criticisms I have faced in the last couple years now seem quite minor," Sessions said. "This has really put it all in perspective." Sessions is now cancer free.

Sessions has adopted a wait-and-see attitude regarding a future career in politics, declining to answer whether he will seek a second term as mayor. "I'm taking it one step at a time," he said. But his experiences have deepened his conviction that every person has a civic obligation to try to improve his or her community. He believes that this obligation extends to young people, even if they have not yet reached voting age. "In government, everything starts locally," he remarked. "I love to take the quote from John F. Kennedy and change it to fit what I think. I always tell young people to, 'Not ask what their community can do for them, but what they can do for their community.' Folks, there are a ton of things that can be done in your community. Whether it is washing windows in downtown or volunteering at the senior center. We as young people have the power to change the world and ourselves."

## HOME AND FAMILY

Sessions still lives at home with his parents and sister, with just a short drive to Hillsdale College. He uses his bedroom as both an office and a study area. Sessions may be in charge of city council meetings, but he notes that "my parents still have the final say in the house."

## FURTHER READING

### Periodicals

*Christian Science Monitor*, Apr. 3, 2006, p.20
*Detroit Free Press*, Oct. 15, 2007, p.A1
*Detroit News*, May 8, 2006, p.A1; Sep. 1, 2007, p.A4
*Junior Scholastic*, Feb. 20, 2006, p.6
*Los Angeles Times*, Nov. 11, 2005, p.A1
*New York Times*, Dec. 15, 2005, p.F1
*People*, Junior Edition, Feb. 20, 2006, p.107
*Toledo (OH) Blade*, Nov. 22, 2005, p.A1

**Online Articles**

http://abcnews.go.com/GMA/story?id=1296769
  (ABC News, "High School Senior Elected Mayor of Mich. Town," Nov. 9, 2005)
http://www.crfforum.org/topics/?topicid=42&catid=8
  (CRF Forum, "Governance: An Interview with Michael Sessions," June 7, 2006)
http://hillsdale.net/stories/112205/news_sessions001.shtml
  (The Hillsdale Daily news online, "Sessions Takes City's Reins," Nov.22, 2005)
http://hillsdale.net/stories/060706/news_20060607015.shtml
  (The Hillsdale Daily news online, "For Teen Mayor, It's on to College," June 7, 2006)
http://www.msnbc.msn.com/id/10004343
  (MSNBC, "18-year-old Mayor Taking His New Job Seriously," Nov. 9, 2005)
http://www.statenews.com/article.phtml?pk=36875
  (The State News, "Meet 18-year-old Michael Sessions...the Mayor of Hillsdale," July 14, 2006)

**ADDRESS**

Michael Sessions, Mayor
Hillsdale City Hall
97 North Broad Street
Hillsdale, MI 49242

**WORLD WIDE WEB SITE**

http://www.ci.hillsdale.mi.us/sessions.htm

## Kate Spade 1962-

American Fashion Designer
Creator of Distinctive Purses and Other Accessories

### BIRTH

Kate Spade was born Katherine Noel Brosnahan in 1962 in
Kansas City, Missouri. She was the fifth of six children in a
close-knit Irish Catholic family. Her father worked for a fami-
ly-owned construction business that built many of the roads
and bridges around Kansas City. Her mother was a full-time
homemaker to Kate, her two sisters, and three brothers.

## YOUTH

Kate Brosnahan was raised in Kansas City, where her parents gave her a practical Midwestern upbringing. Although part of a large family, she still enjoyed one-on-one time with her mother. She treasured mother-daughter visits to a local chocolate shop, where she indulged in Napoleon-style pastries. "It was kind of our time together, and it seemed so special," she recalled.

Kate recalls that she was interested in fashion when she was young, but she wasn't obsessed with it. "When I was a kid, I didn't even know Chanel," the famous French fashion company (pronounced "shuh-NELL"). "I would have called it 'Channel.'" Wanting to distinguish herself from her two sisters, young Kate learned to develop her own style. As a teenager she hunted through local thrift shops for vintage clothes. She learned to appreciate classic styles from the 1950s and 1960s, as embodied by two of her style icons, actresses Audrey Hepburn and Grace Kelly. "My mother thought it was great because a lot of what I was buying were like things she used to wear." Kate also discovered she loved bright colors, such as kelly green and raspberry pink.

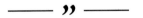

"*I was not obsessed with [fashion]," Kate recalls. "When I was a kid, I didn't even know Chanel [pronounced shuh-NELL]. I would have called it 'Channel.'*"

## EDUCATION

After graduating from high school in Kansas City, Kate Brosnahan entered the University of Kansas. She later transferred to Arizona State University, where she studied journalism and broadcasting. She graduated with a bachelor's degree in 1985.

## MARRIAGE AND FAMILY

Kate Brosnahan met fellow student Andrew Spade while at Arizona State University, when the two of them worked in the same men's clothing store. Kate moved to New York City shortly after finishing college, and Andy joined her there in 1988, taking a job at an advertising company. They became business partners in 1993, and got married the following year. In February 2005 they had a daughter, Frances Beatrix. The couple

*Kate and Andy Spade in the front row of a fashion show in New York City.*

split their time between New York City and their cozy 1870 cottage in Southampton, New York.

## CAREER HIGHLIGHTS

### From Style Reporter to Style Maker

After graduating from college and taking a tour of Europe, Spade moved to New York City. She shared a two-bedroom apartment with three other girls and managed to get an internship at *Mademoiselle* magazine in 1986. Her first duties included fetching coffee at photo shoots, but she soon worked her way onto the magazine's editorial staff. By 1991 she was a senior editor in charge of accessories, which meant she investigated and wrote about the latest trends in jewelry, purses, and shoes.

Despite her expertise, Kate had trouble finding a handbag that appealed to her own personal sense of style. Almost all the purses she saw were made of black or brown leather, while she liked bright colors and different textured fabrics. "I wanted a functional bag that was sophisticated and had some style," she explained. When she thought she might like to leave journalism and work for herself, Andy encouraged her to try creating her own handbags. By then they were sharing a small apartment in SoHo, a trendy

401

neighborhood in Manhattan in New York City; he agreed to support them both for a year while Kate tried her hand at design.

With no background in manufacturing, Kate had a lot to learn before constructing her first handbags. She started with some simple sketches and paper patterns, then checked with producers around New York City to see how much they would cost to make. She cashed out her retirement savings account to fund production, and in 1993 she left her job to focus on her business—but only after asking her boss if they would take her back if she failed. She remembered that "even my mother said I'd gotten cocky— and what the heck was I doing giving up a job with insurance?" Those she encountered in the fashion business weren't very encouraging, either. She remembered that one fabric supplier told her, "Honey, you look like a nice girl. You don't want to get into the business. Settle down." With Andy's support, Kate persisted in the face of discouragement: "Not knowing much about the fashion industry kept me from being nervous," she said. "It kept me from being intimidated."

> " 
>
> *Kate found it reassuring to work with her husband. "Knowing your best interest and the company's best interest is in the forefront of every decision being made without you is really comforting," she explained.*
>
> "

By 1993, the designer was ready to present her bags at a New York accessories show. She considered several names for the label, but finally settled on a combination of her first name and partner Andy's last name. Her first collection, which she called "kate spade," included just six styles of handbags. These boxy but stylish tote bags were made of practical fabrics like nylon, burlap, and linen. Their simple shapes and colorful patterns recalled the classic era of 1950s and 1960s fashion. At that first show she made a sale to Barney's, a local department store, but it didn't cover her expenses. "It was kind of a loss," she recalled. "I thought, 'It didn't work out and now we have to stop.'" The handbags generated such positive buzz, though, that Andy became convinced she was on the verge of success. Before their second show, Kate removed tags from the inside of the bags and sewed them to the outside. The simple black labels, which said "kate spade - new york," charmed fashion editors and led to more sales.

In late 1993, Kate and Andy brought in Pamela Bell as a partner handling production, and in 1994 Kate's old college friend Elyce Arons joined as a partner overseeing sales and public relations. In these early days the couple's small studio apartment was also their workshop; when it was shipping time, they had to find somewhere else to sleep. Cash was even more scarce than space, and Kate and Andy (who married in 1994) had to draw on their own personal savings to buy fabric and pay employees. Luckily, kate spade handbags were gaining more attention: they appeared in more stores, including Bergdorf Goodman, Saks, and Bloomingdale's, and they were featured in fashion magazines and on the arms of several Hollywood celebrities. Revenues grew from $100,000 in 1993 to $1.5 million in 1995, the same year they moved the company into a new space in New York City's flower district.

The year 1996 saw the company, named Kate Spade Inc., achieve several milestones. The company made a profit for the first time, on overall sales of $6 million. Andy made the decision to leave his advertising job and work full-time for the company, becoming creative director and chief executive officer (CEO). Kate found it reassuring to work with her husband. "Knowing your best interest and the company's best interest is in the forefront of every decision being made without you is really comforting," she explained. In 1996 the company also opened its first kate spade store, in New York City's trendy SoHo district. Besides selling merchandise in its own store, the company sold 3,000 bags each to the Saks and Neiman Marcus chains that year. Their year of success was crowned when Kate won a New Fashion Talent Award for Accessories from the prestigious Council of Fashion Designers of America (CFDA).

## Growing a Successful Company

Now that the company was profitable, the Spades worked to increase their business. They moved their flagship store to a larger SoHo location in fall 1997. That year they also opened their first international store, in Japan. In 1998 they expanded further, opening a second U.S. store in Boston and introducing a line of stationery. Kate explained their philosophy in going beyond handbags: "We won't license the name or expand into a new area unless we think we can bring something new to a category that makes it fresh." She picked stationary for her new line because traditional notebooks, diaries, personal organizers, and address books were so dark and plain that she wanted to create brightly colored, stylish, and feminine products that wouldn't look out of place in a kate spade handbag. By the end of 1998 the company had earned nearly $30 million in total sales, and Kate was named Best Accessory Designer of the Year by the CFDA.

In early 1999, the Spades and their partners sold a 56% stake in the company to luxury department store chain Neiman Marcus for $33.6

*Spade shown with a few of her fashionable accessories.*

million. They also expanded the scope of their business, introducing their first line of shoes and branching out into men's accessories with a JACK SPADE store in New York City. JACK SPADE gave Andy the chance to explore his own design ideas, emphasizing high quality products that combined functionality and style. Kate received another honor in 1999 when New York's Cooper-Hewitt Museum (the Smithsonian Institution's national museum of design) included some of her handbags in their first national design triennial celebrating American design excellence.

In 2000 the Spades continued building on their success by adding stores in Chicago, Illinois; San Francisco, California; Greenwich, Connecticut; and Manhasset, New York. The following year they expanded their product line into eyeglasses, both prescription and sunglasses. Then in 2002 they paired with cosmetics giant Estee Lauder to launch "kate spade beauty," a line of bath and body products as well as a signature fragrance of white floral bouquet. The line won a 2003 Fragrance Foundation Recognition Award ("FiFi" Award) for Bath & Body Star of the Year. Although they were working with other companies on these new products, Kate noted that "we want to maintain creative control over everything that goes out under our name—whether we're manufacturing it or letting a partner handle production." These expansions and partnerships were a deliberate business strategy on their part, she explained: "In the short term, it's a great way to challenge ourselves creatively while raising awareness of our brand." The strategy was working; the company, now Kate Spade LLC, had approximately $70 million in sales in 2002.

Another sign that the kate spade brand was increasingly successful was in the number of counterfeit bags that began appearing on street corners—so many that by 2002 the company had hired a specialist to fight the fakes. At one point they estimated that one fake kate spade bag was being sold for each legitimate one. They worked with authorities to seize illegal shipments and let consumers know that counterfeit sales often support organized crime. A genuine kate spade bag is not cheap—prices can range from $150 to over $500—but they cost less than some trendy, high-fashion labels and are designed to become a wardrobe staple. "If you can't keep wearing the things in our line, then we feel we made a mistake," the designer noted. Besides, she added, "I really like the idea of saving for something if you want it."

## Building a Brand to Last

In its second decade as a company, Kate Spade LLC continued to develop the brand. Since 2003, the company has added boutiques in many major American cities, and it began offering sales from its website in 2004. It opened an international flagship store in 2004 in Aoyama, Japan, joining three other stores in Japan, three in Hong Kong, and one each in the Philippines and Thailand. By 2006 the company had expanded to 19 stores (plus four outlet stores) in 15 states, with products available in over 400 high-end department stores and boutiques throughout the U.S. "While we've been relatively conservative" in opening stores, Kate noted in 2005, "retail is important for what you have to say as a company. But nothing is set in stone. When you run a business, you have to be nimble to be successful. I'm not opening stores [just to open them]. We are building stores where our customers are and where they might not be getting the whole [presentation]."

> "For better or worse, we don't do a sweeping theme for each collection. I don't shop that way, so why would I design that way? It's more about different moods," Kate explained. "[If something] will be out of style tomorrow, it won't be added to the line today."

In 2004 the company branched out into items for the home, launching a collection that included bedding, bath items, china, wallpaper, fabrics, and other decorative pieces. While such practical items might seem ordinary, the designer observed that "I don't think you need to neglect the style of something that's functional." Others agreed that Spade had brought style to her new line of home products, which earned a Giants of Design Tastemaker Award from *House Beautiful* magazine, an American Food and Entertaining Award from *Bon Appetit* magazine, and an International Design Award for bedding from *Elle Decor*. For fiscal year 2004 the company generated some $125 million in sales.

The following year Kate and her husband completed a renovation of the flagship store in SoHo to display their entire line of merchandise. The store reflects her eclectic taste: it is decorated with modern art, and it offers kate spade products as well as vintage jewelry and books for sale. "I'm not afraid of experimenting with things," the designer explained. "I don't like being too tightly merchandised. Everything has a common thread. Just because I design doesn't mean I can't appreciate other people's designs. Our customers aren't going to stand still; they need some unpredictability."

——— " ———

*"I'm not afraid of experimenting with things," the designer explained. "I don't like being too tightly merchandised. Everything has a common thread. Just because I design doesn't mean I can't appreciate other people's designs. Our customers aren't going to stand still; they need some unpredictability."*

——— " ———

For fall 2005 Kate created a new line called Collect. The line wasn't a collection of items meant to be worn together; rather, it was inspired by objects the designer herself collects. The handbags in the Collect line are made from more expensive materials, such as snake skin and beaver fur. "We were very conscious of keeping the signature collection accessibly priced," Spade noted. "But with Collect I'm allowing myself to be free and kind of unconcerned about those things. Now I'm thinking, 'Let's have fun.'" She partially attributed this new design approach to becoming a mother in 2005: "There's a bigger responsibility in place and, honestly, I'm not worrying as much. The looseness to Collect—I think it comes out of being a little more relaxed."

## Continuing Success

To date the Kate Spade company has shown no signs of slowing down. Net profits (sales minus costs) in fiscal 2005 were about $84 million, making the company an attractive purchase when Neiman Marcus, itself under new ownership, put Kate Spade LLC up for sale. In late 2006 Liz Claiborne, Inc., a clothing retailer that manages dozens of popular brands, purchased Kate Spade from Neiman Marcus for about $124 million. In announcing the purchase, the president of Liz Claiborne noted that "We are thrilled to welcome this iconic American brand into our Company. . . . Kate and Andy Spade, along with Elyce Arons and Pamela

*Spade was a guest judge on the season three opening episode of "Project Runway," alongside fellow judges Nina Garcia, Michael Kors, and Heidi Klum (left to right).*

Bell, have created a terrific brand with a strong aesthetic and widespread consumer recognition. Our job now is to maintain the essence of Kate Spade while driving it to the next level."

When asked to analyze the reasons behind her success, Kate attributes much of it to her refusal to follow trends or worry about what's "in." When she shops for herself, "I don't fixate on what style a piece is, I buy it for no other reason than I like it." Her own wardrobe is filled with black A-line skirts, capri pants, and sweaters that she accents with color through shoes, handbags, and chunky jewelry. She often uses coats as jackets, wearing them like others might wear a cardigan. She brings the same back-to-basics approach to her designing: "For better or worse, we don't do a sweeping theme for each collection. I don't shop that way, so why would I design that way? It's more about different moods," Kate explained. "[If something] will be out of style tomorrow, it won't be added to the line today." Her designs may be nostalgic, she said, "but I don't want them to look like they came from a vintage store, because then they might as well have." While she still uses some of her original six handbag designs today, she makes them feel fresh and modern by using quirky new colors, patterns, or fabrics. It's this approach that makes kate spade products so appealing to everyday consumers, she argued: "We're not intimidating. I think some people get nervous about fashion because they find it a little scary. But fashion should be enjoyed; it shouldn't be looked at from a jaded, been-there-done-that point of view."

While Kate intends to keep designing for her company, she and her husband also have plans to branch out into other fields. They've already experimented with different media: publishing three books in 2004 with her advice on *Manners, Occasions,* and *Style.* These stylishly designed volumes combined her wit, practical sensibility, love of tradition, and classic style and taste. In 2005, the company debuted the first kate spade music CD, a collection of pop music specially commissioned from the British group Beaumont to be "a nod to '60s cocktail music with a jolt of modern glamour." Since 2001, the JACK SPADE division has produced three short films, as well as several books. Kate Spade herself has appeared on television: in 2002 she guest-starred on the sitcom *Just Shoot Me,* which was set at a fictional fashion magazine and starred her brother-in-law, comedian David Spade (Andy's younger brother). In 2006 she was a guest judge on the season three premiere of "Project Runway," a popular TV reality show and competition for designers on Bravo.

> Kate believes that her products are so appealing to everyday consumers because "We're not intimidating. I think some people get nervous about fashion because they find it a little scary. But fashion should be enjoyed; it shouldn't be looked at from a jaded, been-there-done-that point of view."

One thing that Kate doubts she ever will do, however, is move full-scale into clothing design. She has experimented with the format; in 2004 her company designed uniforms for the short-lived budget airline Song (now part of Delta Airlines) under the kate spade and JACK SPADE labels. In 2005 she collaborated with the international fashion collective As Four on a limited collection of clothing that included shrugs and trenchcoats. But when asked if she would ever create a kate spade clothing collection, the designer said: "I never say never, but I really can't imagine doing it. People are realizing accessories are important now. If I'm in the mood to shop, how fun is a great bag?"

## HOBBIES AND OTHER INTERESTS

Kate enjoys relaxing at her home with her family and their Maltese terrier named Henry. She is also known for entertaining, whether planning a grand party for her husband's fortieth birthday or just a weekend with friends. When she gets away from her business on weekends, she enjoys simple pleasures of reading, walking, or biking into town to browse local shops and antique stores. She often browses flea markets to add to her collection of plates of all kinds.

Kate and her husband also use their company to support charitable causes such as Publicolor, an organization dedicated to sprucing up inner-city schools and community centers with painting projects. The Spades have created a special "publicolor" tote bag and donated 25 percent of its sales to the Publicolor project.

## WRITINGS

*Manners,* 2004
*Occasions,* 2004
*Style,* 2004

## HONORS AND AWARDS

New Fashion Talent Award (Council of Fashion Designers of America): 1996, for Accessories

Best Accessory Designer of the Year (Council of Fashion Designers of America): 1998

FiFi Award (Fragrance Foundation): 2003, Bath & Body Star of the Year, for Kate Spade Beauty

## FURTHER READING

### Periodicals

*Fast Company,* Mar. 2005, p.44
*Forbes,* Dec. 28, 1998, p.86
*Fortune,* Feb. 7, 2000, p.55
*InStyle,* Aug. 2002, p.272
*Kansas City Star,* Nov. 25, 2006, p.E1
*New York Times,* Mar. 12, 1999, p.B2
*People,* June 3, 1996, p.90
*Time,* Feb.16, 2004, p.36
*Vogue,* Aug. 2004, p.200
*W,* Sep. 2005, p.348
*WWD,* July 25, 2005, p.1

## Online Articles

http://money.cnn.com/magazines/fsb/fsb_archive/2003/09/01/350794/
   index.htm
   (CNN Money.com, "Kate & Andy Spade, Kate Spade," Sep. 1, 2003)
http://www.lizclaiborneinc.com/index2.html
   (Liz Claiborne Inc. Press Release, "Liz Claiborne Inc. Agrees to Acquire
   Kate Spade LLC," Dec. 2006)

## Online Databases

*Biography Resource Center Online,* 2007

## ADDRESS

Kate Spade
Kate Spade LLC
48 West 25th Street
New York, NY 10010

## WORLD WIDE WEB SITES

http://www.katespade.com

## Sabriye Tenberken 1970-

German Tibetologist
Founder of the First Tibetan School for the Blind

### BIRTH

Sabriye Tenberken was born in 1970 near Bonn, Germany. Her father was a pianist and her mother was a director of a children's theatre. Her mother gave her the name "Sabriye," which means "patience" in Turkish.

### YOUTH

Tenberken was born with a degenerative disease of the retina, part of the eye. She began losing her sight at the age of two.

For several years she was able to make out colors and faces, but at the age of 12, she became totally blind. Because other children often teased and taunted her, Tenberken worked hard to make it seem that she was not blind at all. She would even get on the wrong bus to avoid asking the driver where the bus was heading. "Not until I accepted my blindness did I begin to live," she has said.

Tenberken's parents sent her to the Marburg Gymnasium for the Blind and Visually Impaired in Marburg, Germany. There she learned different ways to cope with her blindness, like how to use a white cane and how to read Braille. Braille is a form of written language that uses raised dots on a page to create words. Blind people can "read" the words by running their fingertips across the page. But the school taught the students more than coping skills; it also taught them how to have fun, and Tenberken learned how to ride horses, go kayaking, and ski. "That school infused in me all the confidence I could possibly have," she recounted. She read her first book at the school and made friends there. "I had friends. I was equal and happy."

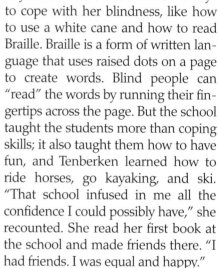

"All of a sudden, for the first time, I discovered I was not alone," Tenberken said about attending a school for the blind. "Teachers as well as students took me seriously for the first time, treating me on equal footing. The friends I quickly made didn't think I was odd. It was the beginning of a new, wonderful life for me."

Years later, Tenberken described how she felt about her early schooling in her memoir, *My Path Leads to Tibet: The Inspiring Story of How One Young Blind Woman Brought Hope to the Blind Children of Tibet.* "When I was very young, my parents discovered I had some eyesight problems. And yet they decided to send me to school like all the other children. This so-called integrated education wasn't ideal, but it was nonetheless very important to me. It enabled me to know the universe of those who can see normally. But all along I felt distinctly different, and I never understood why. Wherever I went, I received privileged treatment. And I noted that some of the teachers addressed themselves to me in a little voice, as if I was helpless. . . . When I turned 12, I went to a special school for the blind in Marburg. That was a revelation. All of a sudden, for the first time, I discovered I was not alone. It was a great comfort when all the other blind students shared their personal experiences. Teachers as well as students took me seriously for the first

*Tenberken traveled through Tibet on horseback in order to evaluate
the needs of the country's blind population. Here, she is shown riding Romeo
through the fields near her farm in Pelshong near Shigatse.*

time, treating me on equal footing. The friends I quickly made didn't think I
was odd. It was the beginning of a new, wonderful life for me."

## Learning about Tibet

Tenberken credits the Marburg school with inspiring her to study Tibetan
culture. While she was in the eighth grade, her class took a field trip to visit
an exhibit on Tibet. The students were allowed to touch religious artifacts,
weapons, and sculptures. They were given a lecture on Tibet's history and
culture. From then on, she wanted to learn more about this Asian country.

Tibet used to be an independent country, but now the Tibet Autonomous
Region is part of China. It is bordered to the north by China and to the
south by India, Nepal, and Bhutan. Tibet is very mountainous and remote, containing the Himalayas and other mountain ranges and many of
the world's highest peaks, including Mount Everest. Political control of
the region has varied: at some points it was independent, and at other
points it was ruled by China. As an independent state, it was a theocracy
ruled by Tibetan monks and led by the Dalai Lama, the spiritual leader of
Tibetan Buddhism.

In the mid-1950s, Tibet and China signed a treaty under which the Dalai
Lama controlled domestic affairs but China controlled foreign and military

413

affairs. But many Tibetans rebelled against Chinese oppression. In 1959, the Dalai Lama (Tenzin Gyatso) fled to India and began a life in exile. From there, he has advocated Tibetan independence and led non-violent opposition to Chinese rule. Since that time, Tibet has remained an autonomous region of China, and the Dalai Lama has continued the struggle for independence, winning the Nobel Peace Prize in 1989. (For more information on the Dalai Lama, see *Biography Today*, Sep. 1998.)

## EDUCATION

After graduating from the Marburg Gymnasium for the Blind and Visually Impaired, Tenberken attended the University of Bonn. There, she was determined to study for a degree in Central Asian Studies, focusing on Tibet. In addition to Mongolian and modern Chinese, she studied modern and classical Tibetan, sociology, and philosophy. She was the first blind person to study Tibetan at the school. But her professors tried to discourage her. The Tibetan language is difficult, and no Braille version existed. But Tenberken was not discouraged. Because there was no Braille version of the Tibetan language, she created one. She also created a Tibetan-German dictionary and, through a computer program she devised, created a way for Tibetan texts to be automatically printed in Braille.

One of her professors offered to take the Braille version to Tibetan authorities, suggesting that they might want Tenberken to visit the country herself and teach it. "It had long been a dream of mine to go to Tibet and make a mark for myself," she recounted. "I couldn't imagine anything more worthwhile than introducing and teaching my reading/writing method to the blind of Tibet!" But the Tibetan authorities were not interested. They did not believe that a blind woman could succeed in such a project. Tenberken earned her degree in Tibetology from the University of Bonn and set out on her plan to visit Tibet.

## CHOOSING A CAREER

In May 1997, after finishing college, Tenberken flew to Beijing, China, to meet with Chinese authorities about using her Braille version of Tibetan. She was told by the China Disabled Persons' Federation that Tibet was not a high priority for them. No care for the blind was planned for another ten years. She was even told that blindness was rare in Tibet. Frustrated, she flew to the city of Lhasa, Tibet, to discover the situation for herself. She met a Tibetan paramedic who told her that blindness was common in the country. Poor diet, widespread vitamin A deficiency, and strong ultraviolet rays because of the country's high alti-

*These Tibetan children, shown in front of the Potala Palace in Lhasa, Tibet, are students in the school run by Braille without Borders.*

tude were the main causes. Tenberken also found that Tibetan society had a strong prejudice against blind people. Many people believed that blindness is a divine punishment for wrong-doing in a previous life or is caused by demons. No charity or medical care organization in Tibet cared for the blind.

Along with two female friends, Tenberken traveled by horseback throughout Tibet to evaluate the needs of the country's blind. Visiting small villages and remote farms, she found many cases where blind children were kept locked indoors for their own safety or because the families were embarrassed by their condition. Other blind children were begging in the streets. When Tibetans were told that Tenberken was blind, they refused at first to believe it. She could ride a horse, and she knew how to read and write. Her idea to create a school for the blind gave many parents hope that their own children might become successful as well.

When Tenberken returned to Lhasa, a local orphanage offered her space to set up a school for the blind. She returned to Germany and, within six months, raised enough money to finance the project. She and her partner Paul Kronenberg founded Braille Without Borders, a group devoted to bringing education to the blind children of Tibet.

415

## CAREER HIGHLIGHTS

### Founding the School

In mid-1998 Tenberken opened the Rehabilitation and Training Center for the Blind in Lhasa, Tibet. The school teaches blind children how to read Braille in Chinese, Tibetan, and English. It also teaches them how to type on a Braille typewriter, how to use a cane to walk, how to cook food, and basic hygiene. There is no charge for the classes or the housing and food the children receive. At any one time, some 30 children between the ages of four and 21 are housed and taught at the school. Many of the teachers are blind children who have already learned Braille. Braille Without Borders prints many books in Braille for use by the children.

—— " ——

*"In the beginning it was horrible," Tenberken said about the early days of Braille Without Borders. "But the obstacles made us stronger. People tried to put limits on me, but limits always show opportunities. I persisted because I* believed *it was possible."*

—— " ——

Students who finish the program are given the choice to attend regular school with sighted children or return to their home villages. For older students, a course in medical massage therapy is also offered.

The project has endured some major hardships. The school had to move from its original location when Tenberken's partner Paul Kronenberg discovered that school funds were being stolen by the director of the orphanage. Later that winter, Kronenberg almost died when he contracted a severe case of pneumonia. And money ran so short that Tenberken was obliged to put all of her own savings into the school to keep it going. "In the beginning it was horrible," she admitted. "But the obstacles made us stronger. People tried to put limits on me, but limits always show opportunities. I persisted because I *believed* it was possible."

The school's annual budget is quite low, only $26,000 a year. Yet, while the Chinese and Tibetan governments now provide some financing for the school, Tenberken and Kronenberg must still spend three months each year in Europe on a fund-raising tour. "The main reason people don't give us money," she explained, "is that we don't raise funds with pity. We don't say, `Pity our poor blind kids.' People find happy, capable children here. But *happy* doesn't really sell."

*Tenberken, Kronenberg, and six blind students achieved an amazing climb of a 23,000-foot Tibetan mountain, which was filmed for the documentary* Blindsight. *In this still from the movie, Tenberken is shown on a training hike prior to the ascent.*

In 2004 Tenberken and Kronenberg opened a training farm for blind adults in Shigatse, Tibet. Here older blind persons are taught basic farm skills so that they can operate a dairy farm. They learn to feed and care for the animals, plant and harvest crops for food, milk cows, and even make cheese. The farm hopes to sell the cheese it produces throughout China in the near future.

### Blindsight

Also in 2004, Tenberken had the opportunity for an incredible adventure. She, Kronenberg, and six teenaged students from their school undertook a three-week climb of Lhakpa Ri, a 23,000-foot mountain in Tibet near Mount Everest. The trip was led by Erik Weihenmayer, a professional mountain climber who is also the first blind man to have climbed Mount Everest. On the expedition, they made use of a number of tools Weihenmayer had invented specifically to help blind people climb safely. Their impressive ascent was recorded by documentary filmmaker Lucy Walker.

The resulting feature was released in 2006 as *Blindsight*. Nominated for several international awards, it won the Audience Award for Best Documentary Film at several notable film festivals, including the 2006 AFI Film Festival, the 2007 Berlin Film Festival, and the Palm Springs Film Festival. In addition, Tenberken wrote a book about the experience, *Das siebte Jahr: Von Tibet nach Indien* (The Seventh Year: From Tibet to India), which is available only in German. In it, she chronicles the climb and profiles the students who undertook the adventure.

### Recent Projects

While her work in Tibet continues, Tenberken has not stopped there. In 2006 Braille Without Borders began construction of the International Centre for Development and Project Planning (ICDeP) in Kerala, India. The need for the new school is clear when viewing statistics from the World Health Organization, cited on the Braille Without Borders web site. Worldwide, 161 million people live with a disabling visual impairment, including 37 million people who are blind and 124 million people with low vision. About 80% live in developing countries.

The new center will teach blind people from all over the developing world how to set up and manage a school for the blind in their own countries. Students will study management, fundraising, public relations, project planning, computer technology, English and communication skills, and other skills necessary to running an organization. The training will enable the students to set up and lead social projects in their own communities. With this new project, Tenberken hopes to educate and empower many more blind people around the world.

## HOME AND FAMILY

Tenberken, who is not married, lives with her partner, Paul Kronenberg. He is Dutch and has worked as a designer and construction coordinator for the Swiss Red Cross and for other organizations. He supervises all construction projects for Braille Without Borders and teaches people bookkeeping and computer skills to run the organization's office.

## WRITINGS

*My Path Leads to Tibet: The Inspiring Story of How One Young Blind Woman Brought Hope to the Blind Children of Tibet*, 2003

## HONORS AND AWARDS

Charity Bambi (Burda, Germany): 2000
Norgall Prize (International Women's Club): 2000
Global Leader of Tomorrow (World Economic Forum): 2001
Zilveren Jandaia (Stichting kerk en Wereld, Holland): 2001
Albert Schweizer Award (Wolfgang von Goethe Association): 2002
Knight (Order of Oranje Nassau, Netherlands): 2003
XX Factor All Star (*Outside Magazine*): 2003
Asian Hero Award (*Time* magazine): 2004
Christopher Award: 2004, for *My Path Leads to Tibet*
European Hero Award (*Time* magazine): 2004
Leile Luce Hadley Award (World Wings Trust): 2005
Bundesverdienst kreuz (government of Germany): 2005
Chomolongma Friendship Award (government of the Tibet Autonomous Region): 2006
National Friendship Award (government of China): 2006
Mother Teresa Award: 2006

## FURTHER READING

### Books

*Contemporary Authors*, Vol. 234, 2005
Tenberken, Sabriye. *My Path Leads to Tibet: The Inspiring Story of How One Young Blind Woman Brought Hope to the Blind Children of Tibet*, 2003

## Periodicals

*Kirkus Reviews,* Nov. 1, 2002, p.1603
*New York Times,* Sep. 20, 2003, p.A4
*O, The Oprah Magazine,* Aug. 2005, p. 222
*Publishers Weekly,* Nov. 11, 2002, p.48
*School Library Journal,* May, 2003, p.181

## Online Articles

http://www.climbingblind.org
   (*Climbing Blind Tibet Expedition 2004,* "Team Profiles," undated)
http://www.oprah.com
   (*Oprah.com,* "Phenomenal Females," undated)
http://www.1000peacewomen.org
   (*Peace Women across the Globe,* "Sabriye Tenberken," undated)
http://www.time.com/time/asia
   (*Time Asia,* "Sabriye Tenberken," Oct. 4, 2004)
http://www.time.com/time/europe
   (*Time Europe,* "The Visionary," Oct. 2, 2004)

## Online Databases

*Biography Resource Center Online,* 2007, article from *Contemporary Authors Online,* 2005

## ADDRESS

Sabriye Tenberken
Arcade Publishing
116 John Street #2810
New York, NY 10038
Blind Without Borders
E-mail: blztib@t-online.de

## WORLD WIDE WEB SITES

http://www.braillewithoutborders.org
http://www.blindsightthemovie.com

## Rob Thomas 1965-

American Author, Television Writer, and Producer
Creator of the TV Series "Veronica Mars"

### BIRTH

Rob Thomas was born on August 15, 1965, in Sunnyside, Washington. His parents, Bob and Diana Thomas, were both teachers. Rob was their only child and he maintained a very close relationship with his parents throughout his youth. When Thomas was 10 years old, his family moved from the Pacific Northwest to Austin, Texas. Two years later they moved to San Marcos, a small town about 30 miles south of Austin, where his parents operated a sandwich shop.

## YOUTH AND EDUCATION

Even as a child, Thomas looked forward to a career as an author. "I've always wanted to be a writer, though the sort of writer I've aspired to be has changed several times," he revealed. "I told my junior high counselor that I was going to be a novelist, but that was when I was bright-eyed and naive."

—————— " ——————

*"I've always wanted to be a writer, though the sort of writer I've aspired to be has changed several times," said Thomas. "I told my junior high counselor that I was going to be a novelist, but that was when I was bright-eyed and naive."*

—————— " ——————

As he grew older, Thomas shifted his sights to journalism. He worked on this goal by writing for his high school paper, and he eventually became the paper's editor. "I'd goof off for three weeks, then my friends who I'd recruited onto staff and I would lock ourselves in and write the entire edition," he remembered. "I have copies of issues in which I've written 14, 15 stories. None of them very good, but I enjoyed seeing my byline."

Thomas was also an outstanding athlete during high school. He played football, baseball, and basketball, and ran track. Unlike the often-alienated characters he has brought to life in books and on television screens over the years, the adolescent Thomas was a straight arrow who enjoyed his teen years. "I played sports in school, liked my parents, cleaved tenaciously to sobriety, and as uncool as this sounds, enjoyed high school."

After graduating from San Marcos High School in 1983, Thomas attended Texas Christian University. A member of the football team, he played as a sophomore before deciding to leave sports behind and focus on his studies. He won a journalism scholarship and later transferred to the University of Texas at Austin. He received his Bachelor of Arts (BA) degree in history in 1987, as well as his teaching certificate.

## EARLY JOBS

Although Thomas had entered college hoping to pursue a career in journalism, by the time he graduated he had his heart set on a life in music. He and some friends had formed a rock band, called Public Bulletin, and by the time he earned his college diploma that group had attracted a modest following. Thomas played bass guitar for the band, but his biggest contribution was as a songwriter. He later admitted that the sound of an audience singing along to his lyrics transformed him. "My life goals changed on the spot," he admitted.

For the next several years Thomas devoted most of his free time to music. On most nights and weekends he could be found on stage at one regional venue or another with his band, which was renamed Hey Zeus in 1988 and Black Irish in 1992. His main source of income during this time was a teacher's salary. "I felt like I was a good teacher, but if I hadn't had my own thing outside, some other aspiration, I would have felt like I was selling myself out," he said.

Thomas's teaching career began in 1988 at John Marshall High School in San Antonio, Texas. In 1991 he moved to Austin, Texas, where he taught journalism at Reagan High School. He enjoyed teaching in part because it challenged him to find creative ways to keep his students excited about journalism. He met this goal one semester by entering one of his broadcast journalism classes in a news production competition sponsored by Channel One, a television network broadcast directly into public schools. His students performed so well that Channel One network executives offered Thomas a job. He accepted the position, in part because he wanted a new challenge and in part because he realized that his dreams of musical stardom were fading. He was encouraged in the career change by his family, noting that "the defining moment for me was when my dad sat me down and said I should write."

## CAREER HIGHLIGHTS

Thomas moved out to California to join the Channel One staff in 1994. His position was as a liaison between Channel One's educational development department and the schools that subscribed to the service. Unfortunately, Thomas found the job to be boring and tedious. "I felt like this job could have been adequately filled by a zealous coat hanger," he recalled.

Thomas's unhappiness with his new job was made worse by the fact that he was no longer working as a musician. "Suddenly, I had this huge creative void in my life," he recalled. "I wasn't doing anything, so I started [a novel called] Rats Saw God: a page a day that filled that hole in my life."

Thomas disciplined himself to write every day, and after 10 months he had completed his first draft. He studied the publishing market and decided to look for an agent. Many writers have great difficulty finding an agent to represent them or a publisher interested in purchasing their manuscripts. But for Thomas, finding an agent and a publisher was easy. "It's funny," the author observed. "I spent nine years beating my head against the wall in this rock'n'roll band, and it took [only] 10 weeks after I had finished my book to get an agent, and 10 weeks after that to get a book contract." He signed a two-book contract with Simon & Schuster, quit his job at Channel One, and returned to Texas in June 1995 to focus on his writing.

### Rats Saw God

Thomas's first novel for young adults, *Rats Saw God,* was published in 1996. It tells the story of Steve York, a California high school senior who has scored high on his college-entrance exams despite a reputation as a flunking-out stoner. A sympathetic counselor challenges him to write a 100-page paper—on any subject—to make up for an English class. Steve decides to write about the experiences that disillusioned him with life and separated him from his father. Steve was a sophomore when his parents divorced and he chose to live with "the Astronaut," as he calls his father. They communicate only through notes and Steve avoids activities he knows his father would find acceptable. Nevertheless, he is a straight-A student until he discovers his girlfriend is having an affair with a teacher. The betrayal devastates Steve, who starts skipping class and smoking pot. But the book ends on a hopeful note, as it becomes clear that the counselor's writing assignment has forced Steve to face the pain in his past, deal with it, and move forward with a greater sense of purpose and maturity.

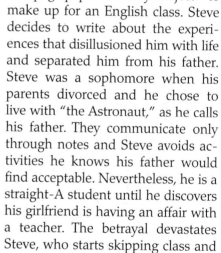

"I didn't think I was writing a young-adult book . . . so I didn't alter anything [in Rats Saw God]," Thomas said. "Teenagers don't live profanity-free, sex-free, drug-free lives."

Thomas's novel was notable both for its sense of humor and its perceptive insights into the thoughts and emotions of teenagers. As a reviewer remarked in *St. James Guide to Young Adult Writers,* "[the] protagonists survive in a high school culture tinged by drugs, sex, and profanity, and Thomas accurately captures the adolescent language they utter and philosophies they follow." Thomas recognized that the strong language and mature themes in his work might raise eyebrows, but he said that "I didn't think I

was writing a young-adult book . . . so I didn't alter anything." Besides, he added, "teenagers don't live profanity-free, sex-free, drug-free lives."

*Rats Saw God* found favor with teen readers, librarians, and critics alike. Writing in *School Library Journal,* Joel Shoemaker called the novel a "beautifully crafted, emotionally charged story" with "layers of cynical wit and careful character development. . . Steve's coming-of-age is not a smooth ballistic parabola, but more a series of explosive changes in relationships. These changes suggest to YA readers that, though complex and difficult, it is this weird willingness to establish interconnectedness that makes being human such a trip. This robust first novel is so hip and cool and strong it hurts." *Rats Saw God* won an American Library Association Best Books Award, as well as several other best book citations and state award citations. It also gave Thomas a big jolt of confidence. "When I finished my novel, I felt like I could read the top young-adult novel out there— my favorite, the one I considered a classic—and felt I could match up to that," he said.

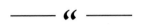

*"For me, coming up with a story idea is the most difficult part of the creative writing process," said Thomas. "If I didn't realize this before, writing a short story collection drove the point home."*

### Slave Day and Other Works

Thomas's second novel, *Slave Day* (1997), also pushed boundaries in addressing issues of prejudice and race. The author uses multiple viewpoints to recount what happens during a school fundraiser, "Slave Day," in which students and teachers in a Texas high school are auctioned off for one day. Keene Davenport, an African-American teen, is offended by Slave Day and tries to organize a boycott. When his protest fails, he ends up "buying" student body president Shawn Greeley, another African American, at the auction. He then has Shawn perform a series of demeaning tasks to show his anger about Slave Day, but the stunt does not turn out as he expects. Other "slaves" and "masters," including a computer geek and the mayor's daughter, an unpopular teacher and a slacker student, and a popular girl and her boyfriend, similarly find their assumptions challenged during the day. "[*Slave Day* is] a cleverly written story that is funny, but that has an underlying serious theme," Judy R. Johnston wrote in *School Library Journal.* "Thomas's quirky humor leads readers and the main characters on a soul-searching experience as themes of equality, racism, feminism, and affirmative action emerge through this intelligently written novel. . . . The final consciousness-raising in the characters' attitudes makes this book a winner. Like Chris Crutcher and Paul Zindel, Thomas has made a distinct contribution to contemporary young adult literature."

Thomas's next book was a short story collection called *Doing Time: Notes from the Undergrad* (1997). Thomas admitted that finishing this book posed a different kind of challenge for him. "For me, coming up with a story idea is the most difficult part of the creative writing process," he noted. "If I didn't realize this before, writing a short story collection drove the point home."

Each story in *Doing Time* follows individual teenagers as they fulfill their high school's community-service requirement. The stories address such serious issues as abuse, poverty, teen pregnancy, and grief. Not only do the students learn more about these issues, they often learn more about their own feelings. In "Loss of Pet," for instance, a library volunteer makes snap judgments about the library's patrons based on their looks or the books they read. She initially mocks a pretty girl for attending a support group for people who have lost a pet, but finds herself unexpectedly moved by the girl's story. Her reaction forces her to reassess her own attitudes. Other characters in the story collection experience similar moments of self-awareness. "Thomas knows the issues that concern kids, and he does a good job distinguishing each character—from bitchy Teesha, who masks her feelings when the group she is with delivers food to her grandmother, to Dwight, who finds joy in himself and in his Mexican roots when he tutors a school groundskeeper," wrote Stephanie Zvirin in *Booklist*. "Thomas has the language and the emotions down just right—and he never forgets that there's hope.

Thomas returned to the novel form for *Satellite Down* (1998), a work in which he drew on his experiences in television to tell the story of one teen's loss of innocence. Patrick Sheridan is 17 when he wins a spot as a student reporter on an educational satellite television show. He leaves his small Texas town and strict parents to live by himself in Los Angeles. At first he his excited by his job, but he becomes disillusioned when he learns the channel is more interested in his good looks than his reporting skills.

He is tempted by alcohol, drugs, sex, and celebrity. But instead of giving in to these temptations, he runs off while in Ireland to explore his family roots. While he finds no easy solutions there, his soul-searching and satirical commentary provide readers with an interesting look into the costs of making your dreams come true. "I know [*Satellite Down* has] a downbeat ending," the author remarked, "but I think there's enough humor and adventure in getting there that it's not a painful ride." A *Kirkus Reviews* critic offered similar thoughts about the novel: "Thomas covers a lot of territory, and Patrick's journeys of the heart are as compelling as his sincere attempts to do the right thing, but readers should be prepared for a raw, ambiguous conclusion."

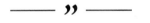

> *Thomas only remained on the staff of "Dawson's Creek" for its first season. "It was a fun year for me, because I got to get out of debt with my first TV job, and I learned a ton."*

Thomas targeted a slightly younger audience in his 1998 adventure novel *Green Thumb* (1998). This tale concerns award-winning botany student Grady Jacobs, who is excited about earning a spot on a scientific mission to the rainforest. But when team leader Dr. Phillip Carter learns Grady is only 13, he gets stuck with meaningless, dirty jobs. Despite all his chores, Grady discovers that Carter is planting genetically engineered trees that are poisoning the rainforest—a secret the scientist would kill to keep. Grady goes on the run, evading wildlife and Carter's henchmen long enough to expose his crimes. Although it differed in subject matter and intended audience from the author's other novels, *Green Thumb* displayed Thomas's trademark wit, along with a flair for action and adventure. "Readers won't be able to turn the pages fast enough," reviewer John Peter wrote in *Booklist*. "Fans expecting another *Slave Day* or *Rats Saw God* are in for a shock."

### Writing for Television and Movies

Thomas's growing reputation as a writer with a knack for reaching teen audiences brought him to the attention of Hollywood. In 1997 he accepted a job as a staff writer for a new television series called "Dawson's Creek." This drama about teens growing up in a small seaside Massachusetts town debuted in 1998 and became an instant hit with teenagers. Some critics complained that the teen characters sounded too articulate for their age. But Thomas said, "I kind of dug writing those kids as though they were college grad students. It was fun and liberating and made for a true sort of writer's show." Although he only remained on the staff of "Dawson's Creek" for its first season, "it was a fun year for me, because I got to get out of debt with my first TV job, and I learned a ton."

That experience would serve Thomas well on his next television job. He had left "Dawson's Creek" because of a fantastic stroke of good fortune: his first pilot script for a television series, called "Cupid," was picked up by ABC to air in the fall of 1998. Two years after moving to Hollywood, executive producer Thomas was now running his own hour-long TV drama. "Cupid" starred Jeremy Piven as Trevor Hale, a charismatic mental patient who insists he is the legendary god of love. He claims he has been exiled to earth and must unite 100 couples with-

*Thomas's first experience in Hollywood was as a staff writer for the TV show "Dawson's Creek," which starred Katie Holmes, Joshua Jackson, James Van Der Beek, and Michelle Williams.*

out using his magic arrows before he can return to Mount Olympus. Psychologist and romance expert Claire Allen, played by Paula Marshall, doesn't believe Trevor but helps him establish a life outside the hospital. Although critics liked the show, ratings were poor and the series was cancelled in February 1999 after 14 episodes.

Thomas was disappointed by the cancellation of "Cupid," but other exciting developments kept him from dwelling on it. In 1999 two films based on Thomas's screenplays were released. One was *Drive Me Crazy*, a teen romantic comedy he adapted from the Todd Strasser novel *How I Created My Perfect Prom Date* (also published as *Girl Gives Birth to Own Prom Date*). Melissa Joan Hart and Adrian Grenier played high school friends from two different social groups who decide to date each other in a bid to make other people jealous. Popular with teen audiences, the movie earned a modest $17.8 million at the box office. Thomas's next screenplay to reach the big screen was the small independent film *Fortune Cookie,* about three

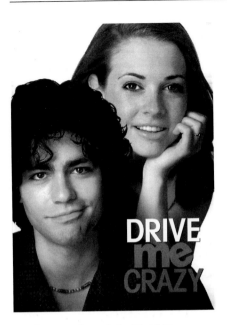

*Thomas adapted the Todd Strasser novel* How I Created My Perfect Prom Date *for his screenplay for* Drive Me Crazy, *which starred Adrian Grenier and Melissa Joan Hart.*

couples at a Chinese restaurant. The movie was not widely seen, but it earned good reviews.

That same year, Thomas was hired by producer David E. Kelley, creator of such award-winning TV shows as "Chicago Hope," "Ally McBeal," and "The Practice," to work on a new detective show called "Snoops." Thomas left the show before it even aired, however. He had wanted to inject more humor into the series, and "[Kelley] and I didn't get on the same page about what this detective show was going to be," the producer explained. This experience taught him an important lesson: "In fiction I am king of this little world," he noted, "[but in television and film] you are one piece in a committee of people producing this thing and everyone has a voice."

Thomas capped off 1999 by signing a four-year development deal with Fox TV that paid him $8 million. For a guy from small-town Texas, such swift Hollywood success was sometimes overwhelming: "I function pretty well knowing what is going on," he said. "But sometimes, just drifting off to sleep at night, it will hit me and make me seize up, and I'll be terrified."

Thomas's anxiety increased over the next four years. Between 2000 and 2003, he wrote 11 pilot scripts for new television shows that languished in "development hell," never making it to a network (for each series that makes it to television, many others are written and have pilot episodes filmed before being turned down). "There were plenty of things that didn't fly, but there was one that literally broke my heart and gave me true writer's block," he remembered. A network had been very interested in a drama series proposed by Thomas. But the network executive who was most intrigued by the series was fired and Thomas's producing partner died unexpectedly of a heart attack. These setbacks doomed the show, leaving Thomas to try again.

### Creating "Veronica Mars"

Thomas's luck finally turned in 2003, when he met with executives for the UPN network to discuss potential projects. During the meeting he mentioned a script he had written for a "teen noir" detective series. "I just started with a vague idea of tackling the noir genre and sticking teenagers into it," the author remembered. "It was one of the first projects I started thinking of visually rather than [in terms of] internalized protagonist dialogue." The image that kept popping up in his imagination was that of a car sitting outside a run-down motel—but the detective sitting in the car is a teenager instead of an adult. Although Thomas first envisioned the character as male, he later decided it would be more interesting to make the character female. The network executives were intrigued, and three days after the meeting they approved production of a pilot episode of the show, called "Veronica Mars." Several months later, the network announced that "Veronica Mars" would debut as a new UPN series in fall 2004.

> *"Unlike a lot of shows, we don't introduce you to the bad guy at the beginning and tell you whodunit," declared Thomas. "We always want Veronica to do something very new and fresh and clever to get to this information, and that's always a challenge."*

The title character, Veronica Mars, is a popular high school girl with a cute boyfriend, loving family, and seemingly charmed life—until her best friend Lilly Kane is murdered. Veronica's father, the local sheriff, accuses Lilly's father of the crime but can't prove his case. Her father loses his job as sheriff, his wife leaves him, and Veronica is ostracized at school. During this time Veronica attends a party and is drugged and raped. The show opens eight months after these events, with Veronica assisting her father in his work as a private detective. Her experiences helping her father show her that harsh truths often lie behind lives that seem perfect on the surface. Played by actress Kristen Bell, Veronica is a pretty girl with a bad attitude—her life has gone so wrong she no longer cares about normal teen problems. "If there's something I've learned in this business," Veronica tells viewers, "[it's that] the people you love let you down." Nonetheless, she still has empathy for people around her. She befriends the outsiders at school and feels sorry for the popular kids with hidden problems, even though they have rejected her.

*Kristen Bell, center, and the cast of "Veronica Mars."*

Thomas admitted that "Veronica Mars" had the potential to be a very dark show. "The network was worried about having a teen show where the protagonist has been raped, her friend murdered, her dad a pariah, her mom disappeared," Thomas noted. "How are you going to be able to handle it and have a degree of humor and warmth?" The humor comes from Veronica's comic observations, which display Thomas's trademark wit. These comic bits work well because Thomas and his writers try to integrate them into the story. "I don't want to write setup, punch, setup, punch, where the joke dictates the scene," he explained, "I want to find comedy in which the drama is actually driving the moment in the scene." According to most critics, Thomas succeeded in his goal of blending wit and dramatic tension. As a result, the show quickly gained a devoted fan base.

Viewers can also find warm moments in the series, especially as demonstrated in Veronica's close relationship with her supportive father, played by Enrico Colantoni. She also displays empathy for the people she investigates. In helping her father with his detective work, Veronica sees that many of the people whose lives seem perfect on the surface are battling their own problems. "Providing this peek behind the curtain not only offers a remedy for those teenage snap judgments, it lends the world of 'Veronica Mars' depth and color," wrote TV critic Heather Havrilesky.

## Mysteries and Teen Troubles

The first season of "Veronica Mars" was dominated by the mystery of the murder of Lilly Kane, and Thomas rewarded loyal fans at the end of season one by having Veronica solve the mystery. He opened the second season by unveiling another mystery for her to solve—this time a tragic accident in which a school bus drives off a cliff. As the season progressed, Veronica found one clue at a time, giving viewers a chance to solve the mystery at the same time she does. That strategy is deliberate, Thomas said: "Unlike a lot of shows, we don't introduce you to the bad guy at the beginning and tell you whodunit. . . . We always want Veronica to do something very new and fresh and clever to get to this information, and that's always a challenge."

Thomas believes that it is not a coincidence that his greatest success in television has been with a teen character. When asked why he writes for young people, he replied, "It has to do with my affection for teenagers. I like people that age. I find them interesting. It's less about writing how they speak than connecting the thematic truisms of people that age." What makes teens respond to his writing is his honest depiction of their lives, even if that makes for a less-than-happy ending. "I feel compelled to include some bit of truth," Thomas remarked. "It's not truth if our endings are always happy."

> *When asked why he writes for young people, Thomas replied, "It has to do with my affection for teenagers. I like people that age. I find them interesting. It's less about writing how they speak than connecting the thematic truisms of people that age."*

Despite its devoted fan base and critical raves, "Veronica Mars" has never been a monster hit in terms of television ratings. Its status for the future became a bit of a mystery in itself in January 2006, when UPN announced that it was merging with the WB Network to form a new television network called the CW. Fans of the show openly worried on Internet fan sites about the show's future. For his part, Thomas projected optimism. He declared that he was hopeful that "Veronica Mars" would not only return for a third season, but that it might run for five or six seasons. "I sort of expect good things to happen," he said. "I don't know where I get it, but I do have a sort of blind optimism." In May 2006 the CW announced that "Veronica Mars" would return for a third season, an announcement that delighted the show's many fans. Their happiness was short-lived, however; after airing 64 episodes, the show was can-celed in 2007.

Thomas has said that he "would love to write more novels," but his film and television work keeps him so busy—and pays so well—that he is unlikely to return to book writing any time soon. Fortunately, he gets just as much satis-faction out of writing for television. "From childhood on, it's always been writing for me," he noted. "I always have to have some big dream, a creative goal to shoot for, and when I'm writing, I feel like I'm reaching that."

## MARRIAGE AND FAMILY

Thomas married Katie Orr, a bookstore manager, in May 2005. Their daughter, Greta Mae, was born that same year. They live in the Hollywood Hills, with neighbors that have included singer Britney Spears and actress Brittany Murphy.

## HOBBIES AND OTHER INTERESTS

Thomas loves to read magazines, especially about pop culture, music, and sports. He also enjoys playing basketball and other sports.

## SELECTED WRITINGS

### Young Adult Fiction

*Rats Saw God,* 1996
*Doing Time: Notes from the Undergrad,* 1997
*Slave Day,* 1997
*Green Thumb,* 1998
*Satellite Down,* 1998

### Television and Film Scripts

"Dawson's Creek," 1997-98 (TV series; staff writer)
"Cupid," 1998-99 (TV series; creator, executive producer)
*Drive Me Crazy,* 1999 (movie; script writer)
*Fortune Cookie,* 1999 (movie; script writer)
"Veronica Mars," 2004-2007 (TV series; creator, executive producer)

## HONORS AND AWARDS

Books for the Teen Age (New York Public Library): 1996-97, for *Rats Saw God*
Best Books for Young Adults (American Library Association): 1997, for *Rats Saw God;* 1998, for *Doing Time: Notes from the Undergrad*

## FURTHER READING

### Books

Hipple, Ted, ed. *Writers for Young Adults,* Supplement 1, 2000
Rockman, Connie. *Eighth Book of Junior Authors & Illustrators*, 2000
Silvey, Anita, ed. *The Essential Guide to Children's Books and Their Creators,* 2002
*Something about the Author,* Vol. 97, 1998

### Periodicals

*Austin American-Statesman,* June 6, 1996, p.E1; Jan. 16, 1998, p. F1; Aug. 11, 1998, p.E1; Nov. 16, 2004, p.E1
*Houston Chronicle,* May 10, 2005, sec. STAR, p.1
*Mediaweek,* May 31, 1999, p.64
*Newsday,* June 3, 1999, p.B35
*Publishers Weekly,* Jan. 18, 1999, p.198
*San Antonio Express-News,* Oct. 14, 1998, p.G1
*Texas Monthly,* Apr. 1997, p.24
*Voice of Youth Advocates,* June 1997, p.88

### Online Databases

*Biography Resource Center Online,* 2005, articles from *Authors and Artists for Young Adults,* 1998; *Contemporary Authors Online,* 2005; and *St. James Guide to Young Adult Writers,* 1999

## ADDRESS

Rob Thomas
CW Television Network
3300 West Olive Ave.
Burbank, CA 91505

## WORLD WIDE WEB SITES

http://www.robthomasproductions.com
http://www.cwtv.com

## Ashley Tisdale 1985-

American Actress and Singer

Star of the Disney Movies *High School Musical* and *High School Musical 2* and the TV Show "The Suite Life of Zack & Cody"

### BIRTH

Ashley Michelle Tisdale was born on July 2, 1985, in West Deal, New Jersey, to Mike and Lisa Tisdale. She has an older sister, Jennifer, who is also an actress.

## YOUTH AND EDUCATION

Tisdale has worked in show business virtually her whole life. "When I was three, I was at the mall with my mom, and this manager came up to us and asked if I wanted to be in commercials," she recalled. This encounter led to a part in a commercial for the national retail chain JC Penney, and from that point forward the youngster knew that she wanted to be an actress.

> "I moved from New Jersey to California, so I know what it feels like to be the girl trying to figure it all out," Tisdale explained. "There was this girl in the popular group who was jealous of me, even though I bought my own clothes and car—my parents didn't give them to me. I never told people in school I was an actress. I'm a girl, and acting is my job."

Over the next several years she appeared in more than 100 commercials, including national ads for products including T-Mobile, KFC restaurants, and Sargento cheese.

In 1993, at the age of eight years old, Tisdale landed the role of Cosette in a national touring company version of the famous play *Les Miserables,* based on the novel by the 19th-century French author Victor Hugo. "My mom threw me into some voice lessons to get me prepared for it," she remembered. "It was a really great experience and so I have sung ever since then. I love to sing." Tisdale left the show after two years and joined the cast of the international tour company for the musical *Annie* for a short time. These stage experiences gave her the opportunity to perform at the White House for President Bill Clinton in 1997. "I was a part of Broadway Kids, which was a bunch of kids who were in Broadway shows, and we sang Broadway tunes and met the president," she recalled. "I was so nervous, but it was really fun."

Tisdale's family moved to Valencia, California, when she was in eighth grade. At first, it was a difficult transition. "I moved from New Jersey to California, so I know what it feels like to be the girl trying to figure it all out," she explained. "There was this girl in the popular group who was jealous of me, even though I bought my own clothes and car—my parents didn't give them to me. I never told people in school I was an actress. I'm a girl, and acting is my job."

Tisdale's acting career continued to blossom throughout her high school years. She landed a small role in the 2001 feature film *Donny Darko* and

*Tisdale with cast members from "The Suite Life of Zach and Cody" (left to right): Cole Sprouse, Tisdale, Zac Efron, Brenda Song, and Dylan Sprouse.*

guest starred on numerous television shows, including "The Hughleys," "Charmed," "7th Heaven," "Beverly Hills 90210," "The Amanda Show," and "Boston Public." Yet she claimed that was actually pretty shy during those years. "Believe it or not I was kind of quiet," she said. "I get that side from my dad. My mom is really outgoing."

Tisdale thinks that her shyness may have affected the way other students looked at her. "In high school people would think I was snobby or didn't want to talk to anybody because I was so quiet. But I like being shy!" Being a cheerleader helped her come out of her shell. "My sister was a hardcore cheerleader and I always wanted to follow her," Tisdale explained.

## Just a Regular Girl

During Tisdale's adolescence, her parents worked hard to keep show business from dominating her life. "I always had a normal life," she said. "I worked at Wet Seal in the mall and went to a regular school. My dad wanted me to know how long it took to make money and not to take anything for granted." Those long hours of work at the local mall still bring back mixed feelings. "I think it was such a great thing to do," she admitted. "I mean, back then I *hated* it. I had to clean up after shoppers—like scraping gum off the floor—so it was definitely a reality check for me." Tisdale also loved to go horseback riding. She went for the first time when she was eight years old, and eventually developed a strong interest in competitive riding. "I rode mostly when I was 12 or 13, and I did it a lot," she revealed. "I loved doing it."

After graduating from high school, Tisdale decided to take a year off before beginning college. "I really believe in listening to your parents, and my parents are into education," she said. "But I was finished with acting projects and done with school, and I said, 'Dad, I want to take a year off.' So I did." During that time, she worked at the mall and thought a lot about her future. "Really, it was so I could take time to think ahead," she said. "It's good to step back and go, 'What do I like? What do I want?' I knew I wanted to keep acting. So I took it seriously and took classes. I knew I had to work to get what I wanted."

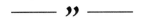

> "I always had a normal life," Tisdale said. "I worked at Wet Seal in the mall and went to a regular school. "I think it was such a great thing to do.... I mean, back then I **hated** it. I had to clean up after shoppers—like scraping gum off the floor—so it was definitely a reality check for me."

## CAREER HIGHLIGHTS

Immediately after high school, Tisdale landed recurring roles on the television series "George Lopez" and "Standing Still." But even as she looked for the part that would firmly establish her name in Hollywood, she encountered doubters. "After I toured with *Les Miserables*, I wanted to come to California and start doing sitcoms and movies," she remembered. "I met with this agency, and they said, 'She's really sweet, but she'll never make it in Hollywood.'"

Tisdale refused to be discouraged by such comments. "I was like, 'You know *what*? I don't *care* what they say,'" she said. "'I'm gonna go for it and take as many classes as I need.' And it's so funny because years later, this same agent was a manager and knew about me because I was working on so many TV shows. He was like, 'Oh, my gosh, she looks just like Brittany Murphy—she's doing so well,' and my mom was like, 'Yeah, I think *you're* the guy that said that she would never work out here.'"

## "The Suite Life of Zack and Cody"

In 2005 Tisdale auditioned for a new Disney project called "The Suite Life of Zack and Cody." This television series revolved around young identical twin brothers living in a luxurious Boston hotel with their mother, a lounge singer. She tested for two roles in the show, London and Maddie, and the producers eventually decided that Tisdale was best suited to play the role of Maddie, the hotel's teenage gift clerk and occasional babysitter for the twins. "I'm really glad that I ended up with Maddie because for fans to first get to know me, I'd rather them look up to this character who is more like me," she said.

Tisdale was very excited to appear on a Disney show. "I love Disney because I'm really, really young still," she asserted. "I never really felt comfortable, even before I was on Disney, doing any type of roles that are really mature. I always wanted to work for Disney my whole life." She admitted that her agent had doubts about taking the role. "My agent did not want me at the Disney channel because I'm older," she said. "But, honestly, I'm not ready for older roles yet, or even the things older girls do. I really am young! All my friends are 16 and 17. I don't go clubbing. I don't drink. I'd much rather have a sleepover or go bowling with girlfriends. I guess you could say I'm not very worldly yet."

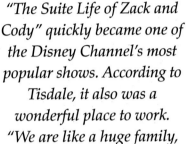

*"The Suite Life of Zack and Cody" quickly became one of the Disney Channel's most popular shows. According to Tisdale, it also was a wonderful place to work. "We are like a huge family, from the beginning, from the pilot," she said.*

When the executives at the Disney Channel decided to add "The Suite Life of Zack and Cody" to their lineup in 2005, the show's producers asked Tisdale to cut and straighten her hair and dye it from her natural brunette to blonde. She agreed to it, but had mixed feelings about the change. "They cut off seven inches and dyed it blonde and began to straighten it twice a week," she recalled. "As it came along, I started to feel doubt, like, 'Oh, did they not like me or my look before?'" Tisdale's doubts about the change intensified when some fans complained that she was trying to imitate another young star, Hilary Duff. "Some of the fans have said, 'Oh, she's just trying to be Hilary Duff,' but me dyeing it blonde, cutting it short, and straightening it—that wasn't even my *choice*," she declared. "That's just for a character. So it's hurtful when people perceive me as trying to be somebody else."

"The Suite Life of Zack and Cody" quickly became one of the Disney Channel's most popular shows. According to Tisdale, it also was a wonderful place to work. "We are like a huge family, from the beginning, from the pilot," she said. "We only had like a week to shoot the pilot—like we bonded. It was just amazing." In addition to her friends on the show, Tisdale has established friendships with several other actresses affiliated with the Disney Channel, including Raven Symone, and the sister team of Aly and A.J. "Once you're in the business, you kind of just get to know everybody," she explained. "You audition with these people, you're friends with these people. I always stay friends with everybody."

> *"It doesn't really matter what everybody else thinks—it's just what makes you happy. Performing is what makes me happy, I couldn't care less if people don't like it—that's fine. I love proving people wrong."*

Tisdale has admitted that it is sometimes easier to maintain friendships with fellow actors because they understand the pressures of the profession. "All my friends are in the business because it's kind of hard," she said. "A lot of people were jealous and didn't understand. I just got to know all these people. It's kind of cool that we ended up on the same channel."

### High School Musical

During the summer hiatus of "The Suite Life of Zack and Cody," Tisdale was determined to keep busy. "I love working, when I'm not working I get so bored," she said. "I was like, what am I going to do for a couple months? I don't know what I'm going to do. So for two weeks on hiatus I was already bored. . . . And suddenly *High School Musical* came around and I went to audition for it."

*High School Musical* was a Disney original film project. Despite her relationship with the studio, Tisdale still had to audition for a role in the film. "A lot of people think [I landed a part in the movie] because I'm on Disney, but I had to go on audition, and callback," she pointed out. "It wasn't like it was handed to me at all. I had to go in there and get it myself."

In *High School Musical,* Tisdale plays the role of Sharpay Evans, a popular but mean girl who plots against two students, Troy and Gabrielle, when they get the lead roles in the school play. Jealous of the talented newcom-

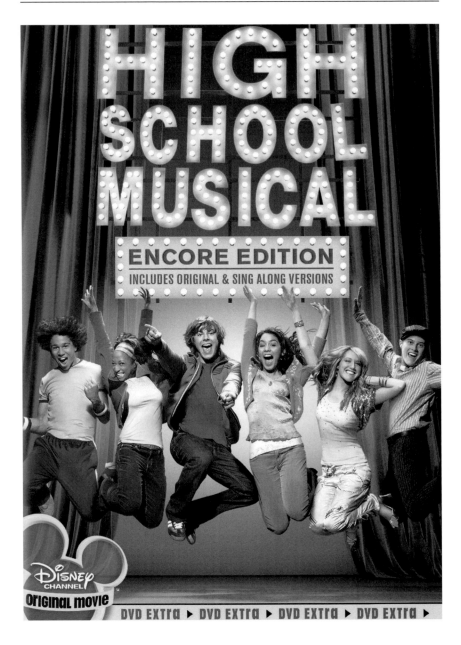

ers, Sharpay and her twin brother Ryan plot to stop Troy and Gabrielle from performing in the musical. "Girls get mean when they feel threat-ened," Tisdale observed. "Sharpay's feet get stepped on, so she gets vi-cious. Mean girls are the same way. I think they're very insecure. They look like they have it all together, but it's a mask."

Tisdale did find an aspect of the character that she liked, though. "[The] thing I can relate to is, she has this *drive*—it doesn't matter if people don't think she's the best dancer or performer, because *she* thinks she is," she said. "It doesn't really matter what everybody else thinks—it's just what makes you happy. Performing is what makes *me* happy, I couldn't care less if people don't like it—that's fine. I love proving people wrong."

To prepare for the role, Tisdale trained very hard with other members of the cast. "I knew when I got the role it was going to be a challenge, but I love challenges," she said. "We had a 'boot camp.' It was like two weeks of dance rehearsal. I'm not really coordinated very well." Tisdale, though, believes that these rehearsals created a sense of warmth and fun on the set that carried over on the screen. "Kenny Ortega [the director] would put together Teen Club Night ... having a little club scene just for us and the dancers," said Tisdale. "That was really cool and I think that's why the experience was so amazing and maybe why this movie has become so successful because they saw how much fun we were having. . . . I think it showed up on screen that we all were having a blast. It looked like a huge party."

*High School Musical* proved to be a tremendous success for the Disney Channel. It quickly became its highest-rated show ever—almost eight million people tuned in for its TV debut, with over 160 million viewers worldwide. It won an Emmy for Outstanding Children's Program and a Teen Choice Award for Choice Comedy/Musical Program. Moreover, the soundtrack to the movie was one of the best-selling CDs of 2006. Ashley freely admitted that the film's popularity caught her by surprise. "I knew it was really good because when we were filming we could just tell it was really good," she claimed. "We had a lot of support from Disney and we had a great director and we trusted him and we knew it was going to be good, but we never knew it was going to be this good. It was really awesome to hear the ratings and the album kind of came from left field, like we did not know it was going to be that successful."

### High School Musical 2

The original movie was so successful, in fact, that the studio immediately planned a sequel. In the new story, school has let out for summer vacation, leading up to senior year. Sharpay and Ryan plan to spend the summer at their country club, where most of the Wildcats manage to find summer jobs. But things become tense as Sharpay schemes to break up Gabriella and Troy. Troy must decide whether to pursue the

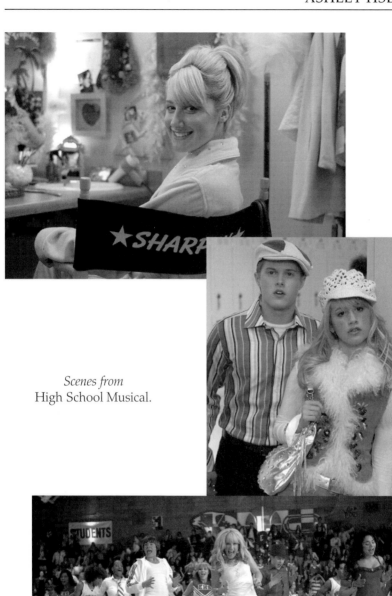

*Scenes from*
High School Musical.

*Summer vacation is a welcome relief in* High School Musical 2.

advantages that are available from Sharpay's wealthy family—even if it means neglecting Gabriella and his friends. It's a difficult summer, especially for Gabriella, but all is resolved as the group participates in the country club's annual talent show. As in the first movie, song and dance numbers abound, and a soundtrack CD was released along with the film.

*High School Musical 2* was released in August 2007 with the original cast. It was as big a success as the original, with over 17 million viewers watching the first run. And many families held viewing parties, which means that the actual number of viewers was most likely even higher. It had more viewers than any broadcast program that week—in fact, it was the most-watched program on cable or broadcast television during the summer season. The *High School Musical 2 Soundtrack* CD also fared well on the music charts. The soundtrack debuted at No. 1 on Billboard's Album chart, with 625,000 copies sold the first week alone. Its first single, the group number

"What Time Is It," hit No. 6 on the Billboard Hot 100 chart. Currently, another sequel is being discussed for 2008.

## Future Plans

Tisdale always hoped to be more involved in music also, and in 2007 she released her first CD. *Headstrong* features pop songs infused with a bit of hip-hop and dance hall. Although it garnered mixed reviews from critics, it was snapped up by her many fans. "*Headstrong* is a chance to get to know me better," she explained. "People know my characters, but they don't know me. I've never really spilled many details about my life in interviews. But on this album I'm talking about what's happened in my life and what is personal to me. I want people to know that I'm a real person, and that I've been through normal situations, like crushes and heartbreaks. I think hearing my stories will help the audience relate better to me."

Reflecting on her own recent accomplishments, Tisdale is happy that her career has evolved the way it has. "You know, I think everybody has their own path," she said. "I'm glad I took this road, where I was struggling at first, because now I don't take anything for granted."

Meanwhile, Tisdale has ambitious plans for the future. "I probably want to do some more movies," she added. "But I always, always, want to have a sitcom. I would love to always have a TV show and then do movies on the side as well. My goal is to win an Emmy one day, not an Oscar."

## SELECTED CREDITS

*Les Miserables*, 1993-95 (stage play)
"The Suite Life of Zack and Cody," 2005- (TV series)
*High School Musical*, 2006 (TV movie)
*High School Musical Soundtrack*, 2006 (CD)
*Headstrong*, 2007 (CD)
*High School Musical 2*, 2007 (TV movie)
*High School Musical 2 Soundtrack*, 2007 (CD)

## FURTHER READING

### Periodicals

*American Cheerleader*, Feb. 2006, p.27
*Bop*, June-July 2006, p.62

*Girls' Life,* Aug.-Sep. 2006, pp.44
*Newsday,* Mar. 1, 2006, p.C14
*People,* Apr. 10, 2006, p.95
*Seventeen,* July 2006, p.104
*Teen,* Summer 2006, p.24
*Tiger Beat,* June 2006, p.10

## Online Articles

http://www.teacher.scholastic.com/scholasticnews/mtm/starspotlight.asp?
   sf=tisdale
   (*Scholastic News Online,* "Star Spotlight: Ashley Tisdale," undated)
http://www.thestarscoop.com/ashley-tisdale.php
   (*Starscoop.com,* "Ashley Tisdale," undated)
http://www.timeforkids.com/TFK/kidscoops/story/0,14989,1169108,00.html
   (*TimeforKids.com,* "The Scoop on *High School Musical,*" Mar. 2, 2006)

## Online Databases

*Biography Resource Center Online,* 2006

## ADDRESS

Ashley Tisdale
Disney Channel
3800 West Alameda Avenue
Burbank, CA 91505

## WORLD WIDE WEB SITES

http://www.ashleytisdale.com
http://www.disney.go.com/disneychannel

## Carrie Underwood 1983-

American Singer
Winner of the 2005 TV Competition "American Idol"

### BIRTH

Carrie Underwood was born on March 10, 1983, in Muskogee, a town in eastern Oklahoma. She grew up in nearby Checotah, a ranching community of about 3,500 people. Her father, Stephen Underwood, retired from a job in a paper mill to raise cattle. Her mother, Carole, is a retired elementary school teacher. Underwood's sisters Shanna and Stephanie were 10 and 13 years old, respectively, when she was born. They are both elementary school teachers.

## YOUTH

Underwood enjoyed a happy childhood in a secure, close-knit family. "I was definitely a tomboy," she said. "I climbed trees, and I'd jump hay bales and play with the cows, and Dad would take me fishing." The Underwood children were also raised in a household that placed great importance on religious faith and ethical behavior. "I was most afraid of the 'I'm disappointed in you' speech," she recalled.

Underwood gave her first public singing performances at age three, singing songs like "Jesus Loves Me" at her family's church, the First Free Will Baptist Church. "I figured she'd make something of [her singing] because she's sung all her life," said her grandfather, Carl Shatswell. "She went to Kansas one time and was singing on the bus. Her grandmother and me, we tried to get her to hush up, but the rest of the folks on there, they wanted her to keep singing. She was just three at the time."

———— " ————

*Underwood enjoyed a happy childhood in a close-knit family. "I was definitely a tomboy," she said. "I climbed trees, and I'd jump hay bales and play with the cows, and Dad would take me fishing."*

———— " ————

Underwood's taste in music was influenced by her parents, who loved "oldies" rock and roll songs from the 1950s and 1960s. She also picked up her sisters' taste for the so-called "hair-metal" bands that were enormously popular in the 1980s. "One of my earliest memories was singing Motley Crue's 'Smokin' in the Boys' Room' when I was five," she recalled. But she also loved the country-western music that poured out of her parents' car radio.

As Underwood grew older, she won the leads in several school musicals. She also became a regular performer at area county fairs and local Lion's Club fundraisers. She pushed her mother to take her to talent contests, though those never turned out quite as she hoped. "I competed in a lot of stuff, and I didn't win. Ever," she recalled. "That was when I was 12, 13, 14 years old. But I didn't need to win. If I got third [place] and got a little trophy or money for school, that made me happy."

When Underwood was about 14 years old, a local admirer arranged for her to go to Nashville to audition for Capitol Records. Underwood dreamed of repeating the success of LeAnn Rimes, who became a country star as a young teenager. But the audition went nowhere. "I honestly think it's a lot better that nothing came out of it now, because I wouldn't have been ready then," Underwood said. "Everything has a way of working out."

## EDUCATION

Underwood was an outstanding student and Honor Society member at Checotah High School. She kept herself busy with basketball, softball, and cheerleading, in addition to her singing appearances at county fairs, school events, and church. She has described her social life during this time as wholesome and low-key. "If we were going to go out, we'd just go see a movie," she said. "We were definitely good kids. We'd all go to church together. Prom night we all went over to my friend's house and drank nonalcoholic champagne and toasted each other."

In May 2001, Underwood graduated second in her high school class, as salutatorian. "After high school, I pretty much gave up on the dream of singing," she said. "I had reached a point in my life where I had to be practical and prepare for my future in the 'real world.'" With this in mind, Underwood enrolled at Northeastern State University in Tahlequah, Oklahoma, only an hour away from home.

In college, Underwood focused on the subjects of mass communications and journalism. "I hoped to get a behind-the-scenes job in Tulsa, Oklahoma, at one of the local television news shows," she recalled. With this in mind, she gained valuable work experience by contributing to student-produced local access TV shows and the student newspaper. She also earned money for college with a variety of different summer and after-school jobs. One summer she served as a page for a state congressman in the Oklahoma House of Representatives. She also waited tables at a college pizzeria and worked for a time at a zoo and a veterinary clinic.

Underwood claims that she came out of her self-described "shy" shell during her years at Northeastern State. After joining a school sorority, She participated in various volunteer programs to collect highway litter and assist hospice patients. During the summer after her freshman year, meanwhile, she mustered up the courage to perform in the Downtown Country show, a country-western music review that included singing, dancing, and comedy. This event placed Underwood on stage in front of audiences that were far larger than any she had seen during her adolescence. "It was mainly there that I learned what it was like to be in front of a crowd," she later declared.

In 2005 Underwood took a year off to make her famous run on "American Idol" and launch her musical career. But as she had promised her family, she then returned to Northeastern State University and graduated magna cum laude (with high honors) with a bachelor of arts (BA) degree in journalism in May 2006. According to Underwood, her journalism classes have been a great help to her now that she is the subject of so many interviews. "I know what the reporters are looking for [in interviews] and I also know when they're trying to make me say something bad," she said. "They'll ask me some hot-button questions, something to get myself in trouble!"

## CAREER HIGHLIGHTS

### Auditioning for "American Idol"

Underwood was a senior in college and only a few credits away from graduation when friends convinced her to audition for "American Idol," a mu-

*"If we were going to go out, we'd just go see a movie," Underwood said about high school. "We were definitely good kids. We'd all go to church together. Prom night we all went over to my friend's house and drank nonalcoholic champagne and toasted each other."*

sical talent contest that had become one of the most popular television shows in the United States since its debut in 2001. "People always told me that I should try out for the show, but I never thought I would be able to handle it," she said.

By 2005, though, Underwood realized that auditioning for the program might be a case of "now or never." "I thought, I'm about to graduate and I don't know what I'm going to do, so why not try out for 'American Idol?'" she said. "What's the worst that could happen? If I don't make it past the audition, nobody's going to know. And I'll get some experience in front of the camera." A few days later, she and her mother drove through the night for eight hours from Oklahoma to St. Louis, Missouri, where regional auditions for the show were scheduled. When Underwood arrived at 8 a.m., she joined more than 100,000 other hopefuls who were auditioning around the country. After another eight-hour wait, her turn finally came. Performing for one of the show's supervising producers, she sang a cover of Martina McBride's "Phones Are Ringing All over Town."

Underwood was sure she had blown the audition. To her amazement, though, she was invited to return the next day to sing for Nigel Lythgoe, executive producer of the program. She belted out "Independence Day,"

*Underwood on stage with other contestants after being named the new American Idol.*

another song by McBride, one of her favorite performers. Lythgoe was sufficiently impressed to pass her on to the next stage in the competition: a performance in front of the show's infamous panel of judges, Simon Cowell, Paula Abdul, and Randy Jackson.

Standing alone in front of the panel, she delivered a spirited version of the Bonnie Raitt song "I Can't Make You Love Me." After she finished, the judges praised her sweet but powerful singing voice and her girl-next-door charm. They then gave her the news that she had been selected to compete on the 2005 version of "American Idol." A short time later, Underwood boarded an airplane for the first time in her life and was whisked off to Los Angeles.

### Triumph on "American Idol"

The next several months were the most stressful of Underwood's life. "Millions of people all over the U.S. saw me do my best and my worst week to week on the show," she pointed out. In addition, her three-month adventure on the West Coast marked the first time that she had been away from home without friends or family. "[The] L.A. lifestyle was new and usually confusing to me," she said. "I learned so much on the show— about myself and about the music/television business."

When the show began, it immediately became clear that Underwood was one of the favorites. Although she was pitted against a group of 12 strong competitors, her country-music style set her apart from most of the other singers. More importantly, her talent and personality caught the attention of the judges early in the show. In one early episode, for example, acid-tongued judge Simon Cowell told her, "Carrie, you're not just the girl to beat, you're the person to beat. I will make a prediction, not only will you win this competition, but you will sell more records than any other previous Idol winner."

Cowell was right. Week after week, she survived as other contestants were voted off the show. Eventually, only she and rock and roll singer Bo Bice were left. On May 25, 2005, Underwood beat Bice to become the fourth "American Idol"-and the first winner with a country music orientation. Underwood's prize package included a recording contract worth at least one million dollars and the use of a private jet for a year, as well as a Ford Mustang convertible. "Two years ago, I was at the grocery store thinking, 'I shouldn't get this cereal—the other one is a dollar less,'" she marveled. "I realize how lucky I am."

> ———— " ————
>
> *In an early episode of "American Idol," acid-tongued judge Simon Cowell told her, "Carrie, you're not just the girl to beat, you're the person to beat. I will make a prediction, not only will you win this competition, but you will sell more records than any other previous Idol winner."*
>
> ———— " ————

### A Rising Pop Star

One month after her momentous "American Idol" victory, Underwood released her first single, "Inside Your Heaven." It entered the record charts as the nation's best-selling song, establishing her as the first country-music artist ever to debut at No. 1 on the *Billboard* magazine "Hot 100" chart. The song's runaway popularity was even more remarkable because relatively few country-music radio stations aired the song.

Seizing on her red-hot popularity, Underwood secured endorsement deals for Sketchers shoes and Hershey chocolate. She also agreed to join fellow "American Idol" contestants on a 44-date concert tour that took her all around the country. Around this same time, she began laying the groundwork for her debut album, called *Some Hearts*.

Simon Fuller, creator of "American Idol" and overseer of her record contract, arranged for Underwood to take part in a weekend "writers' retreat" with some of Nashville's best song writers. During the retreat, *Some Hearts* began to take shape. It was during these sessions, for example, that "Jesus, Take the Wheel" emerged as the album's first single. "[It] was probably the first song I heard that really struck a chord with me," Underwood recalled. "The song tells such a great story."

Underwood was also struck by a song called "Don't Forget to Remember Me." "The first time I heard it, I cried because I was feeling homesick," she recalled. After her mother read the words, she called Underwood to tell her it was "our song." "In that moment, I knew that no matter how hard it would be to get through, I had to record it," she said.

Underwood helped to pick the album's material and co-wrote one of the compositions. "Writing songs is always something that I have been interested in," she said. "But I really didn't feel like my writing chops were good enough yet to write songs for my first album. I did, however, try my best to help. I wanted to help write a song that was strictly for my friends and family in my hometown of Checotah. Obviously, the name of that one ended up being 'I Ain't in Checotah Anymore.' It's basically an account of the things that have been happening to me over the past few months." Of course, the song also conveys Underwood's deep affection for her Oklahoma roots. One of her favorite lines in the song states that "I'd rather be tipping cows in Tulsa than hailing cabs here in New York."

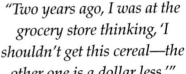

*"Two years ago, I was at the grocery store thinking, 'I shouldn't get this cereal—the other one is a dollar less,'" Underwood marveled. "I realize how lucky I am."*

### Success with *Some Hearts*

*Some Hearts* was released in November 2005 and went straight to the top of the charts, ranking No. 1 in country music and No. 2 in pop music. It sold 300,000 copies in the first week after its release, making it the top-selling debut record ever released by a country recording artist. Industry analysts credited the record's stunning popularity to Underwood's massive exposure on "American Idol" and its selection of songs, which appealed to country- and pop-music fans alike. Underwood acknowledged that she worked hard to please her broad fan base. "Because of the mass audience I

was able to reach with 'Idol,' I wanted to make something everyone could appreciate, not just listeners of country," she said of *Some Hearts*.

By early April 2006 *Some Hearts* had gone triple platinum, which means sales of three million copies. Underwood thus became the first female artist ever to reach the triple-platinum milestone so quickly. Meanwhile, the album's first single, "Jesus, Take the Wheel" topped *Billboard*'s Hot Country Songs chart for six consecutive weeks. Other hit singles from the album include "Don't Forget to Remember Me," "Before He Cheats," and "Inside Your Heaven."

Reviews of the album were mixed. A number of critics dismissed *Some Hearts* as a bland and predictable effort. Eric R. Danton of the *Harford Courant* called it "a slick, polished collection of forgettable, country-lite ballads." But others echoed the more positive comments of music critic Bill

Lamb, who called *Some Hearts* "a well-balanced blend of mainstream pop and country music. . . . Carrie Underwood sounds as comfortable in both pop and country worlds as artists like Faith Hill or Shania Twain." Reviewers such as *Houston Chronicle* critic Joey Guerrain, meanwhile, observed that Underwood's "soaring vocal range . . . takes flight when paired with the right material."

The country music community, meanwhile, embraced Underwood and *Some Hearts* with open arms. In 2006 the Academy of Country Music designated "Jesus, Take the Wheel" as its single record of the year. Academy voters also named her the best female vocalist of the year. In addition, Underwood picked up a Dove award from the Gospel Music Association and awards for best female video and best breakthrough video at the Country Music Television awards.

— **"** —

*"I never thought that any of this would actually happen to me," Underwood admitted. "These kinds of things only happen to imaginary characters on television or in the movies . . . not real people."*

— **"** —

In April 2006 Underwood launched a six-month concert tour to promote *Some Hearts*. A few dates were solo, but in most instances she opened shows for established country superstars like Kenny Chesney. After watching her perform, Chesney expressed admiration for her performing style. "She connects with the audience in ways most new acts take years to develop," he declared. In early 2007, Underwood was thrilled to win three Grammy Awards, for best new artist and for best country song and best female country vocal performance, both for "Jesus, Take the Wheel."

## A Cinderella Story

Underwood admits that she sometimes still can't believe that she went from being an everyday college student to a national music sensation in a matter of weeks. "I never thought that any of this would actually happen to me," she said. "These kinds of things only happen to imaginary characters on television or in the movies . . . not real people."

Underwood acknowledges that the changes to her life have sometimes been disorienting. "After I won the title of 'American Idol 2005,' a whirlwind soon followed. I was swept away to talk shows, photo shoots, and, of course, recording my very first album," she said. But she considers herself to be blessed. "I have known all of my life that being a country music singer would be the most wonderful thing that I could ever do. I am so grateful that I have this opportunity.... Life has changed for the better because I get to do what I love to do."

Success has not affected Underwood's close relationship with her family. In fact, she said that winning "American Idol" has made her appreciate her family more. "I miss home a lot, but I take a lot of it with me," she said. "I call home every day and talk to my sisters. I do get back as much as I can. And I always have with me two stuffed animals from home, a teddy bear and a stuffed lion." Underwood also says that her mother remains the biggest hero and inspiration in her own life.

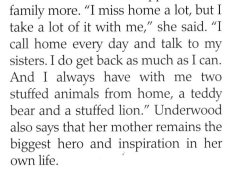

> "I miss home a lot, but I take a lot of it with me," Underwood said. "I call home every day and talk to my sisters. I do get back as much as I can. And I always have with me two stuffed animals from home, a teddy bear and a stuffed lion."

As for her next career step, Underwood hopes to record more of her own songs on her next album. "I think writing is a huge gift, and some people can and some people can't, just like some people can sing and some can't sing," she said. "If I turn out to be a horrible writer then obviously I'm going to leave it up to those who do it best. But I definitely would like to try my best to have a hand in it, because then it's so much more personal."

## HOME AND FAMILY

Underwood owns a two-story house in Nashville that she shares with a dog and two cats. She classifies herself as single but "never not looking." She admits that "my original plan was to get married at 24 or 25, [start having] kids around 27 and be done by 30. I don't think that's going to work out. There's too much going on."

## HOBBIES AND OTHER INTERESTS

Underwood is passionate about animals and animal welfare. Although she grew up in a town where many people made their living in the cattle industry, she became a vegetarian in her teens. "My friends would raise cows.... Then they'd butcher and eat them," she said. "I would feel horri-

*Underwood performing on "The Tonight Show with Jay Leno," October 2006.*

bly guilty and couldn't do it." She has worked in the past for the Humane Society, and in 2006 she became a spokesperson for People for the Ethical Treatment of Animals.

In her spare time, Underwood loves to watch horror movies. She is a big fan of *Star Trek: The Next Generation,* Dallas Cowboys football, and chocolate. Her CD collection includes her three favorite records: *Martina McBride's Greatest Hits; Always & Forever,* by Randy Travis; and *In Your Honor,* by Foo Fighters. It also features music by Green Day, Rascal Flatts, Garth Brooks, Loretta Lynn, and John Denver.

## CREDITS

*Some Hearts,* 2006

## SELECTED HONORS AND AWARDS

American Idol: 2005
Teen Choice Award: 2005, Choice Reality Star—Female
Best Female Video and Breakthrough Video (Country Music Television): 2006, for "Jesus, Take the Wheel"
Best New Female Vocalist (Academy of Country Music): 2006
Dove Award (Gospel Music Association): 2006, Country Recorded Song of the Year for "Jesus, Take the Wheel"
Female Vocalist of the Year (Country Music Association): 2006
Horizon Award (Country Music Association): 2006
Single Record of the Year (Academy of Country Music): 2006, for "Jesus, Take the Wheel"
Top New Female Vocalist (Country Music Association): 2006
Grammy Awards (The Recording Academy): 2007 (three awards), Best New Artist, Best Country Song, for "Jesus, Take the Wheel," and Best Female Country Performance, for "Jesus, Take the Wheel"

## FURTHER READING

### Books

Tracy, Kathleen. *Carrie Underwood,* 2006

### Periodicals

*Girls' Life,* June-July 2006, p.40
*Houston Chronicle,* Nov. 3, 2006, "Star" section, p.1
*People,* June 13, 2005, p.79; Nov. 14, 2005, p.147; Nov. 6, 2006, p.38
*Reader's Digest,* June 2006, p.132

*Self*, Apr. 2006, p.64
*St. Louis Post-Dispatch,* Aug. 31, 2006, p.9
*Teen People*, June-July 2006, p.54; Sep. 2006, p.84
*TV Guide,* June 12, 2005, p.28; Aug. 7, 2006, p.18

## ADDRESS

Carrie Underwood
Arista Records
1400 18th Avenue South
Nashville, TN 37212

## WORLD WIDE WEB SITES

http://www.carrieunderwoodofficial.com
http://www.americanidol.com
http://www.americanidolmusic.com

## Muhammad Yunus 1940-
Bangladeshi Banker and Human Rights Activist
Winner of the 2006 Nobel Peace Prize for His Work
in Fighting Poverty

### BIRTH

Muhammad Yunus was born on June 28, 1940, in the village of
Bathua, near the port city of Chittagong. That area was then in
Eastern Bengal, part of British-controlled India, and is now
part of Pakistan. Yunus grew up in the jeweler's section of
town, with the sounds of street vendors, jugglers, and beggars
right outside his house. His father, Muhammad Dula Mia, was
a goldsmith who kept his jewelry shop on the ground floor.

His mother, Sofia Khatun, was a major influence on Yunus. "Full of compassion and kindness, Mother always put money away for any poor relatives who visited us from distant villages," he remembered. "It was she, by her concern for the poor and the disadvantaged, who helped me discover my interest in economics and social reform." Yunus was the third of 14 children, although five of his siblings died in infancy.

## THE CREATION OF BANGLADESH

The port city of Chittagong is now part of Bangladesh. But at that time, Chittagong was part of India. Beginning in the mid- to late-1700s, much of India was ruled by Great Britain. India was primarily Hindu, although there was also a minority Muslim population. In the 1900s, as India fought for its independence, the minority Muslim population began working for an independent Muslim nation. In 1947 India became independent from Great Britain, and the Muslim nation of Pakistan was formed. But the nation of Pakistan was divided into two parts: West Pakistan, along India's western border, and East Pakistan, along India's eastern border. The two parts of Pakistan were separated by 1,600 miles of Indian territory. At this point, when Pakistan was formed, Yunus was seven.

The separation of India and Pakistan was not smooth. Hindus who lived in Pakistan territory and Muslims who lived in Indian territory began a great migration, with some 13 million people on the move. Terrible violence flared up, and many refugees were massacred. War broke out between the two nations over contested regions. In addition, the new nation of Pakistan experienced tremendous political instability. The two parts of the country were divided not only by geography, but also by ethnic and religious issues. Dissension between West and East Pakistan grew into civil war, and in 1971 East Pakistan declared its independence and became the sovereign nation of Bangladesh.

## YOUTH

Yunus grew up initially in the village of Bathua before his family moved to the city of Chittagong. There, his father was a successful jeweler, but he had only a seventh grade education. Still, he always valued education and taught his children to do the same. Yunus and his older sister, Salam, loved to read so much that they spent part of every afternoon in the waiting room of the local doctor's office, reading the magazines. He and his sister also enjoyed going to the movies, taking pictures with their camera, and eating out in restaurants. His favorite dish was "potato chop," a roasted potato filled with fried onion and vinegar.

## Dealing with Mental Illness

When Yunus was nine, his mother began to act strangely, apparently suffering from mental illness. Mental illness ran in his mother's family—her mother and two sisters had suffered from it—but no doctor was ever able to diagnose or treat it. Yunus wrote about this difficult time in his autobiography, *Banker to the Poor: Micro-Lending and the Battle Against World Poverty*. Here, he described his mother's unpredictable behavior. "Her behavior was increasingly abnormal," he wrote. "In her calmer periods she would talk disjointed nonsense to herself. For hours on end she would sit in prayer, read the same page of a book, or recite a poem over and over without stopping. In her more disturbed periods, she would insult people in a loud voice and use vulgar language. Sometimes she would hurl abuse at a neighbor, a friend, or a family member, but other times she would rant away at politicians or even long-dead figures. Her mind would turn against imaginary enemies and then, without much warning, she would become violent."

The experience was clearly a difficult one for Yunus, who helped his father restrain his mother or protect his siblings from her attacks. His mother gradually lost track of many day-to-day activities, including the children's schoolwork and studies. Still, Yunus demonstrated resilience at an early age. In his autobiography, he recount-

> "Her behavior was increasingly abnormal," Yunus said about his mother. "In her more disturbed periods, she would insult people in a loud voice and use vulgar language. Sometimes she would hurl abuse at a neighbor, a friend, or a family member. . . . Her mind would turn against imaginary enemies and then, without much warning, she would become violent."

ed how he and his siblings learned to treat their mother's illness with a certain humor. "'What is the weather forecast?' we would ask one another when we tried to predict mother's mood for the next few hours," he recalled. "To avoid provoking a fresh bout of abuse, we gave code names to various persons in the household: Number 2, Number 4, and so on."

## EDUCATION

As a young boy, Yunus attended elementary school, called primary school, first at the local village school in Bathua and then in Chittagong. He later

*Yunus with his class in the Graduate Program in Economic Development at Vanderbilt University, 1966. Yunus is in the second row from the bottom, the second from the left.*

attended Chittagong Collegiate School, the rough equivalent of high school. While in secondary school, Yunus joined the Boy Scouts, an American-based organization with troops around the world. With the Scouts, he found a role model in assistant headmaster, Quazi Sahib. "I had always been a natural leader," Yunus said, "but Quazi Sahib's moral influence taught me to think high and channel my passions." He traveled to several other countries with the Scouts and attended the World Boy Scouts Jamboree in Canada in 1955. To return home, he traveled across Europe and Asia by road.

Yunus next attended Chittagong College, where he enjoyed a wide range of creative interests, including theater, art, photography, and writing. In 1957, he enrolled at Dhaka University in the department of economics. He completed his Bachelor of Arts (BA) degree in 1960 and his Master of Arts (MA) degree in 1961. He then spent several years working in business and also as a lecturer at Chittagong College before returning to school.

In 1965, Yunus earned a Fulbright Scholarship to study in the United States. The Fulbright Program, which is sponsored by the U.S. Department of State, is an international exchange program that enables U.S. students, scholars, and professionals to study abroad, and also enables their counterparts in other countries to study in the U.S. The program is designed to foster international relationships and "to increase mutual understanding between the people of the United States and the people of other countries."

The Fulbright Scholarship allowed Yunus to study development economics at Vanderbilt University in Nashville, Tennessee. In the United States, he was deeply influenced by the student activism and civil rights movement of the 1960s. Martin Luther King Jr. became a personal hero. "When I arrived in the U.S. in the 1960s, it was a real shock, coming from a conservative Muslim family," he said. Yunus completed work on his doctoral degree or doctorate (PhD) in about 1969 or 1970 and then was appointed an instructor at Middle Tennessee State University.

Meanwhile, the movement for independence was taking hold in East Pakistan. Yunus returned home in 1972 to help build the newly independent country of Bangladesh and soon became an economics professor at Chittagong University.

## CAREER HIGHLIGHTS

The 1970s, when Yunus was beginning his career as an economic professor, marked a difficult time for Bangladesh. The country was still trying to build an infrastructure after recently becoming independent. Political disorder was ongoing. Then in 1974 floods devastated the grain crop, and a horrible famine gripped the nation. People were literally dying in the streets, collapsing of starvation.

Working as a college professor, Yunus felt frustrated teaching "elegant theories of economics" that did nothing to relieve people's suffering. One day in 1976, he met Sufiya Begum, a 21-year old mother of three who made stools out of bamboo. Because Begum did not have the money to buy her own bamboo, she had to borrow from a trader who sold her finished stools. As a result, she ended up with a profit of only two cents per stool. "Her life was a form of bonded labor, or slavery," Yunus recalled. With the help of one of his students, he discovered that 42 villagers owed a total of less than $27 to traders. "My God. My God," he exclaimed. "All this misery in all these families all for only the lack of $27!" He reached into his pocket and gave his student $27 to distribute directly to the villagers. They could pay him back whenever they had the money. He would not charge interest.

So began Yunus's innovative banking practices. Hailed as the "banker to the poor," he has revolutionized the field of banking by making small loans available to millions of people who had previously been denied credit. Banks traditionally have refused to lend money to the poor because they lack possessions, such as houses or cars, that can be seized if they fail to pay back the loan. Yunus, however, found a new way to guarantee loans, using "borrowing groups" to provide much-needed structure and support.

## Developing a Program of Group Support

Yunus called his experimental lending project the Grameen ("Village") Bank program. Wanting to expand his program, he asked the branch manager of a local bank to loan money to the poor villagers of Jobra. The branch manager told him he doubted the bank would want to lend to people who had no possessions to guarantee payment. Yunus believed that people would pay back their loans because they'd recognize credit as a chance to have a better life. Refusing to give up, he contacted a higher level official at the bank's district branch. Although the bank official refused to lend directly to the poor, he agreed to lend money to Yunus for the villagers. Then Yunus lent the money to the villagers. All the borrowers paid back their loans in full and on time, proving the bank officials wrong.

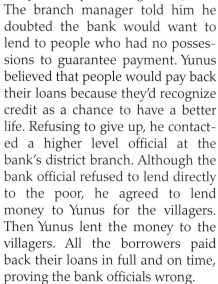

> "Conventional banks look at what has already been acquired by a person," Yunus explained. "Grameen looks at the potential that is waiting to be unleashed in a person. Conventional banks are owned by the rich, generally men. Grameen Bank is owned by poor women."

With this approach, Yunus defied the stereotype of a banker. Many of his lending practices are the exact opposite of those used by conventional banks. "Conventional banks look at what has already been acquired by a person," he explained. "Grameen looks at the potential that is waiting to be unleashed in a person. Conventional banks are owned by the rich, generally men. Grameen Bank is owned by poor women."

From the beginning, Yunus made borrowing groups the centerpiece of his program. "Subtle and not so subtle peer pressure keeps each group member in line with the broader objectives of the credit program," he wrote in his autobiography *Banker to the Poor*. Borrowers come together in five-member groups. Each member must undergo at least seven days of training and pass a test to be approved by the bank. Once the first two people in the group have completed their weekly payments, the third and fourth, and then the fifth, can apply for a loan. Borrowers are required to accumulate savings. Several groups meet together at regional centers, where payments are collected and questions discussed.

Borrowers must also promise to abide by the "Sixteen Decisions." These principles commit members to leading productive and purposeful lives. In his autobiography *Banker to the Poor*, Yunus listed all Sixteen Decisions. The first decision, for instance, reads: "We shall follow and advance the four principles of the Grameen Bank—discipline, unity, courage, and hard work—in all walks of our lives." Other decisions involve matters such as living in a healthy manner,

*Bangladeshi women Monju Begum (left) and Sahera Khatun (right) feed their chickens, which they bought with money loaned by the Grameen Bank.*

keeping family size small, educating children, keeping homes in good repair, and prohibiting child marriage. Some members choose to chant the Sixteen Decisions.

## Loaning to Women

Yunus quickly found a difference between women and men: female borrowers used their loans more wisely than male borrowers did. Male borrowers spent the money on themselves, while female borrowers used it to improve the lives of everyone in the family. However, Yunus knew that it wouldn't be easy to lend money to women in a largely Muslim country like Bangladesh. Many women were afraid to be seen by an unfamiliar man like Yunus, and they were even more reluctant to discuss banking matters with him. Women often told him that they couldn't accept loans because their husbands handled the money. Gradually, with the help of female bank workers, Yunus built up a corps of female borrowers. "Once we were able to convince one woman, our work was half done," he explained. "She

*Borrowers with the Grameen Bank walk to the bank to pay their loan installments in the village of Basta, near Dhaka.*

then was an example that convinced her friends and then her friends' families and so on."

Yunus also faced opposition from resentful husbands and conservative religious leaders. Many husbands, though, became more supportive of their wives' involvement with the bank once their families had enough food to eat. On the religious front, some mullahs (Muslim clerics) preached that Grameen aimed to destroy Islam. Yunus argued back that, in Islamic history, women have long been powerful figures. Nothing in Islam, he said, prevents them from taking loans to lift themselves and their families out of poverty. Over the years, the Grameen Bank's percentage of female borrowers has risen to about 97 percent.

### Expanding the Loan Program

Some skeptics doubted that this system of small loans, known as "microcredit," could work outside of Yunus's own region of Bangladesh. One bank manager, for example, attributed the success of the lending program to Yunus's personality. Determined to prove the naysayers wrong, he took a leave of absence from the university and spread his program to five new areas of Bangladesh in 1982. In 1983, he restructured his bank as an independent institution. As an independent bank, Grameen grew quickly, giving rise to centers all over Bangladesh. The Grameen model has spread to some 100 countries around the world, including the United States.

In 1985, Arkansas Governor (and later U.S. President) Bill Clinton became an admirer of Yunus. Governor Clinton persuaded him to help create a new credit program for low-income people in Arkansas. Critics predicted that such a system would fail in the United States because people were accustomed to large, rather than small, loans. However, Yunus's first recruit— a woman seeking $375 to open a beautician business—proved the critics wrong. Arkansas's Good Faith program grew to reach hundreds of low-income people in the state. Later, Yunus brought a similar program to Cherokee women in Oklahoma. During the next two decades, the idea of microcredit continued to spread.

In recent years, Yunus has added new programs to combat poverty. In 2003, he launched a program focusing on beggars. With the help of interest-free loans, about 5,000 individuals have gone from begging to selling small items such as snacks and toys door to door. He also created a mobile phone company, Grameen Phone. Nearly 300,000 "telephone ladies" provide cell phone service by the minute to the villages of Bangladesh. "This is a form of globalization," said Yunus. "They have the whole world at their fingertips." In addition, Grameen has established two new business ventures. The first is a yogurt factory to produce fortified yogurt, and the second is a chain of eye-care hospitals.

By 2006, Grameen Bank had lent $5.72 billion and claimed a 98 percent repayment rate. Yunus had won the praise of numerous celebrities, including the rock star Bono, TV host Oprah Winfrey, and former president Bill Clinton. In addition, he had won support from members on both sides of the political spectrum. Conservatives liked his message of entrepreneurship and self-reliance, while liberals applauded his commitment to large-scale social welfare.

## Winning the Nobel Peace Prize

On October 13, 2006, Yunus won the prestigious Nobel Peace Prize. The award was divided into two equal parts: to Muhammad Yunus and to Grameen Bank. In awarding the Nobel Peace Prize to Yunus, the committee acknowledged the link between poverty and world peace. "Lasting peace cannot be achieved unless large population groups find ways in which to break out of poverty," the Norwegian Nobel Committee said in its presentation speech. The committee praised Yunus as "a leader who has managed to translate visions into practical action for the benefit of millions of people, not only in Bangladesh but across cultures and civilizations."

As soon as people in Bangladesh heard the news, they started bringing flowers to Yunus's home in Dhaka, the capital of Bangladesh. His phone kept ringing. "This prize is so overwhelming; it will affect our work tremendously," he told a reporter. "It will bring the issues I'm raising to the attention of people who can make a difference in the world."

Yunus received congratulations from people around the world. Former President Bill Clinton had this to say. "Hillary and I first met Muhammad Yunus when I was Governor, and he inspired us to create a micro-finance program in Arkansas based on his model. Muhammad proved that the poor are credit worthy and that a micro-finance effort can be self-sustainable, create growth and spread peace. . . . Because of his efforts, millions of people, most of them women, have had the chance to improve their lives and we are all better off as a result. . . . The committee could not have selected anyone better." And former United Nations Secretary-General Kofi Annan added these words: "Thanks to Professor Yunus and the Grameen Bank, micro-finance has proved its value as a way for low-income families to break the vicious circle of poverty, for productive enterprises to grow, and for communities to prosper. They have provided a powerful weapon to help the world . . . by helping people change their lives for the better—especially those who need it most."

> "This year's prize gives highest honor and dignity to the hundreds of millions of women all around the world who struggle every day to make a living and bring hope for a better life for their children," Yunus said. "This is a historic moment for them."

In his acceptance speech, Yunus emphasized several key points. He called poverty a threat to peace, a potential cause of terrorism, and a denial of human rights. He also said this: "Since the Nobel Peace Prize was announced, I have received endless messages from around the world, but what moves me most are the calls I get almost daily, from the borrowers of Grameen Bank in remote Bangladeshi villages, who just want to say how proud they are to have received this recognition. . . . All borrowers of Grameen Bank are celebrating this day as the greatest day of their lives.

*After receiving the Nobel Peace Prize, Yunus poses with the medal and diploma.*

They are gathering around the nearest television set in their villages all over Bangladesh, along with other villagers, to watch the proceedings of this ceremony. This year's prize gives highest honor and dignity to the hundreds of millions of women all around the world who struggle every day to make a living and bring hope for a better life for their children. This is a historic moment for them."

Yunus argued that change is possible. "We get what we want, or what we don't refuse. We accept the fact that we will always have poor people around us, and that poverty is part of human destiny. This is precisely why we continue to have poor people around us. If we firmly believe that poverty is unacceptable to us, and that it should not belong to a civilized society, we would have built appropriate institutions and policies to create a poverty-free world. We wanted to go to the moon, so we went there. We achieve what we want to achieve. If we are not achieving something, it is because we have not put our minds to it. We create what we want."

Yunus believes that we can eliminate poverty altogether. He hopes that one day, children will wonder why the world allowed poverty to go on for so long. "I firmly believe that we can create a poverty-free world if we collectively believe in it. In a poverty-free world, the only place you would be able to see poverty is in the poverty museums. When school children take a tour of the poverty museums, they would be horrified to see the misery and indignity that some human beings had to go through. They would blame their forefathers for tolerating this inhuman condition, which existed for so long, for so many people."

## MARRIAGE AND FAMILY

In 1970 Yunus was married to a Russian-born American, Vera Forostenko. They had met at Vanderbilt in Tennessee, where both were studying at the time, and then moved to Bangladesh. They had a daughter, Monica, born in 1977. Living in Bangladesh and struggling with the cultural differences, Forostenko felt that the environment was not a good place to raise a child. The couple divorced, and Forostenko moved to New Jersey and raised Monica there.

In 1980 Yunus was married to Afrozi Begum, a physics professor. Begum was a fellow Bangladeshi who had studied in England. She and Yunus had had similar experiences in living both in western and in eastern cultures, which eliminated the issue of cultural differences. They had one daughter, Deena, born in 1986. They live in Dhaka, the capital of Bangladesh.

## HOBBIES AND OTHER INTERESTS

What does Nobel Peace Prize winner Muhammad Yunus do for fun? When Vanderbilt University professor James Foster asked this question, Yunus replied that he spends his spare time "thinking of new strategies to help people help themselves." He also spends much of his time speaking to young people. "I'm encouraging young people to become social business entrepreneurs and contribute to the world, rather than just making money," he said. "Making money is no fun. Contributing to and changing the world is a lot more fun." Lauded as an idealist and a visionary, Yunus describes himself as "a stubborn guy." Throughout his career, he has persevered despite numerous obstacles. "If I feel it in my gut that something is the right thing to do, I do not give it up," he said.

## WRITINGS

*Banker to the Poor: Micro-Lending and the Battle Against World Poverty*, 1999 (with Alan Jolis)

## SELECTED HONORS AND AWARDS

President's Award (Bangladesh): 1978
Ramon Magsaysay Award (Philippines): 1984, for community leadership
CARE Humanitarian Award: 1993
World Food Prize: 1994
International Simon Bolivar Prize (Venezuala and UNESCO): 1996
Help for Self-Help Prize (Stromme Foundation, Norway): 1997
Indira Gandhi Prize (Indira Gandhi Memorial Turst, India): 1998, for peace, disarmament, and development
King Hussein Humanitarian Leadership Award (King Hussein Foundation, Jordan): 2000
Mahatma Gandhi Award (M.K. Gandhi Institute of Nonviolence): 2002
National Merit Order Award (President of the Republic of Colombia): 2003
25 Most Influential Business Persons of the Past 25 Years (PBS and Wharton School of Business): 2004
Innovation Award (*The Economist*): 2004, for social and economic innovation
Nobel Peace Prize: 2006, to Muhammad Yunus and Grameen Bank
Greatest Entrepreneurs of All Time (*Business Week*): 2007

## FURTHER READING

### Books

*Contemporary Heroes and Heroines, Book III*, 1998
*Library of International Biographies—Volume 1: Activists*, 1990
Yunus, Muhammad, with Alan Jolis. *Banker to the Poor: Micro-Lending and the Battle Against World Poverty*, 1999

## Periodicals

*Atlantic Monthly*, Dec. 1995, p.40
*Current Biography International Yearbook*, 2002
*Current Events*, Nov. 10, 2006, p.1
*Los Angeles Times*, Jan. 25, 1998, p.M3
*People*, Oct. 30, 2006, p.120
*Time*, Oct. 23, 2006, p.21
*Washington Post*, Apr. 18. 2004, pp.A1 and A25

## Online Articles

http://www.businessweek.com
(*Business Week*, "Can Technology Eliminate Poverty: Grameen Bank Founder Muhammad Yunus Thinks So. And He Explains Why Changing the World Is a Lot More Fun than Just Making Money," Dec. 26, 2005)
http://www:grameen-info.org
(*Grameen Bank*, "Is Grameen Bank Different From Conventional Banks?" Feb. 2007)
http://www.pbs.org/opb/thenewheroes/meet/yunus.html
(*PBS*, "Meet the New Heroes: Muhammad Yunus," undated)

## Online Databases

*Biography Resource Center Online*, 2007, articles from *Contemporary Heroes and Heroines, Book III*, 1998, and *Library of International Biographies—Volume 1: Activists*, 1990

## ADDRESS

Muhammad Yunus
PublicAffairs Books
250 West 57th Street
Suite 1321
New York, NY 10107

Muhammad Yunus
Grameen Bank Bhavan
Mirpur-1, Dhaka-1216
Bangladesh

## WORLD WIDE WEB SITES

http://muhammadyunus.org
http://www.grameen-info.org

# Photo and Illustration Credits

Front cover photos: Cyrus: HANNAH MONTANA: POP STAR PROFILE copyright © 2007 Disney. All Rights Reserved; Federer: Tom Barson/WireImage.com; Obama: Courtesy of the office of Sen. Barack Obama; O'Brien: Courtesy of CNN.

Shaun Alexander: Peter Brouillet/WireImage.com (p. 11); AP Images (front cover, pp. 13, 21); Kent Gidley/University of Alabama (p. 17); Otto Greule/Getty Images (p. 19); Kevin Terrell/WireImage.com (p. 23).

Carmelo Anthony: Gary Dineen/NBAE/Getty Images (p. 29); Ida Mae Astute/ABC/ Getty Images (p. 31); Syracuse University Athletic Communications (p. 33); Garrett W. Ellwood/NBAE/Getty Images (p. 37); Chris Carlson/AP Photo (p. 39); Jeffrey Bottari/NBAE/Getty Images (p. 43); Garrett W. Ellwood/NBAE/Getty Images (p. 44).

Drake Bell: Chris Cuffaro/Nickelodeon (pp. 49, 53 middle, 55); Nickelodeon (p. 53 top); copyright © 2005 Paramount Pictures (p. 53 bottom).

Chris Brown: Hachi/Zomba Label Group (pp. 59, 66); Scott Gries/Getty Images (p. 64); Alfeo Dixon/copyright © 2006 Screen Gems, Inc. (p. 68; CD: CHRIS BROWN & copyright © 2005 Zomba Recording LLC (p. 62).

Regina Carter: Bill Phelps/copyright © 2007 Universal Music Group (p. 71); Scott Gries/Emigrant Savings Bank/Getty Images (p. 74); Kathy Willens/AP Photo (p. 78); Rick Diamond/WireImage.com (p. 81). CD cover: SOMETHING FOR GRACE copyright © 1997 Atlantic Recording Corporation. Cover design by Elizabeth Barrett. Cover photo by Darryl Turner (p. 77).

Kortney Clemons: Steve Tessler/courtesy of Pennsylvania State University Athletics (pp. 85, 92); Troy Hopkins/courtesy of Soldiers Magazine, March 2006 (p. 88); Carolyn Kaster/AP Photo (p. 90).

Taylor Crabtree: Courtesy Taylor Crabtree (pp. 95, 98).

Miley Cyrus: HANNAH MONTANA: POP STAR PROFILE copyright © 2007 Disney. All Rights Reserved. (pp. 101, 103, 105); CD cover: HANNAH MONTANA 2: MEET MILEY CYRUS copyright © 2007 Universal Music Group (p. 107).

Aaron Dworkin: MacArthur Foundation (p. 111); Maciek Gregorsky (p. 114); Cibele Newman (p. 117); Jeffrey Sauger, Triest Photographic (p. 122).

Fall Out Boy: PRNewsFoto/Virgin Mobile USA, LLC (p. 127); Ken Schles/copyright © 2007 Universal Music Group (p. 129); Scott Gries/Getty Images (p. 137). CD covers:

Wendy Kopp: Jean-Christian Bourcart/courtesy of Teach For America (pp. 253, 255, 258); Elise Amendola/AP Photo (p. 262).

Sofia Mulanovich: Karen Wilson/ASP/Getty Images (pp. 267, 276); Allsport AUS/Getty Images (pp. 272, 274).

Barack Obama: Courtesy of the office of Sen. Barack Obama (p. 279); Simon Maina/AFP/Getty Images (p. 285); Steve Liss/Time Life Pictures/Getty Images (p. 289); AP Images (p. 290); Robyn Beck/AFP/Getty Images (p. 293); Mark Wilson/Getty Images (p. 294). Cover: DREAMS FROM MY FATHER (Three Rivers Press/Crown Publishing Group) copyright © 1995, 2004 by Barack Obama (p. 282).

Soledad O'Brien: Courtesy of CNN (p. 299, 306, 308); AP Images (p. 303).

Jamie Oliver: Courtesy Food Network Canada (pp. 313, 321); courtesy TLC (pp. 316, 322). Book cover: THE NAKED CHEF (Hyperion) copyright © Optomen Television and Jamie Oliver, 2000. Front cover photograph copyright © David Eustace (p. 318).

Skip Palenik: Courtesy of Microtrace (p. 327, 329, 331, 334, 337).

Nancy Pelosi: U.S. Office of the Speaker (www.speaker.gov), (pp. 341, 343, 348); Paul Sakuma/AP Photo (p. 345); Roger L. Wollenberg/UPI/Landov (p. 350); Mandel Ngan/AFP/Getty Images (p. 353); Chip Somodevilla/Getty Images (p. 354).

Jack Prelutsky: Yuen Lui Studio/courtesy of Poetry Foundation.org (p. 359); Elaine Thompson/AP Photo (p. 361). Book covers: A PIZZA THE SIZE OF THE SUN (Greenwillow Books/William Morrow & Co.) text copyright © 1994, 1996 by Jack Prelutsky. Illustrations copyright © 1996 by James Stevenson. (p. 364); THE HEADLESS HORSEMAN RIDES TONIGHT: MORE POEMS TO TROUBLE YOUR SLEEP (Greenwillow Books/HarperCollins) text copyright © 1980 by Jack Prelutsky. Illustrations copyright © 1980 by Arnold Lobel. (p. 366).

Ivan "Pudge" Rodriguez: Steve Grayson/WireImage.com (p. 373); Louis DeLuca/MLB/Getty Images (p. 377); AP Images (p. 379); Al Bello/Getty Images (p. 382); Ron Vesely/MLB/Getty Images (p. 384).

Michael Sessions: Douglas Coon (pp. 389, 392, 394).

Kate Spade: Matthew Peyton/Getty Images (p. 399); LAN/Retna (p. 401); Camera Press/Circe Hamilton/Retna (p. 404); Bravo Photo/Barbara Nitke (p. 407).

Sabriye Tenberken: BLINDSIGHT copyright © 2006 Robson Entertainment (p. 411); Paul Kronenberg (pp. 413, 415); Didrik Johnck/BLINDSIGHT copyright © 2006 Robson Entertainment (p. 417).

Rob Thomas: Kevin Winter/Getty Images (p. 421); copyright © Warner Bros. (p. 429); copyright © 1999 Twentieth Century Fox (p. 430); Robert Voets/UPN. Copyright © 2005 CBS Broadcasting Inc. All rights reserved (p. 432). Covers: RATS SAW GOD copyright © 1996 by Rob Thomas. Cover copyright © 1996 by Simon & Schuster (p. 425); SLAVE DAY (Aladdin/Simon & Schuster) copyright © 1997 by Rob Thomas. Cover photo copyright © 1998 by Hirotsugo Nushioka/Photonica (p. 427).

# Cumulative General Index

This cumulative index includes names, occupations, nationalities, and ethnic and minority origins that pertain to all individuals profiled in *Biography Today* since the debut of the series in 1992.

494

**Pippig, Uta** . . . . . . . . . . . . . . . . . . .Sport V.1
**Pitt, Brad** . . . . . . . . . . . . . . . . . . . . . .Sep 98
**playwrights**
Bennett, Cherie . . . . . . . . . . . . .Author V.9
Bruchac, Joseph . . . . . . . . . . . .Author V.18
Hansberry, Lorraine . . . . . . . . .Author V.5
Hughes, Langston . . . . . . . . . . .Author V.7
Smith, Betty . . . . . . . . . . . . . .Author V.17
Wilson, August . . . . . . . . . . . . .Author 98
**poets**
Alvarez, Julia . . . . . . . . . . . . . .Author V.17
Brooks, Gwendolyn . . . . . . . . .Author V.3
Bruchac, Joseph . . . . . . . . . . .Author V.18
Collins, Billy . . . . . . . . . . . . . .Author V.16
Dove, Rita . . . . . . . . . . . . . . . . . . .Jan 94
Dunbar, Paul Lawrence . . . . .Author V.8
Grimes, Nikki . . . . . . . . . . . . . .Author V.14
Hughes, Langston . . . . . . . . . .Author V.7
Jewel . . . . . . . . . . . . . . . . . . . . . .Sep 98
Lansky, Bruce . . . . . . . . . . . .Author V.17
Martinez, Victor . . . . . . . . . . .Author V.15
Morrison, Lillian . . . . . . . . . .Author V.12
Nelson, Marilyn . . . . . . . . . . .Author V.13
Nye, Naomi Shihab . . . . . . . . .Author V.8
Pinsky, Robert . . . . . . . . . . . . .Author V.7
Prelutsky, Jack . . . . . . .Author V.2; Sep 07
Senghor, Léopold Sédar . . . . .WorLdr V.2
Silverstein, Shel . . .Author V.3; Update 99
Sones, Sonya . . . . . . . . . . . . .Author V.11
Soto, Gary . . . . . . . . . . . . . . . .Author V.5
Stepanek, Mattie . . . . . . . . . . . . .Apr 02
**Polish**
John Paul II . . . . . . . . . .Oct 92; Update 94;
Update 95; Sep 05
Opdyke, Irene Gut . . . . . . . . . .Author V.9
**political leaders**
Abzug, Bella . . . . . . . . . . . . . . . .Sep 98
Amin, Idi . . . . . . . . . . . . . . . .WorLdr V.2
Annan, Kofi . . . . . . . . . .Jan 98; Update 01
Arafat, Yasir . . . . . . . . . .Sep 94; Update 94;
Update 95; Update 96; Update 97;
Update 98; Update 00; Update 01;
Update 02
Aristide, Jean-Bertrand . . . . . . . . . .Jan 95;
Update 01
Babbitt, Bruce . . . . . . . . . . . . . . . .Jan 94
Baker, James . . . . . . . . . . . . . . . . .Oct 92
Banda, Hastings Kamuzu . . . .WorLdr V.2
Bellamy, Carol . . . . . . . . . . . . . . .Jan 06

Bhutto, Benazir . . . . . . .Apr 95; Update 99;
Update 02
Blair, Tony . . . . . . . . . . . . . . . . . . .Apr 04
Boutros-Ghali, Boutros . . . . . . . . . .Apr 93;
Update 98
Brundtland, Gro Harlem . . . . .Science V.3
Bush, George . . . . . . . . . . . . . . . .Jan 92
Bush, George W.. . . . . .Sep 00; Update 00;
Update 01; Update 02
Carter, Jimmy . . . . . . . . .Apr 95; Update 02
Castro, Fidel . . . . . . . . . .Jul 92; Update 94
Cheney, Dick . . . . . . . . . . . . . . . .Jan 02
Cisneros, Henry . . . . . . . . . . . . . .Sep 93
Clinton, Bill . . . . . . . . . .Jul 92; Update 94;
Update 95; Update 96; Update 97;
Update 98; Update 99; Update 00;
Update 01
Clinton, Hillary Rodham . . . . . . . .Apr 93;
Update 94; Update 95; Update 96;
Update 99; Update 00; Update 01
de Klerk, F.W. . . . . . . . .Apr 94; Update 94
Dole, Bob . . . . . . . . . . . .Jan 96; Update 96
Duke, David . . . . . . . . . . . . . . . . .Apr 92
Fox, Vicente . . . . . . . . . . . . . . . . .Apr 03
Gingrich, Newt . . . . . . .Apr 95; Update 99
Giuliani, Rudolph . . . . . . . . . . . .Sep 02
Glenn, John . . . . . . . . . . . . . . . . . .Jan 99
Gorbachev, Mikhail . . . .Jan 92; Update 94;
Update 96
Gore, Al . . . . . . . . . . . .Jan 93; Update 96;
Update 97; Update 98; Update 99;
Update 00; Update 01
Hussein, King . . . . . . . . . . . . . . .Apr 99
Hussein, Saddam . . . . . .Jul 92; Update 96;
Update 01; Update 02
Jackson, Jesse . . . . . . . .Sep 95; Update 01
Jordan, Barbara . . . . . . . . . . . . . .Apr 96
Kaunda, Kenneth . . . . . . . . .WorLdr V.2
Kenyatta, Jomo . . . . . . . . . . .WorLdr V.2
Kim Dae-jung . . . . . . . . . . . . . . . .Sep 01
Lewis, John . . . . . . . . . . . . . . . . . .Jan 03
Mandela, Nelson . . . . . .Jan 92; Update 94;
Update 01
McCain, John . . . . . . . . . . . . . . . .Apr 00
Milosevic, Slobodan . . . . . . . . . . .Sep 99;
Update 00; Update 01; Update 02
Mobutu Sese Seko WorLdr V.2; Update 97
Mugabe, Robert . . . . . . . . . . .WorLdr V.2
Nelson, Gaylord . . . . . . . . . . .WorLdr V.3
Nixon, Richard . . . . . . . . . . . . . . .Sep 94

# Places of Birth Index

The following index lists the places of birth for the individuals profiled in *Biography Today*. Places of birth are entered under state, province, anb/or country.

531

# Birthday Index

## March (continued) — Year

|  |  | Year |
|---|---|---|
|  | Tompkins, Douglas | 1943 |
| 29 | Capriati, Jennifer | 1976 |
| 30 | Dion, Celine | 1968 |
|  | Hammer | 1933 |
|  | Jones, Norah | 1979 |
| 31 | Caplan, Arthur | 1950 |
|  | Chavez, Cesar | 1927 |
|  | Gore, Al | 1948 |
|  | Howe, Gordie | 1928 |

## April — Year

|  |  | Year |
|---|---|---|
| 1 | Maathai, Wangari | 1940 |
| 2 | Carvey, Dana | 1955 |
| 3 | Berger, Francie | 1960 |
|  | Bynes, Amanda | 1986 |
|  | Garth, Jennie | 1972 |
|  | Goodall, Jane | 1934 |
|  | Murphy, Eddie | 1961 |
|  | Street, Picabo | 1971 |
| 4 | Angelou, Maya | 1928 |
|  | Mirra, Dave | 1974 |
|  | Spears, Jamie Lynn | 1991 |
| 5 | Kamen, Dean | 1951 |
|  | McDaniel, Lurlene | 1944 |
|  | Peck, Richard | 1934 |
|  | Powell, Colin | 1937 |
| 6 | Watson, James D. | 1928 |
| 7 | Black, Jack | 1969 |
|  | Chan, Jackie | 1954 |
|  | Douglas, Marjory Stoneman | 1890 |
|  | Forman, Michele | 1946 |
| 8 | Annan, Kofi | 1938 |
|  | Brody, Adam | 1980 |
| 9 | Haddix, Margaret Peterson | 1964 |
| 10 | Bleiler, Gretchen | 1981 |
|  | Carrabba, Chris | 1975 |
|  | Huerta, Dolores | 1930 |
|  | Madden, John | 1936 |
|  | Moore, Mandy | 1984 |
| 11 | Stone, Joss | 1987 |
| 12 | Cleary, Beverly | 1916 |
|  | Danes, Claire | 1979 |
|  | Doherty, Shannen | 1971 |
|  | Hawk, Tony | 1968 |
|  | Letterman, David | 1947 |
|  | Soto, Gary | 1952 |
| 13 | Brandis, Jonathan | 1976 |
|  | Henry, Marguerite | 1902 |
| 14 | Collins, Francis | 1950 |

|  |  | Year |
|---|---|---|
|  | Gellar, Sarah Michelle | 1977 |
|  | Maddux, Greg | 1966 |
|  | Rose, Pete | 1941 |
| 15 | Martin, Bernard | 1954 |
|  | Watson, Emma | 1990 |
| 16 | Abdul-Jabbar, Kareem | 1947 |
|  | Atwater-Rhodes, Amelia | 1984 |
|  | Selena | 1971 |
|  | Williams, Garth | 1912 |
| 17 | Champagne, Larry III | 1985 |
| 18 | Ferrera, America | 1984 |
|  | Hart, Melissa Joan | 1976 |
|  | Villa, Brenda | 1980 |
| 19 | Sharapova, Maria | 1987 |
| 20 | Brundtland, Gro Harlem | 1939 |
| 21 | Muir, John | 1838 |
| 22 | Fox, Paula | 1923 |
|  | Levi-Montalcini, Rita | 1909 |
|  | Oppenheimer, J. Robert | 1904 |
| 23 | López, George | 1961 |
|  | Watson, Barry | 1974 |
| 24 | Clarkson, Kelly | 1982 |
| 25 | Duncan, Tim | 1976 |
|  | Fitzgerald, Ella | 1917 |
| 26 | Giff, Patricia Reilly | 1935 |
|  | Nelson, Marilyn | 1946 |
|  | Pei, I.M. | 1917 |
|  | Welling, Tom | 1977 |
| 27 | Bemelmans, Ludwig | 1898 |
|  | King, Coretta Scott | 1927 |
|  | LaHaye, Tim | 1926 |
|  | Stump, Patrick | 1984 |
|  | Wilson, August | 1945 |
| 28 | Alba, Jessica | 1981 |
|  | Baker, James | 1930 |
|  | Duncan, Lois | 1934 |
|  | Hussein, Saddam | 1937 |
|  | Kaunda, Kenneth | 1924 |
|  | Lee, Harper | 1926 |
|  | Leno, Jay | 1950 |
|  | Lidstrom, Nicklas | 1970 |
| 29 | Agassi, Andre | 1970 |
|  | Earnhardt, Dale | 1951 |
|  | Seinfeld, Jerry | 1954 |
| 30 | Dunst, Kirsten | 1982 |

## May — Year

|  |  | Year |
|---|---|---|
| 2 | Beckham, David | 1975 |
|  | Hughes, Sarah | 1985 |
|  | Scott, Jerry | 1955 |

## July (continued)

| | | Year |
|---|---|---|
| 6 | Bush, George W. | 1946 |
| | Dalai Lama | 1935 |
| | Dumitriu, Ioana | 1976 |
| 7 | Chagall, Marc | 1887 |
| | Heinlein, Robert | 1907 |
| | Kwan, Michelle | 1980 |
| | Leslie, Lisa | 1972 |
| | Otto, Sylke | 1969 |
| | Sakic, Joe | 1969 |
| | Stachowski, Richie | 1985 |
| 8 | Hardaway, Anfernee "Penny" | 1971 |
| | Keith, Toby | 1961 |
| | Kübler-Ross, Elisabeth | 1926 |
| | MacArthur, Ellen | 1976 |
| | Sealfon, Rebecca | 1983 |
| 9 | Farmer, Nancy | 1941 |
| | Hanks, Tom | 1956 |
| | Hassan II | 1929 |
| | Krim, Mathilde | 1926 |
| | Lee, Jeanette | 1971 |
| | Rodriguez, Gloria | 1948 |
| | Sacks, Oliver | 1933 |
| 10 | Ashe, Arthur | 1943 |
| | Benson, Mildred | 1905 |
| | Boulmerka, Hassiba | 1969 |
| 11 | Belbin, Tanith | 1984 |
| | Cisneros, Henry | 1947 |
| | Hrdy, Sarah Blaffer | 1946 |
| | White, E.B. | 1899 |
| 12 | Bauer, Joan | 1951 |
| | Cosby, Bill | 1937 |
| | Johnson, Johanna | 1983 |
| | Yamaguchi, Kristi | 1972 |
| 13 | Ford, Harrison | 1942 |
| | Stewart, Patrick | 1940 |
| 14 | Taboo | 1975 |
| 15 | Aristide, Jean-Bertrand | 1953 |
| | Ventura, Jesse | 1951 |
| 16 | Ferrell, Will | 1967 |
| | Johnson, Jimmy | 1943 |
| | Sanders, Barry | 1968 |
| 17 | An Na | 1972 |
| | Stepanek, Mattie | 1990 |
| 18 | Bell, Kristen | 1980 |
| | Diesel, Vin | 1967 |
| | Glenn, John | 1921 |
| | Lemelson, Jerome | 1923 |
| | Mandela, Nelson | 1918 |
| 19 | Glennie, Evelyn | 1965 |

| | | Year |
|---|---|---|
| | Kratt, Chris | 1969 |
| | Tarvin, Herbert | 1985 |
| 20 | Hillary, Sir Edmund | 1919 |
| | Santana, Carlos | 1947 |
| 21 | Catchings, Tamika | 1979 |
| | Chastain, Brandi | 1968 |
| | Hartnett, Josh | 1978 |
| | Reno, Janet | 1938 |
| | Riley, Dawn | 1964 |
| | Stern, Isaac | 1920 |
| | Williams, Robin | 1952 |
| 22 | Calder, Alexander | 1898 |
| | Dole, Bob | 1923 |
| | Hinton, S.E. | 1948 |
| | Johnson, Keyshawn | 1972 |
| 23 | Haile Selassie | 1892 |
| | Krauss, Alison | 1971 |
| | Williams, Michelle | 1980 |
| 24 | Abzug, Bella | 1920 |
| | Bonds, Barry | 1964 |
| | Krone, Julie | 1963 |
| | Lopez, Jennifer | 1970 |
| | Moss, Cynthia | 1940 |
| | Wilson, Mara | 1987 |
| 25 | Payton, Walter | 1954 |
| 26 | Berenstain, Jan | 1923 |
| | Clark, Kelly | 1983 |
| 27 | Dunlap, Alison | 1969 |
| | Kimball, Cheyenne | 1990 |
| | Rodriguez, Alex | 1975 |
| 28 | Babbitt, Natalie | 1932 |
| | Davis, Jim | 1945 |
| | Potter, Beatrix | 1866 |
| 29 | Burns, Ken | 1953 |
| | Creech, Sharon | 1945 |
| | Dole, Elizabeth Hanford | 1936 |
| | Hayes, Tyrone | 1967 |
| | Jennings, Peter | 1938 |
| | Morris, Wanya | 1973 |
| 30 | Allen, Tori | 1988 |
| | Hill, Anita | 1956 |
| | Moore, Henry | 1898 |
| | Schroeder, Pat | 1940 |
| 31 | Cronin, John | 1950 |
| | Kwolek, Stephanie | 1923 |
| | Radcliffe, Daniel | 1989 |
| | Reid Banks, Lynne | 1929 |
| | Rowling, J.K. | 1965 |
| | Weinke, Chris | 1972 |

## August (continued)

| | | Year |
|---|---|---|
| 27 | Adams, Yolanda | 1961 |
| | Moseley, Jonny | 1975 |
| | Nechita, Alexandra | 1985 |
| | Rinaldi, Ann | 1934 |
| | Steingraber, Sandra | 1959 |
| | Vega, Alexa | 1988 |
| 28 | Dove, Rita | 1952 |
| | Evans, Janet | 1971 |
| | Peterson, Roger Tory | 1908 |
| | Priestley, Jason | 1969 |
| | Rimes, LeAnn | 1982 |
| | Twain, Shania | 1965 |
| 29 | Grandin, Temple | 1947 |
| | Hesse, Karen | 1952 |
| | McCain, John | 1936 |
| 30 | Alexander, Shaun | 1977 |
| | Buffett, Warren | 1930 |
| | Diaz, Cameron | 1972 |
| | Earle, Sylvia | 1935 |
| | Roddick, Andy | 1982 |
| | Williams, Ted | 1918 |
| 31 | Perlman, Itzhak | 1945 |

## September

| | | Year |
|---|---|---|
| 1 | Estefan, Gloria | 1958 |
| | Guy, Rosa | 1925 |
| | Smyers, Karen | 1961 |
| | Trohman, Joe | 1984 |
| 2 | Bearden, Romare | ?1912 |
| | Galeczka, Chris | 1981 |
| | Lisanti, Mariangela | 1983 |
| | Mohajer, Dineh | 1972 |
| | Reeves, Keanu | 1964 |
| | Yelas, Jay | 1965 |
| 3 | Delany, Bessie | 1891 |
| | Finch, Jennie | 1980 |
| | White, Shaun | 1986 |
| 4 | Knowles, Beyoncé | 1981 |
| | Wright, Richard | 1908 |
| 5 | Guisewite, Cathy | 1950 |
| 6 | Fiorina, Carly | 1954 |
| | Friday, Dallas | 1986 |
| 7 | Lawrence, Jacob | 1917 |
| | Moses, Grandma | 1860 |
| | Pippig, Uta | 1965 |
| | Scurry, Briana | 1971 |
| 8 | Prelutsky, Jack | 1940 |
| | Scieszka, Jon | 1954 |
| | Thomas, Jonathan Taylor | 1982 |

| | | Year |
|---|---|---|
| 9 | Sandler, Adam | 1966 |
| 10 | Gould, Stephen Jay | 1941 |
| | Johnson, Randy | 1963 |
| | Wallace, Ben | 1974 |
| 11 | Dworkin, Aaron | 1970 |
| 12 | Yao Ming | 1980 |
| 13 | Johnson, Michael | 1967 |
| | Monroe, Bill | 1911 |
| | Taylor, Mildred D. | 1943 |
| 14 | Armstrong, William H. | 1914 |
| | Koff, Clea | 1972 |
| | Stanford, John | 1938 |
| 15 | dePaola, Tomie | 1934 |
| | Marino, Dan | 1961 |
| | McCloskey, Robert | 1914 |
| 16 | Bledel, Alexis | 1981 |
| | Dahl, Roald | 1916 |
| | Gates, Henry Louis, Jr. | 1950 |
| 17 | Burger, Warren | 1907 |
| | Jackson, Phil | 1945 |
| | Levine, Gail Carson | 1947 |
| 18 | Armstrong, Lance | 1971 |
| | Carson, Ben | 1951 |
| | de Mille, Agnes | 1905 |
| | Fields, Debbi | 1956 |
| | Foray, June | 1917 |
| | Nakamura, Leanne | 1982 |
| 19 | Delany, Sadie | 1889 |
| | Fay, Michael | 1956 |
| | Giddens, Rebecca | 1977 |
| | O'Brien, Soledad | 1966 |
| 20 | Chihuly, Dale | 1941 |
| | Crabtree, Taylor | 1990 |
| 21 | Fielder, Cecil | 1963 |
| | Hill, Faith | 1967 |
| | Jones, Chuck | 1912 |
| | Kiessling, Laura L. | 1960 |
| | King, Stephen | 1947 |
| | Nkrumah, Kwame | 1909 |
| 22 | Richardson, Dot | 1961 |
| | Sessions, Michael | 1987 |
| 23 | Jenkins, Jerry B. | 1949 |
| | Nevelson, Louise | 1899 |
| | Warrick, Earl | 1911 |
| 24 | George, Eddie | 1973 |
| | Ochoa, Severo | 1905 |
| 25 | Gwaltney, John Langston | 1928 |
| | Locklear, Heather | 1961 |
| | Lopez, Charlotte | 1976 |
| | Murphy, Jim | 1947 |

# Biography Today

## General Series

**B**iography Today **General Series** includes a unique combination of current biographical profiles that teachers and librarians — and the readers themselves — tell us are most appealing. The **General Series** is available as a 3-issue subscription; hardcover annual cumulation; or subscription plus cumulation.

Within the **General Series**, your readers will find a variety of sketches about:

- Authors
- Musicians
- Political leaders
- Sports figures
- Movie actresses & actors
- Cartoonists
- Scientists
- Astronauts
- TV personalities
- and the movers & shakers in many other fields!

"*Biography Today* will be useful in elementary and middle school libraries and in public library children's collections where there is a need for biographies of current personalities. High schools serving reluctant readers may also want to consider a subscription."
— *Booklist*, American Library Association

"Highly recommended for the young adult audience. Readers will delight in the accessible, energetic, tell-all style; teachers, librarians, and parents will welcome the clever format [and] intelligent and informative text. It should prove especially useful in motivating 'reluctant' readers or literate nonreaders."
— *MultiCultural Review*

"Written in a friendly, almost chatty tone, the profiles offer quick, objective information. While coverage of current figures makes *Biography Today* a useful reference tool, an appealing format and wide scope make it a fun resource to browse." — *School Library Journal*

"The best source for current information at a level kids can understand."
— Kelly Bryant, School Librarian, Carlton, OR

"Easy for kids to read. We love it! Don't want to be without it."
— Lynn McWhirter, School Librarian, Rockford, IL

### ONE-YEAR SUBSCRIPTION
- 3 softcover issues, 6" x 9"
- Published in January, April, and September
- 1-year subscription, list price $66. **School and library price $64**
- 150 pages per issue
- 10 profiles per issue
- Contact sources for additional information
- Cumulative Names Index

### HARDBOUND ANNUAL CUMULATION
- Sturdy 6" x 9" hardbound volume
- Published in December
- List price $73. **School and library price $66 per volume**
- 450 pages per volume
- 30 profiles — includes all profiles found in softcover issues for that calendar year
- Cumulative General Index, Places of Birth Index, and Birthday Index

### SUBSCRIPTION AND CUMULATION COMBINATION
- $110 for 3 softcover issues plus the hardbound volume

**For Cumulative General, Places of Birth, and Birthday Indexes, please see www.biographytoday.com.**

# 1992

Paula Abdul
Andre Agassi
Kirstie Alley
Terry Anderson
Roseanne Arnold
Isaac Asimov
James Baker
Charles Barkley
Larry Bird
Judy Blume
Berke Breathed
Garth Brooks
Barbara Bush
George Bush
Fidel Castro
Bill Clinton
Bill Cosby
Diana, Princess of
  Wales
Shannen Doherty
Elizabeth Dole
David Duke
Gloria Estefan
Mikhail Gorbachev
Steffi Graf
Wayne Gretzky
Matt Groening
Alex Haley
Hammer
Martin Handford
Stephen Hawking
Hulk Hogan
Saddam Hussein
Lee Iacocca
Bo Jackson
Mae Jemison
Peter Jennings
Steven Jobs
John Paul II
Magic Johnson
Michael Jordon
Jackie Joyner-Kersee
Spike Lee
Mario Lemieux
Madeleine L'Engle
Jay Leno
Yo-Yo Ma
Nelson Mandela
Wynton Marsalis
Thurgood Marshall
Ann Martin
Barbara McClintock
Emily Arnold McCully
Antonia Novello

Sandra Day O'Connor
Rosa Parks
Jane Pauley
H. Ross Perot
Luke Perry
Scottie Pippen
Colin Powell
Jason Priestley
Queen Latifah
Yitzhak Rabin
Sally Ride
Pete Rose
Nolan Ryan
H. Norman
  Schwarzkopf
Jerry Seinfeld
Dr. Seuss
Gloria Steinem
Clarence Thomas
Chris Van Allsburg
Cynthia Voigt
Bill Watterson
Robin Williams
Oprah Winfrey
Kristi Yamaguchi
Boris Yeltsin

# 1993

Maya Angelou
Arthur Ashe
Avi
Kathleen Battle
Candice Bergen
Boutros Boutros-Ghali
Chris Burke
Dana Carvey
Cesar Chavez
Henry Cisneros
Hillary Rodham
  Clinton
Jacques Cousteau
Cindy Crawford
Macaulay Culkin
Lois Duncan
Marian Wright
  Edelman
Cecil Fielder
Bill Gates
Sara Gilbert
Dizzy Gillespie
Al Gore
Cathy Guisewite
Jasmine Guy
Anita Hill
Ice-T

Darci Kistler
k.d. lang
Dan Marino
Rigoberta Menchu
Walter Dean Myers
Martina Navratilova
Phyllis Reynolds
  Naylor
Rudolf Nureyev
Shaquille O'Neal
Janet Reno
Jerry Rice
Mary Robinson
Winona Ryder
Jerry Spinelli
Denzel Washington
Keenen Ivory Wayans
Dave Winfield

# 1994

Tim Allen
Marian Anderson
Mario Andretti
Ned Andrews
Yasir Arafat
Bruce Babbitt
Mayim Bialik
Bonnie Blair
Ed Bradley
John Candy
Mary Chapin
  Carpenter
Benjamin Chavis
Connie Chung
Beverly Cleary
Kurt Cobain
F.W. de Klerk
Rita Dove
Linda Ellerbee
Sergei Fedorov
Zlata Filipovic
Daisy Fuentes
Ruth Bader Ginsburg
Whoopi Goldberg
Tonya Harding
Melissa Joan Hart
Geoff Hooper
Whitney Houston
Dan Jansen
Nancy Kerrigan
Alexi Lalas
Charlotte Lopez
Wilma Mankiller
Shannon Miller
Toni Morrison

Richard Nixon
Greg Norman
Severo Ochoa
River Phoenix
Elizabeth Pine
Jonas Salk
Richard Scarry
Emmitt Smith
Will Smith
Steven Spielberg
Patrick Stewart
R.L. Stine
Lewis Thomas
Barbara Walters
Charlie Ward
Steve Young
Kim Zmeskal

# 1995

Troy Aikman
Jean-Bertrand Aristide
Oksana Baiul
Halle Berry
Benazir Bhutto
Jonathan Brandis
Warren E. Burger
Ken Burns
Candace Cameron
Jimmy Carter
Agnes de Mille
Placido Domingo
Janet Evans
Patrick Ewing
Newt Gingrich
John Goodman
Amy Grant
Jesse Jackson
James Earl Jones
Julie Krone
David Letterman
Rush Limbaugh
Heather Locklear
Reba McEntire
Joe Montana
Cosmas Ndeti
Hakeem Olajuwon
Ashley Olsen
Mary-Kate Olsen
Jennifer Parkinson
Linus Pauling
Itzhak Perlman
Cokie Roberts
Wilma Rudolph
Salt 'N' Pepa
Barry Sanders

William Shatner
Elizabeth George
  Speare
Dr. Benjamin Spock
Jonathan Taylor
  Thomas
Vicki Van Meter
Heather Whitestone
Pedro Zamora

## 1996

Aung San Suu Kyi
Boyz II Men
Brandy
Ron Brown
Mariah Carey
Jim Carrey
Larry Champagne III
Christo
Chelsea Clinton
Coolio
Bob Dole
David Duchovny
Debbi Fields
Chris Galeczka
Jerry Garcia
Jennie Garth
Wendy Guey
Tom Hanks
Alison Hargreaves
Sir Edmund Hillary
Judith Jamison
Barbara Jordan
Annie Leibovitz
Carl Lewis
Jim Lovell
Mickey Mantle
Lynn Margulis
Iqbal Masih
Mark Messier
Larisa Oleynik
Christopher Pike
David Robinson
Dennis Rodman
Selena
Monica Seles
Don Shula
Kerri Strug
Tiffani-Amber Thiessen
Dave Thomas
Jaleel White

## 1997

Madeleine Albright

Marcus Allen
Gillian Anderson
Rachel Blanchard
Zachery Ty Bryan
Adam Ezra Cohen
Claire Danes
Celine Dion
Jean Driscoll
Louis Farrakhan
Ella Fitzgerald
Harrison Ford
Bryant Gumbel
John Johnson
Michael Johnson
Maya Lin
George Lucas
John Madden
Bill Monroe
Alanis Morissette
Sam Morrison
Rosie O'Donnell
Muammar el-Qaddafi
Christopher Reeve
Pete Sampras
Pat Schroeder
Rebecca Sealfon
Tupac Shakur
Tabitha Soren
Herbert Tarvin
Merlin Tuttle
Mara Wilson

## 1998

Bella Abzug
Kofi Annan
Neve Campbell
Sean Combs (Puff
  Daddy)
Dalai Lama (Tenzin
  Gyatso)
Diana, Princess of
  Wales
Leonardo DiCaprio
Walter E. Diemer
Ruth Handler
Hanson
Livan Hernandez
Jewel
Jimmy Johnson
Tara Lipinski
Jody-Anne Maxwell
Dominique Moceanu
Alexandra Nechita
Brad Pitt
LeAnn Rimes

Emily Rosa
David Satcher
Betty Shabazz
Kordell Stewart
Shinichi Suzuki
Mother Teresa
Mike Vernon
Reggie White
Kate Winslet

## 1999

Ben Affleck
Jennifer Aniston
Maurice Ashley
Kobe Bryant
Bessie Delany
Sadie Delany
Sharon Draper
Sarah Michelle Gellar
John Glenn
Savion Glover
Jeff Gordon
David Hampton
Lauryn Hill
King Hussein
Lynn Johnston
Shari Lewis
Oseola McCarty
Mark McGwire
Slobodan Milosevic
Natalie Portman
J.K. Rowling
Frank Sinatra
Gene Siskel
Sammy Sosa
John Stanford
Natalia Toro
Shania Twain
Mitsuko Uchida
Jesse Ventura
Venus Williams

## 2000

Christina Aguilera
K.A. Applegate
Lance Armstrong
Backstreet Boys
Daisy Bates
Harry Blackmun
George W. Bush
Carson Daly
Ron Dayne
Henry Louis Gates, Jr.

Doris Haddock
  (Granny D)
Jennifer Love Hewitt
Chamique Holdsclaw
Katie Holmes
Charlayne Hunter-
  Gault
Johanna Johnson
Craig Kielburger
John Lasseter
Peyton Manning
Ricky Martin
John McCain
Walter Payton
Freddie Prinze, Jr.
Viviana Risca
Briana Scurry
George Thampy
CeCe Winans

## 2001

Jessica Alba
Christiane Amanpour
Drew Barrymore
Jeff Bezos
Destiny's Child
Dale Earnhardt
Carly Fiorina
Aretha Franklin
Cathy Freeman
Tony Hawk
Faith Hill
Kim Dae-jung
Madeleine L'Engle
Mariangela Lisanti
Frankie Muniz
*N Sync
Ellen Ochoa
Jeff Probst
Julia Roberts
Carl T. Rowan
Britney Spears
Chris Tucker
Lloyd D. Ward
Alan Webb
Chris Weinke

## 2002

Aaliyah
Osama bin Laden
Mary J. Blige
Aubyn Burnside
Aaron Carter
Julz Chavez

Dick Cheney
Hilary Duff
Billy Gilman
Rudolph Giuliani
Brian Griese
Jennifer Lopez
Dave Mirra
Dineh Mohajer
Leanne Nakamura
Daniel Radcliffe
Condoleezza Rice
Marla Runyan
Ruth Simmons
Mattie Stepanek
J.R.R. Tolkien
Barry Watson
Tyrone Willingham
Elijah Wood

## 2003

Yolanda Adams
Olivia Bennett
Mildred Benson
Alexis Bledel
Barry Bonds
Vincent Brooks
Laura Bush
Amanda Bynes
Kelly Clarkson
Vin Diesel
Eminem
Michele Forman
Vicente Fox
Millard Fuller
Josh Hartnett
Dolores Huerta
Sarah Hughes
Enrique Iglesias
Jeanette Lee
John Lewis
Nicklas Lidstrom
Clint Mathis
Donovan McNabb
Nelly
Andy Roddick
Gwen Stefani
Emma Watson

Meg Whitman
Reese Witherspoon
Yao Ming

## 2004

Natalie Babbitt
David Beckham
Francie Berger
Tony Blair
Orlando Bloom
Kim Clijsters
Celia Cruz
Matel Dawson, Jr.
The Donnas
Tim Duncan
Shirin Ebadi
Carla Hayden
Ashton Kutcher
Lisa Leslie
Linkin Park
Lindsay Lohan
Irene D. Long
John Mayer
Mandy Moore
Thich Nhat Hanh
OutKast
Raven
Ronald Reagan
Keanu Reeves
Ricardo Sanchez
Brian Urlacher
Alexa Vega
Michelle Wie
Will Wright

## 2005

Kristen Bell
Jack Black
Sergey Brin & Larry
   Page
Adam Brody
Chris Carrabba
Johnny Depp
Eve
Jennie Finch
James Forman

Wally Funk
Cornelia Funke
Bethany Hamilton
Anne Hathaway
Priest Holmes
T.D. Jakes
John Paul II
Toby Keith
Alison Krauss
Wangari Maathai
Karen Mitchell-
   Raptakis
Queen Noor
Violet Palmer
Gloria Rodriguez
Carlos Santana
Antonin Scalia
Curtis Schilling
Maria Sharapova
Ashlee Simpson
Donald Trump
Ben Wallace

## 2006

Carol Bellamy
Miri Ben-Ari
Black Eyed Peas
Bono
Kelsie Buckley
Dale Chihuly
Neda DeMayo
Dakota Fanning
Green Day
Freddie Highmore
Russel Honoré
Tim Howard
Cynthia Kadohata
Coretta Scott King
Rachel McAdams
Cesar Millan
Steve Nash
Nick Park
Rosa Parks
Danica Patrick
Jorge Ramos
Ben Roethlisberger
Lil' Romeo

Adam Sandler
Russell Simmons
Jamie Lynn Spears
Jon Stewart
Joss Stone
Hannah Teter
Brenda Villa
Tyler James Williams
Gretchen Wilson

## 2007

Shaun Alexander
Carmelo Anthony
Drake Bell
Chris Brown
Regina Carter
Kortney Clemons
Taylor Crabtree
Miley Cyrus
Aaron Dworkin
Fall Out Boy
Roger Federer
Will Ferrell
America Ferrera
June Foray
Sarah Blaffer Hrdy
Alicia Keys
Cheyenne Kimball
Keira Knightley
Wendy Kopp
Sofia Mulanovich
Barack Obama
Soledad O'Brien
Jamie Oliver
Skip Palenik
Nancy Pelosi
Jack Prelutsky
Ivan "Pudge"
   Rodriguez
Michael Sessions
Kate Spade
Sabriye Tenberken
Rob Thomas
Ashley Tisdale
Carrie Underwood
Muhammad Yunus